*The People of This Generation*

# *The People of This Generation*

## The Rise and Fall of the New Left in Philadelphia

PAUL LYONS

**PENN**

University of Pennsylvania Press

Philadelphia

10   9   8   7   6   5   4   3   2   1

Published by
University of Pennsylvania Press
Philadelphia, Pennsylvania 19104-4011

Library of Congress Cataloging-in-Publication Data
Lyons, Paul, 1942–
    The people of this generation : the rise and fall of the New Left in Philadelphia / Paul Lyons.
      p.   cm.
    ISBN 0-8122-3715-3 (acid-free paper)
    Includes bibliographical references (p. ) and index.
    1. New left—Pennsylvania—Philadelphia—History. 2. College students—Pennsylvania—
Philadelphia—Political activity—History—20th century. 3. Radicalism—Pennsylvania—
Philadelphia—History—20th century. 4. Philadelphia (Pa.)—Politics and government—20th
century. I. Title
F158.52 .L96   2003
320.53/09748/1109045—dc21                                          2002043043

*This one's for*
*LULA*

# Contents

# Introduction: The Movement and the City of Brotherly Love

## The 1960s: Post-Cold War and Post-Memoir

In the early 1960s a new generation's voice would emerge across the nation, responding to the kinds of themes highlighted in Students for a Democratic Society (SDS) Port Huron Statement of 1962: the threat of nuclear confrontation, the contradictions between American affluence and minority and Third World poverty, the contradictions between American commitments to equality and inclusion and the ugly realities of racism and segregation, and the sense that suburban affluence rested on a mix of hypocrisy, alienation, and meaninglessness. In Philadelphia, that New Left voice would face a number of challenges, some held in common with movement activists nationwide, others specific to this city. First of all, it would need to come to grips with the host of older radical voices that were struggling to recover from the dual blows of McCarthyist assault and the failures of Communism with the invasion of Hungary and the revelations of Stalin's crimes by Nikita Khrushchev at the Twentieth Party Congress in 1956.[1] Second, it would need to determine its relationship to the extensive Quaker organizational structures unique to Philadelphia. Third, young radicals would inevitably and necessarily overlap with and sometimes be at odds with the reform movement as it revitalized the city's liberals. How would New Leftists, who tended increasingly to define "corporate liberalism" as the enemy, accommodate themselves to a liberal reform movement in Philadelphia under assault from the right-wing, ethnic populism personified by notorious mayor Frank Rizzo? Fourth, New Leftists would have to work out relations with the emerging African American activists, beginning with Cecil B. Moore of the National Association for the Advancement of Colored People (NAACP), as well as those involved with the Congress of Racial Equality (CORE) and the Student Nonviolent Coordinating Committee (SNCC). Fifth, those seeking to build a movement based on participatory democracy would have to deal with the ways all the above relations influenced

issues of social class and ethnicity. How would young middle-class student radicals approach local unions and working-class people? How
would they address the "Whitetowners," the residents of the ethnic
neighborhoods belatedly achieving at least symbolic recognition in the
1960s with the elections of Irish American mayor James H. J. Tate and
Italian American mayor Frank Rizzo? Sixth, young New Leftists would
need to figure out how to confront the urban, racial, and ethnic
dilemmas that were occurring in an environment shaped by deindustrialization, as smokestack America was beginning its painful decline.
And finally, New Left radicals, operating in the twilight of the golden
age of American capitalism, would need to come to grips with making
demands on systems, especially city governments, that faced suburban
flight, shrinking revenues, and a consequent deepening of competition over increasingly scarce resources.[2]

I begin with the assumption that one must examine the social and
political movements of the 1960s—what participants characteristically
called the "movement"—in the context of their geographic, political,
and cultural environments. Of course, many movement efforts were
focused not on local but rather on national and global issues, especially when the United States entered the war in Vietnam. But a movement that sought a broader and deeper democracy, at least until the
late 1960s, must be evaluated in terms of how it sought to extend the
boundaries of liberty, fraternity, and equality within its broadly defined community. Too often, accounts of the New Left have emphasized intent and what some call expressive politics—what one sought
to accomplish and how one felt in the effort. It is important to examine these goals within the narrower confines of particular college and
university campuses. But it is also essential to consider what kinds of
effects this eruption of youthful idealism and utopian dreams had on
the politics and culture of the broader local community. I examine
such fundamental questions in the following chapters.

Writing about the 1960s has been affected by two fundamental
changes. The first is more obvious: the initial rush of personal accounts,
memoirs, and histories, written by people who were participant-
observers, has been augmented by the efforts of younger and less
personally involved historians, often doing groundbreaking work in
disaggregating the period through a case study approach. As such, we
now are benefiting from studies of particular campuses, including those
which were out of the media spotlight, outside the bicoastal centers,
and perhaps more representative than elite schools such as Berkeley
and Harvard, which have often received the most attention.[3]

Second, we have now entered the twenty-first century and have
some perspective in looking back at events that occurred nearly half a

century ago. British historian Eric Hobsbawm offers a framework for reflecting on what he calls the short twentieth century, an epoch framed by the Great War at its outset and the collapse of the Soviet empire and of Communism itself at its close.[4] There have been the predictable superficial ideological reinterpretations of the 1960s within what one might legitimately call the End of Ideology II.[5] After all, it is quite reasonable to suggest that the utopian challenges associated with the 1960s are part of a piece with the tragic nightmare that was Communism. There were enough events and episodes, from the Weathermen to the legacy of political correctness, to justify such associations. However, the disenchantment, the sobering brought about by the failures, both economic and moral, of the Marxist-Leninist enterprise, must not be allowed to reduce the distinctive qualities of the 1960s movements to Cold War-style caricature. What remains to be constructed is a nuanced portrait sensitive to the inevitable contradictions inherent in movements for social change and comprehensive enough to consider their destructive dimensions without devaluing their distinctive contributions to social justice and human betterment.

What historians need to do is reexamine those movements and that era—the New Left and the 1960s—with the greater knowledge, empirical and moral, that this short century of totalitarianism and war has yielded. But we must also take into consideration those aspects of the twentieth century in general and of the 1960s in particular that have in some ways increased the amount of freedom, democracy, and ability to pursue happiness, that is, enabling Americans to live longer but also better, to live more freely, more democratically, more inclusively. And some of those benefits require an appreciative examination, certainly not an inquisition, of 1960s movements that helped open the doors of opportunity to African Americans, women, gays and lesbians, and a wide array of other historically mistreated groups. Conservative jurist Richard A. Posner, in criticizing the notion that everything since the 1960s has been moral decay, reminds us that "today's culture does not ridicule obese people, ethnic minorities, stammerers and effeminate men, as the popular culture of the 1950's did, so it may be doubted whether there has actually been a net decline in the moral tone of popular culture."[6] For those who blame the movements of the 1960s for a precipitous moral degeneration, Posner emphasizes "the increased tolerance for people different from the norm, whether in race, religion, sex, sexual orientation or even physical and mental health (no more 'moron' jokes)," concluding that this "will strike most people . . . as moral progress."

## Liberal Consensus and Utopian Challenges, Left and Right

I believe that future historians will look back at the 1960s and its social movements as a critical indicator of the crisis of modern liberalism. In the 1950s and early 1960s most serious commentators assumed that we, not only the United States but also the rest of the developed world and eventually the entire globe, were part of an inexorable process of modernization which required the patchwork, piecemeal strengths of a mixed economy, part capitalist, part planned, and appropriately called a welfare state. Yes, the United States lagged behind our more sophisticated Western European allies—there would be a later version involving Japan in the 1970s and 1980s—but the Kennedy-Johnson years were to help us catch up in the achievement of what LBJ grandly called the Great Society. Not everyone celebrated this antici-pated construction; the Left still dreamed of some kind of workers' state, usually some democratic version of socialism. More powerfully, there were Weberians of various sorts, concerned with the bureaucra-tization of human life itself, haunted by the possibilities of evil as ba-nal, critical of the little houses made of ticky-tacky, the men in gray flannel suits, the organization men, the wasteland of popular culture.[7] But few projected fundamental alternatives; most, in effect, hoped for a Europeanization of American culture. Such critics flocked to the films of Luis Bunuel, François Truffaut, Ingmar Bergman and Fed-erico Fellini, which seemed to embody these yearnings for both au-thenticity and sophistication.

Such projections rested on an economically deterministic approach to history every bit as rigid as Marxism. As has so often been the case, the anti-Communists paid tribute to their ideological adversaries through imitation, from McCarthyism to Walt W. Rostow's theory of economic take-off.[8] Within this modernization model there was no room for ideology, left or right. The New Deal and what Alan Wolfe called the Politics of Growth—Robert M. Collins labels it Growth Liberalism—ostensibly buried both the Communist future and the laissez-faire past.[9] The end of ideology focused on the Left but, pre-cisely in its emphasis, indicated an even greater contempt for the Right. The great liberal critic Lionel Trilling in fact bemoaned the ab-sence of any intellectually vigorous, challenging conservatism; histo-rian Louis Hartz concurred in asserting a singular liberal tradition.[10]

The New Left challenge to that mainstream New Deal coalition, as I will argue, went well beyond the traditional left-wing agenda. As articulated in the Port Huron Statement, it was decisively generational in its outlook and more interested in issues of alienation, community, and meaning than in what C. Wright Mills denigrated as the older labor metaphysic.[11] In its own way, the New Left, not without contradiction, presupposed the modernization model, that is, the permanence of an affluent welfare state, but subjected it to radical critique, in terms of those not yet absorbed, for example, American blacks and the Third World, and, more fundamentally, in terms of those accommodated: "people of this generation, bred in at least modest comfort, housed now in universities."[12]

In this book I tell the story of how the New Left formed, how it operated, how it succeeded, how it failed and then expired, and yet how it continues to live on in a variety of measurable ways in the city of Philadelphia and its environs. Along the way, the reader will encounter considerations of Old Left organizations such as the Communist Party and the Trotskyist Socialist Workers Party as well as their respective youth affiliates; other Marxist-Leninist groups, like the Progressive Labor Party and the National Caucus of Labor Committees (a.k.a. the Labor Committee), which emerged during the 1960s; African American movements and organizations, ranging from SNCC, CORE, and the NAACP to the Black Panthers and campus-based black student groups; hippie cultural rebels, both on and off campus; second-wave feminists; gay and lesbian activists; environmentalists; and liberal reformers. Indeed, the story of the essentially white, middle-class, student-based New Left cannot be told without its being interwoven with the activities and influences of many other social forces and movements. But I have chosen to concentrate on the birth, development, and decline of the New Left movement, meaning the movement for fundamental social change initiated by the civil rights revolution. My focus on the New Left is in no way to be read as a denigration of the importance of these other social movements; indeed, I would suggest that their significance is such that they require more attention than this modest effort can manage.

I begin, in Chapter 1, with an examination of the early history of the Philadelphia chapter of the Committee for a Sane Nuclear Policy, popularly known as SANE, as a means by which to explore the issue of the relations between Old Left and New Left. To what extent was there continuity between Depression-era movements and those that emerged in the 1960s; in brief, to what extent was the New Left "new"? How did the Old Left and Old Left-influenced organizations attempt to build bridges to those coming of age in the late 1950s and early 1960s, inspired by the Montgomery bus boycott, the Greensboro sit-ins, and the freedom rides? What accounts for the apparent disjuncture between radical generations such that the youth movements of the 1960s seemed to operate without significant grounding in the rich if problematic experience of those who came before them?

Chapter 2 is an extensive study of campus activism at the three elite Quaker colleges located in the Philadelphia suburbs: Swarthmore College, Haverford College, and Bryn Mawr College. Such institutions, historically liberal and tolerant, if intensely academic and cloistered, had some of the earliest and most intense New Left experiences, both in terms of civil rights and in response to the Vietnam War. I spend considerable attention in evaluating Swarthmore's role in the creation and implementation of the SDS Economic Research and Action Project (ERAP), an attempt to translate the ideals of participatory democracy into "an inter-racial movement of the poor" in the rundown neighborhoods of nearby Chester. Swarthmore's experiences in Chester in many ways foreshadowed the dilemmas that white, middle-class New Left youth would confront in seeking social and racial justice. The chapter also highlights the highly individualistic qualities of dissent at Haverford and the ways in which one can trace the origins of second-wave feminism at Bryn Mawr.

The very different campus experiences at Roman Catholic institutions of higher learning—LaSalle College, St. Joseph's College, and Villanova University—are considered in Chapter 3. The specifically Catholic aspects of the social movements of the 1960s reveal distinctive patterns, some of which rest on the ways Pope John XXIII and the Second Vatican Council as well as the election of John Fitzgerald Kennedy, the first Roman Catholic president, nourished and influenced campus idealists. This chapter supports the need for scholars of the 1960s to recognize the enormous diversity in student movements, especially the ways in which what was common at liberal institutions occurred later and under greater duress at more conservative schools, particularly those with predominantly commuter student bodies.

Chapter 4 contrasts student politics at the plebeian Temple University and the elite University of Pennsylvania. Also a commuter school, Temple had more remnants of Old Left and liberal activism, a larger number of "red-diaper babies," that is, children of Old Leftists. At Temple, one encounters the universal and surprising lament of all Philadelphia colleges throughout the 1960s—student apathy. How much success did campus activists have in organizing a New Left presence at Temple as they responded to civil rights inspiration and the beginnings of U.S. involvement in the Vietnam War, experienced the rising sensitivity of being an academic enclave surrounded by African American neighbors, and developed demands challenging *in loco parentis* in the name of student power?

In contrast, Penn was a fairly stodgy, fraternity- and sports-centered Ivy League school dominated by the Wharton School of Finance and with no history of either intellectual vitality or political activism. Yet it was at Penn that some of the most important efforts took place, particularly in challenging the university's complicity in secret war-related research. What is most interesting at Penn is the emergence of a dissident subculture, initially more centered on European movies and social satire but ultimately producing many of the activists who helped construct what became Philadelphia's most important peace organization, the Philadelphia Resistance.

The Philadelphia Resistance is the subject of Chapter 5. One of the questions I seek to answer is why Philadelphia's New Left movement never generated a significant SDS presence following the decline of Swarthmore's SDS/ERAP efforts in Chester in 1964. It is here that the institutional and cultural nexus of Quaker institutions, such as the American Friends Service Committee (AFSC), Central Committee for Conscientious Objectors (CCCO), Friends Peace Committee (FPC), and non-Quaker peace organizations like SANE, Women Strike for Peace (WSP), and Women's International League for Peace and Freedom (WILPF), played a critical role. The Resistance, typically New Left in its prefigurative politics, its anti-organizational and direct action strategies and tactics, its libertarian and anarchist spirit, substituted for SDS in the city and, in its emphasis on the war and the draft, avoided many of the ideological pitfalls that plagued other 1960s groups.

Chapter 6 highlights the issue of white antiracism through an analysis of the People for Human Rights (PHR), an organization born in the aftermath of the October 1967 board of education student demonstrations and police repression. The white New Left was forced to come to grips with the centrality of race when Black Power subsumed the more integrationist and nonviolent phase of the civil right revolution. What was to be the role of supportive white activists, no longer able to anticipate "black and white together," at least in the near future, within the struggle for racial justice? PHR embodies how some deeply committed white New Leftists sought to become loyal allies and supporters of the black liberation movement, how they sought to combat white racism, and how they faltered within the dynamics of race, sex, and class.

In the final chapter, I return to all the stories of all eight campuses, examining the late 1960s and early 1970s, particularly as the New Left movement established synergy both among campuses and throughout the region and experienced the fragmenting power of race, gender, and ideological dogmatism and the declining tide of utopian expectations. In many ways, this period was the most impressive in terms of participation, intensity, even accomplishment; and yet it was also, as I will argue, the time when the New Left lost the moral high ground. In the later sections of the chapter, I attempt to evaluate the legacy of

Philadelphia's New Left movement, in terms of both its impact on the area and the ways individual veterans of that movement have attempted to maintain their vision and values in the following decades.

This study is not primarily an oral history, although it is based on dozens of interviews with many of the most important participants in the events considered. Most of what I have discovered rests on extensive explorations in the available archival materials; as such, I approach the interviews in terms of confirmation of what seemed to be the case from the written records. Sometimes the written records require qualification—for example, if, in an organization with both female and male activists, the bulk of its literature was written by men. But faulty, often selective memory requires the social historian to be most careful in the use of interviews often thirty to forty years after the fact.

My goal is to contribute to the developing discussion about the legacy of the white New Left as a critical component of the social movements of the 1960s. We still struggle with the legacy of that era; hopefully, this case study will offer some insight into the complexities, the contradictoriness, and the inspirations that seem to be integral to making sense of those movements and that era.

## The Philadelphia Story

What you, the reader, have before you, then, is an effort to tell the story of the New Left within an important city and its surroundings, operating on a variety of very different college campuses, generating several influential activist organizations, and leaving behind it an impressive range of organizations and institutions, but, more significantly, a cultural and political legacy of protest and dissent in the name of student rights, democratization, social justice, peace, inclusion, and community. What I have attempted to accomplish is to frame how such forces participated in the subversion of what Godrey Hodgson called the liberal consensus and how those challenges are part of what we might more accurately call the gods that failed and, not to be underestimated, the accomplishments of a more inclusive human community.[13]

What was the significance of this set of New Left forces being unleashed in the City of Brotherly Love? The complicated dance of Left, Center, and Right occurred on a particular stage that differed from those of other major cities and of more narrowly circumscribed campuses and campus towns.

The Philadelphia story must be informed by the special qualities that made this fourth largest American city—in the 1950s, it dropped from second and then third as first Chicago and then Los Angeles surged past it—what Sam Bass Warner, Jr., called "the Private City."[14] Historian John Lukacs states, "Interior life was what counted in Philadelphia, including interior decorousness and interior decoration of lives."[15] A number of scholars, most especially E. Digby Baltzell, have emphasized the ways Philadelphia "has suffered from the virus of virtuous materialism for almost three centuries and how its best men, on the whole, have seldom sought public office or positions of societal authority and leadership outside of business."[16] Baltzell cites a politically incorrect friend who observes, "The people in Boston all want to be chiefs, while in Philly they are all content to be Indians." This is not to suggest a particularly democratic core to Philadelphia but rather to an absence of public service and cultural leadership on the part of the Quaker-cum-Episcopalian commercial and then industrial-financial elite.

There were, however, distinctively egalitarian elements. For example, 1950s Philadelphia was a city of small industries, not dominated by a few mega-enterprises.[17] It was a city of neighborhoods spread out over an extensive land area. And, perhaps most profoundly, it was a city of homeowners, with few of the tenements associated with industrial era urban life; Lukacs claims that Philadelphia had a higher homeownership rate than any other comparable city in the world; by 1950, fully one half its families owned their own homes.[18] Middle- and working-class Philadelphians resided in row houses in dozens of neighborhoods with names like Fishtown, Brewerytown, and Manayunk. Some of the economic elite had migrated out to the suburbs like those along the old Pennsylvania Railroad Main Line, but a significant number were settled in enclaves within the city boundaries, in pastoral Chestnut Hill or Center City at Rittenhouse Square.[19]

In the meantime, Philadelphia, from the postbellum era until the 1950s, was dominated by what historian Dennis Clark called "an all but impregnable Republican machine" led by such legendary figures as Boies Penrose and the Vare brothers.[20] What makes Philadelphia distinctive is the longevity of Republican dominance in a national environment increasingly characterized by the loyalty of urban voters to the Democratic Party of Al Smith, Franklin D. Roosevelt, and their heirs. Part of the explanation for this anomaly is Philadelphia's ethnic uniqueness. Whereas Boston elected its first Irish Catholic mayor in the 1880s and never looked back, and New York had the Irish-dominated Tammany Hall, Philadelphia did not have an Irish Catholic mayor until the 1960s. Philadelphia had a lower percentage of foreign born than comparable East Coast smokestack cities and continued to have a large northern European, Protestant working class that provided many of the nonelite leaders of the GOP machine.[21]

Therefore, as one attempts to set the scene for the 1960s in Philadelphia, one must keep in mind the belatedness of the city's embracing of Samuel Lubell's New Deal coalition, both in terms of its welfare state policies and in recognition of its ethnic conservatism. Philadelphians like John B. Kelly, Grace's father, and Albert Greenfield, the Russian Jewish banker and realtor, sought entry into the political and social world of the WASP elite—the Republican Party and the Union League. Both were rejected and subsequently turned toward the more ethnically welcoming Democrats. Greenfield welcomed the party of Jefferson, Jackson, and FDR to its Philadelphia convention in 1936.[22] But such figures weren't able to break the GOP hold on city politics until 1951.

In the late 1940s a coalition emerged, dominated by what Lukacs calls "the Best Men," who led "a civic renaissance" that sped to electoral victory in 1951, ending the sixty-seven-year Republican rule. Philadelphians elected Joseph S. Clark, Jr., a city blueblood, as mayor and Richardson Dilworth, a Pittsburgh transplant and ex-marine, as district attorney under a charter reform platform. This victorious coalition included ethnic elements—Jewish, Irish, Italian, Slavic—that had been so decisive in the triumph of New Deal politics two decades earlier in other cities and indeed throughout the nation. But the leadership remained Anglo-Saxon, and in that were seeds of destruction that would play a significant part in the complicated political environment within which the movements of the 1960s operated.[23]

Philadelphia was changing—finally. Bernard Segal was elected chancellor of the bar in 1952, the first Jew so chosen. The Irish, under the leadership of U.S. Representative William Green, the head of the city Democratic Party, sought to take advantage of the new patronage opportunities offered by the 1951 victories. Blacks like City Councilman Raymond Pace Alexander, Recorder of Deeds the Rev. Marshall L. Shepard, and the Rev. William Gray, newly chosen to join the board of the Redevelopment Authority and soon to be elected to Congress, sought their place in the new Democratic sun. And on the streets of South Philadelphia and in Center City, a rising young Italian American police inspector, Frank Rizzo, began to make a name for himself as the scourge of strip joints and prostitutes.[24]

Philadelphia's ethnic and racial history played a significant role in framing the choices available to what would become the local New Left movement. That Catholics came so late, relatively, to political power affected the ways liberalism came under fire and, necessarily, how a new radicalism positioned itself in the city. Almost as soon as Catholics achieved political prominence, at virtually the same moment as immigrant stock Irish, Italian, and Polish Philadelphians gained control of the machinery of urban politics, they faced a challenge from the even longer and more deeply marginalized African American community. Even without the reality of racism, this set of overlapping demands, expectations, and injuries would have made it most difficult to facilitate a strengthened New Deal coalition.

In addition, Philadelphia liberalism had a decided Quaker and patrician dimension. Its more respectable side was personified by the tandem of Clark and Dilworth, but it included those involved with the Greater Philadelphia Movement (GPM), representing enlightened business interests; planners like Edmund Bacon, central to the reconstruction of Center City; and liberal Democrats, often associated with the Americans for Democratic Action (ADA).[25] The Philadelphia ADA chapter was unique in that it focused primarily on civic reform and less on national and foreign policy issues. GPM and ADA were central players in the 1951 electoral victories and in the subsequent clashes between reformers and machine politicians over the next several decades. Nevertheless, these patrician reformers transformed what had been a private, complacent city. Dennis Clark concluded that

a half century of planning, rebuilding, and controversy had produced a new city image, a rebuilt Center City, but a wide disruption of what was perhaps the single greatest social resource of the city, its working class neighborhoods.
The reformers' emphasis was on revitalization of the business district and of the most visible images of the city, those which might attract new corporate headquarters, conventions, and tourism. The outlying neighborhoods, working and middle class, often felt neglected by the patrician planners.[26]

There were also Quaker-influenced aspects of Philadelphia liberalism. The city was headquarters of the AFSC, CCCO, and Philadelphia Yearly Meeting's FPC. These organizations would play significant roles as foreign policy became more salient, especially as the war in Vietnam became Americanized. But the Quaker influence went beyond issues of war and peace. Quakers helped to shape the ways the city and the region addressed civil liberties and civil rights. Swarthmore, Haverford, and Bryn Mawr Colleges and a host of secondary schools, such as Germantown Friends and Friends Central, added to the institutional structure of Philadelphia Quakerism. As such, many idealists and reformers found employment working for AFSC, FPC, or Friends schools. Such institutions often sponsored and funded speakers committed to social justice and peace or facilitated conferences, research efforts, retreats, and workshops. This influence affected mainstream liberalism in the city both ideologically and ethnically, high-toning it, if

Figure 1. Police Commissioner Frank L. Rizzo observing antiwar demonstrators, 1969. Temple Urban Archives.

you will; it also was an organizational, resource, and financial presence to all young New Leftists seeking funding, places to meet, allies, and sponsors.[27]

It would be difficult to construct a more sharply drawn contrast than that which existed between Quaker pacifism and patrician liberalism on the one hand and Frank Rizzo on the other. The former embodied what Max Weber called a politics of ultimate ends, a priority given to matters of conscience, a high-minded idealism, in part grounded in the luxuries of a privileged social class. Rizzo, in contrast, personified a politics of responsibility—more accurately, a politics of loyalty to one's own, centering on issues of turf and tribal passions. In a variety of ways—with a host of other, sometimes equally salient factors—the tension between these two factions would drive Philadelphia politics, and particularly that of its local New Left, during and following the 1960s.

Frank Rizzo was a critical factor in Philadelphia politics by the late 1950s; by the middle and late 1960s he was *the* dominant issue and story. He dominated mayoral elections for over twenty years, initially as police commissioner, then as a five-time candidate, twice elected. Philadelphia New Leftists and other radicals, whatever their criticisms of mainstream liberals, inevitably were drawn into an anti-Rizzo alliance. As Martin Weinberg, a key Rizzo aide, defined the battle lines,

The row house people and the ethnic community, because of this history of foisting things upon them . . . were ready for revolt. You had this pristine area in Chestnut Hill and Rittenhouse Square, and Society Hill, where Dilworth lived. The division came down to one thing: Economics. On the one hand, you had the white Anglo-Saxon Protestants and the good government Jewish community, and the blacks, and the War on Poverty. And on the other, you had the Italians, the Polish, the Ukrainians, the Germans, the working class Jews, they were getting nothing. Where was the war on *their* poverty?[28]

Frank Rizzo became the embodiment of one side of the culture war as it played out in Philadelphia; as Weinberg suggests albeit with his own spin, the war rested on deeply felt historical injuries and resentments. Consequently, the history of Philadelphia's New Left is bound up with the fate of liberal reform and the long and pervasive shadow of Frank Rizzo's right-wing, ethnic populism.[29]

Such ideological patterns, overlaid with ethnic and social class influences, were exacerbated, as was the case throughout urban America, by race. Like most industrial cities in the northeast, Philadelphia was a major recipient of the Great Migration of African Americans from the south, pulled by economic opportunities and hopes of greater freedom, catalyzed by the world wars, and pushed, especially after 1945, by the mechanization of southern cotton agriculture and intentionally meager and, even then, reluctantly granted social welfare benefits.[30] Between 1920 and 1970, Philadelphia's black population increased from 134,229 to 653,791, from 7.36 to 33.6 percent of the city.[31] Its political leadership remained elite and moderately liberal through the 1950s, increasingly linked to the patrician-led Democratic Party coalition that came to power in 1951.

During the early 1960s, however, Cecil B. Moore became president of the local NAACP chapter. Moore was a flamboyant veteran who quickly clashed with both the white and black establishments.[32] At that time, African American politics, in Philadelphia and throughout the nation, was touched by the rising civil rights revolution, initially focused in the Jim Crow South. Philadelphia blacks had already been challenging traditional racial practices, like the blackface Mummers Parade, the segregated policies of Girard College (a school for male orphans still honoring the racially exclusive last will of its founder), and segregated housing practices, most particularly in new public housing units.[33] But Moore, in the context of freedom rides, children's crusades, and sit-ins, and facing a challenge from a small but aggressive local chapter of CORE, escalated both the rhetoric and the militancy of his NAACP chapter.[34] Clashing with CORE, which he perceived as a rival for the mantle of the most militant and authentic voice of the black community, and with the NAACP's older leadership, whom he viewed as too accommodating, Moore came to personify African American politics in Philadelphia as much as Frank Rizzo was to embody what many came to call white backlash.

The rise of a New Left in Philadelphia thus must be framed within the context of a racial politics dominated by the remarkable and charismatic Cecil Moore. Other forces would take center stage, especially the Black Panthers, who would profoundly influence white radical politics, as well as Swarthmore's SDS chapter, which would launch an ambitious community organizing project in nearby Chester. But in the early 1960s, black politics meant Cecil Moore.

It may be useful to think of Philadelphia politics as distinctively contradictory, even schizophrenic. On the one hand, the city possesses a rich and admirable history of defending civil liberties, especially during the McCarthy-led Red Scare, when the Philadelphia Bar rallied in defense of the constitutional rights of accused Communists during Pennsylvania's Smith Act prosecutions. On the other hand, because of its belated New Deal, its unusual Republican and WASP domination through the 1940s, and its "private city" parochialism, Philadelphia faced incredible barriers to progress in a host of areas, especially public education.[35]

The Philadelphia school district was among the most insular and parochial in the nation. As political scientist Conrad Weiler sharply notes, it "was dominated by a man who had never completed high school, had held the post of Business Manager for thirty years . . . and was obsessed with low taxes and a balanced budget."[36] Add Anderson, described by journalist Peter Binzen as "a penny pincher all his life . . . a ruthless man filled with contempt for 'educators,' " dominated the district through patronage appointments, including those of teachers, from the 1920s until his death in 1962. According to Binzen,

Nobody ever crossed Anderson and got away with it. He became a legendary figure, a Scrooge with rollup desk who blocked all efforts at liberalization and made the school system dance to his tunes. It was during his long rule that . . . janitors were paid more than principals, that per-pupil spending and teachers' salaries sank to national lows . . . that the lawyer who for years had argued the Chamber of Commerce's case against school-tax increases won appointment to the board and became its president.[37]

At one point, the average age of an Add Anderson-chosen board member was over 65. As late as 1965, 63 schools of 266 were built before 1906 and not fire resistant. Moreover, despite the student population becoming majority black by the early 1960s, there were no African Americans appointed to high supervisory positions. Until 1967, the board of education refused to administer any national standardized tests. Indeed, Binzen understates the situation within the district in concluding that the board seemed to be "waging war against change."[38]

Beginning in the late 1950s, with the emergence of Mrs. Albert Greenfield as an influential board member, and continuing into the 1960s, with the revamping of the board under the leadership of Richardson Dilworth and the appointment of Harvard's Dr. Mark Shedd as superintendent, reform commenced. As Binzen noted, however, the new board appointments "reflected the distrust of the reformers, most of them middle-class Protestants and Jews, of big-city mayors, many of them Roman Catholics with working-class antecedents." Binzen concluded, "There was no place on the panel [of the Educational Home Rule Charter Commission] for grassroots Whitetowners or Blacktowners . . . the working-class neighborhoods were ignored."[39] It seemed as if the Add Anderson era had been swept into the dustbin of district history. However, when Frank Rizzo, another high school dropout, emerged, one of his first targets of attack would be Mark Shedd and his band of elite educational reformers.

Indeed, one of the central moments in the story of Frank Rizzo's rise to power—one biographer calls it "one of the most significant days in Frank Rizzo's life"—occurred on November 17, 1967, when the Philadelphia police broke up a student rally at the board of education building that was demanding a more black-focused curriculum and a tolerance of new Afrocentric dress such as Afros and dashikis. In many ways that event serves as a paradigm for the politics of the era: black youth attacked by white ethnic police and defended by patrician, liberal, and radical whites. As they waited, the more than 3,000 students became restless and rowdy, a few climbing on top of cars to speak; police claim rocks and bottles were thrown at them. According to most accounts, Police Commissioner Rizzo gave the signal to charge; several black leaders claim he exclaimed, "Get their black asses!" The melee was brief; the police were efficient. But fifteen were hospitalized, dozens were arrested, and five officers were injured. Spencer Coxe, local head of the American Civil Liberties Union, declared, "I myself was there and saw children fleeing from the police lying on the ground each with three patrolmen beating them unmercifully with clubs." The black community and its white allies called for Rizzo's ouster—by Mayor James Tate, the first Irish Catholic mayor. Board President Dilworth and Superintendent Shedd condemned the police intervention. Tate, in fact, ran for election with a platform pledge to reappoint the police commissioner called by many "the Cisco Kid." Philadelphia's New Deal coalition was fractured and the culture war was on.

It was into this combustible class, ethnic, and racial setting that some of Philadelphia's embryonic New Left activists entered. The first New Left organizing efforts in the city were through the Philadelphia Tutorial Project (PTP), housed at Temple University and initially spearheaded by a New Left leader, Peter Countryman of the Northern Student Movement (NSM), an organization founded to carry the civil rights movement, especially as embodied by SNCC, to northern cities. PTP offered afterschool tutoring services to mostly minority youth, and it was by challenging the inertia of Philadelphia's sclerotic school system that many New Left activists got their first movement experience.[40]

The Rev. Paul Washington, pastor at the Episcopal Church of the Advocate in North Philadelphia and a leader in the developing anti-Rizzo efforts, describes the creation of two other New Left organizations that were inspired by the 1967 event:

One, called People for Human Rights, was only for white people who wanted to work against racism in their own community and to be a support group for Black Power activities. The other, called Philadelphians for Equal Justice (PEJ), was a racially mixed group of citizens who decided to band together to protect black Philadelphians in particular against "illegal intimidation and arrest and almost daily episodes of police brutality."[41]

Washington saw the clashes at the school board as profound demonstration of the developing bifurcation of forces within Philadelphia:

November 17 so clearly showed the division in our city. One the one side were those white people who feared a revolt, and instead of working to eliminate the causes, were calling for police repression. On the other side were black people, with some white allies who were searching for new institutional forms to express their identity and worth.[42]

It was in the context of these racial and class tensions, of a city experiencing the beginnings of deindustrialization, of the clash within a belatedly arrived New Deal between gentleman reformers, ethnic spoilsmen, and African Americans, of the emergence of such strong personalities as Cecil B. Moore and Frank Rizzo, that a New Left took form in the city of brotherly love.

## Chapter 1

# The Old Left and the 1960s

The watershed moment in the origins of the new Left in America was the virtual collapse of the Communist Party in the United States following the Twentieth Party Congress in Moscow and the subsequent Soviet invasion of Hungary in 1956. Within several years Party membership and associated networks precipitously declined and rival left-wing organizations sought to fill the vacuum left by the demoralization of Moscow-driven Communism.[1] The foremost efforts in this direction were undertaken by A. J. Muste, an independent radical and former Communist, who had moved toward a direct action model of pacifism by the 1950s, and by Max Shachtman, also an ex-Communist, whose Independent Socialist League sought to become a third force for democratic socialism between the capitalist USA and the Stalinist USSR.[2] Several groups of Philadelphians—radical Quakers, Shachtmanites, ex-Communists, Trotskyists—showed interest in the several meetings that took place in New York City in 1957–58. But deeply rooted sectarian suspicions, particularly by Max Shachtman and his followers, subverted such bridgebuilding efforts.[3] There was to be no post-Hungary revitalized and reconstructed Old Left.

The shift from an *Old* to a *New* Left occurred in this context and within the developing historical realities of the postwar period: the emergence of a postcolonial Third World distinguishable from U.S. and Soviet interests; the remarkable performance of the mixed economies of the welfare states of the West; the growing sense that the Weberian "iron cage" of rationalization and bureaucracy seemed to make alienation a more salient social phenomenon than exploitation; and the anxiety generated by Hiroshima, what SDS would soon pinpoint in terms of its own historical moment as "the sense that we may be the last generation in the experiment with living."[4] The "oldness" of the Old Left rested on the ways it seemed frozen in Cold War polarities and what C. Wright Mills called "the labor metaphysic." By contrast, the New Left generation's coming of age during the 1950s and 1960s coincided with the success of "corporate liberalism": the integration of previously antagonistic forces, specifically organized labor, into the Democratic Party coalition that had originally been formed during FDR's New Deal. Indeed, the long-awaited merger of the American Federation of Labor (AFL) with the Congress of Industrial Organizations (CIO) in 1955 highlighted what many Leftists perceived as the integration of organized labor as a junior partner to corporate America.[5]

At least as important was the way deeply felt, often traumatic experiences of betrayal and apostasy polluted the waters of any dialogue, not to speak of reconciliation or ideological flexibility, between the Old Left of the Depression and immediate postwar generations. Being *Old* Left meant that one experienced the present through the prism of battles over Stalinism, Spain, sectarian labor conflicts, and rival claims to being the vanguard of the proletariat. Older Leftists were marked by deep and abiding wounds, which never seemed to heal and in fact were re-ignited as every moment in the present ripped apart the scabs of inflamed memory.

In this period of McCarthyism and weakened labor radicalism, there were small but significant civil rights rallies in Washington, inspired by the Supreme Court's 1954 *Brown v. Board of Education* decision regarding school integration and the Montgomery bus boycott of 1955–56. The Prayer Pilgrimage for Freedom took place in 1957, and the Youth Marches for Integrated Schools in 1958 and 1959. These marches were organized within African American communities, chiefly by prominent ministers like the Rev. Leon Sullivan, with white allies in both the liberal and radical communities responding to the call. At the 1957 pilgrimage, which included possibly 5,000 Philadelphians, A. Philip Randolph, a veteran of the sectarian wars among Marxists, "warned Negroes against accepting Communist help in their civil rights struggle." Nevertheless, the *Philadelphia Bulletin* warned, "The Communist Party had been making a big campaign to inject its followers into the pilgrimage." The article conceded that, although Communists had been spotted in the crowd, they had been excluded from the platform.

At the time of these marches, in fact, Philadelphia Communism was in total disarray, with ex-members vastly outnumbering members and the former seeking to reconstruct their lives, find jobs, return to school, and reconnect with their families.[6] The Trotskyists, organized as the Socialist Workers Party, had a small Philadelphia presence, but hardly the weight or numbers to make a significant difference.

The Shachtmanites seemed the most energetic and influential of these Marxist-Leninist groups, in part because of their reputation as principled defenders of democracy, in part because of their ability to attract, at least for a time, a brilliant group of radical intellectuals including Irving Howe and the young Michael Harrington.[7] In Philadelphia, the Shachtmanites were entering their most promising period as they merged in 1958 with the Socialist Party and came to dominate its youth affiliate, the Young People's Socialist League (YPSL, or the "Yipsels" as they were usually called). In the late 1950s and early 1960s, Yipsel youth leaders Martin Oppenheimer, a graduate student in sociology at the University of Pennsylvania, Tom Barton, a conscientious objector from the midwest working for the Friends Peace Committee (FPC), and Leo Kormis, a lab technician at the University of Pennsylvania who would play a significant role in influencing a new generation of campus activists, were able to recruit a number of campus idealists into their circle of radical activities, which included the early years of the Philadelphia chapter of CORE and the promising development of the Student Peace Union (SPU).[8]

The Yipsels are of interest in part because they produced dedicated organizers during the 1950s and early 1960s. Oppenheimer, Barton, and Kormis were children of the 1950s, and those they recruited were of the World War II generation. Such activists, neither Depression generation nor baby boomers, sometimes served as a bridge between the two, but alternatively, as ideological Marxists in an inhospitable period, they could feel a particular impatience with developing New Left sensibilities. Barton, for example, was thoroughly unimpressed in the early 1960s with members of the fledgling Swarthmore chapter of SDS as the latter made connections with the Chester black community, which would help inspire the decidedly New Left Economic Research and Action Project (ERAP). To the ideologically sophisticated Barton, the Swarthmore SDSers were naive, speaking a language he neither respected nor understood. He recalls that he could always engage in ideological banter with his sectarian rivals in the Communist or Trotskyist or social democratic youth groups—"We all spoke the same language," he says, despite hating one another. But with Paul Booth, the young Swarthmore SDSer, he found himself perplexed and bewildered by a rhetoric that seemed to have nothing to do with the familiar Marxist categories of analysis that Barton privileged. "What is he talking about?" Barton recalls. Indeed, Booth, himself a World War II baby, was among the most electorally oriented, most analytic of the Swarthmore SDS activists, characteristically at odds with those envisioning the Chester ERAP as a model for the New Left. But he wasn't a Marxist, at least to Tom Barton's already experienced and ideologically sensitive antennae.

Oppenheimer and Kormis, in contrast, seem to have felt more of a tug of war over their loyalties between Old Left class analysis and the developing New Left emphasis on alienation, direct action, and participatory democracy. Oppenheimer would play a significant role in articulating and teaching the direct action approach of SNCC and CORE; Kormis was respected most of all for the consistency of his deep and abiding commitment to a humanistic socialism based on notions of participatory democracy.[9]

Up until 1963 or 1964, the Yipsel-dominated SPU was positioned to become the dominant and successful progressive student voice on foreign policy issues. It began as a coalition of radical, liberal, and pacifist organizations in Chicago and drew sustenance from the developing criticisms of atmospheric nuclear testing in the late 1950s. This seemed to be a fruitful strategy for radicals seeking to find some wiggle room for a progressive politics in what seemed to most to be monolithic Cold War posturings on both sides. By 1963 it was the largest student-based peace organization in the country, with more than 3,000 members and more than 200 campus chapters. In Philadelphia, SPU claimed 200 members at Temple, Penn, Swarthmore, Haverford, and Bryn Mawr. But the combination of sectarianism, mostly coming from internal struggles within YPSL, and the inevitable loss of focus following the signing of the Nuclear Test-Ban Treaty in fall 1963, led to the collapse of SPU. Once again, the sectarian dogmatism of the Old Left prevented the birth of a promising new coalition.[10]

## Philadelphia SANE

Serving as a catalyst to the rise of SPU in 1960 was the Committee for a SANE Nuclear Policy, quickly called SANE, which had emerged as the most successful organization within an admittedly weak early peace movement. The spark leading to the formation of SANE in 1957 was the accidental scattering of radioactive dust on twenty-three Japanese fishermen in March 1954.[11] The stir over the potential destructive effects of radiation led Lawrence Scott, an AFSC staffer in Chicago, to bring together A. J. Muste, Bayard Rustin, and Robert Gilmore, also of the AFSC, to a meeting in Philadelphia in April 1957. From this meeting came two organizations—one, SANE, created to be a broad-based public education organization, and the other, the Committee for Non-Violent Action (CNVA) to provide more radical pacifists with a smaller, direct-action instrument.[12]

SANE rapidly grew beyond the expectations and the organizational framework of its founders. By summer 1958 there were already 130

chapters and approximately 25,000 members. A Student SANE structure quickly formed as well.[13] Clearly, the call for a halt to nuclear testing had struck a powerful chord among the seemingly disorganized
and demoralized progressives frightened by the McCarthyist Red
Scare and frustrated by the moral placidity of the popular president
Dwight David Eisenhower. In the context of the essential collapse of
the Communist Party and the failure of any other organizational effort
to offer opportunities to the thousands of former Communists left
without institutional support, SANE proved to be an attractive option
for activists concerned with Cold War irrationalities. As such, innumerable individuals with organizational skills, practical political experience,
and a bruised, sometimes humbled, but nevertheless still passionate
set of ideals joined SANE. Most were not former Communists; instead,
the "organizational base" of early SANE remained pacifist, especially
under the influence of the AFSC. There was a concentration of membership and chapters in New York, New Jersey, California, Connecticut, Illinois, and Pennsylvania. Many who flocked to SANE's banner
were nuclear pacifists, that is, those who came to believe that the
threat of nuclear confrontation made world peace a moral imperative,
as well as veterans of world government efforts, such as the United
World Federalists.[14]

In Philadelphia, there was a call for a meeting on May 17, 1960 to
consider the formation of a chapter of SANE. This preliminary meeting, at which national SANE representative Sandy Gottlieb spoke, was
called by Joe Miller and several others, most of whom were veterans
or allies of the Communist Old Left. At a following meeting in June,
considered the first official meeting of a Philadelphia SANE chapter,
Abe Egnal, a veteran of the Old Left, was chosen temporary chair. The
twenty-five who attended the preliminary meeting were now up to
more than fifty. In a reflection of his initial enthusiasm, Egnal exclaimed, "This crowd attests to the fact that millions want peace."[15]
Perhaps more modestly, the gathering suggested that an opportunity
now existed for a coalition of Old Left, pacifist, and liberal activists to
stake a claim to speak for those willing to take a stand against nuclear
terror.

The Executive Board of the Greater Philadelphia Council of SANE
included thirteen members, nine from the Old Left, the remainder ei-
ther Quaker or liberal. The board included Barrows Dunham, the
Marxist philosopher fired from Temple University in the early 1950s,
Ike Freedman of the left-leaning Furrier Workers Union, and such
liberals as Spencer Coxe of ACLU, Norval Reece of Americans for
Democratic Action (ADA), and the well-born Quaker attorney Henry
Sawyer. Two, Abe Egnal and Isadore Reivich, were among the twenty-

six Philadelphia public school teachers fired in 1953 for refusing to discuss their political loyalties, past and present.[16]

Egnal, who would become chairman of both the Main Line-West Philadelphia branch and the Greater Philadelphia chapter, was born in 1908. He was a graduate of the University of Pennsylvania with a B.A. and an M.A. in economics, and had been an activist in the Teachers Union of Philadelphia as a social studies teacher at John Bartram High School until fired. He and his wife Leah joined five others— William and Ethel Taylor, Joe and Eleanor Miller, and Harry Levitan— in signing the charter for the Main Line-West Philadelphia branch of the chapter.[17]

Ethel Taylor, who remained involved with SANE, would also be the long-time leader of the local Women Strike for Peace (WSP) chapter as well as a national leader of that organization. Taylor, who often described herself as "a middle-aged Main Line matron," had previously been active in the Women's International League for Peace and Freedom (WILPF).[18]

Joe Miller, whose brother had been a local Communist Party leader, was a mortgage banker and devoted much of his time and financial networking skills to the peace, civil rights, and social justice movements of Philadelphia from the mid-1950s until his death in 1996. Joe, once described as "a little white-haired man who is creative, warm and filled with hope and energy," and his wife Eleanor, a sculptor, hosted virtually every important progressive fund-raising cocktail party over the next decades at their Center City apartment.[19] The Millers, Harry and Elsie Levitan, Isadore and Elizabeth Reivich, Ethel Taylor, Abe Egnal, and several other veterans of the Old Left would remain mainstays of the Philadelphia chapter of SANE over the next several decades. Some, such as Taylor, would be the key leaders in WSP and WILPF during those same years.

The Greater Philadelphia SANE chapter consisted of Main Line-West Philadelphia, Bucks County, Delaware County, Northwest, Northeast, Center City, and Student SANE branches. Some branches involved larger proportions of liberals and nuclear pacifists, including Quakers and other church-inspired idealists, but the leadership in all instances came from the veterans of the Old Left Communist movement, most of whom were second-generation Jewish Americans. SANE in Philadelphia became an outlet for the remarkable energies and idealism, the organizational skill and experience, of Old Leftists who had been without an ideological home following the virtual collapse of the Communist Party and its front operations, a phenomenon that also occurred in other cities on both coasts where ex-Communists resided.

Just prior to the creation of the Philadelphia SANE chapter, the national organization held a successful rally at Madison Square Garden to coincide with the summit conference planned by President Eisenhower and Soviet leader Nikita Khrushchev. On the eve of the rally, Senator Thomas Dodd, a ferociously anti-Communist Democrat from Connecticut, criticized the rally, pointing to organizers with suspect ideological backgrounds and calling on SANE to purge its ranks of Communists. National SANE had recognized from its initial successes that a variety of radicals, including former Communists, were involved in the formation and development of chapters. One prominent New Yorker instrumental in organizing the Garden rally, for example, had been forced to resign from SANE after refusing to respond to national leader Norman Cousins's questions about his Communist affiliations, past and present. National SANE struggled over the issue before mildly rebuking Dodd and other red-baiting members of Congress and then stating that they welcomed only those "whose support is not qualified by adherence to Communist or other totalitarian doctrine." Such a policy statement, which included a proviso that "persons who are not free because of party discipline or political allegiance to criticize the actions of totalitarian nations with the same standards by which they challenge other nations will not be welcome as members," was distributed to all SANE chapters. Some, especially those in New York, refused to support the statement and were expelled from the organization.

By 1961 the crisis seemed to have passed; the House Un-American Activities Committee's Annual Report stated that SANE was not Communist-dominated.[20] But there had been costs. Many members, including key radical pacifists like Stewart Meacham and Robert Gilmore of AFSC, resigned, as did Muste. Linus Pauling withdrew his sponsorship of the organization.[21]

The Philadelphia chapter seems to have addressed this controversy by voting against the majority policy but not aggressively challenging it. As such, Philadelphia SANE was never threatened with the removal of its charter and expulsion from the organization.[22] In October 1960, Ethel Taylor, the chapter's representative to the SANE national board, reported from the annual national conference about the controversy sparked by Dodd's charges. She noted that the national leadership's recommendation that national and local SANE not play into the controversy "created dissension and a confusion over our best policy, at all levels of SANE (we experienced it in our group) and the inevitable formation of two different positions." In the local discussion following Taylor's report, there was an unsuccessful effort to have the local chapter "express a vote of confidence to the National Committee on its purposes and policy statement." But most members seemed to prefer to take a wait-and-see attitude, urging a renewed focus on the chapter's peace activities. The chapter seemed to opt for evasion over either challenge or compliance.[23]

It is at this moment that one can begin to see the ways the Old Left or, at least, Old Left-dominated organizations, would miss opportunities to attract those of a new generation who came to distinguish themselves as New Left. A younger generation, suspicious of the compromising seemingly inherent in mainstream politics and wary of a politics of deception that seemed simply to reinforce the charge of Old Left opportunism, was looking for a vehicle by which to start afresh.

At the August 7, 1961 meeting in Philadelphia, there was a report on a proposed "Hoot for Peace," to be sponsored by Student SANE. One of the national leaders, Executive Director Homer Jack, had written Ethel Taylor a letter asking that the concert be canceled because of "the irresponsibility of Temple SANE," emphasizing "the fact that the issues of civil liberties and peace should not be mixed." Jack threatened that if the hoot were held, the charters of all Philadelphia area SANE affiliates would be revoked. He also threatened to phone Temple University to ensure that the event was canceled. To Jack, who was operating in the shadow of Senator Dodd's attacks and genuinely concerned with Communist Party infiltration, such events reeked of the old Popular Front.[24]

The controversy began when Jay Mandle, a red-diaper baby whose parents were members of SANE and who was a leader of Student SANE at the University of Pennsylvania, organized the Hoot, which was to be highlighted by the performance of the still-blacklisted Pete Seeger, an Old Left favorite. Mandle had no reason to be concerned as the proposal worked its way through the organization without criticism, indeed with support and enthusiasm. Philadelphia SANE did not object to Mandle's efforts until the Homer Jack directives arrived. In fact, Taylor and another local SANE member had met with Jack to try to persuade him to support the concert. The students were understandably unhappy with the national board's policies and charged that "the National organization was extremely distrustful of student groups." Local leaders felt offended by Jack's demands, but many concluded that "the issue was not of sufficient importance to risk the breaking up of the whole organization." As such, they argued that the concert should be canceled but that a protest letter should be transmitted to the national office. The board minutes state, "Since the peace movement must, to be effective, include elements from both the right and the left, we should be very careful not to alienate any of the elements by our actions." Others, clearly the minority, felt that the actions of the national had already alienated members and consequently weakened SANE, nationally and locally. A few argued that it was more principled to withdraw rather than compromise on this issue, but "it was decided not to take the issue back to the local groups, and to leave the final decision to the students." In fact, Philadelphia SANE had decided to roll with the *dictat* from the national organization, no matter how offensive and insulting they perceived the demand, no matter how hysterical they found Homer Jack's concerns.[25]

The students did speak with Jack; there was some discussion about finding another sponsor. Moreover, chapter head Abe Egnal sent a letter to Jack, Norman Cousins, and Clarence Pickett, all of the national board, stating that "we are outraged when, in an obviously immature manner, we are threatened with separation from SANE. We are further outraged at the insensitivity toward the young people whose careers could be affected by some of the actions threatened." But in the end the Philadelphia chapter of Student SANE canceled the Hoot for Peace.[26]

The Hoot for Peace controversy marked Philadelphia SANE as an Old Left organization, understandably wary of directly challenging McCarthy-like red-baiting and scarred by anti-Communist purges of organizations, especially unions, over the past decade and a half. It also laid bare the tensions within the organization over the extent to which such confrontations were to be avoided. Philadelphia SANE played things safe, albeit with sufficient rhetorical counterattacks to preserve its sense of ideological and organizational self-respect. But such compromises made it an unlikely magnet for the emerging idealism, spurred by the civil rights revolution and the nascent peace movement, of a new generation of Philadelphia activists, red-diaper or not. Young activists, inspired by the direct action authenticity of SNCC and CORE in the sit-ins and freedom rides, would contrast the existential courage they found in the movement with the caution and calculation of those scarred by McCarthyism and trained to value organizational survival over grand but risky acts.

At the same time, the tenacity and relative successes of Philadelphia SANE during the 1960s are striking. At the national level, SANE reached an early peak of success with the signing of the partial Test-Ban Treaty in 1963 and then seemed to flounder in search of a cause.[27] But as early as January 1963 local SANE chapters were highlighting the dangers of U.S. military activities in South Vietnam, proposing "an end of unilateral action" and calling on the administration to "take the initiative for an international conference" comparable to that at Geneva, which had brokered an uneasy coalition government in Laos. SANE warned of the possibilities of "another Korea and even a full scale war with the People's Republic of China."[28]

In this context, Philadelphia SANE opened its first office in Center City in fall 1962, hiring David Eldredge, a history teacher at the George School in Bucks County and a founder of that county's branch, as part-time executive director. A year later, Eldredge took leave from his teaching position to become full-time executive director; a new office manager was also hired. Under Eldredge's leadership, the chapter played a role in a wide variety of peace activities in the period 1963–65, including urging conversion from a war to a peace economy, advocating a more extensive ban on nuclear testing, taking part in Easter Peace Walks, and monitoring the developing crisis in Vietnam, especially when the Gulf of Tonkin incident and the subsequent congressional resolution burst forth in August 1964. The greatest attention, however, went toward working against Barry Goldwater's candidacy for president in 1964.[29]

Electoral efforts, however, did not substitute for the élan produced by the campaign for an end to nuclear testing. Indeed, SANE's national political action director, Sanford Gottlieb, discouraged the Philadelphia leadership from investing too much in local politics, stating his belief that "the peace groups in Philadelphia, in particular, do not speak the same language as the vast majority of their fellow citizens." Gottlieb called on the leadership to expand their base beyond unilateral disarmament people to connect with labor, blacks, and more mainstream liberals. He advised them to drop supporting marginal third-party candidates and, instead, rally behind liberal friends like Senator Joseph Clark.[30] National SANE sought to build bridges to the liberal mainstream; its Philadelphia chapter, driven by Old Left and pacifist longings, ignored such advice but at the same time stayed clear of the more direct action wing of the emerging peace movement. Neither wing had much success in expanding its constituency beyond the self-defined progressives of the white middle classes of Center City, pockets of West and Northwest Philadelphia, and enclaves on the Main Line.

A different sort of criticism from Gottlieb's came from Arthur Shostak, a young radical sociologist at the University of Pennsylvania, who, at a meeting of Turn Toward Peace (TTP), a coalition of peace organizations in which SANE was heavily involved, charged:

(1) There is a feeling of a "party line"
(2) Newcomers feel crudely treated
(3) Outsiders are frightened by the lack of harmony among the peace organizations.
(4) There is a focus on the far-off . . .

(5) A sense of poverty of resources and human talent is conveyed—a few people do a great deal of work.
(6) Self-pity is often expressed
(7) There is no dynamism—a contrast to the civil rights movement.[31]

The minutes note that Shostak's critique "was followed by a lively discussion."

Indeed, the peace movement of the early 1960s struggled with a legacy of mutual mistrust among Old Left, pacifist, and liberal organizations. SPU had collapsed from such divisions; Turn Toward Peace also blew up on the minefields of organizational rivalries and ideological differences. Such self-destructive behavior as described by Shostak often drove younger idealists toward the more clearly defined New Left organizations like the Northern Student Movement (NSM), inspired by SNCC, which established the Philadelphia Tutorial Project in 1961, and SDS, especially at the Quaker schools like Swarthmore, which spearheaded the ERAP in Chester and Philadelphia. Even the anti-organizational, more direct action approach of WSP failed to attract many younger women. The heart of New Left inspiration came from the civil rights revolution, from the inspiration generated by direct action challenges to segregation, economic oppression, and racism, and from the prefigurative establishment of what Movement people called "the beloved community," that is, the circle of friends, and comrades, brought together in struggle to build a just society.

Sociologist and veteran activist Martin Oppenheimer has argued that, whereas Old Left influence on sixties-generation activists was "quite minimal," radical pacifism, especially a commitment to direct action, influenced the civil rights revolution but, less so, the peace movement. I would argue instead that there were Old Left influences, especially over time as a new generation began to look toward Marxism for guidance, but that radical pacifism was more compelling to New Leftists in both civil rights and peace organizations. In Philadelphia, such influence emanated from direct action pacifists, such as Charley Walker of AFSC, Larry Scott and George Lakey of A Quaker Action Group (AQAG), Arlo Tatum of the Central Committee for Conscientious Objectors (CCCO), Haverford physics professor William C. Davidon, George and Lillian Willoughby (CNVA, AFSC, CCCO, AQAG), and, perhaps most important, Stewart Meacham (AFSC), all of whom served as important role models for the New Leftists who would shape the movements of the 1960s.

Organizations like SANE, as well as all other political formations involving Old Left and liberal activists, were incapable of harnessing the idealistic energies of a new generation brought up to value a

Figure 2. Early anti-Vietnam War demonstration, 1966. The young couple on the right are Joan Mandle, who would play a significant role in the development of women's studies at Bryn Mawr College, and Jay Mandle, a leader of Student SANE at the University of Pennsylvania. Robert J. Brand.

contradictory brew of authenticity, absurdity, and angst, a mentality shaped by *Mad* magazine and existentialist writers like Albert Camus, by Holden Caulfield and Lenny Bruce, by Jack Kerouac and Paul Goodman. Young New Leftists loved Woody Guthrie and Pete Seeger, but in "growing up absurd" their generational voices were those of Arlo Guthrie and Bob Dylan. The existential qualities of the New Left, and in particular its demand for authenticity, reflect the ways in which Hiroshima and Auschwitz implanted a permanent shadow of doubt over the quest for "the beloved community." There would always be a self-protective black humor à la *Dr. Strangelove* in the souls of most New Leftists; the Port Huron Statement always rested on the cold fact that these pioneer SDSers looked "uncomfortably to the world we inherit," in large part, because they "were guided by the sense that [they] . . . may be the last generation in the experiment with living."[32]

At the eight Philadelphia area colleges and universities this book will talk about, there was a fascinating range of such voices. From the mid-1950s until 1960, campuses were overwhelmingly apathetic. Nevertheless, during the early 1960s the ice of the McCarthy era began to melt and a new political idealism became ever more apparent in the pages of college student newspapers. At the Quaker-influenced, elite institutions—Swarthmore, Haverford, Bryn Mawr—the influences were the anti-nuclear movement, Third World independence movements, and, most especially, the student-driven, direct action wing of the civil rights movement—the sit-ins, freedom rides, and demonstrations at the nearby Eastern Shore in Maryland. By contrast, at the more Greek-dominated University of Pennsylvania, where social life and sports still reigned, it was the ways liberalism and conservatism were sparked by John Fitzgerald Kennedy and Barry Goldwater respectively. At Temple's more plebeian commuter campus, the initial revival of political idealism centered more on Peace Corps involvement, modest civil rights interests, and, with the Goldwaterite conservatives, anti-Communism and free-market enthusiasm. There was barely anything that could be characterized as New Left at either campus before the U.S. involvement in the Vietnam War exploded in early 1965. At Temple in particular, red-diaper babies, often with Old Left loyalties, jousted for positions at the margins. Interestingly, the Roman Catholic institutions, particularly LaSalle, least so Villanova, began a dialogue about the nature of Catholic commitment and social responsibilities, inspired by both a new Catholic president and, a new pontiff, Pope John XXIII. Whereas energized, radicalized students at Swarthmore would be arrested by the hundreds while joining picket lines at the Franklin School in Chester, a growing number of young Catholic commuters at LaSalle would volunteer their services with local tutoring projects in the North Philadelphia ghetto or consider joining the Peace Corps upon graduation.

As Lyndon Johnson moved toward the decision to commit U.S. air power and combat troops to fight the National Liberation Front (NLF) and the North Vietnamese Army (NVA) in the late winter and early spring of 1964–65, the Philadelphia chapter of SANE was prepared to respond. It already had five years of experience, working with Quaker organizations, WSP, WILPF, liberal reform-minded Democrats, university professors, and young peace-oriented activists in organizations like SDS; moreover, it had five active branches with more than 500 members in the area. It had become the principal arena in which survivors of the Old Left joined with other radicals—Quakers and liberals—to lobby and agitate, albeit carefully, for peace.[33]

An examination of the early history of Philadelphia SANE reenforces the thesis put forth by Nancy Zaroulis and Gerald Sullivan that

The antiwar movement was not a movement of the young, although young people gave it needed energy, served by the hundreds of thousands as its "troops," and provided some of its leaders. It was conceived, nurtured, and largely directed by adults; people over thirty made up a large part of its membership.[34]

At least in the period between the rise of an anti-nuclear testing movement in the mid- to late 1950s and the Americanization of the war in Vietnam in spring 1965, the peace movement was decidedly made up of adults. Zaroulis and Sullivan, however, are mistaken to distinguish SANE so sharply from the Old Left; SANE, at least in Philadelphia, was created and energized by Old Left refugees from the Communist Party, working in alliance with Quakers, other pacifists, some non-Communist Party Old Leftists, and liberals.[35]

In fact, the early New Left was marginal to the emerging peace movement until the SDS anti-war demonstration held in Washington, D.C., in April 1965. Those SDS activists, like Paul Booth, who focused attention on peace issues, were a minority within their organization and do not fit the profile of a prefigurative model of politics suggested by some movement scholars. Booth, who worked in tandem with Philadelphia SANE, was more like a number of other pre-baby boomers with agendas and strategies centered on coalition and electoral politics. His focus was on peace candidates, mostly in Democratic primaries and occasionally running as independents. It was only at the urging of older voices, like the radical journalist I. F. Stone, that SDS somewhat reluctantly planned to respond to the Americanization of the Vietnam War in 1964–65.[36]

Following the military escalation of the Vietnam War, Philadelphia SANE would flourish as a part of the more moderate wing of the anti-war movement, but it would rarely attract to its membership those who came to identify themselves primarily as New Leftists, affiliated with what they began to call "the Movement," an intentionally anti-Old Left, anti-liberal, anti-organizational posture. It would, however, become an essential ally and organizational support system for that younger generation. Indeed, along with the Quaker institutions, Phila-delphia SANE would provide staff positions and, therefore, essential employment and income to many New Leftists.

When Lyndon Johnson began to Americanize the war in March 1965, SANE would join with ADA, FPC, WSP, and WILPF in calling on the president, "while there is still a choice," to be "willing to negoti-ate" and step away from a potential confrontation with China. The ad contained approximately 1,500 signatures, most of them from veter-ans of the Old Left and peace communities, few of them baby boomers. Philadelphia SANE would, however, attract to both mem-bership and leadership a number of those who came of age between the 1930s and 1960s, often liberal academics, ministers, and profes-sional people who had created a life for themselves during the more quiescent 1950s, and who, troubled by the Vietnam War (and often in-spired by the civil rights movement and the War on Poverty), were now ready to enter the fray.[37]

Historian Maurice Isserman correctly suggests that there were sig-nificant continuities and overlaps between Old and New Left, while Oppenheimer offers a valuable qualifier in arguing that such linkages were not decisive. Perhaps the issues should be framed in a funda-mentally different manner. For one thing, we need to pay more atten-tion to those who fall between the Depression generation of the Old Left and the 1960s New Left—activists like Oppenheimer (b. 1930), Barton (b. 1935), and Kormis (b. 1938), who in certain instances were transformed or at least influenced by New Left issues and themes. Within the Philadelphia peace movement, for example, in the second half of the 1960s, a host of such activists, many of them academics, few of them New Left in origins or orientation, took on leadership roles, that is, organized faculty peace organizations, draft counseling cen-ters, and suburban peace centers and helped bridge generational gaps.[38]

Finally, as the case of Philadelphia SANE demonstrates, we need to deepen Isserman's thesis on continuities by asking, not only how the Old Left influenced the New, but how the themes of the New Left, especially participatory democracy, prefigurative politics, and a focus on alienation, affected both veterans of the Old Left and the late-in-arrival adult activists of the 1950s generation, several of whom became mainstays of Philadelphia SANE by the late 1960s. Within SANE by late 1967, for example, one discovers a much more aggressive, militant posture, with one leader going so far as to deny legitimacy to the Eugene McCarthy and Robert Kennedy critiques as insufficiently radical. Such a posture is a very long way from the early 1960s sensibility that found Pete Seeger *too* radical. In some ways nothing had changed; Old Left views simply became more openly stated as the fears of McCarthyism diminished. But at the same time the movements and events of the 1960s were influencing and shaping older voices; indeed, influences appear to have occurred in more than one direction.[39]

## Chapter 2

# The Quaker Schools

The campuses of Swarthmore, Haverford, and Bryn Mawr Colleges are about as far away from the gritty neighborhoods of Philadelphia as one can possibly get. Two of these liberal arts colleges—Haverford and Bryn Mawr—tended to coordinate their student activism; one of them—Swarthmore—was more within the urban orbit of the city of Chester in Delaware County. All three played critical roles in the emergence and development of the white New Left Movement in greater Philadelphia. Swarthmore, for example, was in the vanguard of what became the New Left's early community organizing strategy, the SDS Economic Research and Action Project (ERAP). Swarthmore activists were in the forefront of the efforts of radical students to find a way to break out of what they felt was the ivory tower insularity of their campus to connect with "real people." As such, they pioneered the construction of a cross-class, cross-racial alliance with elements of the black community in Chester. Haverford's activists, less communal and more idiosyncratic, were leaders in the earliest criticisms of U.S. intervention in Indochina. Most striking were the precocious and extraordinary efforts of Russell Stetler, the Philadelphia area's best known and most controversial student antiwar leader through the middle 1960s. Finally, Bryn Mawr, the only women's college considered in this study, provides an avenue to follow the processes by which civil rights and antiwar activists became pioneers in the creation of second wave feminism.

## Swarthmore College

In a 1956 mock election, Swarthmore College students voted for Adlai Stevenson over Dwight David Eisenhower, 375 (53.5%) to 318 (45.2%); that same year the senior class president was future scientist Jeremy Stone, while its most celebrated undergraduate was future P. D. Q. Bach Peter Schickele. This idyllic, leafy campus was "terribly ingrown and self-centered," according to editors of the campus paper, the *Phoenix*. There was a consistent flow of dissident speakers invited to campus—A. J. Muste, Norman Thomas, I. F. Stone, Dorothy Day—but complaints of student apathy ruled, with one editor lamenting, "Even Sputnik is discussed merely as a sort of scientific curiosity." At mid-century, the campus, with a surprisingly strong fraternity presence, seemed dormant, with more energy involved in pushing a very reluctant faculty and administration to establish a Sociology Department than in disarmament and civil rights issues.[1]

In the face of the first sit-ins of February 1960, over one-third of Swarthmore students signed a petition sent to Woolworth's and Kress's to desegregate their southern lunch counters. But when some students joined a solidarity picket in Philadelphia, *Phoenix* editors called their efforts "highly questionable" and concluded that "impulsive reaction motivated by moral indignation . . . may lead to more harm than good" by entrenching resistance and alienating Southern moderates. Indeed the Student Council refused to support the picketers.[2]

Over the next months, as SNCC formed and the sit-in movement spread across the South, Swarthmore began to pay more attention. Swarthmore students participated in some of these events, reporting through the *Phoenix* their sense of excitement and their developing identification with the young civil rights activists. Over the next several years, the Swarthmore experience was comparable to that at most other elite, liberal institutions: idealistic undergraduates would be energized and motivated by the heroism of the civil rights activists, especially those of SNCC and CORE. A small but influential segment would join such efforts by going south to participate in integration struggles, by visiting southern sites to report back to campus about the stirring events, or by examining how such idealism could be invested in more local venues, such as Philadelphia and nearby Chester.[3]

The class of 1964, totaling 259 students, slightly more males than females and 80 percent from public high schools, were selected from an application pool of more than 2,000. That year, 1960, the students overwhelmingly supported Kennedy over Nixon, 69.3 to 28.1 percent; the faculty support for JFK was even stronger, 83.6 percent. Fraternity rush was the lowest in six years—only 59 pledges—and a small group of students, many of them red-diaper babies, including Ollie Fein, Mimi Feingold, and Jerry Gelles, organized a trip to revolutionary Cuba during winter break. Clearly a critical mass was beginning to form—a post-McCarthy cluster of student activists, children of Old Leftists, liberals, and pacifists, who responded to a variety of issues including Cuba, civil rights, and the House Un-American Activities Committee (HUAC). Some were already radical, that is, critical of the capitalist system and knowledgeable about Marxism; others were more liberal, focused on reform, committed to hearing all varieties of dissent from the right as well as left. But the trend was leftward; in March 1961, for example, the Student Council approved a support statement in solidarity with the sit-in movement. And new voices began to emerge who would eventually become leaders of a full-fledged Swarthmore New Left: in 1961 Becky Adams was elected Student Council president and Carl Wittman and Paul Booth joined the editorial board of the *Phoenix*.[4]

Mimi Feingold returned to speak on campus after spending 31 days in jail for participation in the freedom rides, concluding, "None of us had ever experienced such powerful feelings in a crowd, such intensity of belief in what we were doing." It is impossible to exaggerate the significance of such testimony from a classmate, returning from the battle front, reporting, with conviction and exhilaration, on events that seemed so much more relevant than academic life. Penny Patch, who entered the college in fall 1961, recalls hearing Feingold speak of her experiences during the freedom rides:

Mimi was a small woman and she looked tiny at the podium on the stage of that large auditorium. Such a very young woman, only two years older than I was, and look what she had done. I was awestruck. The next step for me into activism just seemed to happen, as if the decision had already unconsciously been made and all I had to do was seize the opportunities as they came along.[5]

Patch would join campus activists in integrationist struggles in Chester and then on Maryland's Eastern Shore before quitting school at eighteen to become "the first white woman working in a SNCC field project in the Deep South."

Swarthmore students, for the most part, took academic success for granted; they had always been high achievers, precociously engaged with demanding readings—it came easily to them. But as children raised with what Kenneth Keniston called the core values of essentially liberal homes, such incipient activists experienced dissatisfaction with the hot-house intellectualism of Swarthmore. The beginnings of a New Left, of a "movement" for social change among white students, began with the experience of going south. Those who went as red-diaper babies, rooted in the old Communist left, returned as something different; they were no longer living in the shadow of their parents' political experiences—Spain, the Popular Front, the Depression, the battles between Stalinists and Trotskyists and Shachtmanites. They now had their own generational experiences in the form of the civil rights revolution, based not in the past but in the present. In brief, they were becoming New Left. Charlotte Phillips, for example, sent reports back from Tougaloo College where she transferred for a year, while Paul Booth wrote a column that focused on what was happening on other campuses. Meanwhile, black and white veterans from the civil rights front arrived on campus to explain, inspire, raise money, and recruit.[6]

In 1962, Swarthmore activists, already involved in local protests in the small downtown of Swarthmore and trying to connect with Chester, became involved in civil rights demonstrations on Maryland's Eastern Shore. For many Philadelphia area activists, these efforts offered the nearest site for participating in the southern movement. A fall 1962 *Phoenix* editorial sympathetically highlighted the "sudden turn" of student activism toward addressing "the Cold War and the oppression of the Negro people" through voter registration, a recently established Chester tutorial project, and disarmament efforts.[7]

By early 1963, battle lines among campus activists were becoming discernible. There was a conservative organization, the Swarthmore Minority Opinion Club, led by Clyde Prestowitz, that protested a speech by Communist Party head Gus Hall; there were a host of liberal activists, including Robert Putnam; there were Student Peace Union (SPU) activists, most of whom were staunch Young People's Socialist League (YPSL) members, who called for a new Labor Party and tended to downplay what they considered to be mere reformist efforts; finally, there were the developing New Leftists, joining the visiting SDS activist Tom Hayden in proclaiming "the end of liberalism," rallying to the Cuban Revolution, beginning to cite Mao Zedong on revolution, and rapidly seeing themselves as the movement. Not only were New Leftists looking more favorably on Third World revolutionaries, but running parallel to their organizing in the South was an existential commitment to put one's body on the line. Mimi Feingold, working with CORE and writing from a Louisiana jail, implored, "Remember . . . no sacrifice is too great for the movement."[8]

In spring 1963, activities intensified in Cambridge, Maryland, as dozens of Swarthmore activists engaged in nonviolent protests under the leadership of Gloria Richardson and the Cambridge Non-Violent Action Committee, which resulted in massive arrests. Five students participated in a SNCC project in Cambridge that summer, including Wittman, Vernon Grizzard, and Connie Brown, all of whom would become leaders in the SDS ERAP efforts. Martial law would eventually be declared, with National Guard troops called in, withdrawn, and sent back in again. Finally, in late July, a Justice Department settlement providing for gradual desegregation in public housing, the establishment of a new biracial committee, and a promise of no further demonstrations brought a halt to the protests. Cambridge, 75 miles from both Washington, D.C., and Baltimore, was unique, according to historian Annette K. Brock. "It was the first grass roots movement outside of the deep South," and attracted students not only from Swarthmore, but also from Brown, Harvard, Morgan State, Howard, and Towson State. For many northern activists, it was the closest battleground in the civil rights struggle.[9]

The beginnings of the Chester demonstrations in fall 1963, only four miles from campus, sparked enormous growth in Swarthmore's New Left. By that time, Paul Booth had become SDS national vice president and a voice for coalition politics in support of peace-oriented candidates in the Democratic Party. Swarthmore's Political Action Committee (SPAC) effectively served as the campus SDS chapter, which provided it with legitimacy and funding not otherwise available. Booth had been a participant in the 1962 SDS retreat at Port Huron, Michigan, which produced the influential statement declaring the birth of an American New Left. SPAC efforts in Chester provided inspirational model for SDS commitment to participatory democracy and what came to be known as an "interracial movement of the poor." Most SPAC activists were working with the Chester Tutorial Project; on campus three key activists—Wittman, Grizzard, and Nick Egleson—taught sections in a SPAC-sponsored seminar on "The Negro in America." And in November the Chester Committee for Freedom Now (CFFN) organized a boycott to protest conditions at the Franklin School, which led to a major breakthrough in both movement visibility and national impact.[10]

Chester, a city of 63,000 residents, almost half African American, was "an industrial city that had specialized in ship-building and oil refining, but with its industry moving out" was deindustrializing. Unemployment was at 15 percent, with blacks out of work at twice that rate. Politically Chester was a smaller, less attractive version of Philadelphia prior to the Dilworth-Clark reform movement of the 1950s: it was dominated by one of the oldest Republican machines in the nation. Chester's blacks were severely underrepresented and, as in most smokestack cities, a number of issues, ranging from job discrimination to police brutality to affordable housing, were beginning to generate insurgent voices. But in fall 1963, Stanley Branche, the executive secretary of the Chester NAACP, who had participated in some of the demonstrations, organized the Committee for Freedom Now of Chester (CFFN) with help from Swarthmore activists he had met in the Maryland struggle.[11]

They targeted the Franklin School, an inner-city elementary school built in 1910—95 percent black, run-down, and overcrowded. An unused coal bin served as the gym, and the entire building contained two bathrooms. There had been a history of parental complaints and administrative inaction. CFFN, seeking an issue that was specifically northern and urban, targeted the school on November 4, setting up a picket line and demanding immediate rectification of conditions and the promise of a new building. The picket line grew from several dozen to about 150 over the next few days, as CFFN waited for a response from the school board. When a week's deadline passed and there was no response, CFFN set up a blockade to close down the school; 400 demonstrators participated and then marched to City Hall to voice their demands. The school board responded with evasion and excuses. The next day, November 12, the blockade resumed, including an occupation of the school board offices, which led to the arrest of 158 demonstrators. After more arrests the following day, the board made several concessions to CFFN, which proceeded to build on its visibility and success to organize block groups in the African American neighborhoods.[12]

Swarthmore's SPAC/SDS activists were exhilarated by their participation in the Franklin actions and by their success in building an alliance with Chester blacks through CFFN. They spoke of Chester as "the first example of the northern movement," as the "Birmingham of the North," and they used their academic skills to develop and implement surveys of Chester's black citizens and of social conditions. During the winter break, 20 to 30 activists worked full-time with CFFN doing voter registration and publicity for a planned city-wide school boycott. As one later prospectus proclaimed, CFFN, with major student input, "could now claim to be *the* movement in Chester":

The Chester movement is now one of the strongest in the country. It can also be called one of the most progressive for two reasons. First, block organizations have rarely been implemented with such success. And second, the thirty-seven demands that CFFN drew up after the Franklin School demonstrations go far beyond the demands of any other Negro movement. They include full and fair employment, equal and improved education, adequate housing for everyone in both public and private dwellings, medical care regardless of ability to pay, as well as protests against the McClure machine, abuse from police, and biased coverage from news media.[13]

Chester came to be seen, initially by the Swarthmore activists and soon by national SDS leaders, as "a case study in community organization."[14]

National New Left activists, mostly involved in creating and building SDS, responded to the Chester events with enormous enthusiasm, and Swarthmore SDS became a national model. What needs consideration is how and why they saw Chester as a model for what became the SDS central organizing thrust—ERAP—initiated in August 1963.

Figure 3. Nearly 300 students from the Swarthmore College SDS chapter march in front of Independence Hall in an early protest against American air strikes against North Vietnam, February 13, 1965. Temple Urban Archives.

ERAP was predicated on the notion of "new insurgencies" as articulated in the SDS pamphlet "America and the New Era," which relied
heavily on the notion of a Triple Revolution of inter-related developments: increasing automation, the rise and centrality of the military-
industrial complex, and the emergence of the Third World and civil
rights movements. The liberal and radical academics and activists who
promoted the notion of a Triple Revolution, which was the focus of a
conference held in June 1963 at Nyack, New York, argued that a severe unemployment crisis was emerging. They anticipated that with
machines replacing humans, public moneys being diverted by Cold
War imperatives, and blacks making demands on the system for opportunity and measurable results, there were organizing opportunities for building bridges between the white and black poor.[15]

For the most part, national SDS leaders like Tom Hayden were
looking for ways to apply the philosophy and strategy of exemplary
organizations like SNCC to urban settings in the north. Like the activists at Swarthmore, Hayden wanted SDS to transform itself from essentially a campus-based, academic discussion group supportive of
other people's struggles to an organization, a "movement" engaged in
the *doing*, in moving past traditional liberalism or Old Left radicalism
toward a kind of direct-action populism. The Nyack conference, which
spawned a National Committee for Full Employment, spearheaded
by the young labor organizer Stanley Aronowitz and economist Ray
Brown, provided a focus and a direction, an escape from the ivory
tower.[16]

The notion of organizing white and black northern residents facing
a long-term downturn in employment opportunities appealed to
those working through ERAP that fall. But ERAP's research dimension lacked early results and suffered from its essentially academic nature. An initial ERAP exploration of white organizing in Chicago,
however, floundered. And then Chester erupted, giving the dominant
action-oriented element in SDS its rationale and inspiration. Kirkpatrick Sale describes how SPAC's Carl Wittman, after orienting SDS
national secretary Lee Webb to the Chester scene, met Hayden and
joined with him in shifting SDS and ERAP to what they began to call
"an interracial movement of the poor," the notion that white student
radicals could work with northern, urban blacks in organizing both
white and black poor. At the December 1963 SDS National Council,
Webb made sure that the Swarthmore-Chester activists, supplemented
by others with analogous experiences and interests, made their presence felt. CFFN's Stanley Branche was invited to make a presentation
on Chester rent strikes. Those skeptical of this romantic "cult of the
ghetto" approach, activists like Al Haber and Steve Max, argued for

either a student or more liberal-labor-peace movement coalition emphasis, but they could not compete with the enthusiasm that fed off the success of CFFN and SPAC in Chester.[17] SDS thus committed itself to challenge what it began to call "corporate liberalism," positioning itself as the advocate of an interracial "participatory democracy" focused on the urban poor.

Both Swarthmore's ERAP in general and its Chester project in particular were formative in the broader development of National SDS and the New Left. Former New Left activist and sociologist Wini Breines defines the New Left in terms of "prefigurative politics," that is, a politics of authenticity, of conflating means and ends, of demanding that one live one's revolutionary values as one engages in revolutionary struggle, of establishing "the beloved community," of inaugurating participatory democracy in the here and now. While recognizing the self-righteousness and impracticality of many SDS ERAPers, Breines writes empathetically of their dedication to transforming our notion of politics from the criteria of "efficiency, efficacy, compromise, discipline and the rules of the game" to an unabashedly utopian vision of politics as building a democratic and just community.[18] In this context, ERAP raised a number of questions that reflected tensions that would plague SDS and the New Left until their respective demise. What did it mean to be white, middle-class activists? Was the college campus a justifiable base for building a movement, or was it a recruiting center for assisting more authentic constituencies in the Mississippi Delta, in the inner city, in the Third World, among factory workers? What was the role of a white, radical intelligentsia in building a movement for social change? In Marxian terms, where was the agent of social change located? If the old labor metaphysic critiqued by C. Wright Mills was no longer operative, what was to replace it?

Early SDS understood what it rejected but was still unsure of what was to replace it. Was it the educated youth called to arms by Mills? Did that suggest what would later be called "new working class" theory, the notion that higher education was the training ground for a more variegated, white-collar, professional working class? Or did it mean that youth were a class, educated or not, insofar as they were unencumbered by institutional and ideological blinders and constraints and consequently open to subversive ideas, especially if, contra the Triple Revolution, the affluent society was forever? Or did it mean that middle-class students and intellectuals had to find a substitute for the proletariat in the poor, in people of color, in what Frantz Fanon called "the wretched of the earth"? And how would activists find ways to meet Tom Hayden's challenge, given the reign of expertise, alienation, manipulation, and self-destructiveness, to create "a new and alternative process that involved people as independent and creative human beings, expressing a new force outside of existing institutions, a society apart from the state, rehabilitating itself from apathy and thus dissolving the immediate structures of its oppression"?[19] Swarthmore SDS struggled with all the above as they moved into the poor neighborhoods of Chester.

New Left activists addressed these questions and issues as they began to identify themselves as part of the "movement." This notion was predicated on the romantic idea of what civil rights activists, especially from SNCC, called "the beloved community," individuals engaged in a movement for social change. As such, the movement was anti-organizational, which is what distinguished the New Left from the older Communist and socialist parties. Perhaps the most revealing difference between Old and New Left was this shift from devotion to the "party" to identification with the "movement." Yet the notion inevitably took on an organizational character that led to rivalries and competition. The young Swarthmore activists identified with SDS, for example, worked cooperatively with and simultaneously found themselves suspicious of organizational rivals like SPU, the W. E. B. Du Bois Club, and the Northern Student Movement (NSM). In some profound ways, those who represented the movement could generate zero-sum battles and feelings of loyalty and betrayal that would put the Old Left to shame.

At Swarthmore, in greater Philadelphia, and nationally, SDSers locked horns with SPU activists loyal to the Shachtmanite YPSL. SPU had its cadre, Martin Oppenheimer and Tom Barton, who were assigned to the Philadelphia peace movement; it also had a number of campus activists like Gail Malmgreen at Swarthmore and Carl Gilbert at Temple. Such activists characteristically viewed the Swarthmore SDSers as babes in the woods, innocents in politics, and petit bourgeois in their seeming obliviousness to Marxism and class analysis. But the success of the Test-Ban Treaty followed by sectarian squabbles within YPSL led to the demise of the SPU and of YPSL itself precisely at the moment when ERAP was being launched as a means to highlight SDS distinctiveness and "new"-ness.[20]

SDS also kept its eye on the Communist Party Youth organization, the W. E. B. Du Bois Club, whose area strength was at Temple University. Swarthmore ERAPer Vernon Grizzard, a key leader in the Chester project, argued for an effort to work with the Du Bois Club, suggesting that there were "large groups of people seriously and constructively dedicated to radical change and people who identify with the communist tradition are in these groups." The Swarthmore SDSers, in establishing a project in Philadelphia under the leadership of Nick Egleson, concluded that they would have to "work closely with the Du

Bois Club people," anticipating somewhat reluctantly that they didn't "have much choice" in the matter. Grizzard later noted, possibly because they had overestimated the Communist presence but also because of the difficulties the Philadelphia project encountered, that an "SDS-Du Bois Club rivalry has not materialized at all" at Temple.[21]

A challenge of another sort came from the Northern Student Movement, a New Left organization established at a civil rights conference at Sarah Lawrence College in spring 1962. NSM, headquartered in New Haven, began with four projects, the most significant of which was the Philadelphia Tutorial Project (PTP). NSM's executive director, Peter Countryman, a charismatic, idealistic activist who took a leave of absence from Yale to work full time in the movement, took charge of the Philadelphia project, which had extensive sponsorship from liberal churches, the school board, the Commission on Human Relations, and the Catholic archdiocese. Countryman recruited twenty activists and hired 175 tutors to work in nineteen centers, mostly located in North Philadelphia but with some initial efforts to establish centers in Chester. As such, when Swarthmore ERAP began to engage with Chester's black community, they discovered a rival with institutional resources and a short but impressive track record of accomplishment.[22]

Countryman knew his SDS counterparts and engaged in intra-movement dialogue over philosophy, strategy, and tactics. In a letter to National SDS leader Lee Webb criticizing SDS arrogance and suggesting limitations in the ERAP approach, Countryman asserted:

It is not the poor who are "deviant," Lee, all of us are, because of this culture—and some of us are beginning to escape our fragmentation and alienation and so on through the process of trying to create a new society. What keeps me going in this is much the fact that because a few of us have changed through the process of being revolutionaries, it is obvious that all of us can.[23]

Countryman, sounding very much more the New Leftist, added,

I think the difference between NSM and SDS thinking is that we are content to simply get people in motion that is personally meaningful and capable of being sustained for long periods, i.e., based on organization. We are much less concerned with where this motion leads people—SDS wants to plan this motion, outfit it into a national strategy.

Webb's response was curt and highhanded: "I really do not have an opinion. I really am too busy trying to build SDS," but he added that he wanted to publish one of Countryman's papers in an SDS medium.[24]

Countryman, who would later become a founder of the important antiracist People for Human Rights (PHR), articulated a strategy and a vision that saw the tutoring experience as a vehicle for community organizing, "Is it conceivable that these students could be used in door-to-door voter education, or in teaching families the rights and responsibilities of renters, or in encouraging and running community rehabilitation campaigns, or in doing tutoring themselves?" As late as mid-1965, Countryman was still exploring ways to build an inter-racial movement based on a pragmatic assessment of everyday reali-ties and limitations, including the difficult questions being forced to center stage by race consciousness.[25]

The Swarthmore SDS group remained the most prestigious of Philadelphia New Left groups in part because it was the most au-tonomous, the least tarred with either Old Left affiliations like YPSL and the Du Bois Club, or more mainstream ones, including liberal sponsorship, like the Swarthmore NSM. SDS was able to present itself successfully as the most authentically New Left in terms of its focus on activism but also vis-à-vis its ideological positioning. SDS correspon-dence suggests an increasingly savvy group of activists sure of their own approach and hardly fitting the notion of a more innocent early New Left. For example, in determining how to engage with Old Left remnants in Philadelphia, Nick Egleson asked, "How much time is it worth putting into talking with these people just for their own educa-tion?" But in particular instances Egleson was wise enough to listen to older professionals like lawyer Harry Levitan, a founder of the Phila-delphia SANE chapter, who, countering the advice of Harlem activist Jesse Gray, urged Swarthmore SDSers to make sure that they had full knowledge of the Chester landlord-tenant laws.[26]

Swarthmore SDSers were neither liberals nor merely existential radicals in the period in which they established ERAP in Chester, Philadelphia, and Trenton. Most called themselves "revolutionaries" and distinguished themselves not only by opting for "action as op-posed to study" but also by looking to Third World Communist revo-lutions as their models: "Mao's efforts in China and Castro's in Cuba to set up a separate society in an area of the country are extended cases of the method of example."[27] Vernon Grizzard also saw SDS's role in radicalizing ERAP recruits as "the second necessity in our work," adding that the organizing experience "will force students to re-evaluate their perceptions about the process of change. And they will be forced to think beyond their ideas about how one should work for change to how one can use power gained from that change."

Despite commitments to participatory democracy and to anti-leadership principles, the Swarthmore group inevitably found them-selves relying on leaders like Grizzard and Egleson and having to deal with the contradictions built on their confidence that they understood revolutionary truths that others—neophytes and local residents especially—had yet to grasp. For example, Grizzard advised insiders, "Please don't print 'For ERAP staff only' on the top of the newsletter. By now everyone knows it's for ERAP staff only, and *saying* that something is secret is just plain dangerous."[28] At another point, Grizzard, sounding very much like a Popular Front Old Leftist, argued that some ERAP literature "had to be tailored to a liberal audience, and thus we did not discuss the real issues, or only obliquely."[29] In this regard, New Left leaders in SDS, despite commitments to participatory democracy and rejection of Soviet-style democratic centralism, found themselves, like the Old Left, sometimes operating on two tracks, one for the insiders, the other for targeted recruits, sources of funding, and possible allies. Especially as New Leftists came to affirm an anticapitalist, increasingly socialist political analysis, inspired by Third World revolutionary movements, they were tempted to hide behind a broadly humanist public face, at least until the mid-1960s.

As early as summer 1964, there was a struggle among key organizers over the relative importance of particular ERAP projects and whether there was a need for a revolutionary party made up of organizers as opposed to a broader strategy involving community organizations, campus organizing, and office staff. Carl Wittman left Chester to join Tom Hayden in what the Swarthmore leader argued was the more significant ERAP project in Newark, New Jersey. Meanwhile the Swarthmore cadre sought to remain the exemplary ERAP model in the summer of 1964 by working with CFFN in Chester and establishing a new beachhead in Philadelphia.

From the start, the Swarthmore SDSers had established a problematical relation with Stanley Branche and the CFFN. They worried about from-the-top linkages in terms of participatory democracy, but understood that it was through Branche that they received legitimation in the black neighborhoods of Chester. Part of the problem was that black politics in Chester remained fluid; CFFN had broken off from the NAACP youth group, and Branche was an ambitious local leader whose shifts in organizational and personal loyalties would plague the ERAP project. A single set of events centering around the initial school boycott set in motion dynamics that the ERAPers found themselves unable to control. They began modestly, committing themselves to building CFFN, become its research arm, and work toward building alliances, especially with whites. And they became the model ERAP for summer 1964, along with Hayden's Newark project and efforts in Chicago and Cleveland.[30]

Almost immediately Chester ERAP had to contend with cooptation.

The city launched a Greater Chester Movement (GCM) in June 1964 and coaxed Branche to join it.[31] As such, ERAP was forced to address issues of race and leadership at the outset of the summer. When the project recruited Don Jackson to the summer staff, project director Vernon Grizzard noted, "there is enough tension so that a Negro on our staff would give us a little extra safety." Jackson, a Chester native with local connections, was a Williams College undergraduate who had taken a leave to do movement work in his hometown.[32]

The situation was compounded by the fact that the two other staffers who were committed to staying in Chester after the summer, Peter Freedman and Molly Pratt, had dated and broken up "in a not-too-pleasant fashion," and Pratt was now seeing Jackson. With Stanley Branche still a force, ERAP found itself relying on Jackson to protect white activists from racial attack. Unfortunately, Jackson didn't always share ERAP's agenda, for example, in focusing on block organizing; more tellingly, he separated himself from ERAP, refusing to see himself as part of the staff.[33]

Despite these difficulties, the project was able to establish twelve block organizations, which met regularly, reaching several thousand residents. The project members anticipated further school actions and possibly an urban renewal struggle in the fall. They had little success with Chester whites and discovered that the project had lost some of its attraction for the students back on campus at Swarthmore. Few seemed willing to stay or become involved. Some of this was a consequence of a rising ERAP self-righteousness about what real political work was. One participant referred to the campus as "this academic flower garden." Indeed, SDS virtually abandoned campus efforts, sometimes sharing "a tendency to write off people who are not organizers." Leaders like Grizzard understood this dilemma: "I am particularly interested in the question of whether a ghetto-jumped chapter loses complete contact with the student body and becomes an in-group."[34]

In 1965, after the project had collapsed, John Bancroft, a Swarthmore activist with some involvement in Chester, noted how SPAC was "viewed quite disfavorably by most on the campus" when he sought to mobilize opposition to the Vietnam War. He added, "All this is most embarrassing to report, since we're supposed to have one of the most radical campuses around." Bancroft would capture part of the problem in suggesting that "maybe Franklin schools don't happen and can't happen every day" and that excessive expectations detracted from the very unexciting grind of political work. Bancroft also criticized a style of politics that had roots in ERAP's origins and deepened as the Vietnam War began to affect student politics, declaring, "In general, the slogan 'action breeds discussion' seems not only untrue, but repulsive in the personal effects it has on people" and concluding that it was "meaningless and quite harmful to scorn liberals and regard them simply as material to be radicalized." Bancroft also attacked an "over-personalization of politics" that inhibited recruits from raising questions.[35]

Such problems, which challenged the very heart of the New Left's strategy in the ERAP projects, meant that activists were unable to penetrate the urban populism they championed. Organizers tried to link up with *authentic*, that is, poor and minority, people; the campus, the working- and middle-class neighborhoods, students not committed to "an interracial movement of the poor" were presumably inauthentic. Meanwhile, during fall and winter 1964 and 1965, the Chester ERAP foundered; reports reached the ERAP national office indicating "ideological differences" within the staff. In October, Jackson, Freedman, and Pratt seemed united in focusing on critical issues:

How do we react to poverty monies? Can (should) we catalyze a anti-negro-Removal mass movement? How important is urban renewal in the urban struggle for change? What does urban renewal mean to financial and political interests? And should we be entagling (sic) ourselves with Stanley Branche and the Committee for Freedom Now again. We are also skirting the old NSM issue—just how much can white students do in a primarily Negro movement? And when does the "inter-racial" angle of our "movement of the poor" materialize?[36]

But Freedman expressed other kinds of frustration to national ERAP head Rennie Davis, pleading for full-time staff to bridge both the strategic conflicts and, perhaps more essentially, personal matters. He lamented, "everything gets personal—e.g., don (sic) whitebaits me." Within a month, Freedman decided to leave the project, feeling that Jackson and Pratt were united against him. Freedman concluded that working in areas with already established leaders, many of whom had their own agendas and some of whom were increasingly attracted to a race-defined politics, was destined to fail. Grizzard, aware of the tensions, noted that the project was too weak and vulnerable to risk a break with Don Jackson. Indeed, Jackson, as the most visible African American close to ERAP, was both essential to and subversive of the project.[37]

By late 1964, little more than a year after the Franklin school demonstrations, the Chester ERAP had entered its "twilight time"; Pratt concluded that it was no longer viable and Jackson, now chairman of the New Independent Committee for Jobs, Homes, and Schools (NIC), a break-off from the now defunct CFFN, began to organize a Ghetto Against Poverty (GAP) program.[38]

In ERAP's newsletter during summer 1965, NSM's Peter Countryman wrote an article on "Race and the Movement" that sought to
explore how the notion of participatory democracy was affected by an
increasingly racial politics. It was a modest, thoughtful piece that focused on the tension between being revolutionary and yet beginning
with people's actual situations and on the dilemmas of seeking to tran-
scend race when it seemed to be so pervasive. Countryman offered no
answers, but insisted that inter-racial efforts needed to be continued.
Don Jackson, now with Chester CORE, responded by attacking "the
immorality, undemocracy, and bad strategy of deploying white kids
and semi-adults into the black ghetto as 'community organizers'," declaring, "In spite of Baldwin, of Malcolm, of LeRoi, of even that
schnuck Moynihan—ERAP does not admit to this TRUTH re racism."
He asked, "What is the answer for the white ERAPers in the ghetto?"
And responded, "Pack the hell up. Get out. Go to work in your own
communities and come back when and if that ghetto gets itself together and invites you (or more likely, your money) back."[39]

And so came to an end the pioneer New Left effort to stretch beyond
the hot-house campus to a nearby impoverished black community.
Was it a failure? Certainly in any narrow sense; as one got closer to the
rise of Black Power, to the 1965 ghetto riots in Watts, to the attacks
on Daniel Patrick Moynihan's *Report on the Negro Family*, all of which
were fermenting and overheating in 1963–64 when ERAP commenced operations, the ideal of an inter-racial "beloved community,"
or of an inter-racial class alliance of the poor sparked by privileged
white undergraduates, was destined for disappointment. Indeed, the
Swarthmore ERAP clearly frames many of the problems the New Left
would face long after notions of participatory democracy had faded
from memory. The activists' ambivalence, mixed with contempt, for
the campus and those residing there ensured that a student movement committed to revolutionary ends would remain marginalized
from both reform-minded and politically apathetic students. But this
did not foreclose all possibilities, nor did it deny the accomplishments
of these most remarkable young people. After all, the Swarthmore
SPAC/SDS group consisted of young men and women aged 18–22,
most of whom were inexperienced. Indeed, those with the most experience, like Paul Booth, were increasingly outside the ideological loop,
marginalized by their belief in coalition politics, by their wariness of
political romanticism. Many would lick their wounds and go on to
other venues, such as organizing against the Vietnam War, but would
also seek answers to the kinds of questions activists like Peter Countryman and John Bancroft had raised. That they failed in Chester is
not particularly notable; in fact, many Swarthmore radical and liberal

activists would continue important involvement in the poor neighborhoods in Chester, at Wade House, for example, in the following years.
It was impressive that these extraordinarily young and essentially inexperienced Swarthmore New Leftists tried and, in most cases, tried
something else and then something else again, not only in terms of
Chester but shortly with a host of other issues. As such they were pioneering participants in a New Left movement that profoundly transformed the ways we approach issues of war and peace, racial equality,
poverty, sexism, homophobia, and the environment. But, indeed, it
had been a rocky, problematical start.

## Haverford: The Case of Russell Stetler

Whereas Swarthmore's Political Action Committee activists inspired
SDS's ERAP, student activism at all-male Haverford College tended to
be more idiosyncratic and individualistic. To most observers of movement politics, Haverford tended to be personified by the mostly pacifist and direct action politics of physics professor Bill Davidon and the
highly publicized and controversial antiwar activities of Russell Stetler,
who as early as 1964 was the best known and, to establishment circles,
most notorious of the campus radicals. Haverford's story in many
ways is embodied in Stetler's remarkable emergence and yet may find
its deeper truths in Davidon's less sensationalist but more ongoing
efforts.

Haverford was an enclave for dissenters during the 1950s, but at
the same time it was a rigorously academic liberal arts college of fewer
than 500 males. In response to the Soviet invasion of Hungary, 310
students signed a petition calling on the college to admit some of the
refugees, but only if they met Haverford's standards.[40] A March 1959
editorial series concluded that "Haverford has recently been tending
toward an inordinate emphasis on the curriculum alone, [and in] de-
priving its students of the opportunity to broaden socially as well as intellectually, is educating only "half the man." Another editorial asked,
"Are there no 'new deals' left to fight for? Are we all members of a generation of complacent conservatives whose only objective is to keep
things as they are?"[41] This, at an historically liberal college which refused Department of Defense funding, and where students were soon
to be energized by the southern sit-in movement to demonstrate
against racial discrimination at local Woolworth's.[42]

Yet Haverford's "awakening" from the doldrums of the 1950s remained relatively oblivious to the Kennedy-Nixon presidential contest, although there was significant interest expressed in joining the
Peace Corps.[43] In fall 1961, William Cooper Davidon, a thirty-four-

Figure 4. Russell Stetler, Haverford College activist and chairman of the May 2d Movement, an early radical antiwar organization. Temple Urban Archives.

year-old physicist who had been working at the Argonne National Laboratory, joined the Haverford faculty. Davidon was extensively involved in a variety of pacifist activities. He would be an inspirational figure to many of Haverford's idealistic undergraduates over the next several decades as he took a leadership role in opposition to the Vietnam War, including tax resistance, antidraft work, and direct action. He served on the national boards of SANE and Resist and joined other peace activists in visiting South Vietnam in 1966.[44]

In 1962 Davidon, who called for unilateral American disarmament, announced plans to leave the United States and settle in New Zealand, declaring, "I can dissociate myself from being one of the murderers. I want no part in preparing for mass murder." He soon changed his mind, mostly due to personal circumstances, and elected to remain within a "self-seeking and profits" centered society. The chairman of Haverford's physics department and his activist wife Ann Morrissett Davidon represented the best in the Garrisonian tradition. Bill Davidon was a radical antinomian offering Haverford students an alternative to the cloistered life. One SDS leader complimented Davidon after experiencing "how close you and some of your students felt to each other. . . . You should know—as I think you do—that you have respect and affection of the students i (sic) talked to (i.e., the radical ones)."[45]

Haverford was among the few American colleges with a liberal, pacifist, and radical presence in the early 1960s. And yet as late as 1962 the college could still see nothing wrong with announcing that "the Old South will be the atmosphere of the Junior Class dance, 'Gone with the Wind'."[46] A small but influential group, however, influenced by activist faculty like Davidon and biologist Ariel Loewy, were about to shake up the institution. This group, often called the Founders Crew, included Paul Mattick, Jr., Class of 1965, and Class of 1966ers Russell Stetler, Joe Eyer, Roger Eaton, and Jim Garahan at its center, with perhaps several dozen on the periphery. All the core Founders except Stetler and Garahan were red-diaper babies, children of Old Leftists, and on scholarship. They were an intellectual elite, eschewing commercial rock 'n' roll for blues and folk and participating in a host of protest activities, including SPU meetings and demonstrations and civil rights efforts in the south and in the environs of Haverford. They were, according to one account, "to the left of most leftists" associated with SDS, but they never formed a chapter.[47]

In March 1964, well before the Berkeley Free Speech Movement erupted, and only months following the school demonstrations in Chester that ignited the Swarthmore student movement and in which most of the Founders Crew were participants, Haverford College made the headlines, at first in the Philadelphia and then in national newspapers. In a story quickly picked up by the European and American press, the Chinese Communist news agency *Hsinhua* reported that Haverford students, through the Student Committee to Send Medical Aid to the Front of National Liberation of South Vietnam (NLF), were seeking to support what Americans already called the Viet Cong. Within days, the committee, at first inaccurately reported as an official college organization and essentially consisting of the five core Founders Crew members, was in the limelight. And one Russell Stetler, a working-class scholarship student from the Roxborough neighborhood of Philadelphia, was front and forward as the chief instigator.[48]

Russell Stetler was Philadelphia's first highly visible New Left student activist. His story is unique and yet reflective of the ways in which Haverford College differed from both Swarthmore and the less elite Temple, as well as from the Catholic institutions of Villanova, St. Joseph's, and LaSalle. He has been described as "a real smart, hard-nosed guy" and as "politically naïve." Perhaps he was both. One old friend adds that he was also "angry and abrasive" and clearly enjoyed his new status among both New and Old Leftists. Stetler was the only child of a conservative Republican churchgoing family. His insular life seems to have been transformed both by his own drive to break from the confines of his conservative Methodist upbringing and through the influence of some close friends and several teachers at Roxborough High School. Most significant was his friendship with the Carner brothers, especially Frank, his closest friend, but also Pancho. The Carner parents were Trotskyists, Old Leftists with commitments to peace, civil rights, and the life of the mind, who provided "an intellectual oasis" for the young Stetler. Stetler, the Carner boys, and Bruce Kuklick formed a small group which was "so intellectually different from the rest of the people they grew up with that they might as well have been from Mars."[49] They were all top-notch students; Stetler edited the school newspaper but resigned when one of his editorials was censored as too controversial. A few teachers, older progressives such as English teacher Howard Carlisle, encouraged the group to think critically. By the time Stetler completed high school, he had become both an atheist and a dissenter. His grades earned him a board of education scholarship that allowed him to attend the very elite and expensive Haverford College.[50]

Almost immediately, Stetler took advantage of Haverford's open and permissive environment to leap into the civil rights and peace movements; by his sophomore year he was chair of the Haverford-Bryn Mawr SPU chapter. It was at an SPU national convention that he encountered the anti-Vietnam War writings of Bertrand Russell, the British mathematician and pacifist. He wrote to Russell, who responded to the young activist with encouragement and suggestions. It would be on the basis of Russell's involvement in seeking to demonstrate solidarity through nonmilitary, medical aid in South Vietnam that Stetler, along with his Founders Crew partners, set in motion the controversy that brought him both notoriety and, inexorably, movement status.[51]

Stetler became a New Left leader in Warholian time. Attending a Yale University conference in March 1964, "Socialism in America," Stetler was elected chairman of the newly formed May 2d Movement (M2M), initially a coalition of very radical activists prepared not only to oppose U.S. policy in Vietnam but to seek solidarity with both the North Vietnamese and the Viet Cong. M2M, at first influenced and soon dominated by a Maoist sect, the Progressive Labor Party (PLP), was a dogmatic bridge between the worst of Old Left turgidity and New Left romanticizing of Third World revolutionary movements.[52] Stetler, who denies ever having been a PLP member, was nevertheless engaged in the intramural struggles of the early New Left over strategy, tactics, identity, and organizational prestige. For example, he was in correspondence with SDS leaders by late 1963 over Haverford's efforts to supply food and clothing to beleaguered Hazard, Kentucky miners. National SDS was seeking to staff the volunteers for the ERAP, which some of the Haverford activists like Eyer joined, but was also concerned already that "there was the possibility that those of us involved would become sort of an 'in-group' or clique."[53]

Stetler, who like most New Leftists experienced frustration with the ways factional fights between the YPSLs and other Trotskyists dominated the SPU and directed it in divisive, ideological directions, was yet a seemingly savvy player in the political game. He spoke of the medical supplies program as a "gimmick" that "makes us into controversial enough figures to be invited to a lot of colleges to stir up talk about Vietnam."[54] Stetler's SDS correspondence suggests a veteran politico aware of national events and key personalities. Even in going to the Yale conference, where his selection as M2M president was at least in part predicated on his outsiderness, his independence from Old Left organizational loyalties, Stetler noted, "My real aim in going is to button-hole people from many different campuses to set up speaking engagements for our Vietnam group."

If he was being used, he was also prepared to use others. In response to questions about whether he was in PLP, Stetler sarcastically asked,

I didn't know SDS has an attorney general; or at least an attorney general's list. So whom do I swear my loyalty? Good old liberal red-baiting! Shades of

SPU! . . . Maybe some day I'll join a "dangerous" organization. But as long as I'm working out of Haverford, the only "dangerous" organizations I'll be in are the ones I start.

Stetler denounced "the destructive game of split the left," defending his M2M leadership and declaring himself "an independent who will work with anybody who will contribute to the results I hope to attain," a decidedly New Left, anti-exclusionary, anti-anti-Communist stance.

Whatever Stetler anticipated was jolted and transformed when in March 1964 the Chinese news agency Hsinhua reported that the Haverford student association supported the NLF. In fact, it was the five campus radicals—Stetler, Eyer, Mattick, Eaton, Garahan—operating through what they called the Student Committee to Send Medical Aid to the Front of National Liberation of South Vietnam, modeled on a Bertrand Russell organization in Britain. By April the news had traveled via Czechoslovakia to the local Philadelphia press. The college may have been embarrassed and made sure that it clarified that the group was decidedly not representing the student body, but it also stood firm on the right of the five to engage in such activities without retribution. However, the Philadelphia board of education, still dominated by old-line traditionalists, was pushed by local veterans' organizations who were incensed that Stetler was a recipient of a city scholarship. They demanded that the board take action and rescind the award.[55]

Stetler received considerable support, an indication that the repressive atmosphere associated with McCarthyism was at least tempering. The college, some faculty from both Haverford and other area colleges, the ACLU, and the Methodist minister from Stetler's church all testified in his behalf at the school board hearings. The most hostile testimony came from a VFW member from Roxborough who apparently blamed the teen-aged Stetler and his friend Frank Carner for trying to influence his daughter. Stetler's ACLU attorney Richard Kirschner was the son of one of Stetler's progressive teachers at Roxborough High School. Stetler also received support from an old high school friend serving in Vietnam who, while critical of Stetler's political views, supported the continuation of his scholarship.[56]

Perhaps Stetler's parents bore the brunt of local resentment, including threatening phone calls. Stetler's testimony before the board was temperate and measured, with no ideological edge or left-wing rhetoric. He did conclude with a forceful denunciation of the board's proceedings, castigating them as "improper and pernicious." In July, the board decided to sustain Stetler's scholarship.[57]

Throughout this controversy, Stetler and his friends pressed on with their activism. In April they spearheaded a "we won't go" ad in the *National Guardian*, 87 signatures from twelve colleges, with nearly half of those signing from Haverford College. The FBI's on-campus investigation of Stetler would stir up civil libertarian resentments, but the issue of medical supplies would fade as the support group concluded that the plan was logistically unworkable. Stetler, however, demonstrated a genius for sustaining a high profile when, in February 1965, he was charged by the FBI with attempting to illegally import a Communist propaganda film—*Heroic Vietnam*—that he was sponsoring on a variety of college campuses.[58]

When the film, which Stetler had received via Cuba, was released and shown at the University of Pennsylvania in March 1965, many students "jeered and ridiculed" it, cheering the arrival of American helicopters and troops in one particular segment. However, back at Haverford, a Student Council poll as early as fall 1964 indicated that a sizable majority (370–255), supported a resolution opposing U.S. policy in Vietnam and calling for a negotiated peace and military withdrawal. And more than 150 students from Haverford and neighboring Bryn Mawr rode the buses to attend the SDS-sponsored Vietnam War protest demonstration in April 1965. Yet one veteran activist, Marty Oppenheimer, a visiting instructor in sociology and already well known for coauthoring a direct action manual for the civil rights movement, criticized "the conservatism and middle-class values that predominate here," concluding that "Haverford's 'radicalism' is mostly a myth."[59]

What was the case? Activists like Oppenheimer and Stetler were alienated from the stubbornly academic culture at the college; they also were developing an impatience with any politics not focused on direct action and revolutionary change. In a letter to a friend, Stetler righteously asserted, "I don't count radicals by the numbers who read unpopular leftist journals. But I count the number of bodies who will create outrage which will build the nation."[60] Here, in a nutshell, is the essence of what became New Left ideology—a politics of authenticity, a rebellion against the life of the mind so quintessential to hot-house institutions like Haverford. It was not as if activists like Stetler abandoned intellectual work—at precisely that moment he was completing a pamphlet "War and Atrocity in Vietnam" and speaking at a host of rallies drawing on his remarkable capacity to dive into both primary and secondary materials relating to the war. But his focus, like that of Oppenheimer and Russell and most of his developing New Left comrades, was on the doing. And his sense that a U.S. Goliath was raining terror on an underdog David blinded him, and many others, to the less inspirational qualities of Ho Chi Minh and his followers. At the same time, he remained strongly committed to domestic civil liberties and democracy in his identification with the early New Left.[61]

To outsiders, Haverford seemed to be a veritable "soviet" of radical activism during the mid-1960s, when most college campuses, including Penn and Temple, were relatively apathetic and apolitical. Most students were certainly liberal; in the campus mock election of 1964, Johnson received 278 votes to Goldwater's 38, with a scattering to third party candidates.[62] There was now a more activist Student Action Committee, which, although choosing not to formally affiliate with off-campus national organizations, became the dominant campus voice for radical change. In addition, the campus now had an alternative to the student newspaper, Joe Eyer's *twopenny press*, a medium for movement news and agitation. Meanwhile the *Haverford News* editorials still complained about campus apathy, and Eyer was already in October 1964 bemoaning that "the student movement of the early sixties could not be rebuilt." It may be pertinent to note that on this strikingly academic campus the death of T. S. Eliot merited a full page obituary with photo.[63]

In academic year 1964–65, Stetler operated more on a national, even international plane than at Haverford. He edited the May 2d Movement's *Free Student*, continued to speak and show the NLF film, and resolved to take a leave of absence from the college to move to New York and teach a course on the war at the new Free University. In October 1965, the school board, supported by Mrs. Stetler, who felt forced publicly to declare her opposition to Communism, rescinded the scholarship. He would return in 1966 to graduate—he already had earned sufficient credits before taking his leave—but his political career now was well beyond the confines of either Haverford or the Philadelphia area. He became Bertrand Russell's personal secretary and executive director of the Bertrand Russell Foundation and played a key role in the War Crimes Tribunal held in Stockholm in 1967. After leaving the foundation, he became a journalist, including a stint at *Ramparts* magazine, and worked as a private investigator during the 1970s. As the nation moved past the tumult of the 1960s, Stetler remained a near-mythic figure to those who watched his meteoric rise as one of the New Left's first "stars," but most lost track of his activities. Since the 1990s he has been involved with considering the fate of death-row inmates through the Appellate Project of the California Bar Association and, more recently, with the Capital Defense office in New York City.[64]

The Haverford story is not reducible to the career of Russell Stetler, although I believe that the college's essentially antinomian radical qualities and traditions made Stetler's idiosyncratic activism emblematic in ways analogous to that of Professor Davidon. To extend this argument, I want to close this section with a brief look at the experiences of Joe Eyer.

Eyer, a red-diaper baby and noted boy wonder, was, next to Stetler, the most visible and best-known Haverford activist. He was elected Student Council president in March 1965 based on his leadership of the Social Action Committee and his editorship of the *twopenny press*. Eyer had been involved in both local and southern civil rights activities in 1963 and 1964, seeking along with Roger Eaton and more than a dozen others from Haverford and Bryn Mawr to establish an ERAP in South Philadelphia based on the JOIN—Jobs or Income Now—concept, but also working with a SNCC project in Savannah, Georgia.[65]

Eyer was a deeply libertarian New Leftist. For example, during a cheating controversy on campus, he concluded, "Causes of cheating should be removed, rather than hurting one who cheats." His campaign for council president emphasized ending campus regulation of student sexual and social behavior. He also submitted sections from a book he was writing to the *Haverford News* as "Letters from the South," which expressed his very personal and idealistic feelings and reflections:

Tonight the KKK is holding a meeting in a nearby park. They may shoot up a few houses or bomb something, so I've got to look out for that, too. I think of myself now as halfway between white and Negro: I always suspect every white I meet. So I am expecting suspicion from every Negro I meet. So I have learned to be very wary of the prejudices everyone has about race. . . . Do not be surprised if I come back with a strange attitude toward all of you: mainly, I will not be accustomed to living with friendly white people.[66]

Eyer, already the experienced New Leftist, pondered whether the integration struggle could be converted into "the political phenomenon of revolution":

But are we going to be able to get Negroes to think in terms of political action to rid themselves of slums, unemployment, low wages—their oppression. If they will then they must think even beyond integration, for then they will HAVE to draw in the poor whites to the struggle, because many of these people are just as downtrodden—and what a change that will be! The poor whites ("rednecks") are now the biggest ideological backlog of racism . . . integration will come first.

Eyer anticipated several years of integration processing before the struggle moved to a newer level: "This will be the real revolution." He saw some of the latter process in the developing voter registration drives, but concluded by noting how exhausted he was from "this cultural poverty" that plagued organizing efforts. This last comment suggests how much even a fairly experienced red-diaper baby such as Joe Eyer was still forming his views, still struggling with how to integrate the excitement of the civil rights upsurge, the recognition, as a radical, that something more fundamental was required, and the personal reflection that at least some of the southern blacks he was meeting were carrying the burdens of centuries of oppression. One must always keep in mind in evaluating New Left political development and consistency that these were very young men and women, sometimes still in their teens, rarely more than their early twenties. They were still growing up at the same time as they were forcing themselves, because of what they perceived as the moral exigencies of the times, to take on grown-up political responsibilities. That there were immaturities is less astonishing than how often these young idealists engaged in the tasks at hand, both in remedying deeply rooted racial injustices and in beginning to confront American bullying in the Third World.

By early 1965, Haverford College was immersed in what most folks would characterize as "the sixties" in ways not yet the case on the vast majority of college campuses. There were Philadelphia City Hall vigils against the bombing of North Vietnam beginning in February; there were *Haverford News* discussions of campus drug use, including hallucinogens; there was coverage of the college's first rock 'n' roll band; there was a call for establishing a quota based on national population distribution to "accept the best Negroes we can find." There were also faculty critics, like economist Holland Hunter, who supported the administration in Vietnam, and student voices like that of columnist Bob Bott, who charged that the developing New Left was "romantic" in its attraction to Maoism and its treks south to participate in civil rights.[67]

Then in early April, a month after taking office, Joe Eyer announced his resignation as president of Student Council. He began by juxtaposing the violent and destructive "existing hierarchy of power" with the newly born movement:

These independent centers of struggle, these people devoted to ideals and a new society, are few now in America; but they have the sympathy and support of the two-thirds of the world's population that starves and is now rising in angry and determined revolt against the old conditions. It is in behalf of these idealists, in behalf of these struggling peoples, in behalf of equality, brotherhood, love and mutual concern between men that I am speaking today.[68]

He spoke of some of the changes in campus rules already achieved, for example, car privileges no longer dependent on grade point average and the creation of student exchanges to southern campuses, or under discussion, such as a student options for exemption from grad-ing. Eyer then declared that his efforts were proving "useless and depressing," turning him as president into "a tool in the hands of the administration," "an informal campus policeman," ending with a curi-ous flourish:

Your president has been required to settle all kinds of petty campus disputes; your president has suffered the harassment of raucous students shouting and beating on his door late at night. Your president has suffered the contempt and indifference of great numbers of the students.

All this in one month! Eyer called Haverford College "an integral part of a corrupt society" that "stands for the status quo and not what might be better." He spoke eloquently of what motivates students to learn, contrasting competitive and intrinsic models; he criticized "publish or perish" pressures on faculty; he deplored student apathy and its resistance to what he saw as necessary social change. But the emphasis remained personal: "I found myself lost in a morass of ac-commodation. . . . I took out all of the stress and strains that resulted on my friends . . . [the process] made me at times . . . imperious, con-temptuous, irrational. It has made me cynical, stolen away what ideals I had." Eyer concluded that he would continue his fight for a better college, society, and world, but that it was not possible as Student Council president. Then he announced his resignation as president. His fellow students, at first stunned, gave him a standing ovation.

I spend considerable time on Eyer's resignation because it so em-bodies central features of both Haverford's radical antinomianism and qualities in the early New Left well before it succumbed to a kind of ideological rigor mortis of recycled Marxism-Leninism and sloganeer-ing. Eyer in many ways embodies the most and the least attractive dimensions of the New Left: its idealism and its immaturity, its com-mitment to tell truth to power, and its self-righteousness. Eyer's state-ment incorporated much of the intellectual atmosphere of the early New Left. One can tease out the influence of C. Wright Mills both in terms of a power elite and in terms of the prospective alliance of the young intelligentsia and Third World revolutionaries; one notes the pedagogical influence of figures like Paul Goodman. Eyer, of course, was not the only student radical to conclude that one must resign from positions of authority because they are coopting and alienating. There is the more well-known case of David Harris, the Resistance founder, resigning as Student Council president at Stanford in 1966 and then doing jail time for his pacifist beliefs.[69]

The Eyer resignation simply offers a window through which one can observe both the moral power and, at the same time, the futile tendency toward a politics of gesture and a certain kind of indulgence. How was one to begin to change this remarkably middle-class, infuriatingly stable America? Many New Leftists, inspired by the heroism and sense of community embodied in the civil rights revolution, seeing similar qualities—from a distance—in Castro's Cuba, Mao's China, and Ho's Vietnam, deeply troubled with the seeming moral opaqueness of so many of their fellow students, teachers, parents, and neighbors, tended to give up on any forms of gradual social change, on any reform agendas—tactics aside—on any belief that liberalism, or social democracy, might still be the vehicle for social transformation.[70]

After all, when Eyer resigned from the presidency, the nation was moving toward something—the end of Jim Crow, through both the Civil Rights Act of 1964 and the Voting Rights Act of 1965. It was in the early stages of the War on Poverty, which would cut the poverty rate in half. Lyndon Johnson was in the midst of building what he called the Great Society: Medicare and Medicaid, urban renewal, aid to education, environmental legislation, National Endowments for the Arts and the Humanities. Yes, there was Vietnam. What did the above ameliorative and certainly insufficient reforms mean when we were beginning to rain down terror in both the Red and Mekong River valleys? As Eyer spoke the nation watched thousands march at Selma, after state troopers had stomped on demonstrators, using cattle prods; they mourned the murders of the Rev. James Reeb and Viola Liuzzo. No one would be convicted; Hoover's FBI would continue to maneuver, to smear, to bug and wiretap, and to blackmail. There were more than enough reasons for New Left contempt of any politics of moderation: the Democratic Convention in Atlantic City where Johnson's forces sought to coopt and placate the Mississippi Freedom Democrats stands as the emblem, the epicenter of such alienation from a "politics of responsibility."[71]

But a consideration of both the Swarthmore and the Haverford experience suggests that many of the qualities that made the developing New Left so attractive and, sometimes, effective, also contained the seeds of its later self-destruction. Eyer's resignation should not be forced to carry such a burden, but it does inform about that antinomian strain—that very American tendency to resolve the tension between living *in* the world but not being *of* the world through withdrawal, even a withdrawal in the paradoxical form of a global populism. The New Left's ambivalence about democracy rests here. Participatory democracy was a politics of authenticity; ERAP and later New Leftists often discovered that only the committed had the time or the interest to invest in such a fusion of the personal and the political; the New Left belief in democracy could only be sustained if one envisioned that "out there," in the Delta, in the ghettos, in Third World revolutionary movements, constituencies existed. And in 1965 that vision was strong and still growing.

The Stetler and Eyer era ended with graduation in 1966; Eyer, selected as an honored senior to give one of the Senior Honors speeches at Final Collection, spoke on "The Necessity of Revolution." Antiwar activism escalated during that year, with professors Bill Davidon and Ariel Loewy leading protests against the Boeing Vertol Helicopter plant in nearby Morton, with fasts for peace, peace vigils, and demonstrations. By the end of the school year, the student newspaper's editorial board castigated the Johnson administration for its policies in Vietnam, but emphasized its commitment to free discussion and its call for all students "to take a stand."[72]

In 1966–67, with the old leadership gone and Davidon on a Fulbright fellowship in Denmark, the campus seemed more culturally than politically rebellious. Drugs seemed to trump activism and editorial laments about student apathy reemerged. Perhaps the despondent words of one student in spring 1967 tells all:

(1) Our protests are serving little more purpose than providing consolation for archeologists of the next millennium.
(2) Most of the voting public supports the war because it "furthers their interests," meaning "protects our suburban homes against the nasty people."[73]

Nevertheless, 35 students participated in the Easter Peace Walk and 140, including Bryn Mawr students, took buses to New York antiwar demonstrations in April. And a Haverford faculty group, through the Canadian Peace Service, sent over $650 for North and South Vietnam medical relief.[74]

In fall 1967, close to 150 Haverford students marched on the Pentagon, with three arrested, and eighteen faculty, including Bill Davidon, signed a Resist statement urging young people to consider refusing to cooperate with the Selective Service system. There were some new voices among the students, mostly well-known ones among the faculty. But as Haverford College entered 1968 it remained a very liberal and academically demanding institution, frustrated with its moral isolation, increasingly attracted to the culturally libertarian call of what would soon be called the freak counterculture, and decidedly American-grown in its antinomian style and rhetoric.[75]

## Bryn Mawr and Second-Wave Feminism

Bryn Mawr College shares much with the Quaker and elite experiences of both Swarthmore and Haverford, but at the same time it stands apart as a women's institution of higher learning. It was the smallest of the Seven Sisters, with an enrollment of about 800 in 1956, including graduate students; the frosh class was 169.[76] In a campuswide poll, the students voted for Eisenhower over Stevenson that election year by a close margin; the faculty, on the other hand, were overwhelmingly for the Illinois Democrat. In the shadow of the McCarthy period, Bryn Mawr seemed precious and intellectual; editorials in the student newspaper, the *College News*, bemoaned Bryn Mawrters' "famous extra-curricular apathy" and lamented: "It is a dry campus; it is a dull community. The energy of a few individuals in a wasteland of tedium and particularization is ineffectual." During the mid- to late 1950s, the paper headlined Beethoven sonata concerts and a wealth of lectures on literature, poetry, and theater; it was a school that prided itself on offering a classical liberal arts education. Occasional liberal speakers visited, but the political tone of the campus was best captured by a petition sent to the National Student Association (NSA) by Alliance, the college's student organization, which, in protesting South African apartheid, stressed "the importance of Western civilization to the natives," who, they believed, were "eager to better themselves."[77]

One of the threads running through all the Philadelphia area colleges from the late 1950s into the 1970s were challenges to *loco parentis* regulations of dress, personal behavior, dormitory restrictions, and social and sexual life. These have particular pertinence at a women's college given that the protective, paternalistic rules were weighted by gender biases. Ruth Rosen, in her history of second-wave feminism *The World Split Open*, evokes the ambivalence of her generation of college women concerning sexual freedoms, referring to what she astutely calls "the hidden injuries of sex."[78] This was before there was a vocabulary of gender, before rape, sexual abuse, sexual harassment, and the very notion of sexism had been raised as issues; before there were challenges to notions of vaginal orgasm; before the formation of the National Organization for Women (NOW) and the emergence of the women's liberation movement. In 1957, Bryn Mawr prominently listed engagements and marriages in the *College News*; students were struggling to persuade the administration to change the time from 11:30 to 10 a.m. when men would be allowed into the women's dormitories.[79]

And yet Bryn Mawr was an essentially liberal institution; along with Haverford and Swarthmore, it refused to accept National Defense Educational Administration (NDEA) loans because of the requirement of loyalty oaths. Thus the winds of change from both the civil rights revolution and the "New Frontier" Kennedy administration began to stir things up on campus. Whereas in 1958, during the Little Rock

School Board controversy, several Bryn Mawrters spoke sympathetically of the white south and saw "strong-arm" federal action as merely
inflaming "their pride and irritation," by the early 1960s sentiment
and allegiance had begun to move overwhelmingly toward the civil
rights activists who led sit-ins and voter registration drives. At the time
of the 1958 Youth March for Integrated Schools, an editorial suggested that the march was "repugnant to nine out of ten students here
on campus" but was troubled by the assumption that "boredom with
the integration-segregation issue was widespread." The editorial writer
spoke of the "fetish for decorum, the unwillingness to become actively
involved . . . prevalent in our generation," but seemed ambivalent, calling for "non-participant support." She concluded, "If sophistication has
replaced zealousness, we are not sure this is bad, but we mistrust it."[80]

But by 1960, with the sit-in movement, the editorial staff invoked

a call for action . . . whether we like it or not, there is no turning back: . . . the
emphasis has been shifted from sympathy to active support. No longer may
we simply admire the tenacity and courage of Negroes sitting-in at lunch
counters, boycotting buses, and attempting to get seats in decent schools. Instead we must be prepared to take positive action, to cease admiring and start
emulating.

Words spilled into action, as Bryn Mawrters began to participate in
demonstrations. Sixty students joined the newly formed Committee
for Action on Civil Rights which, along with Haverford activists, began
sympathy picketing at local chains like Woolworth's that were the targets of the sit-in demonstrators.[81] Some students participated in exchanges with historically black colleges in the south. These were the
kinds of students who strongly supported JFK over Nixon in a student
poll in 1960, while the administration and staff favored the Republican. There was now contested ground at Bryn Mawr; this was the first
phase of what would soon be called "the sixties," a more vital, ideological dialogue over issues of immediate relevance. More conservative students still spoke up, voicing fears that direct action tactics
would alienate southern moderates or that white resistance to black
suffrage was "not sheer bigotry."[82] But there was now a small pocket of
dissent, including a new Bryn Mawr-Haverford chapter of the SPU,
which protested the selling of fallout shelters at Snellenberger's department store in downtown Philadelphia in late 1961.

By 1962, activists like Swarthmore's Mimi Feingold were returning
from the south to talk about their experiences as freedom riders,
while other red-diaper babies like Kathy Boudin, Bryn Mawr Class of
1965, were emerging as leaders of the incipient New Left. In interviews, several undergraduates have recalled how awed they were at

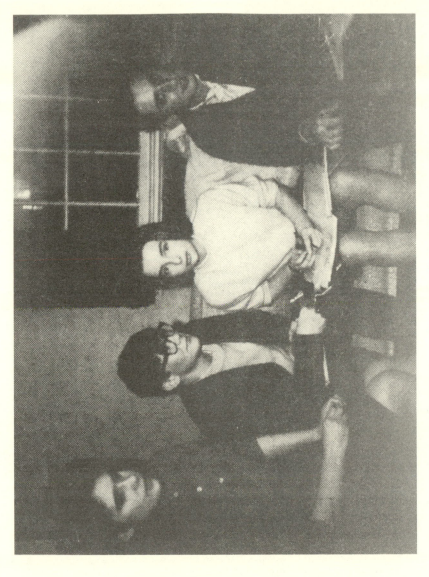

Figure 5. Bryn Mawr's Kathy Boudin and Haverford's Alan Raphael, co-chairs of the Second American Revolution conference, held at Bryn Mawr College in 1964. Bryn Mawr College Archives.

Boudin's intelligence, experience, and commitment.[83] In 1963, activists would participate in the civil rights demonstrations in Cambridge, Maryland, take part in Northern Student Movement-directed tutorial projects in Philadelphia, organize a cooperative house off-campus, bring needed supplies and money to striking miners in Hazard, Kentucky, get arrested in civil rights demonstrations in Chester, and organize a conference called the Second American Revolution at the college, which took place in February 1964.[84]

More than 200 students from dozens of colleges came to the conference, co-chaired by Boudin and Alan Raphael, a New Left activist from Haverford. There were conservative voices, such as segregationist James J. Kilpatrick, but dominating were the more militant words of Howard Zinn, Stokely Carmichael, Stanley Aronowitz, Marty Oppenheimer, and Jesse Gray. With this, Bryn Mawr had most definitely entered the 1960s. And there were other challenges and changes regarding campus regulations; in April, trustees approved men in public areas until 12:30 a.m. on weekends and the wearing of pants and shorts to dinner.[85]

By the end of the 1964 school year, a small yet critical mass of Bryn Mawr students were joining Haverford and Swarthmore activists in movement efforts, both in the south and in ERAP in Chester and Philadelphia. In the fall, a new Social Action Club became part of the Alliance and the *College News* was filled with stories of summer experiences in Chester, New York, and Mississippi. Activists like Edna Perkins, Jeanne Trubeck, Mary Thom, and Ginny Kerr, all Class of 1966, and Jean Hunt, Class of 1967, had joined Kathy Boudin in leadership roles; others like Margaret Levi, Class of 1968, worked with ERAP in Baltimore. And during the fall 1964 term, when Bryn Mawrters voted 476 to 59 for LBJ over Barry Goldwater in a student poll, more than a hundred were involved in a variety of tutoring projects.[86] So when Levi helped organize a Social Action Committee/SDS seminar, "The Meaning of a Liberal Arts Education," in early 1965, there was a rich set of experiences driving the call for Bryn Mawr courses to be more relevant to the real world or even questioning "whether or not it is possible to be simultaneously a political activist and a student."[87]

So it was in an already emerging context of New Left leadership, organizational life, and extensive activism that the Americanization of the Vietnam War lit another spark. That some of the new leaders were the children of Old Leftists is less significant than that they shared with their peers new, inspirational experiences that made them genuinely New Left, that is, led them to place their own experiences in the civil rights struggles in Cambridge, Chester, and the south center stage in terms of strategy, tactics, and notions of selfhood. They identified with a "movement" more than a "party," with a prefigurative vision of a "beloved community" more than of barricades and a factory-centered notion of stages. What they shared, Old and New Left, was an identity as cadre, as an army of revolutionaries, albeit the former were comfortable with violence and the latter posited a "kinder and gentler," though no less militant brand of radicalism.

At the same time, Bryn Mawr's response to the Vietnam War was "confused" and, characteristically, arch, tending toward a rejection of what it called the "extremes" of militarization and withdrawal. How else to describe a campus celebrating the selection of Katherine de Saulles "Kitty" Ellis as best-dressed in a *Glamour Magazine* campus contest while noting that Ellis planned to join the Peace Corps in Africa after graduating. There was a conservative group on campus—eighteen students had attended a Young Americans for Freedom conference in 1962, and there were letters to the editor defending administration policies in Vietnam. But in spring 1965, about one hundred students and faculty went to Washington to march in the first major anti-Vietnam War protest organized by SDS, and the Social Action Committee organized a petition to send to President Johnson protesting the bombing of North Vietnam.[88]

Bryn Mawr's activists did not have the visibility of either Swarthmore's SDS/ERAP group or Haverford's leaders like Russell Stetler and Joe Eyer. Kathy Boudin was its most notable New Leftist; during her undergraduate years she was a campus leader and a founding participant in an emerging circle of activists, most of whom worked with their ideological peers at nearby Haverford, Swarthmore, and Villanova in civil rights, peace, and campus democratization efforts. Certainly as students at a women's college, Bryn Mawr activists were less likely to be noticed among the overwhelmingly male "movement heavies" and by the media. Boudin, despite being a much admired figure, perceived herself with greater ambivalence and significantly less confidence.[89]

In Boudin's 1965 graduating class, 51 percent went on to graduate or professional school, 48 percent decided to enter the work world, and 15 percent of the class planned to be married within the year, intending to combine marriage with either work or study. Some radicalized undergraduates, like Jean Hunt, simply dropped out of school, turning their New Left idealism toward the peace movement and, later, second-wave feminism. Boudin, who had spent the summer after her junior year working with Cleveland ERAP, returned to full-time involvement in the project.[90]

The 1965–66 academic year seemed less intense, perhaps in response to the departure of Boudin, although other area campuses were also quieter. The following year, Bryn Mawr's New Leftists were more successful in organizing opposition to the Vietnam War. Yet there was an abiding frustration with what activists saw as the torpor of the Bryn Mawr experience. Margaret Levi, speaking at a conference on the American university in Los Angeles in the spring, stated that at Bryn Mawr "the level of participation in student affairs is very low. Despite its emphasis on the academic, the school suffers from a lack of intellectualism. Despite its reputation for attracting bright, sensitive girls, its classrooms are dull."[91]

Levi blamed this situation on the absence of "a tradition of participation," a stress on individualism, and a more recent and equally troublesome trend toward "wholesome, well-rounded and stable girls." Levi sharply criticized "the myth that education is the passive acquisition of knowledge." Finally, the Bryn Mawr junior emphasized that the liberalism of the college was contradicted by its intolerance toward other points of view, particularly that of Marxism. Bryn Mawr's marketplace of ideas seemed to confine itself to a liberal-conservative continuum with no legitimation of radical ideas. In a follow-up letter to the editor, responding to criticisms, Levi conceded that Bryn Mawr "is more intellectual and more democratic than most other schools," but that it still needed to do more toward encouraging students to become involved in the larger world. There were some mild successes: during the 1965 Thanksgiving break, 585 Bryn Mawrters fasted to raise money for a SNCC project for unemployed blacks in Natchez, Mississippi, and in early 1966 a letter signed by 200 students was sent to LBJ demanding a bombing halt in Vietnam.[92]

Marty Oppenheimer was a visiting lecturer in sociology that year and bolstered Levi's participatory calls with his own evocation of Paul Goodman's notion of a community of scholars, a participatory democracy in the classroom. Social work professor Philip Lichtenberg called on students to reject becoming "prematurely mature" and "striving for superiority that misses the opportunity to be a fool."[93] Such faculty proddings were consistent with the movement linkage of education and politics, socialization and conformity. Lichtenberg's evocation of the role of the fool captures the ways risk-taking and the joys of discovering subversive avenues of "growing up absurd" had moved to center stage in New Left experience.

Bryn Mawr's New Left activists struggled against the claustrophobia of what they experienced as an essentially smug and privileged environment. Their inspiration came from elsewhere, initially the civil rights movement. Resting on the direct action, participatory activism of those who went south, who joined local organizing and tutorial projects, who spearheaded the opposition of the Vietnam War, who began to question academic authority vis-à-vis curriculum, pedagogy, and campus rules, the New Left was essentially heroic and exemplary, not only at Bryn Mawr but at all the increasingly activist campuses. A small cadre of students were taking risks that rested on clear ethical stances; other students sometimes ignored these challenges, sometimes resented the righteousness of the challengers, but without doubt tended to admire those in the forefront of activism. Leslie Coen, Class of 1966, for example, joined ten other Bryn Mawrters in Cambridge, Maryland, in the integrationist struggles of 1963. She concluded:

I went down to Cambridge certain of the need for integration, but dubious of these methods [of direct action]. Like most Bryn Mawrters I've talked with, I doubted the efficacy, the advisability, of having car loads of college students descend . . . to help older, more experienced citizens in an "internal" matter. I feared a presumptuous attitude on the part of the students, and resentment in the town. But after joining hand-in-hand with Negroes and whites in the most spirited singing that I've ever heard; after having my picket line spit on and jeered at; and, especially, after helping in a perfectly integrated, crowded church kitchen, to serve hot dogs, potato salad, and Cool Aide (sic) to what seemed thousands of enthusiastic people, I realized that this is what must be done.[94]

Such idealism was about to confront the rising anger of Black Power, but it nevertheless still shaped a New Left, which as late as 1967 remained humanistic and ferociously democratic.

Of course that ferocity could alienate peers, as also occurred at both Swarthmore and Haverford. When Drewdie Gilpin, Class of 1968, posted pictures of injured Vietnamese children in Bryn Mawr's Taylor Hall, some students complained about bad taste and covered them up with pieces of paper. Gilpin declared, "War is not in good taste," adding, "My purpose in posting those pictures . . . is not to provoke thought but to inspire action." Gilpin, who became president of the Alliance in 1966, "wondered if students were too busy to think about the war, if they knew nothing about it, or if they just did not care."[95]

At the same time, the New Left was driven by a series of disillusioning experiences, of revelations of corruption and betrayal: secret chemical and biological research on campuses, conflicts of interest between governing board members with real estate and corporate interests and notions of academic freedom and scholarly disinterestedness, government spying. Margaret Levi spent the summer of 1967 working with Operation Crossroads in Uganda only to discover that the CIA was a secret funding source for the program. She was deeply troubled by the ways in which such covert operations shattered the program's reputation for independence from governmental control and may have compromised "African counterparts and friends." Levi's comments remained strikingly non-ideological—she conceded that the "CIA might have meant well by Crossroads" but condemned it for destroying trust.[96]

Cultural challenges deepened in 1967 as students continued to call for less restrictive campus policies, in this case regarding overnight sign-outs to Haverford College, and as the counterculture, including greater discussion of drug usage and more coverage of 1960s rock 'n' roll, became more pervasive. There was still a Bryn Mawr entry to *Glamour Magazine*'s Best Dressed College Girl contest, and skirts were still required for classroom wear, though slacks and shorts could be worn at other times. But the most notable development was the sense, at least among the activists, that they were participating in the creation of a movement. A group of Bryn Mawrters challenged the college to ask basic questions about the Institute for Cooperative Research, a collaborative effort, including Bryn Mawr, that was engaged in secret Vietnam-related defense research. Clearly the battles against Project Spicerack at the University of Pennsylvania were spilling over to other institutions: 260 students signed a petition calling for the college's withdrawal from such collaboration.[97]

Perhaps the peak of this sense of building a movement came between spring and fall 1967, sparked by the April antiwar demonstrations in Washington, sustained by the efforts of the Vietnam Summer project, and extended by the March on the Pentagon in October. One can see during that space of time both the promise and the future troubles of the movement. The critical mass of movement strength occurred precisely as the racial dynamics so central in inspiring its origins and its style turned toward Black Power and as cultural forms of rebellion, especially those relating to drugs, began to intertwine with political forms of dissent. What is most noticeable, parallel to the rising sense of movement strength, is a growing impatience with the slowness of change, especially following the long, hot summer of 1967 in Newark and Detroit. Fueling that impatience was a sense of possibility, driven in part by the growth of the antiwar movement, but also by the sense that youthful rebellion, in manifest forms, was rising. It was the collision between these hopes and expectations and a seeming impotence before the war both abroad and at home, that fueled frustrations and pointed toward the use of more desperate measures. On the eve of the Pentagon March, Bryan Mawrters reprinted an Amherst editorial reflective of such feelings:

Today, nobody talks of a movement whose very beliefs will end the war. There are no illusions that moral acts will end the war. Today, people march to confront the war-makers, not to speak to one another before the United Nations. This march is not a march of hope. It is a march of anger and frustration.[98]

The *College News* was filled with the stories of those who had ventured to Washington, and the commentary from those who just a few years earlier had bemoaned the absence of any sense of social conscience, conveyed how rapidly consciousness could change in times of dislocation and challenge:

Everyone seems to recognize that this is a turning point in the movement, away from peaceful peace rallies and marches, and toward more local and more militant action. We have been marching for over two years and it does not seem to have done much good. Most people involved have expressed a desire for more concrete action, such as draft resistance and civil disobedience in the form of burning draft cards, sabotaging local draft board activities, and perhaps more disruption at the Pentagon.[99]

There was a mixture of exhilaration and deep frustration at the heart of such responses, perhaps driven by the ways the war had come home to roost. People were now dying in the streets of America, and the movement was beginning its turn toward a more Third World, Maoist perspective. In a sense, the New Left was leaping from a kind of homegrown, anti-ideological radicalism clumsily called participatory democracy, jumping past Marxism, with its essentially Eurocentric focus, to a Marxist-Leninist populism marked by slogans like "Power to the People." It wasn't yet there in fall 1967, but the first glimmers had appeared.[100]

As 1968 approached, things at Bryn Mawr had moved a long way from the gentility of the 1950s. Students now demanded that attention be paid to the all-black staff of maids and porters; there was criticism of the "plantation" qualities of the college, with a focus on how poorly such campus workers were paid. Activists attacked the sign-out system as hypocritical, "an anachronism from the days when women were protected, pampered and constantly shaded from the harsh realities of life." They were also demanding that "the stereotype of the woman-as-helpless child" be "eased out."[101] All the contradictions inherent in a movement seeking to make sense of what W. E. B. Du Bois had anticipated as the most salient issue of the century—race—was about to confront head-on the issue of gender.

It is striking, for example, how rarely Philadelphia, including Bryn Mawr, is referred to in any of the more recent studies of 1960s feminism.[102] In fact, the first women's liberation conference took place on September 20, 1969, on Penn's campus; there was a second and larger one, bringing together close to 500 women, on March 21, 1970. By that point there were NOW chapters at Temple and Penn; Penn's Free University and the Philadelphia Resistance's Omega University offered classes in Women's Liberation; there was a strong women's caucus within the white antiracist group People for Human Rights (PHR); Swarthmore had its first women's liberation group; there were African American women's caucuses in the Black Economic Development Committee (BEDC), the National Welfare Rights Organization (NWRO); a Marxist study group made up of feminists existed; there was an Abortion Rights Association spearheaded by Penn graduate Connie Bille Finnerty; and there were approximately a dozen ad hoc women's groups in the region.[103]

At Bryn Mawr, the first meetings addressing women's liberation, which drew more than forty participants, took place in late fall 1969. They were sparked by the leadership of Joan Mandle, a Bryn Mawr graduate student in sociology and a veteran of the New Left. Undergraduate Peggy McGarry called for more women's courses, a women's studies program, and more "action-oriented projects" addressing women's issues. The administration's initial response was, at the least, ambivalent; it canceled the first proposed course, with thirty students preregistered. The students responded with a sit-in, and the college agreed to offer its first course on women's liberation, but specifically *not* to be taught by Mandle. That fall, 1970, Bryn Mawr hired Kate Millett as a visiting lecturer to teach "A Historical and Social Survey of the Role of Women"; two hundred students, including twenty males, were enrolled.[104]

That same year, parietal hours were abolished and the first editorial attacking "sexism," including homophobia, appeared in the student newspaper. Departing President Katherine McBride declared herself supportive of women's liberation and enthusiastic about Millett's course. There was a letter to the editor from Kit Bakke, Class of 1968 and former *College News* editor, supporting the SDS Weathermen faction, noting that it included former Bryn Mawrters Kathy Boudin and Diana Oughton and closing with "To live we must fight." And Wendy Hertzberg's September 18 *News* column was headlined, "Apathy Is Bryn Mawr's Response to Women's Liberation."[105]

## Chapter 3

# The Catholic Schools

Virtually none of the literature addressing student opposition to the Vietnam War or, more broadly, the emergence of the New Left movement, considers the experience of Roman Catholic colleges and universities. There is a marginalized literature addressing Catholic movements for social justice and peace, especially those associated with the Berrigan brothers, Philip and Daniel, and their anti-draft activities. But even the contemporary trend toward shifting attention away from the hothouse environments of Berkeley, Madison, and Cambridge has focused on larger state universities in this period.[1]

In Philadelphia, three Roman Catholic institutions that were shaped by the Vietnam War—LaSalle, St. Joseph's, and Villanova— operated at some distance from the center of the Quaker-led peace work. Swarthmore, Haverford, and Bryn Mawr, all Quaker-based, played significant roles in initiating criticism and opposition to the war and to a host of social injustices, as well, especially racism and poverty. The Roman Catholic colleges, however, never established such profiles, never became centers for dissent and activism. Nonetheless, LaSalle, St. Joseph's, and Villanova were each caught up in the turmoil of the times, driven by similar forces but framed by distinctively Roman Catholic concerns. Catholic campuses were never individualistic or antinomian in their rebellions; they operated within a universe of social responsibility, of corporatism, of loyalties that anchored them to neighborhoods, parishes, rituals, mores, and the tug of 2,000 years of the Church Universal.[2] They were particularly affected by the remarkable emergence of two men: John Fitzgerald Kennedy, the first Irish Roman Catholic to serve as president of the United States, and Pope John XXIII, whose short reign brought a breath of fresh air into the Second Vatican Council, which he created and shaped.[3]

## LaSalle College

LaSalle College, a small (student body of 5,000) Christian Brothers institution located in Philadelphia, was in the 1950s and early 1960s mostly known for its basketball teams. The Christian Brothers were a teaching order "with a real commitment to teaching poor kids" and a more egalitarian bent than existed at many other Catholic institutions of higher learning. LaSalle was a "street-corner" commuter college, most of whose students came out of local Catholic high schools. The political climate was more mainstream than ideologically conservative; most undergraduates were of immigrant stock—Irish, Italian, Slavic—from families that tended to support organized labor and had come, albeit belatedly, to an identification with the New Deal Democratic Party. In the middle to late 1950s, except for some passionate solidarity with the Hungarian freedom fighters, there was little evidence of any interest in either national or international affairs. In the 1960 mock election, students supported John Fitzgerald Kennedy over Richard Nixon by a margin of 843 (78.3%) to 219 (20.3%).[4]

There was a modest increase in campus political controversy and interest in the thousand days of Camelot. The election of an Irish Catholic president, combined with the openness of Pope John XXIII and the Second Vatican Council, seemed to stimulate a greater attention to issues of social conscience on campus. Visitors included voices both left and right, the Catholic Workers' Dorothy Day and conservative scholar Russell Kirk. There was even a brief pro-Castro set of articles in one campus paper, the *Collegian*, before the Bay of Pigs and Cuban missile crisis reinforced the Cold War consensus to which these students from overwhelmingly anti-Communist backgrounds adhered. There were ideologically conservative disciples of William F. Buckley, Jr.; indeed, a new Conservative Club appeared in 1963.[5]

But campus leaders, including the editors of the *Collegian*, remained politically centrist and moderate. For example, when the film *Operation Abolition* was shown on campus, the editorial warned, "Intelligent anti-Communism can not be hysterical." In fact, the editors, seeking more balance, bemoaned that there were no faculty volunteers to speak out against the one-sided House Un-American Activities Committee (HUAC) documentary.[6]

By the early 1960s, LaSalle, influenced by the ecumenical messages of the two Johns, was increasingly drawn to local civil rights concerns as a result of being located uncomfortably close to the North Philadelphia black ghetto, which experienced one of the nation's earliest riots in summer 1964. Some LaSalle students became involved in social activism, although inspired more by Catholic than by New Left idealism.

In 1962, Dennis Clark, director of the Housing Division of the Philadelphia Commission on Human Relations and a spokesperson for the archdiocese, addressed over one hundred students on the moral issue of racial segregation. In fall 1963, a small number of students volunteered to work with the Philadelphia Tutorial Project, an effort organized by the Northern Student Movement to provide extensive supplementary instruction to poor black students in North Philadelphia.[7]

In fall 1964, LaSalle students gave Lyndon Johnson a decisive victory over Barry Goldwater in their mock election, 559–329 (63–37%). The editors of the *Collegian*, however, also stressed "the importance of maintaining the freedom of South Viet Nam" and emphasized the need for a more aggressive policy against Communism.[8] By fall 1965 there was coverage of initial peace protests, some of it harsh: "the Communist influence is all the more sinister and heinous because it uses as dupes and fall guys concerned and intelligent young men and women who are perhaps too naive and idealistic to realize the ends to which they are put." At the annual convention of the National Congress of the National Federation of Catholic College Students, two LaSalle student leaders coauthored a resolution supporting Johnson's Vietnam policies and commending his restraint.[9]

But the response of LaSalle students to the rising challenge of the Vietnam War was complex and remarkably open-ended. On the one hand, there was a massive campaign—Mail Call Vietnam—to send Christmas cards to GIs serving in Vietnam. At the same time, a *Collegian* editorial rejected the pejorative stereotyping of protesters, emphasizing that "we also saw generous young people who conscientiously followed their duty as they saw it." Clearly, the intellectual leadership at the college was feeling ambivalent about this war; they supported the Democratic administration but were troubled by the developing dissent on some campuses.[10]

Two specific instances point out this ambivalence. On September 23, 1965, a member of the Class of 1965, Second Lieutenant James B. Kelly, was killed in action. The Political Science Association sponsored Operation Gift Lift, a donation of gifts to his battery, in honor of Lt. Kelly. One student noted, "The death of Lt. Kelly suggested that perhaps the effort in Vietnam was not really so remote from campus as might have been thought."[11] And in December, Maxwell Taylor received standing ovations both before and after his speech on campus before a supportive audience of 400. Some of a small but now emerging antiwar student group criticized the format of the lecture as inhibiting criticism; only printed questions were allowed. But such voices were few and at the margin; more representative were the six batteries (800 strong) of ROTC cadets parading to the Church of the

Holy Child to attend the Fourteenth Annual Mass of St. Barbara, the patron saint of artillerymen. In May 1966, the first public antiwar activity took place at LaSalle; three students held a peace vigil the same day as an ROTC review.[12]

Most of LaSalle's students simply went about their business—rushing from home to class, often working, focusing on career and family plans, rooting for the basketball team in its intense Big Five rivalries with St. Joe's, Villanova, Temple, and Penn. But a remarkable 32 LaSalle graduates had volunteered for the Peace Corps and were serving somewhere in the Third World by late 1966.[13] The Christmas issue of the school's newspaper reflected a significant shift in social conscience: the focus was on violence and racism. And there was a Special Supplement, "The College Within the City in Crisis," which measured the increasing sensitivity to and concern with racial justice and poverty.[14] By early 1967, the campus seemed split between hawkish and dovish voices, although most students clearly remained on the sidelines. In February, 32 faculty members wired Johnson calling for an acceptance of the Geneva Accords on unification and UN-run elections, a bombing halt, and negotiations with the NLF. This was clearly the largest such faculty expression yet at LaSalle, indicating the growth of a less marginalized minority, at least on the war issue. At the same time, in a campus referendum, students voted 518 (54%) in favor of administration policy, 370 (39%) against, with 68 (7%) expressing no opinion. Moreover, the *Collegian*'s letters column included an increasing number of heated pro and con missives on the war.[15]

In spring 1967, the strands of cultural dissent came together in support of the city's first "be-in," in Fairmount Park. Just as the political rebels of the early 1960s had found sustenance from citywide efforts, (e.g., the Philadelphia Tutorial Project), so the cultural radicals could now join with the developing counterculture of coffee houses, folk and rock clubs, and downtown hangouts. During the Summer of Love, several drank in the new psychedelic street culture of the East Village. Yet the campus remained decidedly mainstream and resistant to all forms of political dissent; a leading faculty dissenter, physics professor Bertram Strieb, complained that posters for the spring 1967 Mobilization in Washington were being systematically torn down or defaced with obscenities.[16]

The Mobilization, the largest demonstration yet, received extensive coverage in the *Collegian*, including by several staffers who wrote as participant observers. The significance of the event can be gauged in part by the response of Thomas A. Downs, Class of 1968, who wrote to the march organizers,

And what a day it was! So beautiful, so purposeful, so memorable. And so many people—what wonderful people!

In order to go to New York, I had to go against my parents' explicit feelings and warnings (I'm still 20). My own conscience came first, however, and now I am more pleased that I lived up to my convictions. Thank you for the chance to be a man.[17]

There was a forum on the war in the fall, featuring the dovish historian Henry Steele Commager and antiwar senator Ernest Gruening, and an anti-draft rally downtown. The existence of this new voice on campus, driven by matters of conscience among Catholics influenced by John XXIII and Kennedy, affected by the anguish of urban racism and poverty right next door to the campus, and attracted to the counter cultural voices challenging all forms of authority—this new voice was still at the margins of an institution like LaSalle, but it was now audible and increasingly assertive. Students expressed enthusiasm for the Beatles' new Sergeant Pepper album, providing on-the-spot reports of the "hippie" Philadelphia Folk Festival, featuring Pete Seeger, and a new Center City head shop. One piece, based on one editor's summer experiences in New York's Tompkins Square Park area, proclaimed, "Something is happening but you don't know what it is, do you, Mr. Jones?" For many at LaSalle, such challenges, from Bob Dylan or antiwar protesters, were intolerable. Mainstream students, as well as faculty and administrators, were not used to being confronted.[18]

In late October, several students, described as "hippies," recently returned from the March on the Pentagon, were harassed, and one was punched in the school cafeteria. The assailant, a fraternity member, exclaimed, "There never was a protest like this in any of the preceding wars. It was my personal feelings that made me hit him. I can see a legitimate protest, but not the characters that are protesting now. When I enrolled at LSC there was none of this element on campus—and I think it's ridiculous." The student, senior Frank O'Hara, was convicted and given a warning by the Student Court in a student-packed hearing room. O'Hara, part of whose defense rested on the fact that he had a cousin serving in Vietnam, added, "I'd hit him again if I was enraged like that."[19]

O'Hara's outrage was not that the antiwar movement had taken over the campus. Indeed, it remained a marginal influence at the end of 1967. But O'Hara was correct; in the early and mid-1960s there were no such voices, or, if there were, they were scarcely audible. Something had changed. There was now a challenge coming from a still mostly liberal but feisty minority of a dozen faculty and possibly a

Figure 6. LaSalle College antiwar vigil, fall 1967. LaSalle University Archives.

hundred students, engaged in civil rights and peace activism, that called for a draft counseling center on campus and the elimination of compulsory ROTC. To give them sustenance, there were off-campus supportive institutions—other colleges; citywide coalitions; cultural enclaves; student newspaper reports on Haight-Ashbury, and Rittenhouse and Tompkins Squares. At the close of 1967, approximately 200 students attended a vigorous, balanced debate on the war in the lunchroom. Certainly the fate of the basketball team, the Explorers, remained higher on the list of campus importance, but as LaSalle approached the traumatic and watershed year of 1968, its student body and faculty were less silent and more iconoclastic than they had ever been in the college's history.[20]

## Saint Joseph's College

Like LaSalle, St. Joseph's College in the early 1960s was better known for its basketball team than for its accomplished Jesuit-trained debating squad. Half its student body (1,400 in 1962) came from several feeder high schools; St. Joe's Prep sent 399, Cardinal Bonner 171, West Catholic 87, Father Judge 46, and St. James 46. In the late 1950s and early 1960s, Hawk Hill, as St. Joe's was often called, was more conservative and traditional than LaSalle. It was a rarity for the college to welcome any speakers with even a mildly liberal perspective; more typical were stirring rallies in support of Hungarian freedom fighters or mourning the death of "a great man," Pope Pius XII, and visits from Dr. Fred Schwarz of the Christian Anti-Communist Crusade. The campus atmosphere, despite the celebrated debate team and an occasional thought piece in the student newspaper, the *Hawk*, was decidedly nonintellectual.[21]

The *Hawk* editorial board supported JFK in 1960 but viewed the election as "Hobson's Choice," saying nothing negative about Nixon. In a campus poll, 66 percent said they'd rather be "dead than red," with 19 percent choosing "life" and 14 percent undecided. The Kennedy Thousand Days did spark an enlivening of campus discourse, with more coverage and commentary on international events and more expressions of idealism, but precious little on either civil rights or on the papacy of John XXIII.[22] In 1962 the Burke Club, with thirty students as members, commenced operations as the campus's center for conservative ideas. They certainly would have shared the contempt expressed in a *Hawk* editorial on "Pseudo-Intellectuals" who "read only those books which they know to be intellectually fashionable: Salinger, Camus, Joyce, Sartre. . . . They assume the cynical pose of one disillusioned with life. They are utterly modern pseudo-intellectuals."[23]

The early 1960s editor in chief, Patrick Temple-West, was an ideological conservative who opposed allowing Communists to speak on campus, arguing that for students to grant free speech to such radicals was "going out of their way to bring about the downfall of American democracy."[24] But there were also signs of change: an editorial opposing Mississippi segregationists; some challenge to the notion that conservatism was compatible with laissez-faire economics; the beginning of tutorial projects in poor black neighborhoods; more coverage of nonmainstream cultural happenings. The assassination of President Kennedy evoked an outpouring of grief, with dozens of reflections and poems. Perhaps reflecting a new idealism, five St. Joe's graduates volunteered for the Peace Corps in spring 1964 (there would be another eleven the next year), while the mostly white student body elected its first African American Student Council president.[25]

When, in 1964, David Marshall, a young philosophy professor, joined the faculty, soon to become a central figure in the small but emerging voices of dissent, the dominant political tone remained centrist to conservative. In the 1964 elections, the students overwhelmingly supported LBJ over Goldwater (59.1 to 40.9%) but also supported Republican senatorial candidate Hugh Scott over his liberal Democratic opponent by a 2 to 1 margin. Within the editorial board, four supported Goldwater and only two opted for Johnson.[26]

When the Vietnam War heated up in spring 1965, 863 St. Joe's students sent a letter to LBJ urging a firm interventionist policy. One editorial writer excoriated "the hysterical and jejeune criticisms from the Exhibitionist Left," while another criticized what it called the "New Rebels," whose "protests carried to excess, including treasonous statements and draft-card burnings." A campus poll taken in late fall 1965 demonstrated a clearly hawkish bent: 54.3 percent (290) supported LBJ's policies, 34 percent (185) wanted a more aggressive policy, 9 percent (51) sought a more dovish posture, and only 1.5 percent (8) argued for withdrawal. That winter, St. Joseph's students sent 500 Christmas cards to Vietnam GIs while columnist Wayne Barrett described Berkeley in late 1966 as "an ugly and sick haven for those with nothing to offer."[27]

There were some campus debates on the war, but the more subtle changes were over dress codes and arbitrary administrative rulings. One outspoken student was denied admission to the campus Jesuit Honor Society by a dean for "disloyalty" to the college. An editorial commentator reflected:

In attempting to provide a Catholic liberal education, St. Joseph's has been steadfastly providing a conservative parochial indoctrination. The question

among student and faculty is not whether this situation exists, for it is generally accepted to exist. The question is whether this is desirable. Is thought
control any less thought control because it is done in the name of the good,
the true, and the beautiful? . . .

Unfortunately St. Joe's would much prefer to produce a Staunch American,
a Loyal Hawk, and an Unswerving Catholic Soul than an agile, questioning, well informed mind.[28]

The 1960s were arriving at Hawk Hill, perhaps belatedly but nonetheless. By the end of the 1967 school year, the student newspaper's adviser
was voluntarily giving up his censoring tasks, and in the fall students
voted 94 percent to end the coat and tie dress requirement.[29]

In 1967, although the campus remained essentially apathetic except
about the varsity basketball team, students raised $500 for an orphan-
age in South Vietnam and more energy and controversy appeared in
the *Hawk*'s columns and letters to the editor. The counterculture had
also become a minor force, providing the spirit behind a pioneering
arts festival on campus. A Martin Luther King, Jr., speech and the first
campus antiwar demonstration suggest both how far St. Joe's had come
and, as at LaSalle, how much resentment that journey inspired.[30]

In early November, Dr. King spoke to an audience of over 1,500 at
the fieldhouse. There was both support for and criticism of King's appearance. Several students commended his support for integration
and equal rights but criticized his advocacy of busing, open housing
laws, and the establishment of a guaranteed income. The letters column was filled with responses, one of which described King as "pro-
Communist"; in the wake of the speech, several alumni canceled
contributions to the college's development fund.[31]

Then, just before the Thanksgiving holiday break, the Ad Hoc
Committee of Concerned Students held a silent vigil, mourning those
who had died due to "the indiscriminate use of napalm." The crowd
of about 250 bystanders became more hostile as the protesters' numbers grew from 25 to 50. They chanted, "Rather be dead than Red"
and, in a cheerleading mode, spelled out napalm, followed by a cheer
of "kill, kill, kill!" Attempts to explain the protest were drowned out by
charges of Communism and cowardice. Finally, at the behest of the
Student Council president, the crowd, which had been drowning out
the protesters with renderings of both the national anthem and the
Hawk fight song, allowed Professor Marshall to explain that the vigil
was not in opposition to the war but, rather, "a vigil in sympathy to
those who have lost friends or relatives in the conflict." A dean refused
to call campus security to manage the crowd; another college administrator exclaimed, "If I weren't an elected official . . . I would make my
feelings and presence felt, physically." The letters column over the

next weeks was filled with mostly anti-demonstrator remarks, including those of a conservative antiprotest leader who suggested that "the demonstrators were taunting the student body to react." Those participating in the vigil, well dressed, wore black armbands with small crosses and held small yellow candles; no Viet Cong flags, no long hair, no revolutionary rhetoric.[32]

One *Hawk* columnist castigated the "basketball-worshipping cafeteria mob," but also charged the demonstrators with self-righteousness, with a refusal to spend time attempting to persuade their fellow students of the validity of their cause. He concluded that "they are now saying that the rest of us are too callous or stupid to know that there is something to be mourned."[33] Nevertheless, the vigil generated sufficient interest that a debate between Marshall and a faculty hawk brought out more than 400 students in January 1968. Marshall did not support immediate withdrawal in his measured comments but rather argued that it was not in the interests of the United States to oppose the self-determination of the Vietnamese people, even if they chose Communism.[34]

Just days after the vigil, Professor Marshall and ten students joined a protest against an area realtor for discriminating against African Americans and Jews. They were part of a larger group from Haverford and Bryn Mawr Colleges.[35] St. Joe's emerging activist contingent was small but had made its presence known as the college entered the tumultuous year of 1968. The small, beleaguered enclave of activist faculty and students at the suburban campus could find some strength in joining with the more energized and experienced movement efforts generated from the elite and Quaker institutions of the Main Line.

## Villanova University

The most Main Line of Catholic institutions, Villanova University, never compared itself with the more plebeian LaSalle or St. Joseph's. 'Nova placed itself in the Catholic elite, which included Georgetown, Boston College, and Notre Dame. It also looked uncomfortably toward its more intellectual and dissident neighbors, Haverford and Bryn Mawr. An editorial in the student newspaper, the *Villanovan*, proudly proclaimed that "the standard of correct living set forth as the ideal of Villanova is that of a Catholic gentleman." Intercollegiate athletics, especially football, basketball, and track, were pervasive emphases, along with a vibrant social life. Villanova, attracting affluent, mostly Catholic students from throughout the nation, placed great emphasis on behavior. Editorialists in the later 1950s, for example, berated beatniks in terms of "the ravings of immature people against order and responsibility," while rock 'n' roll was described as "a cheap form of rhythm which is discordant to the ear of every person that enjoys music."[36]

In a series of articles in fall 1967, at a time when much of the nation's attention was focused on race riots in Newark and Detroit, the emergence of a hippie counterculture during the Summer of Love, and the militancy of the March on the Pentagon, the school paper described the Villanova student as "a conservative thinker—in politics, in dress, and in his outlook on life . . . a man who judges the world as it is, rather than as it should be." The article portrayed the Villanovan's values as "those of middle class America . . . right out of modern suburbia: cars, money, clothes, popularity":

The Villanovan is generally concerned about his social life. He could not be termed a "serious thinker." The main topic on his mind is not Vietnam or the trouble in the cities. Rather, he is concerned chiefly about mixers and parties. He is not overjoyed at having to put much time into his courses. He would prefer planning big weekends of excitement and revelry to having an intelligent discussion with his favorite teacher . . . [he] would rather become an executive than write a book.[37]

There were few signs of intellectual vitality at Villanova in the late 1950s. When the conservative Fulton Lewis III brought the pro-HUAC film *Operation Abolition* to the university in 1961, there were hecklers from the area's pacifist and liberal communities, but more overwhelming was "the latent anti-Communist sympathy of the audience," which responded to Lewis's "formidable array of facts, figures and reports."[38] The overwhelming preponderance of campus speakers represented conservative views; there were few liberal and no radical guest lecturers. However, more slowly and softly than at LaSalle, the influences of Kennedy's Camelot and of John XXIII's Second Vatican Council began to reach Villanova. One editorial spoke, in early 1962, of a revival "of political interest." There was a vibrant Conservative Club, but there were also those who expressed interest in the Peace Corps—81 took the exam in late 1963; eight had joined the previous year; others joined a Catholic version of the corps operating in Mexico or an Archdiocesan Tutorial Program. In the mock election of 1964, LBJ bested Goldwater 946–565 (62.6–37.4%). But the student body of 4,500 undergraduates, including 1,400 business and 1,000 engineering majors, paid little attention to political events. Just as the United States sent its first combat troops to Vietnam, a *Villanovan* editorial complained that "anything is better than the stupefied silence that now prevails on campus."[39]

Students did organize a Christmas Card campaign for GIs; 20,000 were sent. And the Conservative Club sponsored a "books for Vietnam" drive. Letters began to appear in the campus newspaper from graduates serving in Vietnam and sometimes from their families. There was one very critical of protesters from a Class of 1964 alumnus, a second lieutenant in the Marine Corps who was wounded in action near Danang. There were editorials excoriating those Haverford students seeking to send medical supplies to the Vietnamese enemy: "We can only have pity for such individuals who cannot comprehend the importance of even the smallest victory over Communism." And those who demonstrated against the war in April 1965 were decried as "a pitiful corps of individuals whose sole ambition in life seems to be to turn their backs on realities of the world situation." The SDS organizers of the march were called "a motley collection of social pariahs."[40]

These deeply conservative and authoritarian aspects of Augustinian Villanova began to face criticism by 1966, spearheaded by a new, more liberal editor in chief of the *Villanovan* Ron Javers; compulsory class attendance, the severity of the disciplinary code, dormitory rules, even women's rights, all came under scrutiny. In "An Open Letter to the Administration," dozens of student leaders criticized "flagrant examples" of the administration's "ignoring student needs" concerning cafeteria services. For Villanova, this was quite new and daring. The protesters concluded:

We are not out to embarrass the Administration. . . . We are writing this as Christian gentlemen. . . . If the Administration continues its present policies we fear that embarrassment to the Administration, due to forces beyond our control, is inevitable. Hence, we are publishing this letter to temporarily forestall any rash actions by justifiably impatient students.[41]

The first Villanova graduate was killed in action: Albert C. Doody, Class of 1965, a Marine Corps second lieutenant. Dovish critics called for students to consider the Peace Corps over military service; 31 did so by 1966.[42] There were more strains of a Catholic sense of social responsibility and of self-criticism, influenced by the Second Vatican Council. An editorial entitled "Who Is My Brother?" asked, "What would Christ have done in Selma, in Watts, in Washington? He would have realized that all of the preaching in a month of bombings will not soften the hearts of the many bigots who answer the roll call as Catholics." Two articles excoriated Catholic resistance to residential integration and Church racial prejudice in the North. A later editorial, "God on Our Side," ridiculed "Poor Cardinal Spellman," suggest-

ing that "there is no such thing as a 'war for civilization' . . . there will
be no more crusades."[43]

By spring 1967, Villanova's notion of a "Catholic gentleman" had
been at least challenged by what was being called "the Javersonian
Era," after the iconoclastic, outgoing editor in chief of the *Villanovan*,
Ron Javers. The paper's "Story of the Year" was "Student Activism at
Villanova." There was even a new Experimental Free School.[44]

But the enthusiasm of campus intellectuals ran smack in the face of
what was still a conservative and essentially apolitical institution. Few
Villanovans paid attention to the Spring Be-In, Philadelphia's coming-
out party for hippies, and the campus activists organizing for the
Spring Mobilization complained of harassment from the administration at their tables near the college store. The previous spring, administrators had confiscated antiwar literature. In fall 1967, Concerned
Citizens, a new antiwar student group, hardly New Left, prepared "to
take mature, responsible but forceful action" by "nurturing a 'moderate' image," in the face of the "overwhelming odds in Villanova's 80%
'hawk' population."[45]

Many of that hawkish student body greeted the first campus
demonstration ever at Villanova in October 1967 with ridicule and
hostility. A dozen to twenty students and faculty, including priests, organized a vigil. They were peaceful, indeed silent, holding signs that
read, "We are thinking about the War in Vietnam. You are invited to
join us."[46] Then in November there was an anti-Dow Chemical, anti-
napalm demonstration, which drew an even more aggressive response.
The administration limited the pickets to five and warned them
against any shouting; however, a crowd of at least 250 heckled and
jeered, soaked protesters with water, and pelted them with eggs, while
campus security failed to respond to a call for assistance. In one instance, fraternity pledges were ordered to dump water and debris—at
least seven times—from a contiguous building without being re-
strained by campus police. The *Villanovan* spoke of an "ugly crowd"
that "appeared to be getting out of control."[47]

As at LaSalle and St. Joseph's, the watershed year of 1968 approached, and the initial seedlings of antiwar protest at Villanova
faced a vast majority that was not so silent when confronted with challenges to both their complacency and their mainstream values. It was
still risky—indeed, dangerous—to stand up against the war on Roman
Catholic campuses at the end of 1967.

But life would not be the same at such institutions after 1968. Villanova opened its doors to women in 1968 (up to that point they had
only been admitted to the School of Nursing); "The Stewed Tomato,"

Figure 7. Joint Haverford-Bryn Mawr-Villanova banner at the March on the Pentagon, 1967. Bryn Mawr College Archives.

an off-campus coffeehouse, opened for business; the Experimental Free School offered courses on the draft, Quakerism, Karl Marx, and the New Left; and Philip Berrigan came to the university to speak on the topic, "Non-Violence, Vietnam, and the Cold War." It is true that the Villanova fieldhouse was only half-filled to hear "one of America's most notorious anti-war activists." It is also the case that the winter Basketball Edition was a lush and glossy eight pages. But something had indeed changed: the letter-writing campaign of that winter, Mail Call Vietnam, emphasized that it was nonpartisan and that "the soldiers in Vietnam do not set U.S. policy." And at the March on the Pentagon, there appeared a contingent of students carrying a banner, "Haverford-Bryn Mawr-Villanova Students for Peace."[48] What would later be called "the sixties" had arrived, belatedly but nevertheless, at Villanova University; in some very real ways, those "Catholic gentlemen" would never be the same.

All three of Philadelphia's Roman Catholic institutions had entered the maelstrom of the 1960s by the end of 1967. These essentially white, male colleges, the first two working and lower middle class, the latter middle and upper middle, experienced the challenges of the decade through the prism of Roman Catholic values and experiences. By late 1967, there were tentative voices of dissent, but these voices were decidedly moderate to liberal. There was little sign of student radicalism of any type—Marxist, Communist, Maoist, anarchist, or Black Power-oriented. It is important to emphasize how mainstream and conformist these campuses remained in late 1967. The small groups of antiwar activists were deviants, a new and threatening enclave of Catholic humanism. They were respectful, polite, and still strikingly deferential to authorities, and they put themselves at great risk. Both the administration and their fellow students tended to respond to them with a mixture of indifference and hostility. The working-class students at LaSalle and St. Joe's, most of them commuters living at home, were most comfortable in an apolitical environment of classes, family, work, career, and a fierce identification with their respective basketball teams. Villanova's Christian gentlemen were more comfortable with soph hops and junior week partying, with Marine ROTC and football weekends. Neither anticipated the emergence of even a small, marginalized pocket of cultural rebels, civil rights advocates, and pacifist warriors; at their worst, they resented these intruders and made them unwelcome. But the campus heretics, strengthened by their faith and by the surrounding atmosphere of Quaker Philadelphia and the hippie hangout of Rittenhouse Square, of a more cutting-edge radicalism at Swarthmore, and, as we shall see, of rising dissent at Penn and Temple, were ready for more as they entered the late 1960s.

## Chapter 4

# From Subway School to Ivy League

Temple University and the University of Pennsylvania, Philadelphia's dominant Center City campuses, illustrate an important juxtaposition of New Left experience. Temple, though considered by many the Philadelphia equivalent of the City University of New York, only stumbled into 1960s New Left activism, essentially ignoring the growing voices of dissent prior to the Americanization of the Vietnam War in spring 1965. At that time, it had no SDS chapter, and most of the left leadership came from figures like Carl Gilbert, chair of the Student Peace Union (SPU), who maintained affiliations with Old Left issues and styles. In stark contrast, it was the conservative, stodgy Penn that emerged in the late 1960s to most successfully shape New Left movement efforts in the city. Although dominated by professional schools, a lively fraternity culture, and big-time athletics, Penn nevertheless gave birth to the most important cohort of New Left activists in the Philadelphia area.

## Temple University: Subway School from McCarthyism to the Rise of the Movement

During the mid-1950s, Temple was a politically quiescent urban commuter school with small, isolated enclaves of activist liberals plus the remnants of a shattered and defensive Old Left. In 1953 the trustees of the privately operated but state subsidized university had fired Barrows Dunham, chair of the philosophy department, for invoking his Fifth Amendment rights before the House Un-American Activities Committee, prompting the American Association of University Professors to censure the school in 1956.[1]

At the same time that campus radio station WRTI banned rock 'n' roll, some of the campus survivors of the McCarthy purges organized the Three Arrows Club, whose purpose was "the study of democratic socialism and other contemporary problems." There was also a Thomas Jefferson Club, affiliated with Americans for Democratic Action, and a chapter of the Student League for Industrial Democracy.[2] Twenty Temple students under Three Arrow sponsorship journeyed to Washington, D.C., in 1957 for the Prayer Pilgrimage for Freedom, but the Student Council ruled out of order a resolution that requested funding for part of the bus fare on the grounds that the civil rights rally, called in support of implementation of the Supreme Court's 1954 *Brown* decision on school integration, was a non-campus activity.[3]

There was little activity beyond occasional speakers sponsored by the above groups until the early 1960s. The editorial page of the *Temple University News*, mostly mainstream, mildly liberal Democratic, complained about student apathy but had little expectation of response. In fall 1961 there was a small stir when national SANE pressured a cancellation of a Student SANE-sponsored "Hoot for Peace" performance at Temple by the blacklisted Pete Seeger. Temple Student SANE chair Diane Post protested that the "conservative" national leadership "feel that civil rights and peace are two separate issues" and the Tyler (Temple's art school) Student Council sent SANE a letter criticizing its role in the cancellation. McCarthyism indeed still cast an oppressive shadow over anything that might be construed as pro-Communist. But changes were on their way.[4]

The SPU held its first meeting that fall and began campaigning for a nuclear test-ban treaty. Chaired by Carl Gilbert, Class of 1965, it stepped forward as the most active, progressive campus organization for the next few years. It began to hold biweekly meetings, brought in prominent speakers like radical pacifist David McReynolds, and addressed the salient issues—nuclear testing, U.S.-Cuba tensions, and opposition to Kennedy's fallout shelter program.[5]

Such views were challenged most forcefully by Eugene Eisman, an anti-Communist liberal, who criticized direct action protests against nuclear submarine missiles and argued that the "real heroes" were in "far-off Vietnam . . . 10,000 heroes . . . who have made a full commitment to a just cause." There were also the beginnings of modest volunteer activities, including the Philadelphia Tutorial Project (PTP) created by the Northern Student Movement (NSM) in 1962. The PTP, headquartered at Temple, recruited 175 tutors at nineteen centers to assist 375 public school students.[6]

The Kennedy era, in terms of both civil rights and foreign policy, lifted the campus out of the political apathy and timidity of the mid- to late 1950s. Editorials and opinion columns became more politically focused as the outside world began to penetrate the still essentially quiet North Philadelphia campus. Other small but noticeably more frequent signs included a black SNCC activist who returned to campus to discuss voter registration in the south, an emerging interest in the folk music scene, the establishment of a YPSL (Yipsel) chapter with close connections with the SPU, and an increasingly visible and militant CORE chapter.[7]

In the fall term of 1963, Gail Paradise from national SPU spoke at a local chapter gathering of 25 and urged the United States to withdraw from South Vietnam. But despite some civil rights activity the campus remained oblivious to political concerns. The most visible SPU leaders, Gilbert and Bob Kernish, were now on Student Council, but the biggest news item during the winter was a panty raid involving about 500 students.[8] During spring term, Gilbert, a red-diaper baby and Yipsel activist, took a stand against a Student Council withdrawal of an invitation to segregationist Mississippi Governor Ross Barnett, arguing for the value of a diversity of views. Gilbert was a Third Camp advocate, that is, a militant Marxian socialist who sought a radically democratic alternative to both U.S. imperialism and Stalinist totalitarianism. As such, he held principled positions that the university should stand as an open forum for ideas, even those, *especially* those, as offensive as Barnett's.

Gilbert began a regular op-ed column "On the Left" in late 1964, which helped to make him the most notable voice of radicalism at Temple over the next few years. In 1964, the Philadelphia Yipsel chapter was suspended for refusing to support Lyndon Johnson for president against Barry Goldwater. The ideologically focused Gilbert argued, "Re-electing Johnson would be worse than electing Goldwater. He is moving the U.S. toward state capitalism." The Temple Yipsels soon vanished, with Gilbert shifting his considerable energies to a short-lived Independent Socialist Club chapter and then to SDS.[9]

At the same time, a new campus CORE chapter formed, headed by Ellen Goldstein, an ally of Gilbert's. Also, a new organization, Social Service in Action, brought three Mississippi Freedom Democratic Party activists, including Philadelphia native Larry Rubin, to campus and sent food and clothing to demonstrate solidarity with Freedom Summer. Following the North Philadelphia riot of the preceding summer, the small civil rights activist contingents divided energies between southern and local racial injustices. As a result of the 1964 riot and the increasing sensitivity to Temple that existed in the midst of the North Philadelphia ghetto, activists began to focus attention on the complaints from neighbors about the university's expansion—past, present and future. A crowd of 300 heard NAACP local leader Cecil Moore criticize Temple's relations with the North Philadelphia black community.[10]

But prior to the Americanization of the Vietnam War in February and March 1965, the Temple campus for the most part ignored these small if growing voices of dissent. There had yet to be any discernible New Left presence on campus. It did not have an SDS chapter, and most left-of-center leadership came from veterans like Gilbert, who were associated with Old Left issues and styles. In contrast to figures like Mimi Feingold or the ERAP activists at Swarthmore, who engaged in direct action in civil rights struggles, Temple's radical voices seemed on the sidelines—commenting, theorizing, talking, but not *acting*. They seemed more interested in being ideologically sound than in having a practical impact. Indeed, they were often ineffective. Student government refused to recognize campus CORE and rejected Gilbert's motion to support the kinds of freedoms advocated by the Berkeley Free Speech Movement (FSM), although it also refused conservative calls for disaffiliating from the National Student Association (NSA).[11]

When U.S. air power responded to the Viet Cong attack on Pleiku in February 1965, some faculty voices were raised. History professor S. M. Chui argued that the bombing of North Vietnam was counterproductive; political science professor Charles Joiner countered by supporting administration policy. In March a new faculty group, the University Faculty for Peace in Viet Nam, formed, led by speech professor Herb Simons. Campus debate escalated that month as 500 students listened to philosopher Sidney Hook, at Temple as lecturer in residence, excoriate Berkeley demonstrations as a "disgrace," followed by Communist Party theoretician Herbert Aptheker's lecture, attended by 200, which called Marxism "the greatest force in the modern-day world." At the least, the spirit of a repressive McCarthyism was fading. Civil rights activism also advanced with the establishment of Conscience, a group of 60 students committed to working for racial justice in the contiguous North Philadelphia black community. Conscience held a rally attended by 400 students, at which Dick Gregory was featured but failed to show up; toward the end of the term they brought out 120 students to engage in a neighborhood clean-up effort. By fall 1965 there was considerable coverage in the campus newspaper of student involvement in the local North Philadelphia community, including a summer camp project for local children and the PTP's ongoing efforts.[12]

On campus, life heated up considerably as Haverford activist Russell Stetler, already well known for organizing efforts to send medical supplies to Vietnamese insurgents, narrated a National Liberation Front (NLF) film, *Heroic Viet Nam 1963*, which had been seized by U.S. Customs and subsequently released. Some in an overflow crowd of 600 challenged Stetler's pro-Viet Cong comments, but others rallied to his defense.[13]

One thousand Temple faculty and students would march from Barton

Hall to Independence Hall to protest the murder in Selma, Alabama, of the Reverend James Reeb, who had earned a master's degree in theology in 1956 at the Broad Street campus. Speech professor Herb Simons, linking the struggle in the South with race relations closer to home, exclaimed, "We must erase the image of the 'closed gates' of Temple University—An image of a white island in the black ghetto."[14]

In April, 800 students and 75 faculty members attended a teach-in to protest U.S. Vietnam policies. This impressive showing suggested that the New Left movement had finally arrived at Temple. The teach-in was organized by the new Faculty-Student Committee for Peace in Vietnam, in coordination with analogous and synchronized events at Penn and Swarthmore. Interestingly, Carl Gilbert expressed disappointment "that the demands of the demonstration are so moderate," calling for immediate U.S. withdrawal and "non-violent civil disobedience." Speakers included A. J. Muste, chair of the Committee for Non-Violent Action (CNVA) and long-time radical pacifist. The teach-in, which began at 8:45 A.M., continued until 2:30 A.M., when only 100 participants remained. English professor Robert Edenbaum, spokesman for the teach-in, concluded that the turn-out was "disappointing but respectable," a sentiment shared by several others. But the editors of the *News* thought otherwise: "Never in the history of Temple University has there been such an encompassing change in outlook among students and faculty as there as been in the past few months' political awakening." They were particularly struck by the "more amazing" active involvement of many faculty in the protests. However disappointing compared with other campus efforts, Temple certainly seemed to have entered the "sixties" at long last.[15]

SDS made its first appearance at Temple with a May rally protesting U.S. military intervention in the Dominican Republic. Carl Gilbert was among the chapter's leaders, but there were a number of new voices, both graduate and undergraduate. But whereas two SDSers were elected to Student Council that spring, students voted 698–292 in support of administration policy in Vietnam. Campus interest in the subject seemed to deflate quickly as a debate between the antiwar professor Herb Simons and the hawkish professor William McKenna managed to draw only 75 listeners.[16]

In the fall, the Temple SDS Student Committee for Peace in Viet Nam (SCPVN) sponsored a rally and then a march to City Hall to hear Stetler, Staughton Lynd, Carl Oglesby, and others during the International Days of Protest.[17] SCPVN did not monopolize discourse; in October a group calling itself Responsible Students for Vietnam Policy (RSVP), formed, and the Alpha Epsilon Pi fraternity hung a banner "Kill the Cong" from their North Broad Street house. Such pro-war efforts increased in November, when Alpha Chi Rho joined Mail Call Viet Nam to collect 15,000 Christmas cards to send to GIs in Southeast Asia, and pro-war students staged a rally of 750 to show their strength. A coalition of hawkish students, including RSVP, Young Americans for Freedom (YAF), the Young Democrats Organization (YDO), and the Temple University Republican Organization (TURO) held another rally, which despite the rain drew 200 to Barton Mall. In December, 132 students gave blood to show their support for GIs. The newspaper's letters column was filled with both pro- and antiwar expressions. The former tended toward support of the administration, including one describing a twelve-year-old pen pal of a Marine stationed in Vietnam and another by Betty Zakroff Halstead, former editor in chief, Class of 1963, reporting from Vietnam for UPI that morale was high and that GIs resented home-front protests.[18]

In late 1965 and early 1966 the counterculture began to appear for the first time. Following three drug busts, the *Temple University News* headlined "Narcotics Seen Widespread at U." An editorial noted that drugs had become "a real problem," with "Marijuana as easy to buy as alcohol."[19] There was not yet, however, any suggestion of a countercultural voice in letters, columns, or news articles. Mostly, this characteristically apathetic city campus was being drawn in, somewhat reluctantly, to the controversies over Vietnam and civil rights. Its moral center in late 1965 remained mainstream, middlebrow, and loyal to the Democratic Party that had brought together immigrant stock Jews and Catholics under the banner of the New Deal and the New Frontier. A larger proportion of students, though far from a majority, were becoming engaged, most typically in liberal, occasionally conservative, activities, characteristically ameliorative, pragmatic efforts in nearby poor neighborhoods, in other pockets of poverty in the nation, and in developing Third World nations. As such, Temple's essentially secular political dynamics, including a sizable Jewish component and a small but critical cadre of red-diaper babies, were more liberal, but only marginally so, than Catholic LaSalle and St. Joe's.

The rise of dissident groups led the *Temple University News* to run a special on "The Activists" in early 1966.[20] The report suggested that, of Temple's 10,000 students, about 300 were politically engaged, with only 30 as leaders of seven organizations, left and right. YAF leader John J. McKelvie claimed 20 members and voiced a sly commitment to the principles of "participatory democracy" in arguing that "we would neither welcome nor reject" members of the extremist John Birch Society. The report characterized SDS/SCPVN as "the most vocal of the campus political groups," describing it as "new left" in having "no formal ideology" but instead focusing on "direct action to bring about immediate change."

The chapter claimed 25 active members, 15 "nominal" members, and about 100 sympathizers. Its executive committee included Carl Gilbert, Mel Pine (an evening student), and Frank Carner, a graduate assistant in English. The campus paper noted that SDS/SCPVN "suffers from factionalism," with a split over support or nonsupport of the Viet Cong. Such factionalism rested on tensions between Third Camp Yipsels like Gilbert, who carried deep suspicions of any political formations smacking of Stalinism, and the developing New Left identification with the heroism of the Viet Cong and other Third World insurgents.[21]

The January report stated that CORE was the "smallest' and most "inactive" of the organizations; Campus Americans for Democratic Action (CADA) was described by its leader Mark Dimirsky as "a force of moderation on the left," and clearly divided on the war; TURO, with 112 members, was strongly pro-war but self-described as "strictly middle-of-the-road with a slight liberal tendency"; and president Irv Ellis of the YDO, with 150 members, noted "that the campus is nominally Democratic," and, playing future politician, that his group was "progressively conservative liberal." Ellis added that YDO worked with Republicans and conservatives to support the war, but emphasized that they also defended the rights of protesters. Ellis admitted that some of his members opposed LBJ's policies but that most of those had resigned from YDO to join antiwar organizations.

There was also "the only strictly ideological club," the Independent Socialist Club (ISC), described by chairman Carl Gilbert as having "a third camp orientation" in opposition to "the power blocs of the Soviet Union, China and the United States." ISC claimed about 20 members. Gilbert, described as "the best known student politician," called himself "a democratic socialist and revolutionary pacifist." Mel Pine, SCPVN chairman, referred to Gilbert as "a kind of elder statesman" among activists, adding, "Some consider Gilbert to be part of the 'old left.' He used to be much too rigid and doctrinaire for the new left (SDS-SCPVN). As of late, SDS has become more rigid than he. Nevertheless, Gilbert is not on the 'in' of the new left."

Gilbert, responding to being called old guard, countered, "at 22?" Yet Pine's somewhat patronizing comments suggest a changing of the guard, one in which new forms of dogma were replacing older ones.

There were other liberal social action groups operating on campus: Conscience, Project Head Start, Volunteers in Service to America (VISTA). Conscience, the only one that was founded locally, worked in

North Philadelphia on housing, youth and recreational efforts. In addition, in February 1966 150 students expressed interest in joining the Peace Corps. As at Temple's sister commuter colleges LaSalle and St. Joe's, a small but growing number of idealistic students were seeking out modest ways to right wrongs.

The combined impact of Vietnam, civil rights, especially as it turned its attention to northern discrimination and poverty in neighborhoods like North Philly, and a variety of cultural challenges made for a fundamentally changed campus by 1966. There would be calls for a new free university, the W. E. B. Du Bois Club would seek chapter recognition, and thirty student activists would picket graduation speaker U.S. Vice President Hubert Humphrey to protest the war. This was still a relatively quiescent, apolitical campus, but most markedly the last remnants of the McCarthy era were being blown away. A campus editorial proclaimed "Recognize Du Bois Club," a defense of the right of students to join the youth group of the Communist Party, U.S.A. If anything, with a caveat to conservative currents, the most striking quality of the mid-1960s at Temple was its essential liberalism, that is, the commitment of a critical mass of students to joining the struggle to make the nation live up to its ideals of equality of opportunity, free speech, and democratic participation. There were, of course, developing but still marginal New Left currents, and many of the activist groups were led by Old Left veterans like Gilbert and several others with backgrounds in the various Communist and Socialist movements. But the dominant strain, albeit soon to be challenged by a series of traumatic events, was moderately liberal.[22]

A few more organizations joined the contest for domination over student politics in fall 1966. There was the Trotskyist Young Socialist Forum (YSF) and, finally, a recognized Du Bois Club, led by ponytailed English graduate student Jim Quinn. But the campus was minimally responsive—only 75 turned out for a rally sponsored by SDS and the Du Bois Club, which was heckled by hawkish students. There seemed to be more attention paid to counter-cultural events, particularly a Philosophy Club-sponsored presentation that, by advocating the use of LSD, brought out a crowd of 150. One of the speakers was Ira Einhorn from the Philadelphia Psychedelic Center, already becoming the leading countercultural voice in the city.[23]

In late 1966 Student Council held another referendum on the war, which demonstrated how mainstream if ambivalent students were. Of only 373 respondents, over 65 percent of the males declared their willingness to serve if drafted. Sentiment, however, was turning against Johnson; his policies were opposed 58–42 percent, but a quarter of LBJ's critics wanted all necessary means to be used to achieve victory while only 10 percent supported the immediate withdrawal of U.S. forces. Another 15 percent called for a bombing halt and UN arbitration. Whereas the campus paper's political editor called for victory in Vietnam, seven Student Council members, including president Phil Robinson, sent an NSA-sponsored letter to LBJ expressing their "concern" over the war.[24]

Perhaps the most striking and noticeable change in academic year 1966–67 was the greater visibility of dissident faculty. Herb Needleman on the medical school faculty spoke on several occasions about his involvement with Physicians for Social Responsibility and his own Committee of Responsibility to Save War-Burned and War-Injured Vietnamese Children. Despite right-wing hecklers and occasional noise from Harrisburg legislators, the mid-1960s, at least at Temple, encouraged more confidence that dissent was less likely to face the kinds of repression and retribution of just a few years before. In February 1967, Bob Edenbaum announced the establishment of a draft-counseling center on campus. Most notably, there were 60 faculty sponsors of the center, 21 of them from the increasingly dovish English department. Faculty, most of whom had been too young for the radicalism of the Depression Era, many of whom had been focusing on earning degrees, gaining tenure, and beginning their own families during the McCarthy period, now saw an opportunity, inspired in many cases by this new breed of activist students, to stand up and be counted. Such faculty visibility with no seeming retribution from Temple's administration measured the distance from McCarthy era timidity; undergraduates began to assume faculty dissent as a norm. And that dissent extended beyond speech to action.[25]

On March 1, 1967, the campus erupted when a disappointingly small SDS-led rally ran into unanticipated opposition. The demonstrators were booed by many in the tiny crowd when a spokesperson called for supporters to picket an ROTC-sponsored display of Vietnamese Communist military equipment in the Mitten Hall Great Court, a facility used by many students for lounging and socializing. When the demonstrators entered the hall, followed by hecklers, they held up their antiwar signs. At this point, several hundred students "gathered and began hooting and jeering," and some tried to seize or rip apart the signs. The security guards sought to persuade the protesters to leave, but they were adamant. More physical confrontations followed, with some bystanders catcalling, "How long has it been since you took a bath?" Confrontation resumed the next day as SDSers, joined by the Du Bois Club and YSF among others, returned to face about 75 members of the Booster Club, who held signs reading "End the War in Mitten Hall," "A Pink Student Is a Yellow Red," "Kill the

Cong," and "Peace Creeps Go Home." A *News* editorial highlighted the fact that the demonstrators lacked a permit for their protest and, consequently, were acting illegally, but, seeking balance, noted that the administration seemed to engage in favoritism in granting use of the hall. The editors came down strongly in favor of the need for a place where students could engage in free and open discussion of all issues and called on the Student Council to examine relevant regulations.[26]

Such antiwar episodes were preparatory for the April 15 marches and rallies in New York and San Francisco. At Temple, there were an anti-military ball, a teach-in and debate, and a host of creative arts events, all sponsored by SDS, the Du Bois Club, YSF, and the regional faculty peace group called the Pennsylvania Universities Council on the Problems of War and Peace. Plans were coordinated with other area campuses, including Penn and Swarthmore. The campus paper provided extensive coverage of the events, both locally and nationally. However, the teach-in drew only 150 students to hear a slew of speakers criticize Johnson administration policy. The critics ranged from Communist Party columnist Victor Perlo to the Southern Christian Leadership Conference's James Bevel, national director of the Spring Mobilization Committee, which had organized the national events. There was no heckling, no counter-demonstrators, no physical confrontation, perhaps because the pro-war students, all forty of them, held their own "win-in" sponsored by YAF. One observer, reflecting on the teach-in, concluded, "To a student not deeply interested in the Asian controversy, the ten-hour succession of anti-administration speakers probably was boring."[27] In part, such ho-hum responses reflect how routine and accepted such events had become since 1965. They also suggest how difficult it was to sustain visibility and involvement on a commuter campus.

Yet the granddaddy of Temple activists, Carl Gilbert, described as "still chairman of the now inactive Independent Socialist Club," bragged about "the development of a left wing on campus that never existed before." SDS seemed, however, to be the most significant if ideologically muddled group. Ellis Zelmenoff, a Temple SDS leader, stressed the centrality of participatory democracy to his organization: "SDS believes a basic change in our society has to be made if problems like war, racism, and poverty are ever to be successfully dealt with." But Zelmenoff added that, even though a "person who believes a basic change is necessary is a radical," he identified SDS as an organization of radicals and liberals, without addressing the inconsistency of including the latter. He emphasized that SDS was "not a Communist group with a capital 'C'," leaving open non-Stalinist Marxist alternatives but specifically excluding the Soviet and Chinese systems.[28]

By spring 1967, Temple SDS faced two related dilemmas. The first was the developing contradiction between the ideology of most of its leaders, which was an anti-Stalinist brand of Marxism with increasing interest in Third World varieties, especially those in Cuba and Vietnam, and its public rhetoric, which was more pragmatic, liberal, and humanist. This contradiction was exacerbated by a certain manipulation on the part of SDS leaders, many of them red-diaper babies and comfortable with Marxist analysis, who intentionally downplayed their leftist beliefs as they "brought along" less sophisticated recruits. This was not true of Gilbert, who was always open about his Third Camp Marxism, but Gilbert's "granddaddy" status, a mixture of respect and contempt, stood on the seemingly old-fashioned nature of his ideology, personality, and rhetorical style. The second dilemma was the tension between the successful emergent presence of a left-wing voice on campus and the limits it faced, given the still mainstream, liberal, and essentially apathetic and sometimes hostile responses it met from most students. The sixty students who disrupted a Temple basketball game to protest the Mitten Hall display of captured Viet Cong weapons, for example, were made to feel unwelcome, and isolated, while the much-discussed Free University, after registering 1,000 students, fell apart because of poor planning and improper scheduling.[29]

And yet 1,000 had registered. Something was stirring. As the Spring Mobilization of 1967 in New York City generated the largest antiwar demonstration in American history, Philadelphia's hippies, 1,500 strong, came out for the first countercultural "Be-In" in Fairmount Park. And when Allen Ginsburg offered a poetry reading at Temple that fall, he drew a packed house of close to 2,000.[30]

The activists from SDS and the youth groups of the Old Left began the academic year of 1967–68 knowing that they had established a beachhead at Temple, but fully aware that they had yet to figure out how to build a solid student movement. There clearly was a left wing at Temple, but not yet a movement; indeed, the student organizations, including SDS, were built for the most part by activists tied to Old Left analysis and style and, perhaps most significantly, without the two ingredients that most distinguished the New Left from its forebears. The first missing ingredient was a set of experiences, characteristically within the civil rights movement, that marked the generational turn, that is, a means by which a new generation of activists could trump an older one, thus fundamentally shifting the central issues away from the past and into the present. New Leftists at Temple and nationwide simply began to ignore Old Left concerns, such as the centrality of the working class and the importance of a vanguard party and organizational forms. The second missing ingredient was the experience of putting one's body on the line, the existential commitment to act. The Swarthmore SDSers had such experiences, but at Temple, while there were glimmers, campus radicals seemed more the heirs of an older tradition taking advantage of new conditions than the pioneers of a distinctively New Left politics. Activist students at the more elite Philadelphia schools had gone south; had traveled to Cambridge, Maryland, to fight segregation; had joined with black insurgents in Chester to protest inadequate schools. Their newness was precisely their personal experience in direct action; it provided them with credentials that could trump both Old Leftists and liberals. Temple's activists brought such New Leftists onto campus, but they themselves were not personally influenced by such viscerally powerful experiences.[31]

During summer 1967 Carl Gilbert offered some indication of such a shift in his "On the Left" column. Gilbert excoriated whites for their indifference to the conditions that led to ghetto riots: "America, that is the overwhelming majority of white people, were home watching TV and could care less." He asserted that "the books of the struggle are *The Autobiography of Malcolm X* and Frantz Fanon's *The Wretched of the Earth*." At the same time as he affirmed Black Power, Gilbert showed his more traditional older left sensibility by warning, "There is still some time left for one to stop listening to 'Sergeant Pepper's Lonely Hearts Club Band' for a little while and hear the sounds of a going storm."[32] Gilbert, after six years at the Broad Street campus, was soon to depart for Toronto to begin a doctoral program there. He had remained a Yipsel at heart, ideologically consistent and essentially deaf to the countercultural sounds that shaped much of New Left sensibility.

In another interesting indicator, the Temple SDS chapter joined a national SDS call for the abolition of the NSA. Until 1967, it had been the student conservatives who had attacked NSA affiliations; now, after the revelations of CIA funding in *Ramparts* magazine, the New Left jumped all over the clearly tarnished organization. Temple's Student Council president Stephen Finestine, however, continued to defend Temple's affiliation with NSA.[33] Though students showed increasing interest in doing community work in North Philadelphia and in establishing a student cooperative, they had little patience for what seemed to be the wasteful irrelevancy of student governance. The new editor in chief of the paper, Shelly Goldberg, asked "How free are we?" in her first editorial, examining the pervasiveness of the draft issue and highlighting the decision of former graduate student Robert M. Eyer to move to Canada. She asked,

If Eyer and others like him have found that they have no choice but to leave the country because of the frustrations and obstacles placed in the way of staying and working to alter the system, does this not indicate a need for a revision, or at least a long hard look at the system?[34]

In asking "what kind of country are we living in?" Goldberg was raising the kinds of questions that began to dominate the campus discourse. News editor Kitty Caparella joined three others in a walk-out at a U.S. Student Press Association meeting in Williamsburg, Virginia, after receiving copies of an LBJ speech defending administration policy in Vietnam. The willingness of more mainstream students to engage in such public protests over issues like the war was escalating.[35] The question was whether campus radicals would be able to take advantage of this rising iconoclasm, this erosion in the liberal consensus.

As the mood on campus became more critical, more focused on New Left issues of empowerment (including the creation of an anti-draft union group), Temple held its first "bitch-in," organized by an ad hoc Committee for Student Participation and Representation and spearheaded by activists like Jim Quinn and Susan Borenstein from the Du Bois Club and Ed Aguilar from SDS. The event encouraged students to vent about bookstore and cafeteria prices and what seemed to be institutional and administrative contempt for student concerns. The 450 who attended heard Quinn assert about the cafeteria concessionaire, "Slater food is like the war in Vietnam. It goes on and on."[36]

A few days later, 400 attended a four-hour speak-out on Vietnam, an event coordinated with the upcoming March on the Pentagon in Washington. Twenty faculty members, joining Resist, declared that they would engage in civil disobedience; the News editors applauded the faculty's commitment as a "question of conscience." In this context, the Ad Hoc Committee at Temple (ACT), through its acting chair Shelly Brick, announced plans for a "brown bag boycott" of the Slater-run food services beginning October 31. This was not Vietnam or racism or ghetto poverty, but it was an issue that spoke to the everyday experiences of Temple students.[37]

The News editors published a front page endorsement of the boycott and an estimated 2,000 students either sat in or refused to use the cafeteria on November 1. ACT, building on its initial success, demanded that new university president Paul Anderson make public the contract between the university and the cafeteria concessionaire. Anderson countered by creating a liaison committee to discuss student demands, but ACT, by a 59–18 vote, spurned the offer and refused such participation, instead escalating the conflict.[38]

On November 16, eight ACT leaders, including political science teaching assistant Ed Lambert, were suspended for violating a ban on protests within the cafeteria. Both the new liaison committee and the campus newspaper criticized Anderson and asked for a delay in the suspensions. At faculty request, Anderson put the suspensions on hold, pending hearings. Meanwhile, 750 students picketed the cafeteria.[39]

At this point, with the hearings postponed, a split developed between moderate and radical student elements. The campus newspaper editors criticized ACT for the first time, charging that it was losing sight of the issues that had led to the boycott in the first place. The editorial suggested that ACT leaders were using the boycott to further their own political ends. Within a few days, the boycott was over. The administration had coopted the boycott by offering a liaison committee and responding to the moderate student and faculty request for a reversal of punitive suspensions.

The more militant leaders of ACT shifted attention to the creation of a student union, but an initial meeting was described as ending "in chaos and shouting," with sharp disagreements "between factions."[40] Despite urgings from the Faculty Senate Steering Committee not to test the free speech issue in Mitten Hall, seven of the suspended students spoke up following an outdoor rally. The News continued its criticisms of ACT leadership sectarianism: "The storm has blown over. Why start it over when a workable means of easing grievances exists? Could it be a play for attention?"

As the fall term ended, it was clear that the dynamics of campus politics had changed. The activists operating through ACT, those still involved with SDS, the Du Bois Club, and the newer Student Mobilization Committee (SMC) that emerged out of the national protests in April, augmented by many new faces without experience in the seemingly glacial building of a radical student movement, were engagé. Events, both national and local, were drawing Temple University into sharper and more ideologically and emotionally drawn controversies. The March on the Pentagon was both a catalyst and an indicator of a more militant mood; even the NSA troubleshooters called in to advise what became ACT urged the group to act, not talk. In fact, ACT's militancy strengthened Temple's moderates and liberals, who now occupied a center considerably to the left of where it had been just several years past.

While the "brown bag boycott" unfolded, the campus was facing rising challenges from African Americans, both on and off campus. There was now a Black Student League, which refused to allow whites to attend one of their events, as well as North Philadelphia black activists threatening to burn down the campus if the university didn't respond to their demands. The civil rights movement seemed over; the era of Black Power had begun. The white director of the new

Figure 8. Paul Goodman, radical author of the influential *Growing Up Absurd,* speaking at a 1968 Temple University rally protesting the non-tenuring of professor Sidney Simon. Robert J. Brand.

Student Community Action Center, established to administer student voluntarism in poor, black neighborhoods, resigned and requested that his successor be black; he joined local black activists in demanding academic credit for community work and the creation of a Black Studies program controlled by African Americans.[41]

The political and cultural environment, nationally and in Philadelphia, speeded up as Temple entered the tumultuous and traumatic year of 1968. Nationally, the Tet Offensive finally shattered Lyndon Johnson's liberal consensus on the war and, inevitably, his domestic reform agenda. Liberals suffered the loss of their most eloquent voices—Martin Luther King, Jr. and Robert Kennedy. Student radicals began to move toward a more confrontational approach, which made the leap to advocating revolution inspired by Ho Chi Minh, Fidel Castro, and Mao Zedong—"Two, three, many Vietnams." And after all the tumult, in many ways because of the tumult, Richard Nixon was elected president of the United States.

At Temple, education professor Sidney Simon was denied tenure for refusing to give grades. The administrative decision led to student protests, including a massive teach-in featuring SDS leader Carl Davidson and noted writer Paul Goodman. A reconstructed ACT called Committee for Action (CFA) issued eight demands, including not only that Simon be tenured but also that a quarter of the next freshman class be African American. The rhetorical level rose; there was a more confrontational style, influenced in part by the Columbia University building occupations. (These and the police actions that followed marked an important turn in New Left campus-based strategy and tactics. The idea of a military grounded in the notion that the university was merely an instrument of imperial power began to shape student radicalism.)

President Anderson spoke to hundreds of students at a forum in Mitten Hall, but when he had finished and most of the audience had departed, activists, frustrated at what seemed to them to be administrative manipulation, staged an overnight sit-in, making new demands. Anderson foolishly persuaded a judge to issue a broad and vague injunction against all campus gatherings; five days later it was rescinded.

In this instance, Temple's administration had responded to student challenges clumsily. The injunction incensed most faculty and drove more moderate students into the arms of the radicals, who at that moment were effectively marginalized by Anderson's words. If he had ignored their precipitous sit-in, there would never have been a rallying to the radicals. Instead, Anderson gave them a victory they had not earned, and he added fuel to the fire by refusing to honor several of the leading activists already selected as outstanding seniors. As at many other campuses, administrative ineptitude played into radical hands. Administrators reacted, Pavlovian style, with repression when students, unable to mobilize a majority of their classmates, engaged in what were the desperate acts of a frustrated minority. Unfortunately for the activists, administrators caught on and began to avoid such over-reactions.[42]

Did Temple now have a New Left movement? Certainly more so than in the preceding years. Leadership included a combination of Old Left, increasingly Du Bois Club activists with less experienced, more instinctively militant students. Although the rhetoric was more militant, it was not yet dogmatic or hackneyed; for example, there were not yet a "Power to the People" style or even much evidence of a romantic revolutionism. Temple SDS member Ed Aguilar, for example, wrote a series of articles in the *News* that called for student power and a more socially responsible university, but remained committed to a humanist discourse:

A university's most basic function is to disseminate knowledge. This doesn't only mean the academic kind, for M.A.'s and B.S.'s and Ph.D.'s are meaning-less unless people can use their knowledge in relevant ways. It means knowl-edge of the facts, situations and events that directly affect our lives now and how such facts relate to the experience of the people around us. College can be a humanizing or dehumanizing experience depending on how well the university carries out this vital function.[43]

Aguilar reflected a more socialist perspective, but one not laden with either Marxist-Leninist or nihilistic assumptions. He argued that the New Left's

primary purpose is not to end the war, but to change the system that makes such neo-colonial wars both possible and necessary. In addition to anti-draft resistance . . . other tactics have been based on the idea that the white poor and working class communities as well as those in the white-collar "new work-ing class," must organize themselves, if change is going to come.[44]

At the same time, others, less patient and less grounded, began to lose any expectations that such change was possible.

As on many campuses in the late 1960s, the radical students de-pended on a variety of circumstances in order to flourish: the ways ongoing events, such as the war, the ghetto riots, two traumatic assassi-nations, the delegitimatizing revelations about authority (CIA links with the NSA), and, most especially, heavy-handed responses from college administrators pushed more moderate to liberal students into alliances with the radicals. All these factors were compounded by the rebellious sensibilities of the growing counterculture. By fall 1967 Philadelphia had its first underground press, *Yarrowstalks* and the *Distant Drummer*. As a part of the spring 1968 struggles, the *Temple Free Press*, created by leaders of ACT and CFA in response to administrative censoring of the *News*, emerged as the voice of increasingly radicalized students. The *Free Press* journalist-activists, initially a coalition of political and cultural radicals, increasingly became a vehicle for the most revolutionary voices, not only at Temple but within the larger youth movement in Philadelphia.[45]

As the student subculture's center of gravity, at Temple and elsewhere, shifted to the left, the developing New Left movement began to range farther from what had become a more liberal campus mainstream. As administrators like Paul Anderson discovered the strategic advantages of cooption over repression, as students seemed more open to the kinds of critiques activists like Aguilar were offering, indeed precisely as Temple seemed to be becoming a little less of an apolitical, subway-commuter college, those who dominated the *Free Press* escalated the rhetoric and began to argue for revolutionary Communism with a strong Third World flavor. The results would be predictable. Temple's New Left activists, despite promising developments in 1967–68, would share in what seemed to be a deepening youth rebellion, both against the war and against the mainstream culture, in the late 1960s and early 1970s. But they were never able either to build a campus movement or, as the *Free Press* aspired, to link with white and black working-class and poor constituencies off-campus. That story unfolds in Chapter 7.

## From Ivy League to New Left Leadership: The University of Pennsylvania

In the early 1960s, a local observer would likely anticipate that either Swarthmore or Haverford would produce the most influential student-based activism. Temple, with its small core of red-diaper babies, might also have been considered a possible source of movement leadership. But, remarkably, by the late 1960s it was the significantly stodgy, conservative, essentially anti-intellectual University of Pennsylvania, more notable for its professional schools, especially the Wharton School of Finance, its dominating fraternity culture, and its efforts at big-time athletics, that emerged to shape and direct New Left movement efforts most successfully.

In preparing for the 1965 school year, the *Daily Pennsylvanian* (*DP*) headlined "Berkeley Type Revolt Still Unknown at Penn." There had been some student protests at the university over the location of a new arts building and concerning dormitory rentals, but the *DP* suggested that the tumult at Berkeley had contributed to the Penn administration's willingness to listen and negotiate with students. Reporter Robert A. Gross described the campus as "quietly and moderately in flux," with "only an alienated fringe find[ing] the University's structure unacceptable."[46]

An alienated fringe could scarcely be uncovered in the midst of what one observer described as "the Conservative Tradition of the University of Pennsylvania" during the middle and late 1950s. One of the few—mostly bohemian and aesthetic—voices of dissent was Derek S. B. Davis, who satirized the "Beaten Beatniks" overwhelmed by an "intellectual conservatism" that was "all the rage here." The campus seemed to be dominated by Greeks, jocks, and the utilitarian pursuit of careers. One *DP* editorial bemoaned the "intellectual ennui" driven by the fraternities, which corralled 45 percent of undergraduates and "comprised the most unenlightened, unstimulating large unit in the University," mostly concerned with sports, partying, and drinking.[47]

At the same time, there were pockets of intellectual energy and hints of dissent, certainly emanating, unremarkably, from the newspaper staff, from the influence of both radical Quaker and Old Left voices, and from a few academic departments such as Oriental Studies (Dirk Bodde, Allyn Rickett, and Jonathan Mirsky), Architecture (Robert Venturi), and Communications (Gilbert Seldes), and by the presence of Robert J. Rutman (Chemistry), a McCarthy era survivor and peace activist. Penn also was pulled in a more ideologically conservative direction by the presence of the Foreign Policy Research Institute, directed by Robert Strausz-Hupe, and by the rise of a student conservative movement.[48]

In the early 1960s, similar to what occurred at many campuses, ideological definitions sharpened and became more visible as John Fitzgerald Kennedy entered office and the civil rights revolution entered a new phase with the Greensboro sit-ins and the freedom rides. Some Penn students joined pickets at the local Woolworth's, while the *DP* provided more coverage of both local and national civil rights demonstrations. There were demands that the university remedy racially discriminatory practices in housing and construction. And a local tutorial project, Tutorial for Higher Education and Social Exchange (THESE), working at predominantly black West Philadelphia High School, emerged as an outlet for student idealism.[49] The campus independents, long dominated by the Greek-led Red and Blue, the primary campus organization, seemed to gain some feistiness in their still marginalized status. But the election of Candace "Cappy" Bergen, the beautiful daughter of Edgar, as Miss University seemed to ignite the campus more than civil rights or peace activism.[50]

The first significant student protest occurred in response to the environmental destruction anticipated by the building of the new Fine Arts Building in November 1964. Four hundred students, supported by at least a dozen faculty, rallied to the new All-University Ad Hoc SOS Committee against what they called a "poorly sited, architecturally inadequate, and esthetically objectionable" design. Leadership in the struggle came from graduate students in Fine Arts, who, after petitioning and demonstrating, discovered that the university administration did not seem to be open to negotiations and was operating "in bad faith." When construction began, SOS, having failed to halt or modify the plan, launched Operation Green Belt, a sly and imaginative call for students to paint a variety of trees on the ugly plywood walls surrounding the building site. But three students—from Wharton no less—were arrested for just such a painting caper.[51] In some ways this small conflict sparked the emergence of Penn into the 1960s, especially insofar as it began to subvert the presidency of Gaylord P. Harnwell.

The Penn activism of the early 1960s tended to be dominated by Old Left-affiliated organizations and activists, especially Shachtmanites and Trotskyists, and traditional political liberals. Cultural protests, as with the beginnings of SOS, were decidedly high-toned and essentially esthetic. But with the overreaching arrests and suspensions in response to Operation Green Belt, the university administration left itself open to being portrayed as petty, humorless, and quite ridiculous.[52] Indeed, underneath the seeming complacency of the campus, forces were beginning to converge. That coming together included a cultural and bohemian component, a long-time anti-Greek independent streak, powerful impetus from the civil rights revolution, and, finally, in 1965, the Americanization of the Vietnam War.

Dan Finnerty, a self-described Air Force brat who entered Penn in fall 1962, characterized the campus as "a '50s kind of environment." But he found an enclave of dissent, deviance, and cultural vitality at the Christian Association (CA). While most undergraduates were joining fraternities, cheering on the Quakers on the gridiron, carousing at the annual rowbottom riots, preparing for careers as pre-law, pre-med, pre-dent, engineering, or accounting majors, a small group of somewhat liberal, somewhat bohemian rebels found a home at the CA.[53]

The CA had representation of nine clergy from a variety of denominations. One of them was the Rev. John M. Scott, who became rector of St. Mary's Episcopal Church and Episcopal chaplain at Penn in 1962. Scott had arrived in Philadelphia already an activist in battles against racism. He quickly entered the struggles in nearby Chester over overcrowded, inadequate schools in black neighborhoods, joining the demonstrators, getting arrested, spending five days in jail.[54] Scott would remain in the forefront of a variety of social justice struggles at both Penn and St. Mary's until his retirement in 1993. He was joined by the Rev. Richard Fernandez, another activist minister who later became national chair of Clergy and Laymen Concerned.[55]

The CA was not simply a social gospel-based enclave of activist clergy; rather, it nurtured both civil rights and peace-oriented activism. There was also a more cultural dimension to the CA; it offered a space in which cultural rebellions gestated. Finnerty recalls the importance of movies, mostly European films like Alain Resnais's *Night and Fog*, as well as the works of Antonioni, Fellini, de Sica, Kurosawa, Bergman, and Truffaut, and British films like *Look Back in Anger* and *Loneliness of a Long-Distance Runner*. Gathering at the CA were the kinds of youth who, somewhere between early adolescence and college graduation, discovered Salinger and Camus, jazz and folk music and rhythm 'n' blues. They were encouraged by "hip" ministers like Presbyterian Ted Kachel to create, in 1964, the Underground, a "satirical review extraordinary," managed, written, and performed by a group of wickedly funny undergrads, including Finnerty and Bob Brand, both of whom became leaders in campus political movements.[56] One student enthusiast described these events:

How can I convey the fact that the Underground is basically a warm experience? How many students have been to Quaker meetings with a foot of snow on the ground outside, with a crackling fire in the fireplace, with the warmth of good fellowship in the air, with the dusty air sliced into shafts by refracted sunlight? Those students will know what it is like at the Catacombs Friday nights, and then some.

What was occurring at the Catacombs, the CA's coffeehouse at 36th and Locust Streets, was the emergence of a critical mass of youth, supported by sympathetic and role-modeling adults, who began to see themselves as an alternative to the Red and Blue, the traditional fraternity- and jock-based undergraduate elite. It became a space for art exhibits, a stage for poets and folk singers, a soapbox for all kinds of agitation, a film forum, and a meeting place of students involved in anything from CORE and NAACP to SPU and YSA. The Catacombs scene encouraged those who grew up with Lenny Bruce, Beyond the Fringe, *Mad* magazine, and Nichols and May to make fun of the straight, square, often hypocritical world around them.

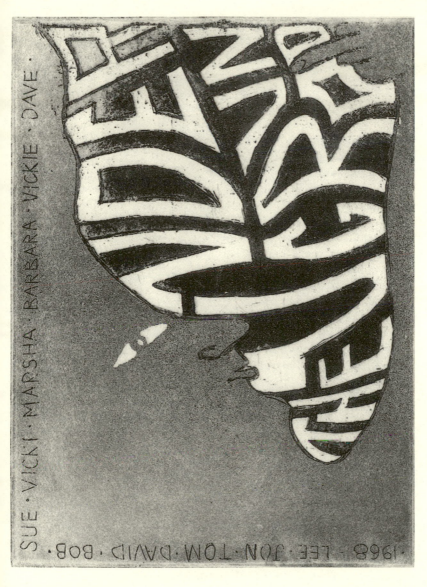

Figure 9. The Underground, which started in 1964 as a "satirical review extraordinary," became a center for an emerging campus alternative to jocks and Greeks at the University of Pennsylvania. Adam Corson-Finnerty.

The Underground, codirected by Lee Eisenberg and Jon Takiff, satirized Greek life with the serial "Fratman and Snobbin, Pledge Wonder," performed "Edward Albee's Adaptation of Mary Poppins" and "Baines in Toyland," and lampooned racism, the Vietnam War, the city of Philadelphia, Hollywood movies, pompous professors, liberals, jocks, and, indeed, themselves. They were irreverent, silly, sophomoric, pun-crazed, and over the top. As one of their self-mocking songs put it, "Hello Apathy, Good-bye Pain." But this troupe of CA staff and students was in the process of challenging those who had dominated Penn—and most American campuses—in the postwar years. They would not win this battle. Indeed, most Penn students remained mainstream and moderate, career-oriented and conventionally ambitious. But those who created the Underground and hung out at the Catacombs were part of what became a serious challenge to the hegemony of Penn Greeks and jocks.[57]

The radical presence beginning to appear at Penn was nourished by other supports as well as those at the CA. There were Old Left remnants and some red-diaper babies, as well as Quaker-based radical pacifist elements. In the early 1960s Penn had an active NAACP chapter, which Bob Brand, arriving from Long Island already a civil rights activist, joined. Marty Oppenheimer, a graduate student at Penn in sociology, along with his friend the radical pacifist George Lakey, worked part-time for the area's Central Committee on Conscientious Objection (CCCO) and then with the AFSC Peace Education section, while leading the Shachtmanite Independent Socialist League (ISL) and helping to establish SPU and CORE chapters. Someone getting involved in peace or civil rights activity would have access to people like Bob Rutman, who was a victim of McCarthy era blacklisting before becoming a Penn professor and SANE leader, and to Charley Walker and George Willoughby, long-time peace activists and direct action advocates.[58]

The fact that Penn was in West Philadelphia in the midst of a number of working-class and poor black neighborhoods bolstered interest in the civil rights movement. The campus NAACP chapter pressured the university to deliver on the integration of construction crews working on campus; activists like Oppenheimer and Brand joined some of CORE's sit-in protests at construction sites elsewhere in the city. Others followed the lead of the Rev. Robert C. Chapman, an African American Episcopal priest on the CA staff and campus advisor to the NAACP, along with John Scott, at the Chester demonstrations. And then there was Steve (later Kiyoshi) Kuromiya, Class of 1966, a Japanese American interned as a child during World War II, who was beaten unconscious but nevertheless returned to join the march at Selma, Alabama, walking beside the Rev. Dr. Martin Luther King, Jr.[59]

There were also campus-centered developments, like the SOS protests against the construction of the Fine Arts Building, protests against on-campus discrimination (especially that of fraternities against blacks and Jews), and criticisms of gender segregation. It was not until August 1962 that women were fully integrated into the staff of the *Daily Pennsylvanian*; undergraduate women were also denied the right to live in apartments, unable to have women-only curfews lifted, and denied participation in the student government until 1966.[60]

There were clearly a series of developments, on and off campus, that prepared the activists at Penn for the events precipitated by the Vietnam War in the late winter of 1965. There had been some early protests against U.S. involvement in Vietnam on the Penn campus, including several organized by the SPU in fall 1963. Professors in Oriental Studies like Dirk Bodde and Jonathan Mirsky called for negotiations and withdrawal following the assassination of Ngo Dinh Diem. The SPU, still a relatively marginal Old Left-dominated coalition and beginning to fade from the scene following its success in catalyzing support for the Nuclear Test-ban Treaty, sponsored a rally that attracted more than fifty listeners but that also experienced heckling from a hostile crowd. In fall 1964, just prior to the sending of U.S. troops and the beginning of the air war against North Vietnam, Penn students supported Lyndon Johnson over Barry Goldwater by a 3-to-1 margin, although SPUers, led by Trotskyists Robin Maisel and Frederick Feldman, picketed a pre-election LBJ rally at Convention Hall.[61]

At the same time that DP editorials criticized Johnson's Vietnam policies and the SPU, with some faculty support, called for the United States to withdraw from Vietnam, the editors spoke critically of the "chaos" at Berkeley: "We fear . . . that the situation has become so disordered that rational discussion can not proceed. . . . We ask . . . that the students temper their protest with a view to the political realities of their situation."[62] Penn prided itself on its capacity to resolve issues amicably. The sense noted above that Penn was not Berkeley, that the "Penn student today fosters realistic attitudes, shuns abstract theories, impractical solutions," rested in large part on the belief that the university administration had a "willingness to compromise and to include students in its decision-making apparatus."[63] But the larger environment was shifting. A new generation of students were making new demands—for input into campus discrimination practices, campus building plans, campus *loco parentis* rules, campus responsibilities for issues of social justice and peace. Penn's administration under the presidency of Gaylord Harnwell had passed some early tests but was about to be pushed beyond the boundaries of its traditions of academic deference and hierarchy.

This new generation or, more accurately, this soon to be highly visible cutting-edge of a new generation, is appropriately designated New Left insofar as it focused on a politics of authenticity, a prefigurative strategy that privileged direct experience "on the barricades" over study groups, electoral activities, and sectarian quabbles.[64] It appeared as if Old Left youth, associated with the SPU and either Trotskyists or Shachtmanites, were leading the struggles, at least in terms of U.S. foreign policy, through the mid-1960s. But newer voices like Bob Brand found the SPUers to be "limited"; he preferred to work directly with civil rights groups involved in direct action, to get involved with the Committee on Miners, which sent supplies to striking workers in Hazard, Kentucky, and, most of all, to become part of the Underground satirists. He was high energy, bright, and full of mischief. Old Left debates over ideology and history seemed stale, boring, irrelevant. Who needed it?[65]

In addition, some of those Old Left voices, particularly those who were of the in-between generation, coming of age after World War II and during the McCarthy era, were offering a different model of leadership and direction. There were the activist clergy at the CA. There were experienced activists like Marty Oppenheimer, who went to Greensboro, North Carolina, in 1960 to write his dissertation on the emerging sit-in movement organized by what became SNCC. Oppenheimer and fellow sociology graduate student George Lakey were part of "the middle left generation . . . small in number, theoretically undernourished, and pessimistic." But Greensboro, where CORE trainers were called in to organize workshops in nonviolent civil disobedience, inspired Oppenheimer not only to write his dissertation but also to write and publish through AFSC the influential *A Manual for Direct Action*, coauthored with Lakey. Oppenheimer, who recalls the importance of "the era of coffeehouses," of salons in Powelton Village as a New Left was nearing its birth, and who would break with his Shachtmanite loyalties, served as an older head to many of the younger activists.[66] A more influential figure at Penn was Leo Kormis, a lab technician on campus, involved with CORE, SPU, and the beginnings of an SDS chapter. A number of key leaders of Penn's New Left, like Brand and Josh Markel, stress the influence of Kormis, a veteran of the sectarian wars who seemed able to communicate a compelling commitment to democracy of the participatory kind and to tolerance and openness to a new generation of activists. As Brand notes, "Leo hung out with us."[67]

Perhaps the central event at Penn inaugurating a New Left, parallel to the explosion of Vietnam as an issue, was the initiation by Dan Finnerty of Project Mississippi. Finnerty, a regular at the Catacombs and an Underground "ham," had taken time off from school to travel, ending up in San Francisco just when the Berkeley Free Speech Movement erupted. Finnerty did not become a participant, but on returning to Penn quickly became the local expert on Berkeley, speaking at the Catacombs and then at the University of Delaware before a packed house. There he met a number of civil rights activists who persuaded him to join them in the Selma march of March 1965. That series of events, climaxed by the violence directed against fellow student Steve Kuromiya and the situation he encountered in Shaw, Mississippi, where displaced African American tenant farmers, evicted for striking for minimum wages, were living in an inadequate tent city, "shocked" Finnerty and led him to initiate what came to be called Project Mississippi.[68]

In October 1965 Finnerty, the project coordinator, announced a campus-wide campaign to raise $10,000 for the construction of a community center and to send twenty campus volunteers to help build it. Finnerty received support from the university in the form of a co-chairmanship from an administrative vice president and a university chaplain. But the project quickly became controversial when Project Mississippi requested supportive funding from both the Men's and Women's Student Government organizations (MSG, WSG) and some students raised questions about the propriety of university funds, $1,500 from each government organization, being used for non-university purposes.[69]

The *DP* editors rallied in support of funding the project, and Yale Rabin, a senior planner with the university, agreed to become planning director. Eventually both student governments helped fund the project, after weeks of discussion and despite maneuvers led by conservative and some mainstream Red and Blue student representatives. Project Mississippi always held the high moral ground in the controversy, with opponents resorting to legal and bureaucratic tactics to stall, divert, and frustrate closure. As such, the controversy worked in the interests of the civil rights activists, who were able to rally much of the student body, including Greeks, to their standard. At this point, the activists had placed mainstream and conservative students on the defensive. One editorial noted that another student-run program, the Tutorial for Higher Education and Social Exchange (THESE), which worked with students at West Philadelphia High School, received funds. Both THESE and Project Mississippi extended the moral reach of Penn to the civil rights revolution, both in terms of addressing poverty and its consequences, especially regarding education, and in terms of dealing with racial discrimination.[70]

On December 27, the twenty Penn faculty and students arrived in Leland, Mississippi, where they helped construct a 1,900-square-foot community center. More than 2,500, mostly Penn people, contributed to the project, which also received grants from America's Conscience Fund through the auspices of the CA's Dick Fernandez and local support from the Delta Ministry of the National Council of Churches. One student was struck by SNCC's Curtis Hayes's introductory comments, "Challenging us as white Northern liberals, who he claims are the greatest enemy to the Movement since we're making things easier without changing anything."[71] Finnerty noted that, whereas in the north discrimination is "corporate and clothes itself in a variety of 'defensible' positions," in Mississippi "the 'evil' is personal and open":

A student who begins work in the North can become hopelessly confused, entangled in the mesh of well meaning statements and hidden discrimination. Students like ourselves, who begin and learn in the South find—as students did from Harvard, Berkeley, Oberlin—that the Northern Ghetto opens up, becomes more comprehensible. We become more sensitive to the feelings of a people still left out of their society. The cries against police brutality, the frustrations, the riots, all can be seen from a new perspective. Then we are able to begin in the North.[72]

Students returned from Project Mississippi to form the Penn Rights Council (PRC), which immediately decided to picket the Federal Building in Center City to protest another eviction of blacks, in this case from an Air Force building in Greenville, Mississippi. This followed the disbanding of the campus NAACP chapter. The PRC founding was not smooth and consensual and, indeed, pointed to some of the dilemmas white civil rights activists would increasingly face in the second half of the 1960s. Was the council to be "liberal" or "radical"? Was its purpose reforming or "tearing down the existing social structure," as one of the black participants advocated? The issue was tabled.[73]

As activist students like Finnerty and Brand were engaging in civil rights activities, the Vietnam War erupted as a major issue on campus, especially when radical students uncovered university complicity in some of the worst aspects of U.S. military operations—chemical and biological weaponry used to defoliate crops. With this new target, Penn's student movement moved sharply from liberal to radical and fully into the New Left.

Robert A. Gross's August 1965 *DP* article anticipating that Penn would remain "quietly and moderately in flux" and decidedly less "chaotic" than Berkeley could not have imagined the extent to which the grounds were being laid for the rebellions and turmoil just around the corner.[74] The beginnings of the Americanization of the war in Vietnam in February and March 1965—the start of the bombing of North Vietnam called Operation Rolling Thunder and the sending of the first combat troops—set off protests by both faculty and students at Penn. A crowd of 150 gathered at an SPU-sponsored rally at Houston Hall Plaza as early as February 11, and several days later forty-six faculty telegrammed President Johnson, urging him to negotiate rather than escalate the war.[75] There were several hawkish articles and letters, a mildly critical editorial, but attention was not yet on the war. The campus activists, for example, supported an Emergency Civil Liberties Committee (ECLC)-sponsored "Democracy on the Campus" conference in late March at the CA, which featured Joan Baez and focused on the Selma march and antidiscrimination efforts in the area.[76] However, matters escalated, as they would on most elite campuses, when faculty members Robert Rutman and Jonathan Mirsky organized a teach-in on April 8, supported by sixty faculty and featuring the veteran radical pacifist A. J. Muste. The teach-in, supported by a *DP* editorial and coordinated with efforts to join the April SDS march in Washington, brought out 1,200 participants.

The teach-in marked the changes that had been slowly unfolding in greater Philadelphia and at Penn over the past five years. First of all, it was coordinated with other teach-ins at Swarthmore and Temple. Swarthmore's Paul Booth was a featured speaker, as Haverford's Russell Stetler had been at the "Democracy on the Campus" conference in March. Civil rights efforts in Chester, Philadelphia, Maryland's Eastern Shore, and the deep south had brought together students from several of the area's institutions, most especially Swarthmore, Haverford, and Bryn Mawr, but always with some Penn and Temple people and occasional participants from the Catholic colleges. The SDS/ERAP included students from a variety of schools. The small enclave of rebels and activists of the late 1950s and early 1960s were expanding and deepening, making contacts, building networks, seeing one another at conferences and workshops and coffeehouses and folk clubs and showings of the best European movies. The CA served as such a center at Penn, but its core activists were increasingly in touch with dissidents at other institutions, including radical pacifists associated with the AFSC, CCCO, and FPC, and Old Leftists involved in SANE, SPU, and ECLC. As such, when 1,200 students showed up for the Penn teach-in, there was a developing critical mass of activists with experience in civil rights and peace work discovering that their own campus was not so apolitical and stodgy as it had appeared just months before. Between the Berkeley Free Speech Movement and the teach-ins, movement activists at elite schools like Penn could imagine for the first time that they were, if not a potential majority, a significant and growing minority on their campus.[77]

And yet Penn was still a fairly mainstream campus—the Gross article of that summer is emblematic—as it entered the fall term of 1965. A few activists, like Bob Brand, had returned from support work with the Mississippi Freedom Democrats at the Democratic Party National Convention in Atlantic City; the SOS continued its protests over the Fine Arts Building; antiwar activists formed the University Committee on Problems of War and Peace (UCPWP); and there was the first drug arrest. But Penn was still dominated by the Red and Blue organization and its 34 fraternities.[78]

Then all hell broke loose on October 11, 1965, when the Philadelphia Committee to End the War in Vietnam (PCEWV, on campus CEWV) charged Penn's Institute for Cooperative Research (ICR) with engaging in chemical and biological warfare research directed toward application in the Vietnam War. Historian Jonathan Goldstein, a participant in the Penn battles over ICR, has written the definitive article on the Summit-Spicerack controversy of 1965–67.[79] Despite having been involved in chemical and biological warfare (CBW) research for more than a decade under the leadership of professor of chemistry Knut Krieger through the ICR and ranking eleventh among universities on the value of Department of Defense (DOD) contracts, Penn had not been challenged about the propriety of such research until undergraduate Robin Maisel, a Trotskyist activist and YSA member, working in the university bookstore during the summer of 1965, discovered that many of the books being ordered by the ICR touched on Vietnamese politics and rice crop diseases. Maisel communicated his suspicions about Vietnam-related CBW research to historian Gabriel Kolko and history graduate student Jules Benjamin, both of whom were already active in CEWV. Benjamin sent materials about two of the major CBW projects, Project Summit, which involved "analysis of air-delivered CBW agent-munition combinations in counterinsurgency," and Project Spicerack, which engaged in similar research for the Air Force, to *Ramparts* magazine and *Viet-Report*, both radical antiwar organs. Allegations were also made by University of Michigan psychology professor Richard Mann at an international teach-in in Toronto attended by a significant number of Penn activists.[80]

CEWV confronted Penn President Gaylord Harnwell with their charges and called for the termination of such contracts and for the closing of ICR. Harnwell and Professor Krieger defended the research, confirming the existence of the projects. As Goldstein frames the controversy, the campus began to organize into factions. Kolko's

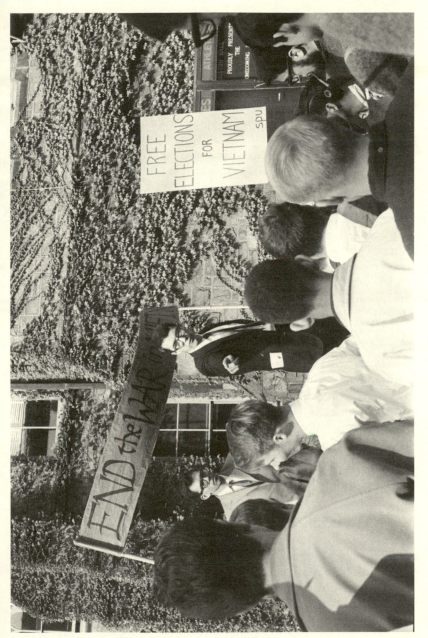

Figure 10. A 1965 anti-Vietnam War protest at the University of Pennsylvania, organized by the Student Peace Union. Robert J. Brand.

UCPWP group opposed Vietnam-related research, classified or not, on moral grounds. More moderate to liberal faculty opposed secret research and called for ground rules that mandated full disclosure through traditional scholarly channels. Harnwell supporters among administrators and faculty defended ICR research as both consistent with academic freedom and essential to the national interest. Finally, there were a variety of student responses, parallel to those noted above, including a newly formed SDS chapter, co-chaired by Anita Diamondstein and Andrea Balis, which worked with YSA, UCPWP and CEWV, and a new Young Americans for Freedom (YAF) chapter, which supported Harnwell.[81]

Despite the massive attendance at the spring teach-in, Penn remained fairly mainstream. The *DP* editors, supporting disclosure, declared that it was "no time for emotionalism" and that the controversy should be addressed with "moderation and reason." A small student poll in mid-October indicated that 84 percent supported administration policies in Vietnam. And a coalition including 32 fraternities, 11 sororities, and MSG began a campaign to indicate their support of administration policy and of U.S. troops by purchasing 10,000 Christmas cards to be sent to GIs in Vietnam. They eventually sold more than 18,000. In this regard, Penn was closer in sentiment to non-elite Temple and the Catholic colleges than to the Quaker-related schools on the Main Line. But Penn was now contested terrain, with the once complacent Greeks forced to assert their predominance. The campus, once somnambulant, was now politicized and alive with controversy.[82]

During the winter of 1965–66, campus activists were immersed in the ICR controversy, protests over the war itself, an antiwar fast, the Fine Arts Building protests of SOS, Project Mississippi plans and travel, the creation by SDS of the Free University, Penn Rights Council demonstrations, in addition to ongoing events like the Underground revues at the Catacombs and organizational meetings. But there was little sense of elation. Dan Finnerty expressed his amazement "at the undergraduate's deep feelings of powerlessness."[83] Yet just a few days before, 1,000 demonstrated at City Hall Plaza and 300 marched to the ICR; a week later, 45 from CEWV joined a protest at Vice-President Hubert Humphrey's visit to Convention Hall. Meanwhile, Amy Lowenstein, a senior in the College for Women, a Trotskyist leader, and a CEWV activist, was sentenced to 75 hours of unpaid labor for an alleged altercation with campus security while she was hawking copies of *The Militant* and the *Young Socialist* in the dorms. And, in a measure of the resentments among some traditional students of the rising challenge from activists, at a demonstration protesting ICR chemical-biological warfare research, hecklers disrupted the event, destroyed signs, and beat some people up.[84]

The CEWV, which organized the protest, charged that campus police condoned and even encouraged the disruptions, during which ten signs were torn and two activists knocked to the ground. One student emphasized the developing split:

There are double, divergent tendencies on this campus which are developing into a severe split: on the one hand, Tutoring boards, Project Mississippi, concern over the University's ICR policies, the Vietnam teach-in have involved more students in actively questioning constituted authorities; on the other hand, there are groups trying to revive "cane marches," old songs, and other traditions. This latter group must of necessity not question administration authority for it is to the administration that this group looks for approval.[85]

This was certainly the case. But there were more than two tendencies at work. The efforts of the increasingly New Left activists were moving the arguments, political stances, identifications, and involvements leftward. Previously moderate students could shift to the right in reaction against the activists, but more seem to have shifted toward a greater acknowledgment of the value of activism and a politicization that moved them, if not to joining SDS, then toward the dovish wing of the Democratic Party. Within a few short years they would rally to Gene McCarthy and Bobby Kennedy. For example, the *DP* editorial excoriated what it described as "the most disgusting, shocking thing we have yet seen at this University." The editors condemned "the ignorant boobs" who outnumbered the demonstrators and asked, "Where were the campus guards?" And in January 1966 the MSG passed a resolution supporting professors at St. John's University in New York who were on strike to protest the firing of 31 colleagues.[86] So long as the movement activists were able to sustain the high moral ground of academic freedom, freedom of speech and assembly, and equal opportunity, so long as they were able to point to the contradictions between the proclaimed values of established authority, on campus and in government, and behaviors like classified research, germ warfare, and bullying smaller nations, the New Left grew in terms of activists, supporters, sympathizers and allies.

President Harnwell proclaimed that ICR research had no direct relation to the Vietnam War and denied that there were plans to transfer ICR projects to the new consortium called the University City Science Center (UCSC). However, activists challenged Harnwell's assertions and engaged in a silent picket of fifty against ICR during the Founder's Day ceremonies in late January 1966.[87] Harnwell persuaded the majority of the faculty to support a resolution establishing the obligation of faculty to pursue all forms of research so long as the results were made freely available. However, the mainstream faculty developed their own criteria, which tightened and clarified the specifics of what it meant by publishable research and opposed all contracts that suggested outside agencies could be the gatekeeper of what was deemed publishable. The Kolko group had no faith in Harnwell's promises and suspected that the administration would humor the mainstream faculty but continue to follow their own interests in protecting classified research.[88]

During this struggle, student activists picketed, demonstrated, and held "weekly bitch-ins" at Houston Hall's open plaza every Tuesday at 11 A.M., a time when no classes were scheduled. These events focused on war-related research but also emphasized calls for the U.S. to withdraw from Vietnam. By late 1966 the *DP*, a shade to the right of the protesters, called for "de-escalation coupled with negotiation," a unilateral bombing halt, recognition of the Viet Cong, and inclusion of Communist China in the negotiations.[89] New Left activists, while more radical, remained plain-speaking, focusing on the damage U.S. efforts were imposing on the Vietnamese people, on the Viet Cong's peasant base of support, and on the corruption and venality of the Saigon regime. There was no Marxist-Leninist rhetoric; there was little rhetoric at all.[90]

Indeed Robert A. Gross's August 1966 overview of campus activism highlights the changes that had occurred in a year. Now he stated that "the spirit of Berkeley" had spread to Penn with

a growing minority of students . . . rebelling against the less intellectually committed, associational values of Penn's past and . . . seeking an educational experience more challenging and more oriented to individual needs, more aware of its relations with the non-campus world. An intense meritocracy . . . is beginning to replace the older, more leisurely aristocracy (and) the life of the "Greek" has less meaning for students and serves more often as a means rather than an end.[91]

This was an insightful analysis insofar as Gross highlighted that the changes occurring went beyond those associated with protest and rebellion to what he called the "new achievement-oriented student." Penn may have been late in joining this transformation, which was initiated by the GI Bill and the democratization of higher education it inspired.[92]

Intertwined with the rise of the counter-culture was also the stripping away of the last remnants of the pre-World War II WASP domination of elite education. Many of Penn's rebels, disproportionately Jewish, were simultaneously demanding more from their courses, for example, more seminars and colloquia, and more from themselves, for example, the proposals of the Student Committee for Undergraduate Education (SCUE), which included a pass-fail option, a Free University, and the end to *loco parentis* regulations. This meritocratic turn also included integrating women into the university; in late 1966 Penn elected its first woman student body president, Barbara Berger. Aspects of the hippie subculture would divert some of this energy in a more playful and mischievous direction, one that indeed challenged and tried to subvert meritocratic and work-ethic ideals. Gross recognized that the majority of Penn's undergraduates felt caught between these contradictory currents. He also emphasized that the estimated 300 to 350 activists "generally turn out to be the most academically-committed members of the student body."[93]

Although Harnwell claimed to have abolished the ICR in late 1966, the contracts for Projects Summit and Spicerack continued, and the latter was renewed in March 1967 to be sustained through the new UCSC. News of these events reunited moderate and radical faculty and students, who forced the cancellation of Spicerack. In spring 1967 there was a teach-in at Penn on CBW and the establishment of a new student organization, Students Opposed to Germ Warfare (STOP), which opposed the transfer of Project Spicerack to the UCSC. Faculty and student activists also participated in the massive national efforts of National Vietnam Week, which culminated in large demonstrations in New York and San Francisco.[94]

STOP, led by Josh Markel, Class of 1968, occupied Harnwell's office in late April. The campus activists had clearly shifted their tactics toward a direct action model, spurred by Harnwell's seeming duplicity. They received close to total support from the *DP* editors, who felt less inclined to give Harnwell the benefit of the doubt any longer. The old, patrician order was crumbling.[95] Yet the faculty remained divided and increasingly rancorous over how to respond to Harnwell's maneuvers. Finally, a key administrator and ally of the faculty moderates, Provost David Goddard, facilitated a delay in the demand for a condemnation of the president if he did not immediately terminate Operation Spicerack. That maneuver allowed the Board of Trustees to terminate all secret defense-related research, not transferring it to the UCSC. Goldstein concludes, "No other American university, at the height of the Indochina conflict, decided to make any such clear break with classified research."[96]

The summer *DP* issue's theme was "The Year That Berkeley Came to Penn."[97] And in the early fall there was further evidence of radicalization and rising militancy. Thirty-five Penn activists signed a "We Won't Go" petition in the student newspaper, declaring their refusal to serve in the U.S. military if drafted; a month later the list expanded to 81. Lawrence Elle, a Penn activist, represented a new organization, the Philadelphia Anti-Draft Union, at a rally of 200. Markel, becoming more of a leader, especially with the graduation of Finnerty and Brand, both of whom remained on campus as graduate students, cochaired with Marty Goldensohn the Vietnam Week Committee that planned for activities in coordination with the March on the Pentagon. During the academic year 1967–68, there would be more focus on anti-draft, direct action demonstrations, especially as some key Penn leaders such as Markel and Goldensohn made their own choices to resist compliance with Selective Service. During that year both Bob Brand, then teaching at the Mantua-Powelton Mini-School, and Philip Pochoda, a sociology instructor and faculty leader in antiwar activity, returned their draft cards to Selective Service. In November 1967, activists engaged in a sit-in to prevent the Dow Chemical Company and the CIA from recruiting on campus.[98]

By that point, a new radical organization, the Philadelphia Resistance, a chapter of the national anti-draft movement that began on the West Coast, would begin to become the epicenter of the white New Left antiwar movement within and around Philadelphia. The Philadelphia Resistance was born out of the Vietnam Summer project, which brought together many of the antiwar constituencies from campuses, traditional peace groups, Old Left organizations, and neighborhood-based groups. Increasingly, in 1967 and 1968, the developing campus movements and individuals began to join forces in city-wide efforts.[99]

At the end of academic year 1967–68, activists at Penn chose to hold their own "Vietnam Commencement" as an alternative to the traditional graduation exercises. The program was a measure of how significant the movement had become at Penn. It was chaired by Philip Pochoda, with introductory comments from CA's Rev. John Scott. Marty Goldensohn spoke for the Class of 1968 and Dan Finnerty and Robert Rutman spoke in recognition of the 125 students and faculty who signed a pledge to refuse induction into the military because "Our war in Vietnam is unjust and immoral. As long as the United States is Involved in this war I will not serve in the Armed Forces." Five others signed "individually amended versions" of the above and sixteen signed but wished that their names not be made public. Another 190, mostly faculty, signed a support of draft resisters statement, 22 signed amended versions, and 23 signed but preferred to remain anonymous.[100] This event and response indicates how deeply the movement, especially its antiwar emphasis, had penetrated the formerly stodgy, careerist, mainstream currents of the University of Pennsylvania.

Within Penn's student movement there were a number of positions contesting for hegemony. First of all, there were Old Left elements,

Figure 11. University of Pennsylvania students, wearing gas masks in protest of the war, walking to commencement exercises in 1967. Temple Urban Archives.

most particularly the Trotskyists, whose YSA was most active. Unlike Temple, where the Communist Party and its fronts played a significant role, and other local institutions, where there was no discernible Old Left influences, Penn always included a YSA presence under the leadership of Fred Feldman, Amy Lowenstein, and Robin Maisel. Maisel's role in uncovering Project Spicerack strengthened YSA's position. However, the Trotskyists, partly because of their Old Left style, both culturally old-fashioned and politically hierarchical and inherently manipulative, were never able to dominate Penn's campus movement. The war-related and other issue-specific groups, such as campus NAACP, Penn Rights Council, Project Mississippi, SOS, CIC, CEWV, the New University Party (NUP), and STOP, all essentially pragmatic, minimally ideological coalitions of action-oriented students, remained most salient and resistant to sectarian takeover.

An effort to organize an SDS chapter at Penn experienced some success, especially in 1968–69, but for the most part the campus New Left movement remained ad hoc and fluid. We have a portrait of the SDS chapter in early 1966 from *Philadelphia Bulletin* reporter Eugene L. Meyer, who posed as a graduate student and attended chapter meetings.[101] At that point, there were 54 members, although only about two dozen attended most meetings. Meyer described them as "a clean-cut bunch of idealists with little use for sloppy dress and appearance . . . [who] lacked the hard-headed, no-nonsense militancy of their more radical contemporaries at Penn." Penn's SDSers eschewed ideology and exclusion. The temporary chair of Penn's chapter was twenty-eight-year-old Leo Kormis, a lab technician and experienced Old Leftist of the Shachtmanite variety, who by 1966 embodied for many members the spirit of democratic socialism. The chapter included Bob Brand, then a junior and also member of campus NAACP, and Fred Feldman a YSAer and law student.

Interestingly, the chapter had been debating how to respond to the presence of an Air Force recruiter on campus. The group could not come to a consensus between those who argued that such a presence made the university complicit regarding the Vietnam War and those who urged debating the recruiter under a banner of free speech to all. The issue was tabled; by 1967–68 a more direct action, less civil libertarian approach would prevail among Penn's activists. There was criticism of the ways Old Left turf wars between Communists, Trotskyists, and Progressive Laborites were damaging national organizational efforts regarding war protests, but there was also frustration expressed by Albert C. Lowenstein, a senior, about the group's "hang-up" on "participatory democracy." In the midst of the discussion, six activists from the Philadelphia Area Committee to End the War in Vietnam, led by Penn graduate student Joel Aber, its chair, "barged in" to disrupt the meeting. But discussions continued on the ICR war-related projects, on campus regulations, and on the Free University.

At a later meeting, there was a discussion of the NLF, popularly known as the Viet Cong. Meyer notes, "Only a few openly approved of the Viet Cong. Many felt that a Viet Cong victory and takeover after U.S. withdrawal would result in a vicious despotism." One member, Jay R. Mandle, a graduate student in economics, "expressed the uneasy consensus": "We're faced with a hideous situation. There will be no democracy in Viet Nam as long as the U.S. is there, and there will be no democracy under the Viet Cong." At the same time, SDS strongly supported withdrawal of all U.S. forces, rather than the milder pro-negotiating positions taken by less radical, more liberal critics "because peace in Viet Nam for the Vietnamese is more important than democracy."

SDS at Penn was unable to withstand the pressures both from more direct action advocates, who criticized the chapter for remaining a debating society, and from those whose ideological radicalization led them to embrace Third World revolutionaries, especially in Vietnam, China, and Cuba, and to abandon what they increasingly perceived as "bourgeois" democracy and "bourgeois" civil liberties. In its later 1968–69 reincarnation, Penn SDS would perceive itself as revolutionary along Maoist lines.[102]

Dan Finnerty, the founder of Project Mississippi and a leading activist, wrote of his own radicalization in March 1966 as being reinforced by what he experienced in the south. He saw automation as making it likely that displaced southern blacks migrating north would be trapped in ghetto poverty. He criticized the ways "the Establishment" was manipulating all reform efforts, from the War on Poverty, which was controlled by city bosses like Daley of Chicago, to Head Start in Mississippi, where "Movement people" were being thrown out by more timid whites in league with reactionaries like Senator James Eastland.[103]

Finnerty kept a diary from late 1966 until summer 1967 that is suggestive of how white student activists were struggling with how to respond to what they perceived as fundamental social injustices. Finnerty challenged the notion that his was the "protest" generation, lamenting that "boys my age are going off like automated sheep to kill & be killed in a war that is so obviously wrong." He viewed grown-ups as perhaps worse—"our people, so stupid, so afraid of dissenting from what everybody else believes . . . march off in grey flannel suits and die."[104]

Finnerty had little confidence in the Old Left's proletariat, whom he skewered, after a evening out to dinner:

They were mostly working class types, the sort that possibly support the war and would riot if a Negro moved into their neighborhood. They were loud, and their kids were pushy and the total effect was like a Macy's bargain basement sale. All were quite concerned to get their money's worth and they heaped up their plates like refugees who had no plans for food to arrive again. I confess that one reason they irritated me is because their greed is only more crudely expressed than mine is—yet I wanted to get my money's worth too.[105]

Like many New Leftists, Finnerty was notably anti-ideological. There is virtually no discussion in his diary of radical theory, Marxist or otherwise, and there is an impatience with "these great academic types" involved in the antiwar movement as well as SDSers, who are described as "sloppy and silly." Finnerty did not seem to have a model of social change, although he leaned toward a post-scarcity framework. Several of his friends worried that the "bored and pampered masses" in such an affluent world would be subject to elite manipulation, that is, bread and circuses. Finnerty recognized the snobbery of such views and added that from a global perspective post-scarcity talk seemed parochial—"there is plenty of work to do," he concluded, mentioning guaranteed education (sixteen years) for all, universal health care, conservation, pollution abatement, urban reconstruction, and confronting the human and social problems that not only would not be eliminated but might increase. He focused on global needs, with professionals working in developing nations, albeit within a non-patronizing model of reciprocal learning.[106]

Finnerty was clearly less "radical" than many other Penn activists such as Brand and those like Josh Markel who would become members of the Philadelphia Resistance. He was more inclined to work at the edges of student government, to bridge between reformers and radicals, although he was very critical of "navel-watching" students and the fraternities, which were "choaking (sic) this campus." His visions of the good society remained essentially liberal. But as late as 1967 such views were part of an evolving New Left still struggling with how to effect fundamental social change. Some activists were exploring what came to be called New Working Class Theory, including emphasis on students as workers in training and universities as the sites for the creation of this more variegated proletariat.[107] But the pressing nature of the war and the rising tide of ghetto riots made it increasingly difficult for young activists, attracted to direct action authenticity and feeling the need to act, encouraged by the rapid growth of varieties of dissident youth, much of which was drawn to the counter-culture, to engage in long-term planning. Soon many would be caught up in a contradictory but potent mix of revolutionary anticipation and existential despair, of investment in Third World liberation movements, and frustration with "white backlash" and Richard Nixon's successes in mobilizing a movement of "the great silent majority," precisely those Finnerty had characterized so pejoratively.[108]

It is important to understand that New Leftists were simultaneously concerned with themselves, with their own futures, careers, love lives, and, clearly, draft status. Finnerty spent much of his senior year debating whether to go to graduate school, where to go, what to study, how it would relate to his political values. He explored fellowships and considered foreign travel, especially through the Peace Corps. He was strikingly honest about his own ambitions:

Now what I want is influence and power, I love getting up in a meeting and controlling its direction by my ideas and my personality. Certainly I've enjoyed being in student government, as silly as it is, and if I could actively get in a real legislature, I would have a ball—cause there I'd find some real issues. . . .
    I would like to be a Senator or a Representative—my experience in the Student Gvmt gave me a feeling for that. There's nothing I like better than speaking to an Assembly and trying to influence people to my point of view— and in getting things done. Let's face it, I'm an organizer, and I should be a politician, except I can't see any way to do it. Perhaps I'm flattering myself in thinking that I could never make it in the normal channels because I'm too radical. But what I've seen of my conformist society leads me to fear that I may be right. Perhaps with the breakup of the Cold War, yesterday's heresy will become tomorrow's Truth and people like myself will be considered quite establishment. Why not?[109]

He often targeted anti-Communism and the ways "it has strangled and stifled" society. Underlying his criticisms was a deep disappointment with America: "God damn it! Our country has never lived up to its ideals."

Think about the possibilities for change if we could get over our communist "hang-up" and start talking about what benefits people and what doesn't. And, Lord, let me never get caught in the trap of "proving" I'm not a "communist" by playing to anti-communist fears. . . . Don't make me compromise like so many have done for fear of being called "reds." Even if they know they are right.

He especially feared that an American withdrawal or compromise in Vietnam might revive McCarthyism.[110]

Finnerty anticipated that if he were drafted he would refuse to serve and be forced to spend several years in prison. He rejected fleeing to Canada because "though I get hostile to my country and feel alienated, I still want to change it." This son of a career military officer even considered joining the Air Force OCS, noting that "military people are generally more democratic and varied than IBM employees or business-men generally." But he added that he would refuse to be complicit in the Vietnam War. With his movement friends he struggled with the moral dilemma of personal responsibility in tension with societal function—*someone* would still be dropping the bombs even if he personally refused.[111]

Finnerty received the Stephen Wise Award for his work with Project Mississippi. At the luncheon honoring him for his contributions to intergroup understanding, he suggested that the abolition of Greek life at Penn would contribute to such understanding. He added that the award should have gone to more deserving students like Rick Baron from the tutorial project or Tom Perloff from CIC; his own work was "a one-shot deal." Meanwhile, he continued to write term papers, worry about his future, and engage in a wide variety of activities both within and outside student government, especially the struggle over Project Spicerack.[112]

After graduation, Finnerty stayed on at Penn as a graduate student. He was at odds with some of the developing political changes, including the mystique of Black Power and the welcoming of ghetto riots as incipient revolutionary acts. He "saw no purpose in a riot if it had no rational goals," concluding that "I'm not prima facie against violence but when I see it working to no good purpose I have no use for it."[113] In this regard, Finnerty was increasingly out of synch with much of the New Left as it entered 1968. In an essay that year, he lamented "a growing tendency in the antiwar movement toward making police-demonstrator clashes a part of the tactics," concluding that "the anticop crusade is not only foolish and counter-productive, it is damned dangerous as well." He affirmed the legitimacy of blacks as a colonized people responding to the police as an occupying army, but questioned the validity of the white middle class excoriating working-class cops who are not responsible for poverty, racism, or the Vietnam War. Finnerty warned of the self-fulfilling prophecy of defining the police as the enemy. Sounding more like an orthodox Marxist—which he was not—he declared, "The short-term 'respect' we would gain from black militants by confronting cops is not worth the further alienation of the white working class. . . . Our 'Enemies' should be the people who gave the orders, not the pawns who followed them through." He added that "romantic minorities" engaging in daring, provocative actions could undermine efforts to build a more popular movement and criticized those who were increasingly viewing large, peaceful demonstrations as "old-fashioned and insignificant."

Finnerty was one voice within the contested terrain that existed at Penn in the latter 1960s. For example, the editors of the *DP* criticized the Vietnam Week Committee for opposing the right of the Marines and Dow Chemical to recruit on campus. As the movement shifted "from protest to resistance," as direct action came to the fore, as activists felt the need to act, given what they perceived as the life-or-death realities of both Vietnam and the black ghettos that exploded during the summer of 1967, tensions developed over the notion of the university as an open market of ideas.[114] The New Left was rapidly moving away from the kinds of libertarian commitments embodied in the Free Speech movement toward a less than coherent mix of direct action radicalism and various forms of Marxism. Meanwhile, the Penn campus remained dominated by the old guard—the Red and Blue—which swept to victory in the student government elections of February 1967, although some dissidents, like Josh Markel, were elected as well. In April a referendum calling for the United States to withdraw from Vietnam was defeated.[115]

In addition, the terrain had shifted by early 1968. The bohemian qualities encouraged at the Catacombs and a host of off-campus coffeehouses had been transformed into a much broader cultural challenge by those increasingly called freaks or hippies. For example, the Free University, started in 1966 by SDS activists, proudly asserted its commitment to ideological diversity, offering a course on the Vietnam War by the dovish Jonathan Mirsky as well as one on Communism by William Kintner, the anti-Communist deputy director of the Foreign Policy Research Institute. Most courses focused on political and economic subjects. However, by the end of the year some founders were expressing disappointment at the results—poor attendance, low standards, and "a paucity of creative thought." Others disagreed. Some of the dispute seemed to be about the changing interests of those teaching and participating. There was now a more countercultural flavor, marked by the fact that one of the most popular courses had become "Evening with Ira Einhorn." There was now a psychedelic subculture at Penn, overlapping sometimes uncomfortably with the New Left movement. Einhorn, a longtime presence at Penn, was rapidly becoming a hippie guru, an entrepreneur of the counterculture.[116]

Penn's activists had to react to a variety of transformations and new demands by 1968 in addition to that personified by Einhorn. The war went on and on, with casualties rising. Despite greater success in terms of those participating in antiwar demonstrations, locally and nationally, there did not seem to be any end in sight. And the draft was beginning to affect some of Penn's finest. Equally significant was the shift in civil rights toward Black Power militancy. Many of Penn's activists and their supporters were involved in a variety of local community-based projects. But ameliorative interventions such as tutoring and modest health-care and housing efforts did not seem to speak to the rising rage embodied by the riots, which began in places like North Philadelphia in 1964, reached new levels in Watts in 1965, and then exploded in Newark and Detroit in 1967. In fall 1966, the issue of black power came to Penn. Forty activists, white and black, argued over two hours in a meeting "marked by sarcasm and a lack of communication" between Black Power militants and old-style integrationists. The *DP* reported that

> At one point, a white member of the audience said, "I've been working down in the South . . ."
> Clay [Leonard Clay, coordinating secretary of the Penn Rights Council] interrupted, saying, "Good. You're one of the last white liberals."[117]

The next week, local activist Walter Palmer, speaking before the Tutorial Board and a mostly white audience, attacked "the perpetual genocide against all black people," and Oliver W. Lancaster, coordinator of the Philadelphia School Board's Office of Integration and Intergroup Education, spoke of tutors' "paternalistic attitude" toward black students.[118] Penn's white activists were being forced to rethink their ways of reaching out to the black community. And they were pushed farther and deeper by the deteriorating racial climate within the city of Philadelphia.

On November 17, 1967, the Philadelphia police, commanded by Police Commissioner Frank Rizzo, broke up a student rally at the Board of Education. The students were making demands in the spirit of the new Black Power emphasis—courses on black history, tolerance of black style. The more than 3,000 students did get restless, but most observers concluded that Rizzo's order to disperse the crowd led to an ugly scene of racial epithets and beatings. From this point on, Frank Rizzo became the central figure in Philadelphia politics, and both liberal and radical white activists would have to shape their racial strategies and tactics with him in mind, indeed, at center court.[119] Two movement organizations were formed in response to Rizzo's actions: one, Philadelphians for Equal Justice (PEJ), committed to protect citizens, especially people of color, from police brutality, harassment, and illegal arrests; the other, People for Human Rights (PHR) a white support group supportive of Black Power and seeking to confront racism in their own communities.[120]

Many of Penn's New Left activists became members of one or both of these organizations. Events at Penn would follow the trajectories at many elite campuses in the latter 1960s, but by 1968 there existed a larger, citywide context and critical mass.

As Penn's New Leftists entered the watershed year of 1968—Tet, the assassinations of Martin Luther King, Jr. and Robert Kennedy; the continuing riots following King's murder; the upsurge in student radicalism and militancy marked in the United States by the Columbia University building occupations and internationally by what Stephen Spender would appropriately call "The Year of the Young Rebels"; the clashes at the Democratic Convention in Chicago; the election of Richard Nixon in November—there would be a variety of responses and directions taken. Finnerty's was only one and not the most representative; what all Penn's New Leftists shared was a sense that the stakes had gone up, that the war was seemingly interminable, despite Lyndon Johnson's acceptance of negotiations, that the racial tensions were deepening, especially in the city of Philadelphia under its very powerful police commissioner Frank Rizzo, that the culture seemed up for grabs, as the Great Silent Majority clashed with the movement and the counterculture.[121]

Penn's New Left activists would branch into a variety of activities. Their most significant impact would be in the two organizations that emerged in 1967 and 1968 to address the most salient issues facing the New Left, the Vietnam War, and racism: The Philadelphia Resistance and People for Human Rights.

## Chapter 5
# The Beloved Community Goes to War

In the early 1960s, prior to the Americanization of the Vietnam War, the peace movement in Philadelphia focused attention on the struggle to eliminate or at least reduce nuclear testing. The participants in this effort were mostly a hardy band of pacifists, Old Leftists, and liberals. They included what *Greater Philadelphia Magazine* called "the peace-mongers," living in the city with a claim, based on its Quaker institutions, of holding "the title of America's peace capital."[1] The article described the "religious pacifists," with a specifically Quaker motivation, as well as the Fellowship of Reconciliation (FOR); "the emotional pacifists," a sexist category including both the Women's International League for Peace and Freedom (WILPF) and Women Strike for Peace (WSP); and "the rational pacifists," including the Committee for a Sane Nuclear Policy (SANE) and the United World Federalists (UWF). It estimated that there were 20,000 peace activists in the region, a strikingly high estimate seemingly based on the assumption that all 17,000 Society of Friends members were committed to the cause. The oldest parts of the movement were the Peace Committee of the Yearly Meeting of the Society of Friends (FPC), the Peace Education Committee of the AFSC, and the CCCO. But there were also more radical, direct-action oriented Quakers associated with the Committee for Non-Violent Action (CNVA) and the Peacemakers.[2]

The non-Quaker segments of the peace movement were spearheaded by SANE, WILPF, WSP, and, among a younger generation, the Student Peace Union (SPU). The movement's estimated membership was

| WILPF | 750 |
|-------|-----|
| WSP | 1,000 (mailing list); 500 "dependable cadre" |
| SANE | 1,500 (mailing list); 400 "paid membership" |
| UWF | 2,000 |

The article noted the four student peace groups—SPU, WSP, Student SANE, and the Young People's Socialist League (YPSL)—at

Penn, adding, "Haverford, Swarthmore and Temple were also peace-hotbeds."[3] In fact, peace activity, while on the upswing, was fairly limited. At a peace vigil at Independence Hall on September 16, 1961, 33 of 129 registrants were listed as members of WILPF; no other organization included more than 4. At the more successful Turn Towards Peace–sponsored Easter Peace Walk of April 21, 1962, the majority of the 407 registrants came from WILPF (76), SANE (48), SPU (38), WSP (35), FPC (24), and FOR (19).[4] It would appear that at that peak moment in the anti-nuclear testing campaign, Quakers and Old Leftists *were* the peace movement.

A 1964 Labor Day rally—"for economic security, peace and freedom"—offered a measure of pre-Vietnam activism. The coordinator of the rally was SANE's chair Abe Egnal. The sponsors included not only a few mostly progressive union locals and the visible peace groups but also some representation from the black community—for example, the Congress of Racial Equality (CORE) and the Urban League—as well as voices from the student movement, including the Northern Student Movement (NSM) and Philadelphia Jobs or Income Now (JOIN), an SDS-sponsored organizing project. Those attending the meetings and taking responsibility for the demonstration were mostly veterans of the pacifist movement—for example, Egnal, George Lakey (FPC), Ethel Taylor (WSP), Dave Eldredge (SANE), and Mickey Metelits from the Independent Citizens Committee (ICC), a Communist Party front. But there was also representation from the budding New Left, including Steve Gold from the Philadelphia Tutorial Committee and NSM, as well as Russell Stetler from Haverford and Nick Egleson from Swarthmore, both student activists involved at that point in summer Economic Research and Action Projects (ERAP).[5] As such, prior to the eruption of the Vietnam War, the peace movement had been at least partially transformed by the civil rights movement and the early New Left. Perhaps George Hardin, the veteran Quaker activist, had been too precipitous in declaring in 1963 that "the day of the mass demonstration is over," although he was on to something in his anticipation of a new concentration on "face-to-face confrontation."[6]

When the United States sent its first combat troops and initiated the sustained bombing of North Vietnam—Operation Rolling Thunder—in March 1965, the Philadelphia peace movement—SANE, FPC, WILPF, WSP, and Americans for Democratic Action (ADA)—reacted with participation in local and national demonstrations and a letter to President Johnson published in the *Philadelphia Bulletin*. It was a moderate plea, headlined, "While There Is Still a Choice in Vietnam—America Must Be Willing to Negotiate," with statements of support

from Pope Paul VI and senators Mike Mansfield (Dem., Mont.) and
Ernest Gruening (Dem., Alaska). The signatories included a preponderance of veteran pacifists, liberal academics, and many Old Leftists,
but few New Leftists or civil rights activists.[7]

That summer, local activists organized a "street speaking" project.
The leadership came from Dave Eldredge of SANE and Mickey Metelits
of ICC. The project sent out teams of speakers into several neighborhoods to carry antiwar petitions, organize local meetings, and make
opposition to the war more visible. The results were, at best, modest.
Between 1965 and 1967, however, the antiwar movement grew as the
war escalated, most particularly among idealistic students and disillusioned liberals. The traditional voices—pacifist, Old Left, and liberal—
grew stronger and more militant, but the new energy came from the
campuses.

At all moments during the Vietnam War period, from the early
1960s through the middle seventies, the organizational supports remained the Quaker-based organizations, SANE, WILPF, WSP, and a
host of Old Left—mostly Communist and Trotskyist—groups and
their fronts. They were the folks who operated the phones, sold the
tickets for bus trips to Washington and New York, and took responsibility for logistics, legal complications, and finances. In late 1966,
George Hardin spoke of "the fantastic changes going on in the peace
movement," including the emergence and growth of new direct action
groups, like A Quaker Action Group (AQAG); the growth of activism
among Roman Catholics and Episcopalians; and the rise of student-
based New Left groups. He reflected that the approaches of the early
1960s, especially vigils and teach-ins, "seem sort of quiet and placid,
even a little old-fashioned," and that one should anticipate more polarization, "an intensification of the personal dilemma," and more
secular-based dissent.[8]

Hardin's projections seemed to be fulfilled by active participation of
the Philadelphia Mobilization Committee (PMC) in the massive April
1967 demonstration in New York City. The Spring Mobilization, as it
was known, was the largest outpouring of opposition to the war to
date and was highlighted by Rev. Martin Luther King, Jr.'s forceful
public denunciation of U.S. policy. It was here that the protesters
moved beyond calls for peace negotiations—a position still held by
many moderate doves—to a call to "end the war now." PMC's composition, including at least forty-three groups, reflected the growth of
organizational strength in Philadelphia. Most noticeable were the
campus-based groups—for example, the University of Pennsylvania
Committee to End the War and Temple SDS—as well as the openly

sectarian groups, such as the Trotskyist Young Socialist Alliance (YSA), the Socialist Workers Party (SWP), and the Communist Party and its youth group, the W. E. B. Du Bois Club. The committees, those doing the real work in organizing the event, were staffed mostly by the pacifist and Old Left veterans. The bus tickets sold give an excellent sense of the diversity of participants:

| | |
|---|---:|
| University of Pennsylvania activists | 200 |
| Swarthmore College | 100 |
| Sholom Aleichem Club (an organization of secular, Old Left Jews) | 100 |
| Student Mobilization Committee (headed by a Du Bois Club leader) | 150 |
| Student Mobilization Committee | 200 |
| Germantown Peace Council (a neighborhood with a history of civil rights and peace activism) | 316 |
| Trade Unionists for Peace (a Communist Party front) | 100 |
| Mainline Area (headed by an Old Left veteran) | 150 |
| North Philadelphia (headed by a Trotskyist leader) | 105 |
| WILPF-Old York Road (suburban) | 100 |
| Congress of Racial Equality (CORE) | 60 |
| Chester County Society of Friends | 100 |
| Walter Palmer (a black activist) | 100 |
| Temple University | 100 |
| Women Strike for Peace | 200 |

For many participants, it was their first experience in the peace movement, and it shattered many of the cold war stereotypes of peaceniks and other sorts of agitators. The buses were filled with idealistic students, longtime pacifists with their children, and older people with liberal or Old Left histories.[9]

## Vietnam Summer in Philadelphia

The turnout of hundreds of thousands of people for the Spring Mobilization sparked national antiwar leaders to consider immediate follow-up action. In particular, they attempted to model the success of the 1964 Mississippi Freedom Summer with a nationwide organizing effort called Vietnam Summer. The project sought to recruit an army of students to reach into communities with petitions, draft counseling, canvassing, and general efforts to mobilize those turning against the war but not yet activated. One of its founders and codirectors was

Richard Fernandez, executive officer of Clergy and Laymen Concerned About Vietnam (CALC) and formerly a staffer at Penn's Christian Association (CA).[10]

In Philadelphia, responsibility for the coordination of Vietnam Summer was given to Bob Brand, already a veteran civil rights and antiwar activist and recent graduate from Penn, and someone Fernandez knew very well from his CA years:

Very sharp guy, can talk with different kinds of people. More pragmatic than ideologically oriented—wants to get projects started—Worked with ghetto people but comes from middle class. . . . Can easily communicte (sic) will (sic) mid-class groups. Is flexible—good sense of humor.[11]

Brand was hired in late May to coordinate community-based projects with the promise of two additional staffers and funding for some of the local project organizers. The Vietnam Summer Committee evolved from the Spring Mobilization coalition, with six initial target areas, an arts project, and proposed draft counseling and draft resistance programs. There was much activity in June, with Brand traveling throughout the state to facilitate projects and submitting reports to the Cambridge, Massachusetts, headquarters about how things were progressing.[12]

Philadelphia's Vietnam Summer Committee included many names representing organizations that had been critical to peace work since the early 1960s: Mary Morrill, Carolyn Berger, and Helen Evelev from WSP; George Hardin from FPC; Abe Egnal from SANE; and younger Old Leftists like Fred Feldman from YSA and Sandy Patrinos from the CPUSA. But there was also a host of newer voices representing the campuses, both faculty and students, as well as of new cultural radicals: Jonathan Goldstein of Penn SDS, Lawrence Elle of the Philadelphia Anti-Draft Union, and Ralph Flood from Temple University and the Universities Council on Problems of War and Peace. Also on the list was Tony Avirgan, representing the Germantown-Mount Airy Vietnam Summer project.[13]

Avirgan would become one of the most influential peace activists in the city over the next several years. He was a twenty-three-year-old ex-jock and college dropout who had become a successful motorcycle racer but broke his back in a serious accident. Exempt from the threat of the draft because of his injuries, Avirgan then proceeded to have a successful career in market research and sales. His business partners, wanting to learn more about what seemed to be the changing attitudes of young people in the context of SDS, the Free Speech Movement, and early anti-Vietnam protests, subsidized Avirgan in late 1965 to travel to places like Berkeley, where he began to undergo a remarkable transformation. Most interestingly, the events in Indochina led Avirgan and his two partners to an unusual arrangement: a salary and car for one year for Avirgan to engage in anti-Vietnam War activism.[14]

Avirgan came to Philadelphia and walked into the AFSC offices, where he met a kindred spirit, Martha Westover, an Oberlin transfer and Swarthmore senior volunteering at the desk. The two of them agreed to work together in the Northwest section of Philadelphia in Germantown and in East and West Mount Airy, politically liberal neighborhoods with histories of community efforts to maintain racial integration. As such, Avirgan, with a church-subsidized storefront office on Germantown Avenue, became the head of the developing Vietnam Summer efforts in Germantown-Mount Airy.[15]

The Philadelphia Vietnam Summer project was also visible in Center City (downtown); West Philadelphia, Spruce Hill-University City, and Mantua-Powelton Village (all near the University of Pennsylvania); the Northeast (a middle-class quasi-suburban area divided between Jewish and Catholic neighborhoods); and Logan-Olney and East Oak Lane (both racially mixed areas north of Temple University). There were other projects in Camden and Medford across the river in New Jersey, as well as in Wilmington, Delaware, and nine suburban areas of Montgomery and Delaware counties.[16]

Brand submitted reports on the progress of the projects in mid-July. Some registered frustration—for example, at the slowness of Center City in challenging "fink reform Democrats" to come take a stand on the war and in reaching out to "neighboring white working class areas," as well as annoyance because some project leaders weren't giving top priority to the project. But other reports, like that about the Northeast, indicated more enthusiasm:

The project is just getting underway, and is fairly small right now (10 people). It is run by a beautiful couple who live and have always lived in the great NE (the Great NE is Yahoo center of the world). They have canvassed once, are scared shitless, but will persevere. Hopefully, they aren't too afraid, a couple of local NE high school students will join the project next week. I spoke to them at a draft conference and they seemed interested.[17]

By late July, Avirgan had moved to a more citywide leadership position. The most active efforts seemed to be in the Mantua-Powelton project, where a racially diverse leadership operated a lively newsletter, focused on draft counseling, and began to address larger social issues like poverty, unemployment, and racism; the Center City and University City groups, which held lots of block discussions and weekly house meetings; and the Main Line project, with 90 volunteers, 40–50 canvassers, and a newsletter.[18]

At the summer's end, Vietnam Summer's leadership hoped to extend operations for most projects into the fall. Tony Avirgan, funded by the Friends Peace Committee, agreed to run the Philadelphia office. Ed Lambert, a Temple University graduate student and staffer at the Germantown-Mount Airy project, anticipated that the National Conference of New Politics, scheduled for Chicago in September, would serve as a catalyst for broadening the scope of what he hoped would become "more truly community organizations."[19]

## Fall 1967

The events of summer and fall 1967, however, would enormously complicate such aspirations. The discovery of the hippie counter-culture, especially in the Haight-Ashbury section of San Francisco, collided with the summer of the most ferocious and ominous ghetto violence in Detroit and Newark. Those like Lambert and Avirgan, who attempted to build a more broadly based social movement in late 1967–1968, were, in part, responding to "the long, hot summer" and its implications. For most white New Leftists, the riots intensified pressures to reorder national priorities, end the war in Vietnam, and focus attention on the issues of racism and poverty here at home. Newark and Detroit not only brought the war home, deepening the sense of violence associated with America's legacy of racism, but also made it increasingly difficult for white activists to engage in a politics based on long-term strategies of social change.

By fall 1967, most New Leftists had clearly rejected reformist strategies for some variety of post-capitalist, socialist alternatives. They viewed corporate liberalism as the primary adversary (in so doing dangerously underestimating the revitalization of conservatism) by linking the domestic failures of Johnson's Great Society and War on Poverty programs with the immorality of the Vietnam War. As New Leftists, they did not look to Moscow for inspiration but were increasingly attracted to the Communist models offered by Third World nations like Vietnam, China, and Cuba. They were particularly enamored with the notion of wars of national liberation, that is, guerrilla wars, embodied by Ernesto "Che" Guevara, the Argentinian revolutionary who fought with Fidel Castro and died in the Bolivian jungles. In many ways, this Third Worldism was just reaching a take-off stage in fall 1967 as the national antiwar movement prepared for the March on the Pentagon.[20]

This rising radicalism was intertwined with a deepening frustration over the movement's demonstration-based strategy. For two years, the New Left and its allies had marched, demonstrated, held vigils, hawked petitions, and tried electoral options; meanwhile, the death toll in Vietnam for both GIs and Indochinese rose, and now there were people dying on the streets of Detroit and Newark. For young, idealistic activists—white and mostly middle class—it was increasingly difficult to justify their relative privilege removed from both battle-fields of high risk and mortal danger. Many asked, "What am I willing to risk while young people are dying on the streets here and in Viet-nam?" As such, there was a powerful impetus to escalate the militancy of protest—"from protest to resistance."[21]

This more militant, direct action notion came to the fore during the spring 1967 national demonstrations, which included the first draft-resistance activities. The outpouring of people to those demonstra-tions illustrates another, contradictory dimension of what New Leftists felt by fall 1967. It seemed that their antiwar sentiments had achieved a breakthrough, if not perhaps to a majority of Americans, at least to an enormous and growing minority, especially among the young. Much of this breakthrough took the form of culturally rebellious youth, on campuses and increasingly within the high schools, who were attracted to the emerging trinity of "sex, drugs, and rock 'n' roll," who had been turned on to the coming together of the Beatles and Bob Dylan and Allen Ginsberg, who smoked pot, considered try-ing acid, and were letting their hair down, dressing more in costume, and, recalling Marlon Brando in *The Wild Ones*, rebelling against what-ever was available. To white New Leftists, this cultural rebellion was both exhilarating and frustrating. Were these hippie freaks amenable to the movement goals of socialist reconstruction and Third World solidarity? Who knew? But, at the very least, they seemed alienated from the Establishment, viscerally anticapitalist, and racially enlight-ened. Surely change was the order of the day, and the possibilities seemed compelling.[22]

The National Conference of New Politics (NCNP) added another complication to the movement brew: African American militants domi-nated what was meant to be a coming together of a post-liberal elec-toral politics based on opposition to the war and a reordering of domestic priorities. Instead, most white participants were intimidated into yielding to black demands for control over the platform. It was a special and pathetic moment in the development of what writer Tom Wolfe would wickedly satirize as the "Mau-Mauing" of guilt-ridden whites. Perhaps more significantly, it was a critical moment in the ero-sion of the high moral plane upon which both the civil rights move-ment and the New Left had stood. The presumed courage of activist whites would be challenged by their tendency to yield, not because of agreement, but on the basis of the fear of being perceived as racist. The era of Black Power, with all its inevitable testings and reversals of

domination and humiliation, with all its brilliant assertions of pride
and all its mischievous "runnin' up the side of whitey's head," had entered center stage. No more "We shall overcome" or "Black and white
together," or so it seemed as figures like Stokely Carmichael, Rap
Brown, and the Black Panthers became the most vocal and publicized
tribunes of black America.[23]

So as Tony Avirgan and Martha Westover and others sought to extend the gains of Vietnam Summer into the fall, they had to come to
grips with the local versions of these national developments. The fault
lines had changed; they were deeper and more cross-cutting, problematical, and contradictory. There was the tension between ending
the war and ending the system the war embodied, between educating
one's fellow citizens and more desperate efforts to gain attention. How
could one build a movement, build the "movement," as the war in Indochina came home to urban, racialized America?

In Philadelphia, these questions had distinctive if shared dimensions. By fall 1967, there was a significant antiwar organizational
structure made up of Quaker, pacifist, Old Left, and liberal components, all of whom believed in fairly mainstream avenues of protest
and were uncomfortable with a direct action strategy, uneasy with the
new Black Power militancy, and bewildered and distressed by the
emerging hippie counterculture's embrace of drug experimentation,
casual and open sexuality, and deviant dress. How was the movement
to absorb or embrace or criticize cultural rebels? How was it to respond to the rising and voluble demands of African American militants? Some of the patterns that emerged clearly had generational
determinants: the white New Leftist baby boomers were more likely to
at least feel comfortable with longer hair, more expressive language,
casual drug usage, and sexual and residential experimentation. But
this was not consistently the case: the younger partisans of Communist
and Trotskyist organizations remained essentially straight; and a not
inconsiderable proportion of older activists, especially those one generation removed from the baby boomers, played catch-up. They were
often products of the 1950s who had lived the work ethic in their academic careers and had made fairly conventional marital choices. All of
a sudden, their involvement in movement activities thrust them into
intimate contact with a host of transgressive options and temptations,
the seeming opportunity to retrieve and relive a youth that had been
burrowed in term papers, dissertations, diapers, and a host of other
sacrifices. Such opportunities touched both men and women, but,
predictably, took on the gendered characteristics of open marriages,
professorial indulgence with students, divorce, communal living, and
remarriages.

Some of these tensions became apparent at the early meetings of the Vietnam Summer planners. For example after the initial two meetings, George Hardin of the Friends Peace Committee noted that the sessions were "poorly disciplined, dominated by students or young people." He complained, "Representatives of organized peace work were distraught, and inclined not to cooperate." The minutes concluded:

Hardin is tired of the six major peace organizations (all with staff, budgets of some size, and three with fifty-year histories) out-voted by the small, chiefly student-type outfits (two or three of which confess to being only half a dozen members). Other people are beginning to see the point.[24]

At the same time, these tensions must not be exaggerated, since many were the consequence of a feeling-out process during which experienced activists expecting some deference had to deal with new voices, some of which were disrespectful. Indeed, the lines were not consistently generational, since some of those calling for a more militant, direct action approach were pacifist veterans.

Tensions over race were probably the most salient. In Philadelphia, fall 1967 brought forth, in the person of Frank Rizzo, the polarizing forces and political alignments that would define much of the city's politics for the next decade. There was no escaping the rise of Rizzo as urban populist and avenger, hero of the white ethnic neighborhoods. He was quite clear in what he opposed, what he was determined to crush: those unwilling to play by the traditional rules defined by family, church, school, and work. He blamed the permissive liberals, the demagogic black militants, the immoral hippies, and the subversive New Leftists for what he perceived as threats to public order. And, indeed, Rizzo's challenge forced those groups, more attractively self-defined, into uncomfortable alliances with one another. Over the next decade, the defining characteristic of Philadelphia politics was: where do you stand on Frank Rizzo, for or against? There was no middle ground. You either gave him voice to represent the "Great Silent Majority" or you joined forces to construct an alternative majority, held together by little more than a common enemy. As such, Center City liberals and moderates, ADAers, ACLU advocates, reform Democrats, and mainstream black Democrats joined, uncomfortably, with militants, radicals, and freaks.[25]

## The Philadelphia Resistance

Such alliances were made most clearly manifest in the Philadelphia Resistance. The motley group that ultimately became the Philadelphia Resistance included Tony Avirgan and Martha Westover, as well as a number of Penn activists: Bob Brand, Dan Finnerty, Josh Markel, Eva Gold, Dina Portnoy, Mike Griecen, Candy Putter, Marty Goldensohn, and Paul Golden. Among the most important leaders within the group was Judy Chomsky, a college graduate, married with children, who had walked into the Germantown Vietnam Summer office and developed immediate rapport with Avirgan and Westover. Also central to the group was Lisa Schiller, a high school dropout from a working-class Catholic family, rebellious and wild, who, virtually adopted by Chomsky, quickly began to take over essential office operations—the ex-hippie as organizational whiz. There were also important older members and supporters like Episcopal Urban Missioner David Gracie, Haverford physics professor Bill Davidon, and Swarthmore Russian professor Thompson Bradley.[26] At first Avirgan, Westover, Chomsky, and their developing circle assumed that they would continue Vietnam Summer, expanding it to include grass-roots electoral activities and a more multi-issue community organizing. They participated in the organization of the Philadelphia Area Draft Council, worked with the silent vigils many church-based activists were organizing, attended the National Conference of New Politics in Chicago, and, most of all, worked with the Philadelphia Mobilization Committee in planning the March on the Pentagon to "Confront the Warmakers."[27]

Avirgan saw the emergence of the Philadelphia Resistance as a pragmatic decision for those who chose to focus their attention to the war. The Resistance was a national movement organized initially out of Stanford University by David Harris and other radical pacifists. It initiated antidraft actions, including the handing in and burning of draft cards at the March on the Pentagon. In an organizational pamphlet, "What Is Resistance?" it was described as "a national movement which aims to challenge the Selective Service System by taking the position of complete and open non-cooperation with the draft." After national draft-resistance actions, including Philadelphia in October and December 1967, provided some visibility for the new organization, the Vietnam Summer project decided to become the Philadelphia Resistance in January 1968.[28]

The Philadelphia Resistance sought to integrate the direct action, antinomian emphasis on "individual acts of conscience" with "a movement [that] aims for political effectiveness . . . based on a radical critique of American society and foreign policy." They focused on the draft

because it is an integral part of a system that pursues a brutal war in Southeast Asia, that actively opposes attempts at social revolution in the underdeveloped world, that exploits the black people of America, that maintains institutions over which ordinary citizens exercise virtually no control.

They framed the draft as an instrument of social control, based on a 1965 government document that stated:

One of the major products of the Selective Service classification process is the channeling of manpower into the many endeavors, occupations, and activities that are in the national interest . . . The process of channeling by not taking men from certain activities who are otherwise liable for service, or by not giving deferments to qualified men in certain occupations, is actual procurement by inducement of manpower for civilian activities which are manifestly in the national interest. . . . Young men would not have pursued a higher education if there had not been a program of student deferment.[29]

This manipulative and prejudicial core of the draft process inspired many in the Philadelphia Resistance to reject what they acknowledged as their class privilege, the 2-S deferment.

The Philadelphia Resistance saw itself as an integral part of the developing movement as it shifted "from protest to resistance" in 1967 and early 1968. Its early participants were closely aligned with, indeed had some overlapping membership in, People for Human Rights (PHR), which, in response to police attacks on black students at a Philadelphia school board meeting in November, determined to create a white, antiracist movement organization. Members of both groups were organized into communal living arrangements in the Powelton Village neighborhood, adjacent to both Drexel and Penn campuses.

Resistance activists were influenced by Marxism, which by 1968 was increasingly the lingua franca of the movement. They were part of a New Left increasingly enamored with Third World national wars of liberation, particularly that of the Vietnamese, but also of the Cubans and Chinese. At the same time, they were "anarchists, anarcho-syndicalists," according to Avirgan, whose daring and humor made him a natural leader of this essentially anti-organizational circle of brothers and sisters. The Philadelphia Resistance never descended the slippery slope to a dogmatic and manipulative Marxism-Leninism more intoxicated by sloganeering and sacred texts than with effective practice. In this sense, Avirgan was the embodiment of the Resistance. He was not an academic, prone to leap from the cloistered and suffocating ivory tower to what too often turned out to be action for its own sake. Nor did he immerse himself in the arcane and esoteric canon of revolutionary Marxist theory. Avirgan was instead focused on the war and organizing resistance to it, period.[30]

Philadelphia never developed a strong SDS presence in the 1960s despite innumerable attempts—at Penn, Temple, and Swarthmore—to develop one. Part of the reason seems to have been the inevitable

Figure 12. Judy Chomsky (middle) and Dina Portnoy (seated) in the offices of the Philadelphia Resistance. Robert J. Brand.

Quaker influence on the city's radical politics. The Quaker organizations with which George Hardin identified were the backbone of much of the movement; they characteristically supplied and subsidized the office space, the equipment, the technical apparatus, and the paid jobs that sustained activists like Marty Oppenheimer, Tom Barton, Tony Avirgan, Martha Westover, and so many others. And they were always there; they were the ongoing, stable institutional structure that New Left activists ridiculed, denigrated, exploited, but finally relied on. Whatever else happened as the world seemed to be turning topsy-turvy, there would always be the Quaker organizations, especially the AFSC and FPC. It would be difficult to measure the influence of Quakers on the more secular peace organizations—SANE, WILPF, WSP, FOR, CCCO—but there is no question that they were a complicated and sometimes uncomfortable mix of religiously driven pacifism, Marxist-based radicalism, and, to a lesser extent, liberalism.

Those who formed the Philadelphia Resistance, however, were not interested in Quaker-based activism. In fact, emerging almost simultaneously, even before the Resistance, was a specifically Quaker alternative, A Quaker Action Group (AQAG), formed in July 1966.[31] Lawrence Scott, a longtime Quaker activist and founder of both SANE and CNVA, initiated the call for a specifically Quaker, nonviolent, direct action organization committed to a radical revolutionary transformation of the United States. Their focus, as with the Resistance, was the war in Indochina. Their first ventures were the very well-publicized *Phoenix* voyages, three of them, to deliver medical supplies to war victims in both North and South Vietnam. AQAG also was heavily involved in the Poor People's Campaign, in protests and projects regarding U.S. policies in Latin America, and in inspiring the very effective and moving reading of the names of U.S. war dead at the fall 1969 Mobilization in front of the White House.[32] Scott's approach was for AQAG to be a "channel for individual and group concerns that take the form of nonviolent action, nonviolent resistance or civil disobedience." Although AQAG included non-Quakers, Scott was sustained in his efforts by veteran Quaker activists George and Lillian Willoughby, Ross Flanagan, Lynne Shivers, George Lakey, Charles Walker, and Swarthmore graduate Bob Eaton.[33]

Eaton had participated in campus antiwar activities at Swarthmore with the Student Political Action Committee (SPAC) and SDS and had traveled to Hazard, Kentucky, to deliver supplies to striking miners, but his heart was essentially radical Quaker, as were his primary affiliations with FPC, CNVA, CCCO, and finally AQAG. He worked with the Swarthmore ERAP-SDS people in Chester, coordinating volunteers for the Robert Wade Neighborhood House, and was arrested for

engaging in direct action protests at the Boeing-Vertol Helicopter
Plant in 1966. Eaton, the youngest crew member at 23 and chosen because of his sailing experience, joined the first *Phoenix* journey in early
1967. Later a flier promoting speaking engagements exclaimed,
"Well, this guy Bob is something of a charismatic figure, and he has
quite a lot of experience and good sense packed into 24 years."[34]
Eaton's draft resistance began in 1966 and played a central role in
both AQAG and the Resistance's efforts through 1969, when he was
convicted and imprisoned for his noncooperation with the Selective Service System. Eaton was a member of both organizations and
certainly among the most admired activists in the Philadelphia area.

Most of those who joined the Resistance, however, were uncomfortable with AQAG's Quaker essence; indeed, many were of Jewish back-
ground and decidedly secular. But the Resistance and AQAG would
work together, cooperating in their direct action efforts and their draft
counseling and resistance and sharing a commitment to a prefigurative political life so characteristic of the New Left, that is, living revolutionary values while engaged in revolutionary practice.

Over the next several years at least until the end of the war, the
Philadelphia Resistance took a leadership role in movement activities,
especially but not restricted to draft and peace work. There were a
host of challengers, both comradely and contentious, who sought the
mantle of New Left leadership. Certainly there were always the youth
groups of the Old Left—the Communist Party's W. E. B. Du Bois Club
and later the Young Workers Liberation League (YWLL), which had a
presence particularly at Temple University, and the Trotskyist Young
Socialist Alliance, which played a significant role in the chemical-
biological weapons research struggles at Penn. But none of these
groups could escape the ways in which their parent parties stifled innovation and remained congenitally insensitive to American rhythms
and expression, although they did play important roles in the broad
local and national demonstration-grounded mobilization coalitions.[35]

There were also newer versions of Old Left styles, most prominently the Progressive Labor Party, Youth Against War and Fascism,
and the Marxist-Leninist products of the SDS self-destruction: the
Weathermen, RYM2 (Revolutionary Youth Movement), and the Labor Committee. None of these generated more than blips on the organizational radar screen, and all of them made it easier for mainstream
apologists to marginalize radical viewpoints.[36] Philadelphia's most important Marxist-Leninist group was the *Philadelphia Free Press* people
(Freep), led by Bill and Judy Biggin. The Freep evolved out of Temple
University demonstrations against cafeteria services; a group of radicals, including Bill Biggin (a graduate student in biology), Jim Quinn

(then a Du Bois Club leader), and Temple undergraduates Rick Rubin and Art Platt, started the *Temple Free Press* in May 1968. The paper became the *Philadelphia Free Press* in 1969 as it radicalized, with the more culturally oriented editors starting their own paper, the *Plain Dealer*, in early 1970.[37]

The Freep, like most of the late 1960s communized groups, was more Leninist than Marxist and more Maoist than Leninist. Most of its followers eschewed the stodgy and gray Communism of the Soviet Union, instead romanticizing—from afar—the more utopian Third World liberation movements and governments. It was the era when all too many New Leftists succumbed to the mystique of Maoist communitarianism, inspired by the courageous resistance of the Vietnamese Communists to American domination and seduced by the idealistic rhetoric of Mao's Great Proletarian Cultural Revolution. It was a time when a number of Philadelphia New Leftists journeyed to Cuba as members of the Venceremos Brigades to participate in Fidel Castro's ultimately unsuccessful efforts to massively increase the yields of the sugar harvests. The heroes of the day were Fidel, Che Guevara, Mao, Régis Debray, and, to some, even North Korea's Kim Il Sung and Albanian dictator Enver Hoxha.

It would be all too easy simply to ridicule such misplaced allegiances as merely another episode in the Left's tendency toward Stalinism and totalitarianism. Such loyalties were dreadful, obscene, and finally, pitiful. But they also were part of the efforts of New Leftists to find their way toward a strategy of radical reconstruction, a model of a post-capitalist society. The Marxist-Leninist-Maoist groups, confronting the intransigence of the war and the seeming collapse of liberal efforts in the late 1960s and early 1970s, frustrated by the inadequacies of an anti-ideological, existential radical politics they associated with early SDS, felt the need to return to Karl Marx. Alas, they rarely took more than brief glances at "the young Marx," associated with a humanistic critique of alienation, and leaped directly to the most reductionist versions of Leninism and Maoism.[38]

This development, barely discernible through 1967, erupted during the traumatic and watershed year of 1968. Until spring 1967 it was still possible for individuals in the emerging New Left to engage in long-term strategies of fundamental social change based on innovative revisions of Marxism and a host of other critiques. The most promising, perhaps, was the call for a reconfiguration of Marx's notion of the proletariat to include all employees, all salary- and wage-earners, under the category of "the new working class." This argument, which seemed to be gaining strength in 1967, allowed campuses to be encompassed in the New Left call for social change. Students were not

petit bourgeois or privileged or "niggers"; they were workers in training within a developing post-capitalist economy.[39]

But the pressure of events—the riots in Detroit and Newark; the intensification of the war; the developing white backlash as measured by
figures like George Wallace and, in Philadelphia, Frank Rizzo; the assassinations of Martin Luther King, Jr., and Robert Kennedy; the rise
of a hippie counterculture proclaiming a post-scarcity, hedonistic
"greening" of America; the turn in African American politics from an
integrationist and ameliorative approach to one emphasizing confrontation, Third World identity, and revolution—all made it extremely difficult for white New Leftists to engage in a political praxis
that anticipated a majority constituency bound together as workers
and citizens.[40] In the most tragic sense, young activists, pressured by
the rush of events, with minimal guidance from the more experienced, were prone to abandon the democratic project and the possibility of persuading their fellow citizens of the moral necessity of
building "the beloved community." Some found refuge in a reversion
to the most simple-minded notions of the proletariat. Others leaped
into the most puerile generational notions of a "Woodstock Nation"—
of, in effect, Peter Pan as the "New Socialist Man." Many looked to the
exotic, the Other, in the Third World, in African America, or Native
America, eschewing "white-skin privilege." And there were those who,
with little consistency or thought, mixed and matched some or all of
the above. What made the Philadelphia Resistance distinctive was that
its members found a way to connect to indigenous traditions of dissent
and conscience, which facilitated their ability to maintain the high
moral ground of the early movement. In the early and middle 1960s,
both the civil rights and New Left movements gained influence to a
large extent because they spoke truth to power, because they pointed
out the contradiction between American ideals and American practice
and demanded that those contradictions be resolved. Those who returned from the southern antisegregation struggles; those who stood
up for the underdogs of the world, the nation, and, close to home, the
campus; those who put their bodies on the line for their beliefs, were
admired by many who could not take such stands. Many observers,
both on campuses and in the larger society, admired the young idealists who stood up for liberty and democracy, even if they remained on
the sidelines. But to the extent that movement activists were evoking
deeply felt values—participatory democracy, equal opportunity, voting rights, freedom of assembly, or free speech on campus—they were
able to maintain some degree of the heroic though they might annoy,
even anger others. The hostility faced by the movement, especially
in its formative years, cannot be underestimated; nevertheless, its

strength was always its capacity to stand on the high moral ground of the most cherished of American principles. By the later 1960s, many New Leftists, in frustration and, indeed, self-righteousness, abandoned some of these principles, thereby yielding the high moral ground. In desperation, they reached for solutions and strategies that too often were contemptuous of "bourgeois" principles of free speech and assembly, democratic elections, tolerance, and a deeply felt patriotism.

The Philadelphia Resistance rarely succumbed to these degenerations. They spoke in clear, direct, expressive, and often funny ways. They did romanticize Third World liberation movements; they did struggle with establishing honest and respectful relations with militant black organizations, like the local branch of the Black Panthers or the local chapter of the Black Economic Development Conference (BEDC). But this "band of brothers and sisters" came closer than most to a prefigurative politics in which they lived what they believed, by teaching and advocating in word and deed. As a result, they were without doubt the most admired and respected white New Left activists in the Philadelphia area from 1968 through the end of the Indochina wars. Why that was the case merits consideration and analysis.

The Philadelphia Resistance focused most of its attention on activities addressing the Vietnam War, most especially draft counseling, draft resistance, public education, and demonstrations, including direct action protests. During its first year—that extraordinary watershed year of 1968, during which the nation went through the trauma of two assassinations, the driving of a president from office, escalating campus confrontations, the tumultuous Democratic Convention in Chicago, and the election of Richard Nixon as president—the Philadelphia Resistance engaged in organizing three major draft-card turn-in demonstrations; joined others in protesting the establishment of martial law in nearby Wilmington, Delaware; protested Democratic Party presidential candidate Hubert Humphrey's and vice presidential candidate Ed Muskie's visits; engaged in demonstrations at at least five draft boards; cosponsored protests against city schools; and organized a protest against war toys. And this was just the surface of their activities.[41]

The Philadelphia Resistance was never a membership organization. Rather, it was a prefigurative community of activists, many of whom lived together in several housing collectives in the Powelton Village neighborhood near the Penn campus, all of whom sought to live the values of the revolutionary society they worked to bring forth. There were twelve full-time staff that first year, paid (most of the time) $25 a week; in addition there were at least another two dozen people who identified with and worked extensively as part of the Resistance, including academics like Davidon and Thompson, clerics like Gracie, and wives and mothers like Judy Chomsky. It became a tight band of brothers and sisters very early, based on the intensity of their commitments, the risks they were willing to take to fulfill those commitments, and the shared sense of who they were, what they were about, and why they were so engaged.[42]

The Resistance, unlike many other New Left groups in the late 1960s, never lost its sense of humor. On July 11, 1968, some of them, at the suggestion of Paul Golden, protested the sentencing of Resist leaders Benjamin Spock, William Sloane Coffin, Michael Ferber, and Mitchell Goodman by climbing " a dozen statues of famous Americans, mostly Revolutionary heroes and [placing] . . . gags over their mouths." Resistance activists also allowed for sports activities and played football games against Young Americans for Freedom (YAF), the Trotskyists, the *Philadelphia Inquirer*, and local high school student activists.[43]

As Christmas approached, twenty Resistance activists sang carols, performed satiric skits, and tried, unsuccessfully, to give out holiday cookies to police officers at the Roundhouse, Philadelphia's police headquarters. They proclaimed: "While we have had confrontations with the police, we do not regard the men of the police force as our enemies, nor do we feel that they are the initiators of the policies of repression which we object to."[44] Such a gesture, however tongue in cheek, reflected attempts to come to grips with the increasing tendency among white New Leftists to imitate the increasingly brutalized rhetoric and dehumanizing views of the Black Panther Party and other black militants toward police and was compounded by the beatings Resistance activists received from Frank Rizzo's police. For example, during Vice President Humphrey's visit, Tony Avirgan, Richard Gale, and Jeff Jaffe were "beaten and hauled away while trying to cross 16th Street" following what seemed to be the singling out of protesters for violating restrictions on signs and areas of access.[45]

Dan Finnerty was one of the Resistance people who cautioned against what he called "this anti-cop crusade," suggesting that it was a risky way to "gain credence" among black militants. Yet Finnerty tried to walk a tightrope in defending the Panther use of epithets like "pig" while denying such use to whites. He stressed that the average police officer was not the cause of poverty, racism, or injustice, and that peaceful demonstrations were more likely to win over new recruits. That such advice was as applicable to black as to white activists was perhaps too risky a deduction for even the most sensible movement activists.[46]

Figure 13. The Philadelphia Resistance softball team. Robert J. Brand.

The dilemma was caused by the increasing tension between efforts to build the movement, on the one hand, and, on the other, feelings that desperate measures were necessary—indeed, imperative—in desperate times. Following the violence at the Democratic Convention in Chicago, antiwar economist Douglas Dowd, in a reprinted article in the *Philadelphia Resistance Review*, saw worse ahead "because we are outnumbered, and they are terrified. And they are armed." Dowd believed that whites would now join blacks as targets of police vigilantism and emphasized the urgency activists faced to "stop fascism": "We can't wait for the straight people to opt to join us. We have to help them. The Resistance must speak out to straight people, not just to itself."[47] In the same issue, an anonymous commentator concluded, "Anyone who doubted that a revolution can take place in this country can just look at Chicago. They can see not only that it can happen but that it will happen. And we can thank Daley and his pigs."[48]

Such a profound misreading of the Chicago events rested, at least in part, on an apocalyptic sensibility among the New Left that equated the United States with Nazi Germany. When Wilmington, Delaware, was under martial law, one Resistance member concluded, "It may be that Wilmington is an experiment in military and social control that will be repeated elsewhere, and this in some sense can be viewed as a model city, its rulers as the vanguard of corporate fascism."[49] To the extent that the United States was perceived to be in a revolutionary moment with either fascism or socialism as the options for the immediate future, activists had little patience for the slow and grinding work of democratic politics. As much as the New Left gravely erred in misapplying a Maoist version of Marxism-Leninism to the United States, it compounded the mistake by exaggerating the repressive forces of a tumultuous era and perceiving those forces as indicators of an incipient fascism.

In late 1968, four Resistance members journeyed to Montreal for the Hemispheric Conference to End the War in Vietnam. In many ways, however, it was a demoralizing event, "another fiasco of left divisiveness and petty-factionalism," reflecting "the complete insensitivity of each faction to the position of the others." There was a radical caucus and a black caucus and a Third World caucus, each with nonnegotiable demands. Resistance member Josh Markel found the workshops useful but was aghast at the Sunday plenary, where Latin American student radicals seized the moment to chant against American imperialism with raised fists. Markel asked, "At whom were these demonstrators aimed? Who among the audience needed to be convinced?" He also noted the conference's discomfort with the issue of Soviet behavior in Czechoslovakia, wryly noting, "Somehow it is hard to see the

Maoists as great champions of Czechoslovakias (sic) fight for civil liberties." Markel concluded, "There is not one spector (sic) haunting the world. There are two. The spector of Vietnam and Czechoslovakia."[50] The Philadelphia Resistance struggled with these issues more than most New Left organizations. They were torn between their libertarian-anarchist beliefs and their admiration for the Third World revolutionaries playing David against the American Goliath.

One of their most exemplary actions took place in August 1968 following the Soviet invasion and occupation of Czechoslovakia, which "offered itself as the perfect opportunity for Resistance to show its opposition to authoritarianism from the left or the right." Bob Brand and Leo Kormis proposed liberating the offices of the Soviet news agency Tass in Manhattan. They planned to surprise the occupants and attempt to send a teletype message of solidarity to the Czech people. Of course, they understood that they were unlikely to succeed; the point was to gain public attention. Indeed, their arrival had been tipped off to the press and, thus, to security at Rockefeller Center, where Tass was located. They did, however, persuade Tass to seem to send their message via teletype. But more significant was that at least one New Left group cared about the crushing of the Prague Spring government of Dubček and Svoboda, who took seriously the ways in which what all too many were calling "bourgeois" civil liberties were, in fact, essential to the radical vision of the good society. It was a rare and emblematic moment that helps to explain the Resistance's moral cachet in Philadelphia.[51]

At the same time, the Resistance found itself romanticizing Third World revolutionaries, especially the Vietnamese. In September 1968, Paul Golden and Thompson Bradley traveled to Budapest with other New Leftists to meet with Vietnamese Communist representatives. Both were uncritical and in awe of the Vietnamese they met. Bradley accepted without question the Vietnamese claims of a strengthened NLF presence in South Vietnamese cities following the Tet Offensive and the morality of NLF assassination policies. Golden wrote of "the Vietnamese putting us to shame" in terms of their seriousness and preparation.[52] Two years later Tony Avirgan and Martha Westover went to Indochina. Avirgan wrote: "There are no beggars, prostitutes or drug addicts on the streets of Hanoi. There are also no people without homes." He was struck by the "incredibly strong solidarity and unity of purpose" of the Vietnamese people, as well as their treatment of minorities and their collectivization successes, and only experienced some frustration in trying to persuade them that not all Americans opposed their government's policies. Like so many movement visitors, Avirgan found it difficult not to be swept up by the heroic resistance of the Vietnamese to American bullying and terror.[53]

The Philadelphia Resistance also faced agonizing choices in attempting to be a part of the broader struggles in the city, especially those addressing race and racism. In August 1970 they participated in the Philadelphia Regional Conference, which embodied a "microcosm of problems facing the radical movement in this country" and included antiwar, black, labor, and women's groups. On the last day, chaos erupted, initially when Roxanne Jones, the Philadelphia leader of the local chapter of the National Welfare Rights Organization (NWRO), interrupted a workshop report that was stating its support for a $5,500 guaranteed national income. Jones attacked the conference for "talking big but not acting." Other women present connected Jones's attack to the marginalization of women's issues at the conference. It wasn't so much the issues as the tone, the single-minded anger: "there was not enough mutual respect or trust to allow for this kind of orderly proceeding. Each special interest group felt (all with some justification) that their vital interests had gone unrecognized."

If that was not enough, Mike Tinkler, a particularly abrasive representative of the Labor Committee, a Marxist-Leninist break-off from SDS, rose to challenge the funding aspects of the $5,500 demand. Bob Brand, frustrated over time with the Labor Committee's tendency to be obstructionist, "snickered and loudly interjected a sarcastic comment that the only correct position was that of the labor committee." At that point, Tinkler challenged Brand's earlier call that proposals must originate only from the group affected by the proposals, noting that "one wouldn't necessarily entrust the decision making in a mental hospital to the inmates." Brand, of course, disagreed in the spirit of empowerment. And, almost inevitably, most of the participants proceeded to excoriate Tinkler for comparing the oppressed, those on welfare, and minorities to the mentally incompetent. Following some heated argument, a black Communist decided that Tinkler's insults to black women required a beating. Only the intervention of co-chair Mohammed Kenyatta, the black leader of the Black Economic Development Conference, and some other cooler heads prevented "a mini-race riot." Tinkler left and the meeting calmed down.[54]

Such confrontations had become all too common since the New Politics Conference in fall 1967. The Resistance struggled both to maintain comradely relations with such volatile participants as Roxanne Jones and Mike Tinkler—and many others—and also to sustain its own organizational and ideological integrity. They saw value in that "white radicals feel more guilty than ever about their role with regard to black people." But they understood that such feelings obscured the need to address the perception of white workers that a guaranteed national income was morally outrageous only in part because they would be paying for it with their taxes. The Resistance understood that, short of socialist revolution, a strategy was needed that brought poor and working-class whites and blacks together. It wasn't entirely satisfactory for the Resistance to argue that joining forces to oppose the war and shift defense spending to domestic needs was the answer. That would not be sufficient to attract those white, working-class ethnics rallying to Frank Rizzo, many of whose sons were most vulnerable to the draft. But they were on the money to bemoan that it "is a pity that so much energy is wasted in fighting over abstraction."[55]

The Philadelphia Resistance survived such encounters for the most part through their focus on a primary target—the war—and a series of ongoing antiwar activities that kept them more pragmatic and, perhaps more significantly, on a more human scale than most of their organizational rivals and allies. For one, the young men of the Resistance were directly engaged in their own battles with the Selective Service System. Tony Avirgan had returned his draft card in 1967; he was indicted in mid-1968. Bob Eaton had returned his the year before. When any local draft resister was called before the criminal justice system, the Philadelphia Resistance was there in solidarity. When Dick Jennings refused induction in summer 1968, the Resistance created a "Chain of Life" by which he was linked to eight activists, with another seventy in support. Resistance people helped organize the visit of over 1,000 activists to both Allenwood and Lewisburg federal prisons at Christmas 1968. Resistance activist Paul Golden showed up for his induction supported by the George Fencl Memorial Draft Refusal Jug Band & Storm Door Company, "Resistance's answer to the Chester American Legion's OPERATION SENDOFF." In this instance, the Resistance was poking fun at Fencl, the head of Philadelphia's Civil Disobedience Squad and the figure activists dealt with the most in the planning and executing of demonstrations and marches in the city.[56]

The Resistance's efforts at humor and solidarity helped to soften the grim realities facing so many young men. When Bob Eaton was sentenced to three years in prison in August 1969, there were 100 supporters in the courtroom and another 300 standing vigil outside, twenty of whom had chained themselves to the young Quaker when he was arrested. The court heard testimony on Eaton's behalf from Pastor Martin Niemoller, who had spent eight years in a Nazi camp; Devi Prasad, the Gandhian leader of War Resisters International; and

Vo Van Ai, a Vietnamese Buddhist. Eaton's own words reflected the ethos of both the Resistance and AQAG:

The issue before this court today is a political one. My crime has transgressed against no human being. It has openly challenged the political order of this society. I think, on balance, the courts of this land failed us in dealing with the great issue of slavery. The courts have played a passive role in confronting major social issues facing us today. . . .
    Many of us refuse complicity with a conscripted society because our government will not act to remove this evil from our society. This has involved open and civil disobedience to certain laws. This is a serious act. But written law is not an absolute in a free society.[57]

In addition to supporting draft resistance, the Resistance organized a series of ongoing activities, including distribution of draft information to GIs at the Philadelphia Airport every Sunday. One of their most important creations was the Monday night Resistance dinners, initially at their offices in Center City and later at St. Mary's Episcopal Church near the Penn campus, during which food and drink were offered along with political presentations from local and visiting activists and scholars as well as occasional entertainment. Resistance people also leafleted the city's main induction center every morning, handing out wallet-sized cards to inductees; at one of these early events, Police Commissioner Frank Rizzo punched Tony Avirgan in the face.[58] Such activities were institutionalized expressions of solidarity and of the prefigurative politics that the Resistance attempted to express. Solidarity was indeed integral given the Resistance's high-risk, high-wire act.[59]

The Resistance also opened an alternative educational institution, Omega U., in fall 1969, with over 300 participants in eleven courses. There were policy meetings the first Thursday of the month and many fundraisers—art sales, party boutiques, rock concerts—for this cash-desperate collective often unable to cover its minimal needs. Resistance veterans always looked forward to the annual Resistance picnic at Judy Chomsky's house—with pool. The work was often exhausting and sometimes demoralizing—when demonstrations fizzled, or when ultra-Left groups threatened to subvert events, or when a young recruit committed suicide. The ability to have fun, to *make* fun, to enjoy life to its fullest, to poke holes in pretense, to adhere to Emma Goldman's notion of revolution requiring music and dancing, to raise a banner, "Beat Army, Beat Navy, Join the Resistance," during the annual Army-Navy game at Philadelphia's Memorial Stadium—all helped to build solidarity, loyalty, and comradeship among the several dozen Resistance staffers and the several hundred more who identified with the organization.[60]

Figure 14. Philadelphia Resistance activists engaging in an antidraft demonstration featuring the George Fencl Memorial Draft Refusal Jug Band & Storm Door Company (Fencl was the head of the Philadelphia police's Civil Disobedience Squad). Robert J. Brand.

The Resistance established a cooperative print shop, Resistance Graphics, which printed movement literature, holiday cards, wrapping paper, and calendars. It also produced literature on corporate complicity and worked with the AFSC project National Action/Research on the Military-Industrial Complex (NARMIC) to develop slide shows on antipersonnel weaponry. In both of these activities, Resistance women like Martha Westover, Sue Levering, Eva Gold, and Judy Adamson took the lead.

The Resistance also joined up with other peace groups, including AQAG, to form the Weekly Action Project (WAP) in late 1969 to address "the growing mood of frustration" that was leading all too many activists toward either violence or retreat. The WAPs were weekly nonviolent, direct action events geared to sustain movement morale and maintain pressure on the war machine through corporate boycotts, guerrilla theater, and talk-ins at draft boards. In response to the new lottery system, WAP held lotteries to determine which draft board to close down in the following weeks. Resistance engaged in its own draft counseling, including a focus on assisting GIs, but participated in the citywide Draft Information Center as well.[61]

As part of a countercultural movement in which marriage and monogamy seemed passé, Resistance activists struggled with gender issues, attempting to live revolutionary values in their communal lives and in their decision making. There was drug usage and sexual experimentation; there were some personal disasters. Nevertheless, the core of Resistance activists seemed able to explore the interconnections of the personal and the political without the disastrous results experienced by some local radicals more enamored of the cultural revolution.

Powelton Village was one of the sections of the city that offered support if not encouragement for countercultural life styles. Indeed it was in this neighborhood that Ira Einhorn, Philadelphia's most well-known hippie and cultural radical, resided with his girl friend Holly Maddux, whose body was stored in a trunk in his home until it was discovered and he was arrested in 1979. Resistance activists knew and sometimes worked with Einhorn. In what became known as the "Warlock Affair," the Warlock Motorcycle Club twice showed up at the Resistance offices demanding compensation for alleged damages to their motorcycles during a peace rally, which they somehow blamed on the pacifist group. On the second occasion, they punched a staffer and engaged in other threatening behavior. Facing such obvious blackmail, the Resistance, counseled by Einhorn, chose to stage a benefit to raise the money instead of pressing charges. The benefit was staged at St. Mary's, but the Warlocks never showed up; the money remained in escrow.[62]

Mark Morris design

YOU ARE CORDIALLY INVITED TO

# RESISTANCE DINNERS

## EVERY MONDAY ❈ 6:00 P.M.

| JULY 3rd | JULY 10th | JULY 17th | JULY 24th | JULY 31st |
|---|---|---|---|---|
| at St. Mary's Church, 3916 Locust St. War of the Backseat Generals, color documentary on Laos | at Germantown Presbyterian Church, Greene and Tulpehocken Karl Hess will give an anar- chist perspective on the elections | at St. Mary's (see July 3rd) City Wide Meeting on the Indo- china Sum- mer Project | at St. Mary's (see July 3rd) Ron Whitehorne and David Levine will sing some Labor History | at St. Mary's (see July 3rd) Cora Weiss of the Committee of Liason will disuss recent information about P.O.W.'s |

THERE WILL BE NO DINNERS HELD IN POWELTON
VILLAGE. FOR FURTHER INFORMATION CALL PE 5 1350

Figure 15. The Philadelphia Resistance held weekly dinners every Monday, usually at St. Mary's Episcopal Church on Penn campus. Eva Gold and Josh Markel.

Figure 16. Lisa Schiller, Resistance office manager. Robert J. Brand.

Figure 17. Josh Markel, Penn student leader of STOP and Resistance staffer. Robert J. Brand.

Resistance women were slow to respond to the emerging women's liberation movement. For example, at the Counterinaugural in January 1969, Resistance staffer Lisa Schiller noted: "Marilyn Webb spoke concerning the women's liberation movement. Her speech was not well received by the crowd, which wanted to get into the streets."[63] In fact, at that event the New Left veteran Webb had heard male radicals yell, "Fuck her! Take her off the stage! Rape her in a back alley! . . . Take it off!" She was followed to the stage by Shulamith Firestone, who attacked male chauvinism as the crowd "booed and shouted obscenities." Many of the involved feminists gave up on movement men at that point, with the final straw being a threatening phone call to an ultraleftist woman: "If you or anybody like you ever gives a speech like that again, we're going to beat the shit out of you."[64] Resistance women were late in focusing on gender issues because of their deep commitment to war-related and draft-related activities. They were also wary of what they perceived as the racial and social class exclusivity of early women's liberation. In fall 1969, for example, they criticized a women's liberation conference for the "conspicuous absence" of "black women and women over thirty years old" and expressed impatience with the conference's focus on the emotional problems of white, middle-class women. Instead, they called for more fundamental struggles for adequate housing, nutrition, and education for nonwhite, nonelite women and their families. Resistance women were sensitive to the ways antidraft efforts tended toward a kind of elitism and increasingly sought to break out of white privileged isolation by organizing in the public and parochial schools, developing special efforts to reach out to draft-eligible minority and working-class youth, and organizing at GI coffeehouses, especially at New Jersey's Fort Dix.[65]

In addition, Resistance women were clearly unhappy with the mixed messages directed toward the men who attended the women's liberation conference, noting that "we were already exclusive enough" and arguing that men should be welcomed as participants. With women like Chomsky, Schiller, Portnoy, Westover, Putter, and Gold heavily involved in the day-to-day operations of the Resistance, they felt little need to have a separate women's caucus or to initiate critiques or confrontations with the Resistance men. This was an unusually strong and confident group of women with very clear goals and targets. There were, of course, sexist experiences, but the group seemed to address them directly and often with both camaraderie and, always, humor. As a result, although there were casualties and bruisings, the organization was able to weather the initial hurricane of feminist assertion collectively. As with so many other self-destructive possibilities, Philadelphia Resistance seemed impervious to the heavily ideological, divisive posturing of both the worst of Marxism and the worst of the women's liberation movement. Most of them simply remained activists who kept their eyes on the prize of ending the war and offering services to those at risk of falling in the war's destructive path.[66]

Between 1968 and 1975—when the Indochina wars culminated in Communist victories in Vietnam, Cambodia, and Laos—the Philadelphia Resistance was the most significant New Left antiwar organization in the city. SDS never took hold in Philadelphia, despite promising starts at Swarthmore in the mid-1960s and serious efforts at Penn and Temple throughout the decade. By the later 1960s, the white New Left had both splintered and moved toward either turgid Marxist-Leninist dogma or nihilistic confrontation. The splintering included the most promising and, finally, successful challenges to the status quo: the women's movement; the gay and lesbian movements; the Black Power movement and the wide variety of efforts toward inclusion and diversity that it inspired; and the environmental movement. But these movements require stories of their own, which can only in part be tracked through the history of the white New Left. That part of the New Left, with the striking exception of the Philadelphia Resistance, faltered in the later 1960s, losing much of the moral high ground it had gained through its ideas about participatory democracy, its commitment to racial justice, its critique of American bullying in Indochina, and its exemplary actions in pursuit of living those ideas and ideals.[67]

The Philadelphia Resistance embodied the best of what has always been the American radical tradition—conscience, individualism, and anti-statism. They were the New Left's version of "the best and the brightest," many of them starting their activist lives at the University of Pennsylvania. They maintained effective relations with the older adult wings of the peace movement: the Quakers; the left-liberals and pacifists of SANE, WILPF, and Women Strike for Peace. They were able to be both critical of and yet willing to work with the various Marxist-Leninist sectarians—the Communists, Trotskyists, and various post-SDS factions. Mostly, they kept their focus—ending the war and rallying those who refused to be complicit in its operations. And they were *there*, at all times, helping to organize demonstrations, leading direct action efforts, reaching out to those seeking counsel about the draft (including those within the military), rallying to those who engaged in resistance and noncompliance, holding dinners and classes and fundraisers and parties and football games, and seeking to link up with the broader movement, especially in terms of racism and poverty.

Most spectacularly, the Philadelphia Resistance was centrally involved in organizing the October 15, 1969, Moratorium Day rally, "the most massive antiwar demonstration in Philadelphia history," with an estimated 100,000 participants throughout the region and approximately 25,000 at JFK Plaza in Center City. It was a day of high school walkouts but also official peace-related programs at both public and Catholic schools; parades to the Plaza from Penn, Temple, and Drexel Universities; vigils and fasts; readings of the war dead; and Roman Catholic masses. The Resistance concluded, "One of the finest aspects of Vietnam Moratorium Day was that it attracted the middle class and the middle aged":

Businessmen conducted a noon service in the City Hall courtyard not far from the rally site. Marching to the rally were contingents from the Housing Association of Delaware Valley, Child Guidance Center and the Health and Welfare Council. Seventy-five workers from Graduate Hospital walked to JFK Plaza carrying picket signs with crutches attached. White-coated medical students were stationed on street corners . . . distributing literature linking the war with the domestic health crisis.[68]

As opposed to many other parts of the country, in Philadelphia, in part because of the Resistance, antiwar radicals embraced, rather than criticized, the more dovish Moratorium. They saw it was a part of the effort, consistent with the more militant Mobilization, to reach out to those thus far hesitant, tentative, and suspicious of the peace movement. They did not condemn or ridicule the more moderate voices that had previously invested in Eugene McCarthy and Robert Kennedy or had voted for Hubert Humphrey the previous year; they understood that ending the war required a strategy of inclusion and generosity. And it worked.[69]

The Resistance understood the practical need to build a majority movement; however, their essential values and ideology as a nonmembership vanguard committed to direct action cut against such a goal. It would not be fair to blame the Resistance for the failures of the Philadelphia New Left movement. Indeed, it is difficult to imagine how any group could have effectively fended off the self-destructive and self-isolating aspects of the New Left.

One of the Resistance's major goals was to demonstrate solidarity with GIs, especially through the establishment of a GI coffeehouse near Fort Dix and through provising counseling for those seeking information about conscientious objection and desertion. The Resistance's efforts challenge the conventional notion that peace activists mistreated GIs; indeed, it is overwhelmingly clear that they acted on the principle that, whereas the Pentagon and the top brass were morally culpable for war policies, enlisted and drafted military personnel were to be treated with respect and empathy. The slogan "Bring the Boys Home" was apt in assessing how the Resistance saw themselves in solidarity with the grunts.[70]

The Resistance sought many times to establish strategies for the long haul, anticipating the end of the war. In late 1969, they sought, unsuccessfully, to situate their antiwar activities within "the context of a whole series of social and political ills to which men, as moral agents, are obliged to respond."[71] They offered two policy statements. The first, and more countercultural, was penned by Mark Morris and began with the statement that the "internal combustion engine has turned out to be a great mistake" and should "be outlawed." It concluded with calls for free bicycles, free drugs, optional work, the abolition of money and taxes, and environmental protection.

The second, proposed by a much weightier leadership group, including Bill Davidon, Tony Avirgan, Judy Chomsky, Paul Golden, Robert Green, and Josh Markel, began with a declaration of moral agency, the existential call to "free ourselves and our society from the stultification of passive obedience to illegitimate authority." As such they highlighted ending U.S. military involvement in Indochina and allowing the Vietnamese to achieve self-determination, and they critiqued U.S. efforts worldwide "under the banner of a paranoiac anticommunism" to protect an economic elite interested in domination of the Third World. The proposal went on to argue that defense spending should be shifted toward meeting human needs, all fairly conventional radical proposals, couched in moral but not self-righteous language. But then the statement called for "an end to Dehumanizing Institutions Such as Prison and the Military," revealing the Resistance's basic libertarianism and the ways it was attempting to link up with the black liberation movement, especially in excoriating "the basic criminality of a society built on gain at the expense of others," and in calling for an end to racism and a coming to grips with a history of "liberal rhetoric" masking the "brutal realities" of Indian genocide, the internment of Japanese Americans during World War II, the oppression of women, and "the use of nuclear weapons, napalm, chemical agents and other horrors of technological warfare against Asian peoples." The proposal closed by returning to the Resistance's core identity: resistance to military conscription and to the military itself, joined with calls for similar actions against economic exploitation—an anticapitalist logic without the mention of capitalism—against FBI and police harassment and repression, and for school and college direct action against racism and both military and corporate complicity. The statement closed, arguing that antiwar and antidraft activism had led the Resistance to oppose broader forms of oppression, with the Third World liberation mantra, "We will dare to struggle. We will dare to win."[72]

Despite its very American style and its pragmatic politics, the Resistance inevitably was shaped and influenced by the turn in the movement toward a Third World model of revolution, which included an emphasis on human will and agency, a rejection of liberal reform, and a privileging of nonwhite, non-middle-class constituencies. It never resolved the tensions between such Maoist influences; its more libertarian-communal beliefs, which appealed to a hothouse segment of the white middle class; and its deeply egalitarian, democratic efforts to build a majoritarian movement. In the end, its essential utopianism remained in conflict with its pragmatism. It was the best of the vanguard groups but still suffered from the limitations of such bottom-line elitism. Within the constraints of these tensions and contradictions, however, the Philadelphia Resistance stands out as exemplary among all white New Left efforts: its members stayed the course; they did good deeds; they never lost their humanity; they held to the high moral ground; and they kept their sense of humor in times of enormous stress, frustration, and rage. For all of that, they have much to be proud of—they were effective in helping to limit the even greater destruction of life and the environment that the wars in Indochina could have wrought. And they now stand as part of the legacy of democratic resistance to unjust authority that has always been the hallmark of the best of American activism.

## Chapter 6
# The Politics of White Antiracism: People for Human Rights

Although the Philadelphia Resistance concentrated most of its attention on the war in Indochina, it also worked with other activist groups who were focusing on domestic social issues. Of these groups, People for Human Rights (PHR) emerged as the most vocal. In its effort to join the New Left and Black Power movements, PHR also was perhaps the most divisive. By virtually all accounts, the inspiration for the emergence of the social movements of the 1960s was the civil rights revolution. Rebels without a cause watched—often on television—dignified, courageous African Americans assert their rights to the vote, to equal opportunity, to be respected as citizens and human beings. Early indicators of the emerging New Left sensibility like the Port Huron Statement demonstrated how an affluent, educated generation "was penetrated by events too troubling to dismiss":

First, the permeating and victimizing fact of human degradation, symbolized by the Southern struggle against racial bigotry, compelled most of us from silence to activism. . . . The declaration "all men are created equal . . ."rang hollow before the facts of Negro life in the South and the big cities of the North.[1]

The statement, in seeking "alternatives to helplessness," took note of how the civil rights movement demonstrated "that there can be a passage out of apathy" and added that events like the sit-ins and the freedom rides "challenged a few thousand liberals to new social idealism." The notion that one can change history seems to require the emergence of some social agency, like the labor movement of the 1930s and the African American freedom movement of the 1950s and 1960s, to give flesh to the democratic ideal. The early civil rights movement revitalized a democratic project battered by McCarthyism, Stalinism, and elitist notions of mass society. In light of Freedom Summer and other events, perhaps the people, or at least some significant segment, could push the nation toward what New Leftists called "participatory democracy."[2]

The history of the New Left remained closely intertwined with the African American struggle, especially as the latter changed from its early nonviolent integrationism to a more rhetorically militant and nationalist period. In several specific ways, the emotional dynamics of the white New Left was highly sensitive to the moments of hopefulness and despair, as well as to the ambivalent relationship black activists had with the United States. Very early on, in Philadelphia, the politics of race began to shape the ideology, strategy, and tactics of the New Left movement.

At the national level, the critical years were 1964 and 1965. It was at that point that the greatest triumphs of the civil rights revolution occurred, including the Civil Rights Act of 1964 and the Voting Rights Act of 1965. But already there were signs of discord, misunderstandings, and tragedy. After more than three hundred years of race-based enslavement, followed by de jure and de facto segregation, including job and housing discrimination, violations of citizen rights to the vote, intimidation, physical abuse, literal terrorism and lynch law, it would have been remarkable if African Americans had been able to adhere to the model of nonviolence embodied by Martin Luther King, Jr. In a characteristically American blindness to the weight of history, white liberals and radicals hoped against hope that the nation could escape the thunder of three hundred years of oppression and move into the sunshine of human rights.

In my personal experience, I recall attending a speech at Rutgers University by James W. Silver, a history professor at the University of Mississippi and the author of *Mississippi: The Closed Society,* an account of his experiences in Oxford as a white advocate of racial integration. Silver, forced to flee the state under threat of assassination, came to Rutgers University to inform us of how totalitarian and terroristic Mississippi had been but also about a remarkable, if haltingly slow, beginning of progress, of enlightenment. The year was 1964.[3] The audience, mostly white undergraduates, seemed to take inspiration from the hard-earned hopefulness of this courageous southerner. We wanted to believe that a significant point had been reached in our nation's racial history. But at that moment, during the question-and-answer period, a young black man from the back of the audience asked whether Silver expected him to be spiritually uplifted by the idea that the deep south would soon be comparable to the north, which was without Jim Crow but still suffocated by inner city slums, dilapidated housing, inferior schools, high unemployment, and demeaning welfare. "Is this supposed to get me excited and inspired?" I did not want to hear this young man from Jersey City at that moment; I knew his words were true and yet I sought at least a moment of optimism and, perhaps, self-congratulation. I suspect most of the white audience shared my feelings. Professor Silver, in response, made only the absolutely truthful and yet inadequate assertion, softly spoken, that, yes, there was lots of work to still to do but that it was an extraordinary accomplishment to begin to bring the deep south into the modern American world of equal opportunity.

This experience epitomizes the tensions that would begin to emerge as black and white activists sought to take the next steps in fulfilling the promise of Dr. King's dream. On the one hand, there were those within the larger society who were reluctant to embrace even the nonviolent, integrationist logic of the two federal laws and hardly open to coming to grips with demands addressing poverty, unemployment, and racism. Already by 1964, Alabama governor George C. Wallace was demonstrating in the Democratic primaries the presence of what many observers began to call "white backlash." Although well *before* affirmative action and busing, the sentiment was related to rising challenges in most northern cities, including Philadelphia, about realtor discrimination, red-lining practices by lending institutions, hiring discrimination at publicly funded jobs such as construction, and dismal and inferior public schools.[4]

Philadelphia's racial, ethnic, and political history made such racial reactions more probable, if not inevitable. A city with such a belated liberal Democratic Party ascendancy experienced immediate contested terrain between good-government Anglo patricians and their affluent Jewish allies; newly empowered ethnic Catholics (first and foremost the Irish but also Italians), Slavs, and working-class Jews; and, last, increasingly impatient African Americans, inspired by the civil rights revolution to demand their place at the table.[5] As such, it was a city defined by the battles between such powerful figures as the reformers Joe Clark and Richardson Dilworth, ethnic pols like Bill Green, Senior, charismatic NAACP head Cecil Moore, and emerging urban populist Frank Rizzo.[6]

It was within this ethnic and political environment that white New Leftists grappled with the issue of race and racism. The Swarthmore SDSers working in Chester in 1963–64 were immediately forced to adjust their expectations and inchoate strategies and theories to racial realities. One report lamented the unpleasant necessity of blending "centralized control" with their more preferred participatory democratic model, given what they perceived as the apathy of black residents:

The majority of the people in the block organizations lack experience in a successful democratic group situation. They lack faith in, and commitment to, operating in this fashion. They cry again and again that they want "a leader, a leader," someone to do things for them. They lack the faith in their ability to accomplish things without a charismatic leader who can do this. People are not coming out of the block in terms of the numbers that the objective political situation would demand. Yet alternatives to a grass-roots democratic movement, which could meet the needs of the political situation might mean the departure of our program from its central ideal of grass-roots democracy.[7]

The Philadelphia SDS/ERAP initiated in 1964 by Nick Egleson and Connie Brown had even less success in connecting with local black or working-class residents.[8]

Philadelphia-based New Leftists had also been involved with civil rights activism through the Northern Student Movement (NSM), an organization that emerged out of a 1962 conference at Sarah Lawrence College sponsored by the New England Student Christian movement. NSM established the Philadelphia Tutorial Project (PTP)—one of four—with a prestigious set of sponsors including the Rev. Leon Sullivan of Zion Baptist Church and Dennis Clark of the Catholic Interracial Council. Two of the Yale-based founders of NSM—Thomas Gilhool and Peter Countryman—played considerable roles in the early successes of PTP.[9]

There was, as noted in Chapter 2, some rivalry between SDS and NSM. Peter Countryman and SDS's Lee Webb clashed over the issue of what in other quarters would eventually be called the culture of poverty. Countryman argued that ghetto blacks were no more "deviant" than white, privileged activists, and that indeed both suffered from "fragmentation and alienation." His confidence was formed from the belief that, since some movement activists already "had changed through the process of being revolutionaries, it is obvious that all of us can."[10] Countryman, who became the most influential leader of both NSM and PTP, was impatient with the ideological rigidities of SDS, specifically, their commitment to a particular form and process of building an interracial movement of the poor under principles of participatory democracy. Countryman preferred an ad hoc pragmatic strategy of beginning with where people were and moving them forward. He felt that it was more important to offer a service than to be diverted by irrelevant issues of process. He banked on training tutors, on establishing a "personal relationship" in tutoring, on bonding between idealistic but well-trained tutors and poorly educated but motivated students. Together they would build a movement to transform education in Philadelphia, with the students themselves becoming tutors, and therefore activists, in their own communities.[11]

Both New Left projects, especially that of the Swarthmore SDS in Chester, had to deal with cooptation by mainstream organizations, including African American allies less concerned than idealistic undergraduates with issues of "selling out." They also had to deal with racial tensions within their staffs. PTP was stronger in that it was, from the outset, an alliance between radicals and liberals with strong support from the Roman Catholic Church, black ministers, and liberal human rights organizations.[12] But it finally had to address what some ERAPers described as "the old NSM issue—just what and how much can white students do in a primarily Negro movement?"[13] By the mid-1960s, such questions had become virtually rhetorical. Movement activists were forced to address the challenges posed by Black Power, the painful recognition that blacks and whites would not be arm-in-arm together as the civil rights revolution shifted gears. It was a gut-wrenching experience for many white activists with deep commitments to racial integration.

## The Detroit Experience:
## David Gracie and People Against Racism

The Philadelphia story actually begins in Detroit where an organization called People Against Racism (PAR) was formed in 1966.[14] The leading spirit in this development was a New Left activist named Frank Joyce, who in October 1965 began what he called Friends of NSM. FNSM was to focus its attention on the white racism that "permeates the economic, political, educational, religious, and social institutions of the entire nation" and that "perpetuates the helplessness and hopelessness of black people." The FNSM statement of purpose asserted that "black people will be free only when they equitably control . . . those institutions which influence their lives." It saw the Northern Student Movement as consistent with "a national movement of black people to acquire power" toward the end of community control. In that spirit, FNSM saw itself as a "nucleus of a movement of whites and Negroes . . . in communication with the ghetto-based movement" and able to "support and interpret its efforts" and "take initiative in our own communities in confronting others on the issue of racism." Its goals included the provision of financial and other support for NSM and the Adult Community Movement for Equality (its Detroit affiliate), support of the black movement in general, education of whites about racism and black history, the raising of the issue of racism in white communities, and the taking of action regarding manifestations of racism locally and nationally.[15]

FNSM met several times in the fall and distributed a newsletter, with Joyce chosen as chairman and a young Episcopal priest, David McI. Gracie, as vice chairman. By late winter 1966, FNSM had transformed itself into People Against Racism (PAR), with essentially the same anti-racist statement of purpose. Clearly, in response to the Watts riot and the rise of a Black Power consciousness, PAR positioned itself to organize those "white people who have been identified with the 'Civil Rights Movement' [who] are often left feeling offended, baffled and paralyzed" by this nationalist turn. PAR asked, "What is the role of whites who genuinely want to be part of the struggle?" As such, PAR was on the cutting edge of the agonizing struggles of radical and liberal white activists, New Left and otherwise, to sustain and even deepen their commitments to racial equality following their virtual expulsion from civil rights organizations like SNCC, CORE, and other groups turning from integration toward versions of autonomy and exclusion.[16]

PAR quickly became involved in a project to transform the teaching of racism and black history in the public schools, "especially in white suburbs"; engaged in solidarity efforts regarding police behavior; attacked the local war on crime as racist; ran a summer seminar on racism for white students; and joined Gracie in supporting the Freedom School established by striking black students at Northern High School.[17] Gracie, a 1954 graduate of Wayne State University and a working-class Detroit native, had returned from military service to work for the Detroit Human Relations Commission for two years before enrolling at the Episcopal Theological School in Cambridge, Massachusetts. He was ordained in 1961 and was assigned initially to a small country church. Following what he describes as a "transforming" experience of being selected on the basis of his involvement in the Episcopal Society for Cultural and Racial Unity to be an honorary pallbearer at Mississippi civil rights leader Medgar Evers's funeral in June 1963, Gracie became rector of an interracial church in Detroit. The church, St. Joseph's, became the site of the Freedom School established by the Northern High School protesters.[18]

A tall, handsome Scotsman, Gracie further increased his visibility as a clerical activist by his involvement in the creation of a draft counseling service. Then the Detroit ghetto riot erupted in July 1967, and he led efforts to organize emergency relief to local residents. At that moment, the Rev. Robert DeWitt, bishop of the Episcopal Diocese of Pennsylvania, recruited Gracie, whom he had known during his Detroit years, for an experimental ministry as Urban Missioner.[19] At his farewell dinner in Detroit, Gracie asked,

How far can one effectively challenge an institution from within? Or how far can one go down the path of division and conflict without violating love? And can a community of love be of any effective help to those who are backed into a corner and must fight to survive?[20]

Tough questions from the increasingly radical priest who had come to the conclusion that the Detroit riot was "a call to repentance, perhaps a final call to this nation." In his final Detroit sermon, Gracie called on his flock to repent from consumerism; from violence, especially "the violence of our armies, of our police, and the 'frozen violence' of our institutions which crushes the lives of the poor in our land"; from "our neglect of the poor"; and finally from "the domination of the poor by the wealthy, of blacks by whites."[21]

## Gracie Comes to Philadelphia

David Gracie arrived in August 1967, direct from the Detroit riot in which forty-three died, in a Philadelphia whose 1964 riot had contributed to the ascendancy of police commissioner Frank Rizzo. Within a relatively short time, Gracie would become a leader in both the antiwar and antiracist movements. Helping to create and direct the two most significant movement organizations, the Philadelphia Resistance and People for Human Rights, he was, without doubt, one of the most influential and controversial political actors in the city.

Bishop DeWitt certainly understood the implications of recruiting Gracie. DeWitt had himself arrived in the diocese in 1964, whereupon he had immediately become involved in controversy. Following ghetto explosions in Chester, DeWitt had rushed to Harrisburg, literally rousted Governor William Scranton out of bed to intervene on behalf of the Commonwealth of Pennsylvania, and sought to introduce interracial dialogue and reconciliation. That same year he supported picketing Girard College, a private school for orphans restricted by Stephen Girard's nineteenth-century will to white males only. DeWitt also was an outspoken critic of Lyndon Johnson's interventionist policies in Vietnam.[22]

Within months of his arrival, Gracie clashed with conservative members of both Episcopal clergy and laity. Presiding at a draft-card burning demonstration in October 1967, he was arrested for advocating breaking the law and was subsequently criticized within the diocese for a lack of patriotism. Many called for DeWitt to fire him, or at least muzzle him. Support came from 129 area faculty members, who submitted a letter of support to the bishop, stating:

Father Gracie has seen fit not to walk away from his responsibility to these young men. Is he to be honored less than the priest who refuses to recognize the dilemma? Or is the alternative silence? The resurgence of vitality in the churches in the last few years is directly related to the growing number of clergymen who will not be silent about what they believe; it is not those who speak out who are irresponsible. To silence a David Gracie is to destroy just that vitality that has been so valuable to church and community.[23]

Gracie's growing importance in Philadelphia's New Left circles became apparent when, within a year of his arrival, he was honored on his thirty-sixth birthday by the Philadelphia Resistance. Two hundred supporters gathered at the First Unitarian Church in Center City, and testimonials were delivered by Roxanne Jones, leader of the Philadelphia chapter of the National Welfare Rights Organization; local hippie luminaries Ira Einhorn and Don Coleman; and David Rudovsky, a young attorney working with PHR, which Gracie had helped establish based on his Detroit experiences. Gracie himself spoke about "the problems of an anti-imperialist movement in a non-European culture" that "must develop a new set of priorities in order to identify with the colonized peoples of the Third World countries." One sympathetic reporter noted:

He asked us to consider whether we could arouse a new sense of commitment and the ability to risk our own security for such change in this society. He closed with a quote from Jan Myrdal: "Love us when we're dirty. Everybody loves us when we're clean."[24]

As the tensions of racial conflict rose, it was around this remarkable man that a group coalesced to form People for Human Rights.

The long, hot summer of 1967, including the terrible riots in Detroit and Newark, stands as a watershed in the development of the white New Left. Certainly the challenge of Black Power had been brewing for several years; SNCC and CORE had already shifted from integrationist to nationalist stances. The ghetto uprisings beginning in 1964, including that in North Philadelphia and the Watts riot of 1965, had shifted the racial climate toward a more confrontational, mistrustful, and increasingly chiliastic mood. The white New Left struggled with these developments. The more reformist Vietnam Summer reflected the ambivalence of reaching out to mainstream voters, appealing to the conscience of the nation, door-to-door, in the spirit of the 1964 Mississippi Summer project. Such an approach was hampered by the escalation of the war, the increasing radicalization of the movement and the shift "from protest to resistance," which had little patience with reaching out to white, middle-class, often suburban moderates and liberals. In a summer workshop, SDS's Tom Hayden spoke contemptuously of such people, suggesting that if they hadn't

Figure 18. The Rev. David McI. Gracie, Urban Missioner of the Episcopal Diocese of Pennsylvania, antiwar activist and co-founder of People for Human Rights. Robert J. Brand.

already recognized the immorality of the war in Vietnam, they were ethically hopeless, beyond redemption. From that posture, it was only a short distance to viewing such people as the enemy.[25] Then Detroit and Newark erupted.

The summer riots of 1967 made it exceedingly clear that America was engaged in a two-front war that compelled idealistic white New Leftists to come to grips with apocalyptic possibilities, matters of life and death. Time seemed to be running short—time to build interracial coalitions, to engage, educate, persuade, compromise. Some imagined a revolutionary moment and emphasized what appeared to them to be a global shift toward Third World liberation struggles, a Maoist turn in which the countryside rallied against the privileged First World cities and suburbs. Some connected such expectations with movement growth on campuses, especially among the counterculture. At the same time, intertwined with this sense of revolutionary expectation was a deep and bleak apocalyptic despair, a sense of defeat in the face of the endlessness of the war in Southeast Asia, of the futility of protest, of a rising white backlash embodied by George Wallace and at local levels by figures like Louise Day Hicks in Boston, Anthony Provenzano in Newark, and Frank Rizzo in Philadelphia.[26]

It was in this political and emotional climate that one of the most polarizing events in recent Philadelphia history occurred. On November 17, 1967, approximately 3,500 African American high school students demonstrated in front of the Board of Education building, demanding more black history and Swahili language courses in the curriculum, as well as dress code revisions that allowed for African-style clothing and hair. Philadelphia school superintendent Mark Shedd, a reformer brought in by the Richardson Dilworth-dominated board, had agreed to meet with representatives of the students. As the crowd swelled and became restless, a few students climbed on a car and broke off the antenna. What then transpired remains subject to contradictory recollections of various eyewitnesses. Police argue that students were getting out of control, throwing rocks and bottles at them. Others suggest that the crowd was, at worst, getting rambunctious, and that the initiative for assault came from the police. Some witnesses claim that Police Commissioner Rizzo yelled, "Get their black asses!" as the police went into action. One African American student described the melee:

I ran. I was scared, really scared. I saw the cops take a young kid off the steps. They just pulled him off the steps, dragged him down the steps, and they pulled him into the street, and they just beat him with clubs. We saw blood flying all over the place. And I yelled, "Look there's a cop," because he was looking at us. My friend looked at him. The cop looked at her. I didn't move. And he ran past me and caught her and beat her all around the head. She went to the hospital. Boys were running all around on top of cars, trying to get away from the cops. It was crazy. It was just hundreds, hundreds of cops.[27]

The attack lasted a few brief minutes, although some enraged students headed into Center City, where they punched some innocent pedestrians. Five officers reported injuries, fifteen students were hospitalized, dozens were arrested. The School Board riot further exacerbated racial and ethnic tensions in the city, especially given the fact that just weeks before James Tate had been elected mayor to a considerable extent on the coattails of his police commissioner Frank Rizzo. To racial moderates, liberals, black activists, and movement people, a Rizzo-dominated city served as a catalyst to action.[28]

In many ways, the School Board confrontation set in motion the dominant political and racial dynamics of the city for the next decade: Rizzo/anti-Rizzo. At the student level, the turn toward Black Power solidified, as they soon demanded exemption from saluting the American flag, the teaching of black history as a major subject by black teachers only, the removal of police and security from all schools, and the assignment of black principals to black schools.[29] White moderates and liberals began to look for candidates who could defeat Rizzo as his intention to run for mayor in 1971 became clear. Caught between these impulses, movement activists joined in the liberal electoral efforts but looked beyond them to ways they could demonstrate their solidarity with black Philadelphians. As African American activist and Episcopal priest Paul Washington defined the deepening polarization:

On the one side were those white people who feared a revolt, and instead of working to eliminate the causes, were calling for police repression. On the other side were black people, with some white allies, who were searching for new institutional forms to express their own identity and worth.[30]

## People for Human Rights

It was this wider constellation of forces that prompted the organization of People for Human Rights in the winter of 1967–68. The founding spirits of PHR included its Detroit inspiration, Frank Joyce of People Against Racism, recently arrived PAR leader David Gracie, and veteran New Left activist Peter Countryman, founder of the Northern Student Movement and the Philadelphia Tutorial Project. Countryman and Joyce had both struggled to find a way for white activists to respond to both the rise of Black Power and the explosiveness of inner-city ghettos through an essentially white antiracist organization. As late as summer 1966, as civil rights organizations such as

CORE and SNCC moved toward racial exclusiveness, both Joyce and Countryman remained committed to an interracial movement and palpably in anguish over the viability of whites remaining involved in black community efforts.[31]

PHR was formed at a meeting in early December 1967 at the Denbigh Conference Center, an Episcopal Church retreat in the affluent suburb of Radnor in Delaware County, by a wide-ranging mixture of radicals and liberals, movement people, and those with more mainstream electoral priorities, some of whom were moving toward or had already arrived at a position that was revolutionary and anti-capitalist, and others who remained hopeful that the nation could fulfill its democratic promise within the prevailing system. The leadership—Joyce, Countryman, Gracie, and Ron Whitehorn—tended to be more radical, while key supporters like the attorney Robert Sugarman, NSM veteran Tom Gilhool, and PTP staffer David Hornbeck remained essentially reform-minded. PHR was a white support group working with and most often following the lead of African American allies ranging from Roxanne Jones of the Philadelphia chapter of the National Welfare Rights Organization (NWRO) to Mohammed Kenyatta, head of the local Black Economic Development Conference (BEDC), from Episcopal clergy Paul Washington and James Woodruff of the Episcopal diocese to Reggie Schell of the local Black Panthers and local activist Mattie Humphreys.[32]

One PHR member, Mary MacColl (later Wentworth) recalls Peter Countryman speaking at that initial gathering:

Peter stood at the portable blackboard, mounted on a large easel, with chalk in hand, drawing a good-sized triangle. As he worked, he explained, "Our society is structured like a pyramid."

He drew a line across the inside of the triangle at the very top, leaving just the tip above the line. "At the top is the ruling class—very wealthy white people. Most of them have inherited wealth and basically run the country."

About a fourth of the way down, he drew a second line, noting that this section represented the upper class—larger than the ruling class but smaller than the middle-class grouping below it.

Since a triangle grows wider towards the bottom, the lower sections were larger than the ones above. He labeled the fourth section from the top the "working class" and at the very bottom drew a line making a pencil thin section at the base. "This," he said, "represents the caste of color which includes the twenty million black people in the United States."[33]

The focus of the discussion was on the ways the "whole society weighs on the black people at the bottom, keeping them down." Admitting the apparent simplemindedness of the design, Countrymen emphasized the ways in which a racial caste system generated inferior schooling, housing, health care, and employment opportunities. Mac-Coll remembers concluding, "Poor working-class whites might have lives as deprived as blacks, but they, at least, could pride themselves in knowing that no one was ever going to call them 'nigger.' " She, along with others in attendance, was asking herself what this group of white activists could do to defeat this racist caste system. One way, according to Countryman, was to make a commitment to "working within white society to eliminate racism and supporting the Black Liberation Movement, i.e., the empowerment of black people." The other was to establish People for Human Rights as an affiliate of PAR. The decision to take a more inclusive name was a mark of independence, an assertion that perhaps the Philadelphia chapter was more advanced than that in Detroit, particularly in recognizing the ways that whites, too, experienced oppression in their opposition to the Vietnam War.[34]

Within months of its founding, PHR was a functioning organization of a few dozen activists and a total of approximately fifty members. The founding cohort created an open, fluid framework based on their admiration for SNCC and SDS, ironically at a moment when SDS had degenerated into Marxist-Leninist factions and SNCC, on the verge of collapse, had decided to merge with the Black Panther Party.[35] PHR set up a steering committee open to all and three standing committees—Education, Health and Welfare, and Police. Members pledged monthly contributions to sustain the organization. According to Mac-Coll, those who joined

were mainly middle-class professionals who interfaced with blacks as social service and community mental health workers, teachers, housing advocates, legal services lawyers, ministers, heads of settlement houses, professors of religion, political activists, and students. Many others supported our work but for professional or personal reasons remained off-stage.[36]

PHR also sponsored lots of workshops to train members in black history and antiracism and organized demonstrations, including one at St. Ladislaus Roman Catholic Church to protest the role of its priest in persuading his good friend Mayor James Tate not to displace fifteen white families from an area chosen for the expansion of an overcrowded high school. PHR wanted to call attention to the fact that ten times that number of black families had been displaced in West Philadelphia redevelopment projects. This focus on discriminatory practices drew little more than hostility from the white parishioners of St. Ladislaus.[37]

On April 4, 1968, the Rev. Dr. Martin Luther King, Jr., was assassinated in Memphis and the nation experienced another agonizing series of ghetto explosions. In Philadelphia, Mayor Tate declared a limited state of emergency that restricted public gatherings to no more than eleven, while Delaware governor Charles Terry, Jr. called up the National Guard in anticipation of violent responses in the city of Wilmington. The Guard remained on the city's streets for nearly a year. PHR reacted to these security measures by working with a variety of groups to protest the Wilmington occupation; plans for a sizable protest march were canceled only when a new governor recalled the troops. PHR also demonstrated at the home of South Philadelphia Representative William Barrett to protest what they argued was the unconstitutionality of Mayor Tate's proclamation. They demanded that Barrett support the legislative objectives of the Poor People's Campaign, which had been launched by Dr. King to address the festering urban poverty which seemed to fuel the riots. Twelve members were arrested for refusing to disperse.[38] It was in response to the King assassination that Ron Whitehorn, a VISTA worker working with black youth in the Powelton section, joined PHR at the urging of Steve Gold, one of the founding members. Whitehorn would become one of the leaders of the organization over the next several years.[39]

During the next year, PHR became involved in a host of local issues. They protested a Chamber of Commerce Man of the Year award to Commissioner Rizzo, and offered as an alternative a mock, no-frills dinner at a local church. PHR activists were also involved in protesting against a controversial crosstown expressway that threatened working-class and minority housing; they participated in a Temple University conference protesting police brutality and testified at City Council hearings against cuts in the budget of community mental health centers.

The year 1968–69 was the peak of PHR's activism on a number of fronts related to racism. They organized high school students in establishing a bookstore/storefront as a center for antiracist learning as a part of the establishment of the Liberation High School project and participated in protests against Democratic presidential nominee Hubert Humphrey's speech at the Spectrum. There were demonstrations at a suburban Protestant church, including disruptions of ceremonies, to protest the complicity of a congregant in violating the United Farm Workers national grape boycott organized by Cesar Chavez. In an effort that paralleled the Resistance's satiric bent, PHR engaged in a sing-in at the *Philadelphia Inquirer* to protest editorials and employed guerrilla theater to protest the National Guard occupation of Wilmington. In a whirlwind of energy, PHR took responsibility for training whites in antiracism for the Episcopal Society for Cultural and Racial Unity (ESCRU) national conference in Philadelphia, joined a solidarity demonstration in support of the occupation of the State Office Building offices by the local branch of the NWRO in demanding $50 disbursements for winter clothes, and organized a protest against a *Philadelphia Magazine* swimsuit cover featuring a scantily attired white woman flanked by two black men.[40]

These activities were interwoven with ongoing meetings of the three action committees, a host of lectures and presentations both as a form of PHR internal education and as outreach to the larger community, karate classes at the YMCA, and their second and third annual organizational retreats. At the second retreat in Stroudsberg, Pennsylvania, a women's caucus was formed. Several women, including Mary Mac-Coll, had tried to raise questions about gender inequities, such as exclusive male leadership, meeting times difficult for women with children to attend, insensitive comments, and a sense that recruitment of new members was focused on males. They wrote a short position paper for a spring 1968 meeting, which the men ignored, and it was thus at the Stroudsberg retreat that the caucus was created. Unlike the Philadelphia Resistance, in which there seemed to be a capacity for developing and articulating a feminist consciousness, PHR experienced painful and divisive conflict over issues of gender. According to one veteran of both organizations, the PHR male leaders were more prone to sexual promiscuity, including the indiscriminate propositioning of female members, whereas Resistance males were more serially monogamous. According to Mary MacColl, the climate of what she called "male bonding"

was unreceptive, sometimes even hostile, to our active participation in the discussion, never mind hearing our ideas for action. A woman could garner attention if she were speaking about arrangements for a potluck dinner or a Saturday night bash or a housekeeping problem in the office—nonpolitical tasks that were seen as our domain. But when it came to political topics, the patriarchy had defined our role as that of listener/silent observer. Allowing us into the arena as equal participants would not only eliminate the audience but would enlarge the pool of players competing for dominance within the group.[41]

In addition to its difficulty in dealing with gender issues, in the late 1960s PHR quickly became a deeply ideological organization prone to dogmatic positions, which would eventually lead to its demise in the early 1970s. Characteristic of many New Left groups, PHR was moving toward a Maoist version of Marxism-Leninism. In their study groups, members read Frantz Fanon and Eldridge Cleaver, identified with Third World liberation movements and the Communist leadership of Vietnam, China, and Cuba, and anticipated that, short of revolutionary upheaval, the United States was facing a fascist future. The

*PHR Newsletter* included enthusiastic reviews of William Hinton's *Fanshen*, a pro-Maoist account of revolutionary change in a Chinese village, and reports from activists returning from visits to Vietnam and Cuba.[42] On the one hand, there was a powerful identification with revolutionary possibilities; on the other, there was despair over the rising tide of reaction at both local and national levels, especially the popularity of George Wallace during the 1968 elections, the Wilmington occupation, the election of Nixon as president, the repression of the Black Panthers and other black militants, and the prospect of Frank Rizzo's becoming Philadelphia's next mayor. On a radio broadcast, PHR's David Gracie castigated a caller as a fascist when she identified herself as an Episcopalian and a Republican who supported Lyndon Johnson because she supported all elected presidents.[43]

This apocalyptic turn in PHR as well as much of the New Left was reminiscent of many Old Left moments when the term "fascist" was promiscuously applied to one's adversaries and when Communists underestimated the resiliency of "bourgeois democracy," that is, the constitutional protections of speech and assembly. Historian Leo Ribuffo defines "brown-baiting" as the promiscuous and demagogic tendency of progressives to paint all conservatives with the brush of fascism. This phenomenon, associated with the Depression era, repeated itself during the late 1960s and early 1970s. All calls for "law and order," for greater police protection from both urban riots and the rising rate of violent crime, were perceived as moving the nation closer to fascism.[44] It is clear that the combination of the rising crescendo of ghetto riots, the presidential victory of the deeply hated Richard Nixon, and the seemingly never-ending violence of the Indochina wars weighed heavily on movement activists, already impatient with the seeming feebleness of liberalism.

There was a decidedly New Left cast to these developments. Mary MacColl recalls, "We weren't going to make the mistakes of the old lefties by forming a political party. By making our politics relevant and by establishing alternative institutions, the old system would wither away." New Leftists, although mistrustful of organizational answers, were increasingly attracted to the creation of their own revolutionary institutions.[45]

There was also a deepening belief in PHR that the United States was becoming two nations, one retreating toward repression, the other seeking liberation; one consisting of those resisting racial justice, the other made up of African Americans and their white allies. PHR members possessed a determination to fight racism, not only among the white working and middle classes but also within themselves. They strongly proclaimed the centrality of the notion that "if you weren't part of the solution, you were part of the problem." Kayla Weiner wrote about how PHR members were failing to "live by our ideals," in part "because our racist institutions fucked-up the system [and] successfully dehumanized all of us (black and white). We really don't know what 'to be human' is." Weiner referred to the ways members rarely listened to one another because they were "conditioned into not revealing our true thoughts and feelings" out of fear of being seen as weak. Her train of thought led to profound challenges to the integrity of the individual and the value of privacy:

We've talked of the evils of people going off to their little cottage with white picket fence, two cars, and the two-point-five kids and not caring about anything but their own pleasures. We've passed that, in that we do care about others but are still guarding our own pleasures. How many of you love music but have never gone beyond sharing it with one or two people? How many of you shared your favorite poem or special spot in the park? Along the same line is the question of individuality which we have decided is not meaningful in our time. Yet we have not begun to try new patterns. How many of us will take our problems to a group? How many groups are ready to deal with someone else's problem? How many are ready to subject their job or vocation to a group decision? I'm not sure group decisions are the answer, but individual or "friend" decisions are not. Who has a new pattern we can try for a new society?[46]

Such prefigurative notions of politics permeated much of the New Left precisely as it was becoming increasingly attracted to Maoist ideas of cultural revolution.

The difficulties of engaging in a politics to eradicate racism, end the war, and radically transform an essentially capitalist society were compounded by this simultaneous and daunting imperative to change oneself, to purge oneself of all vestiges of a corrupt culture. For example, Weiner struggled with the PHR conclusion that the public schools were "evil," arguing that "we don't hate the motherfucker enough" to think more seriously about "counter-institutions." She asked, "Are counter-institutions to be merely alternative institutions, or are they to confront the system?" These were exceedingly difficult issues to address for PHR and other New Left activists with children; at its heart it set the countercultural tendency toward retreats and enclaves against the more New Left commitment to participatory democracy and political struggle.[47]

It was a heavy burden for PHR members to confront white racism and other manifestations of capitalist oppression in the wider society while simultaneously transforming themselves to participate in the future post-capitalist society and culture. The rise of the women's caucus enhanced expectations, sometimes producing breakthroughs and sometimes explosions of frustration. The women demanded that sexism be framed in the same terms as racism, that is, as a dehumanizing ideology and behavior that deformed all people, especially all men. When Peter Countryman reported that Northeast Catholic High School for Boys had invited PHR to offer several antiracism sessions to the students, the anticipated enthusiasm was marred by the caveat that the Jesuit school would only accept male speakers. Countryman at first argued for a pragmatic response: shouldn't PHR take advantage of the offer to further the goals of antiracism? But MacColl and others asked, "If we had been told that we were not to bring any blacks with us, wouldn't we have refused?" Countryman was persuaded, and PHR included women as discussion leaders. The Jesuits also yielded. But other concerns were not resolved in such a conciliatory fashion. At one point, PHR women threw a large rock through the front window of the Powelton commune where one of the male leaders with a reputation for manipulative sexual promiscuity resided. Trying to live the revolution mandated extraordinarily selfless behaviors; few were able to live up to such demands.[48]

## BEDC and the Reparations Movement

PHR's Maoist turn intensified in 1969 and 1970 with increasing involvement in the Black Power movement. This involvement crystallized when the organization fully embraced the reparations demanded by the Black Economic Development Conference (BEDC), a national organization led locally by the forceful and charismatic Mohammed Kenyatta. On April 26, 1969, James Forman, longtime SNCC leader, presented the Black Manifesto to the National Black Economic Conference meeting in Detroit. The Manifesto was directed to "the White Christian Churches and the Jewish Synagogues in the United States of America and all other racist institutions." It called for "Total control as the only Solution to the Economic Problems of Black People," given that the United States was "the most barbaric country in the world" and that those committed to the manifesto "have a chance to help bring this government down" by "whatever means necessary, including the use of force and power of the gun to bring down the colonizer." Referring to African Americans as "the Vanguard Force," it advocated "an armed confrontation and long years of sustained guerrilla warfare . . . dedicated to building a socialist society" within which "white people . . . must be willing to accept black leadership." The Manifesto demanded $500 million in reparations, "15 dollars per nigger, with the moneys distributed to pay for a Southern land bank, publishing operations, a research center, organizing training, a strike and defense fund, and cooperative ventures both here and in Africa." The Manifesto was signed by twenty-four African American leaders, including Fannie Lou Hamer, Julian Bond, Ken Cockrel, Vincent Harding, Forman, and Kenyatta. The Conference adopted the Manifesto, and Forman made it public at a disruption of services at Riverside Church in New York on May 4. Over the following months, BEDC confronted the National Council of Churches and most of the mainstream Protestant denominations with the Black Manifesto and its demands.[49]

After becoming the leader of the Philadelphia chapter of BEDC, Mohammed Kenyatta, a twenty-five-year-old Baptist preacher, participated both locally and nationally in the provocative and disruptive actions of the organization. BEDC demanded that the wealthy Episcopal Church commit $60 million, plus 60 percent of the profits on its assets, matched by an accounting of exactly what assets it held. Paul Washington of the Church of the Advocate in North Philadelphia recognized that the "frightening rhetoric" of the Manifesto's demands had "tremendous shock value," and affirmed its consistency with social justice: "Was this extortion, plain and simple, or was it a prophetic call to move beyond charity to a just sharing of resources with those who had been shut out of the system for so long? I heard it as prophecy."[50]

Washington's views were at least in part shared by Bishop Robert DeWitt, the head of the diocese, as well as by David Gracie and James Woodruff, the activist Episcopal priests. In July 1969, Kenyatta formally demanded reparations from the diocese; DeWitt invited him to a Diocesan Council meeting where the majority of participants resisted BEDC's demands. Washington stalked out and resigned from the Council in protest. But DeWitt persisted and, at the May 1970 diocesan convention won a commitment of $500,000 to a grant program to be administered, not by BEDC, but by a group of black Episcopalians and called, not reparations, but restitution. There was less bridge building at the national level, especially after Kenyatta seized the microphone, leading to a physical struggle, a walkout of black and some white participants, and a final vote to grant $200,000 as seed money to the National Committee of Black Churchman. During the tumultuous meetings, Washington exclaimed, "White people cannot set the agenda for this church. Black people must set the agenda for this church and for this nation. And since you refuse to deal with our agenda, I have no choice but to call upon all blacks to leave this convention."[51] These confrontations left no one satisfied. The mainstream of the church was attacked from both sides, viewed as patronizing and engaged in tokenism by BEDC and its allies; perceived as cowardly and willing to succumb to blackmail by its more conservative members.

PHR served as BEDC's primary white support group in Philadelphia. They were asked by BEDC to show solidarity by joining the building takeover at Cookman Methodist Church; one PHR leader recalls feeling "honored" by the call. One PHR member's wife was actively involved with BEDC. PHR included within their educational outreach the advocacy of the Black Manifesto's demands.[52]

## Two Nations?

One must recall that in the late 1960s it appeared as if racial civil war was possible. Few anticipated that the ghetto riots following Martin Luther King's assassination in 1968 would be the last of the major eruptions; most, from all ideological perspectives, feared that the nation was in for a continuing pattern of "long, hot summers." Many white activists, liberal and radical, found themselves responding to black demands as a means of preventing race war and what some anticipated as a genocidal onslaught from whites responding to those who irresponsibly invoked racism, like George Wallace and Frank Rizzo. It was an environment in which the young, handsome, and urbane John V. Lindsay became mayor of New York in part based on his promise to engage in conciliatory politics, both symbolic and programmatic, to fend off a major riot. It was a period when at Cornell University armed African American students seized a building, made demands, received considerable concessions, and marched out, weapons in hand. Conservative writer Tom Wolfe would effectively satirize this moment as "radical chic," skewering a Black Panther fund-raising cocktail party at the home of Leonard Bernstein. It was a time when the critic Susan Sontag proclaimed, "The white race is the cancer of the human race." Indeed, it was a time of extraordinary psychodrama, when the weight of hundreds of years of racism and oppression suddenly began to lift, tempting African Americans, who were filled with a complicated and contradictory mix of exhilaration, expectation, impatience, anger, and delicious pleasure in turning dominance on its head, to engage in a politics of gesture and defiance. It was a time when whites, appropriately and legitimately seeking remedy for that weight of racism, sometimes succumbed to masochistic self-contempt. How was this not to be, given the burden of three hundred years of oppression? Black and white together faced the fury of long-suppressed desires for vengeance, of bold self-assertions of racial pride and solidarity. Only with the greatest of wisdom and patience, the influence of dozens of Kings and Nelson Mandelas, of Abraham Heschels, Marian Wrights, and Peter Edelmans, of Barbara Jordans, could the nation have moved forward without succumbing to payback and backlash. That this moment coincided with the violence of Indochina and the beginnings of economic malaise only make it less likely that the thin reed of understanding would hold. It was bound to disappoint both parties. It was inevitable, necessary, and unbearably, poignantly, deeply tragic.[53]

Those involved with white antiracist organizations like PHR were compelled to their activities by the kinds of concerns voiced by the Kerner Commission Report, which warned of the United States becoming two societies, racially divided. In fact, the reality was contradictory, simultaneously promising and desperate, beginning to deliver on long overdue promises of equal opportunity and yet seemingly unwilling and thus unable to come to grips with the devastating economic consequences of slavery, racism, Jim Crow, and, more recently, deindustrialization. When Martin Luther King's open housing efforts in Chicago in 1966 were met with ferocious, enraged white residents, when his attempts to begin to focus the nation's attention on social class and poverty through his Poor People's Campaign floundered, both black and white activists turned toward more radical, militant, and, unfortunately, rhetorical alternatives. Bayard Rustin's call for a renewal of the liberal-labor alliance in support of a Freedom Budget was compromised by his support for Lyndon Johnson's war in Vietnam, by the increasing rejection by movement people of what they called "corporate liberalism," and by a deep and intense fury at those, like LBJ and Rustin, who, in the words of Carl Oglesby of SDS, broke their American hearts. As many Americans moved politically either right or left, the liberal center faltered. Weighed down by the albatross of war, its pragmatics of ameliorative, peaceful reform had fewer and fewer takers.[54]

## The Black Panthers in Philadelphia

For white movement activists focused on antiracist politics, there was no group more quintessential than the Black Panther Party of the late 1960s and early 1970s. Philadelphia's Panther chapter, not one of the organization's more successful, was formally established in early 1969. Reggie Schell, a sheet-metal worker and veteran, was impressed by the Panthers' armed demonstration in Sacramento protesting antigun legislation and helped form the Philadelphia chapter, becoming defense captain.[55] The Philadelphia Panthers started with breakfast programs, weapons training, and protests over instances of police misbehavior, particularly the killing of Harold Brown by four highway patrolmen. Schell's group put up wanted posters for the patrolman who allegedly gunned Brown down as he begged on his knees for his life. The contradictoriness of the Panther movement as a whole is manifest in the Philadelphia chapter. On the one hand, the Panthers impressed a number of local activists with their dedication and seriousness. Moreover, the harassments and raids of Panther offices by Commissioner Rizzo's police generated feelings of solidarity and acts of support by such organizations as PHR and Philadelphians for Equal Justice. It is an indicator of the desperation of the times that the Panthers' homicidal intimidation and threats, such as putting a price on the heads of policemen, and the brutalized language, for example, cops as "pigs" to be "offed," did not lead many movement activists to morally distance themselves from the Panthers. Too many New Leftists were glibly quoting Maoist mantra that "power grows out of the barrel of a gun" without a scintilla of a notion of Communist governments' crimes and mass murder.[56]

The Black Panthers were a contradictory mix of revolutionary party, reformist community organization, and bravado street gang. That they were nationalists seeking alliances with whites, joined by their romantic Marxist-Leninist-Maoist Third World ideology, made them compellingly attractive to PHR and other movement radicals. In many ways, the white movement exacerbated some of the Panthers' least attractive qualities, making it more likely that they would grow too fast and be unable to manage the entry into their locals of *agents provocateurs* and sociopathic hoodlums. In Philadelphia their face-off against Rizzo made them all the more glamorous, sexy, and seductive, perhaps especially to highly educated white youths suffocating from the intellectualism of the cloistered academy.[57]

During summer 1970 the Black Panther Party announced that its Revolutionary People's Constitutional Convention would be held in Philadelphia beginning September 5. Commingling the Panthers and Frank Rizzo would have been enough to signal potential trouble, but the announcement came in the midst of what appeared to many to be a concerted campaign by law enforcement organizations throughout the nation to strike out at the police-baiting black revolutionaries. Perhaps the most sensational and murderous moment was the gunning down of Fred Hampton by Chicago police in a predawn raid on December 4, 1969.[58] To exacerbate matters, on the weekend prior to the convention, a Fairmount Park police sergeant was murdered in a guardhouse, two other policemen were shot in a patrol wagon, and two others were shot during a seemingly routine roadside questioning involving armed felons. In this climate of mounting paranoia, Commissioner Rizzo launched early morning raids on three Panther offices, in North Philadelphia, West Philadelphia, and Germantown. The raids received massive local and national publicity when a photo went out on the wires of arrested Panthers forced to strip naked for a search. The insensitivity of many movement activists to the murder and wounding of police, to the risks that were a daily reality to those patrolling those mean streets whose despair and pain had not been determined by anything cops controlled, was more than matched by the vengeful reaction of Rizzo and his supporters, who seized the moment as an opportunity to intimidate and terrorize dissidents.

Those who acted most responsibly were mainstream authorities who ensured that the Panther convention would proceed without incident at Temple University and the Church of the Advocate. Indeed, federal judge John Fullam issued a restraining order against the Philadelphia police vis-à-vis the constitutional rights of the Panthers and their supporters, concluding, "A madman out of control shooting at policemen is not much more dangerous to the community than a policeman who loses control and goes shooting up people's houses and raiding them."[59]

The convention itself was somewhat anti-climactic. Michael Tabor of the New York Panthers spoke for more than two hours, during which he suggested a way to respond to a cop who challenged you in broad daylight:

come sundown, come sundown, when the streets are dark and deserted, and you go up on the roof, and you take your action out, fix up your sights, put your index finger on that trigger—that's self-defense, that's self-defense. Because if you don't get *him*, he's gonna get *you* the next day.[60]

The crowd, about half white and half black, applauded approval. Tabor, soon to be a fugitive from justice as he fled to Algeria, evoked the optimistic Maoist rhetoric increasingly comfortable to the movement, of an America built on genocide, from Plymouth Rock to Vietnam, but nearing its demise, with "one foot in the graveyard."

The most deflating moment was clearly Huey P. Newton's speech, delivered on tape. He spoke of "a nation conceived in liberty and dedicated to life, liberty, and the pursuit of happiness . . . in its maturity (becoming) an imperialist power dedicated to death, oppression, and pursuit of profits." According to local Panther leader Reggie Schell, most of his speech, abstract and disorganized, fell flat: "What he said just lost people. When he spoke to the people at that session, he spoke to ordinary people way over their head."[61] The audience, made up of an impressive number of neighborhood blacks, movement activists, and what journalist Nora Sayre described as "spaced-out teen-agers" and "white revolutionary trippers who appeared half-stoned," were part of an apocalyptic moment, mixing images of the barricades with anticipations of concentration camps and genocide. All this in the shadow of the Kent State and Jackson State killings of students, the Panther-police confrontations, President Nixon's demagogic appeals to his "great silent majority" of white backlashers, and a Third World revolutionary offensive highlighted by the Vietnamese Communist successes, the romance of Mao Zedong's Cultural Revolution, and Fidel Castro's efforts to achieve economic independence through massive increases in sugar production, all predicated on Che Guevera's notion of a selfless, altruistic "new socialist man." As historian David Farber concludes:

In their horror over the war in Vietnam, in their often ignorant and misplaced enthusiasm for revolutionary struggles abroad, and in their zealous attempt to repudiate their own "white skin privilege" in a society that had been built on racism, a tiny group of extremists lost their grip on political, social, and global realities. They and their black revolutionary allies managed to inject a poison into American political life which only served to weaken the antiwar movement and all other progressive forces struggling for social justice. Their fanaticism gave credibility to the hard-line forces that wanted to put a stop to all forms of dissent in America.[62]

Philadelphia survived the convention, although the Panthers, rocked by police repression, the erratic behavior of leaders like Newton, and the self-destructiveness of its more *lumpen* recruits, were soon to recede in importance. PHR actually was quite ambivalent about the Black Panthers, its reservations driven in part by Detroit founder Frank Joyce's close relationship with black activist and BEDC leader James Forman. According to Philadelphia PHR members, Joyce was critical of the Panthers, basing his position on their conflicts with Forman. Not all PHR members felt that way; PHR leader Ron Whitehorn's wife, Rosemary Mealy, was actively involved with the local Panthers. Joyce, though, held strongly to the position that African Americans were the vanguard of revolution, aligned with global Third World forces; according to one former member, he was "a jealous guardian of anti-racist purity." Peter Countryman, "the most commanding presence and ideological leader" in Philadelphia, in contrast, was rapidly moving toward the view that revolutionary change required the inclusion of the countercultural white youth, brought into alliance with white and black movement activists. PHR was successful in focusing on its practical agenda of political education, solidarity with local black militants, involvement in efforts to limit police misbehavior, and generally comradely liaison with major movement concerns, especially the war. But these fissures concerning strategy and audience, including that of the increasingly militant women's

Figure 19. Ron Whitehorn (left), activist with People for Human Rights, and Paul Golden, a member of Philadelphia Resistance. Robert J. Brand.

liberation caucus, was inexorably moving the organization toward disintegration. It was losing its liberal wing as its Third World, countercultural, and finally more traditional Marxist-Leninist class analyses confronted one another. The latter view, championed by Ron Whitehorn, who was focusing on working with white working-class youth, expressed concern about what it perceived as "anti-working class politics." Eventually, Countryman drifted from the organization, traveling to Cuba in 1970 as part of the Venceremos Brigade. By 1971, PHR had ceased to exist, with those adhering to its ideological perspectives going their respective ways.[63]

That year, Philadelphians elected Frank Rizzo as the first Italian American mayor of the City of Brotherly Love. His young aide Martin Weinberg, son of a working-class Jewish Democratic Party pol and a former high school basketball standout, described the strategy in terms of the tensions between "the row house people and the ethnic community" who were "getting nothing" and the liberal alliance of WASPS, Center City Jews, and African Americans. He asked, in the name of the neighborhoods, "Where was *their* war on poverty?" Weinberg cited local pol and Representative Bill Barrett, who understood the need for a candidate who would appeal to that social class—and racial—resentment.[64]

Philadelphia, a city that had just fallen below two million people, losing 3.3 percent of its population in the 1950s and 3.7 percent in the 1960s, but with a increase of 10 percent among blacks, a city facing deindustrialization and racial strife, had its largest turnout—65 percent of eligible voters—in the Democratic primary, where Rizzo, the law-and-order candidate of the ethnic neighborhoods, defeated young Kennedyesque Bill Green (129,000) and the African American Hardy Williams (45,000) with 177,000 votes, almost 50 percent of the vote. In the general election, running against patrician Republican Thacher Longstreth, Rizzo, effectively playing the man of the people, won easily, despite losing all but one black ward.[65] The New Deal coalition of liberal professionals, ethnic Catholics, and minorities, belatedly triumphant with the Dilworth-Clark successes of 1951, had lasted just twenty years. Philadelphia had given way to the new political reality of ethnic populism.

## Chapter 7

# The Rise and Fall of the New Left

To examine the history of the New Left movements on college campuses in the late 1960s and early 1970s is to enter a minefield of interpretative brawls and extraordinarily contradictory developments. First of all, there is the ideological battlefield on which conservatives and some liberals see utopian dreams descending into a nihilistic nightmare, the "dark side" of illiberal egalitarianism. Opposing this assault are several versions of left-of-center reconstruction: first, an argument that affirms the early democratic promise of the New Left but regrets the degeneration of idealism as organizations like SDS embraced Third World versions of Marxism-Leninism and, at worst, Weatherman terrorism; second, a point of view that is kinder and gentler to both the radicalization and the heightened militancy of the later period of 1968–73, seeing it as appropriately responsive to the times; and third, a critique of the limitations of the early New Left and a defense of the later movement, particularly insofar as it moved away from a white old boys' network toward an affirmation of Black Power, feminism, gay and lesbian rights, and environmentalism. These last two views reflect a fundamental disagreement about the value and consequences of what came to be called "identity politics."[1]

Such ideological battles rest on what are, indeed, contradictory developments that had become clearer by 1968. By that most traumatic year—which included the Tet Offensive, LBJ's decision not to run, another summer of ghetto riots following the assassination of Martin Luther King, Jr., the escalation of campus confrontations following those at Columbia University, the assassination of Robert Kennedy, the Democratic Convention in Chicago, the Soviet invasion of Czechoslovakia, the Black Power protests at the Mexico City Olympics, student rebellions throughout the world including a near revolution in France, and, finally, the election of Richard Nixon as president—the American New Left had framed its decision to shift "from protest to resistance" in increasingly ideological terms.[2]

In looking at the eight campus movements in greater Philadelphia, the following themes predominate, beginning in 1968 and extending into the early 1970s:

1. The rise of an increasingly Maoist version of Marxist-Leninist ideology within the leadership of SDS and other New Left organizations.
2. An increase in the willingness of New Leftists to engage in direct-action confrontations with government, military, corporate, and educational institutions. Such actions were characteristically nonviolent, but there was a deepening tolerance for those who began to embrace the use of revolutionary violence.
3. The growth of a liberal student activism, both aligned with and yet in tension with the New Left. This important development included the responses of students to the Eugene McCarthy and Robert Kennedy primary campaigns, the 1969 Moratorium efforts, and the 1972 George McGovern presidential campaign.
4. The emergence of a Black Power-based African American student movement, which sought an increase in black enrollments, the development of supportive services, the hiring of black faculty and staff, and the creation of various versions of Black Studies curricula and departments.
5. The emergence of Third World movements inspired by the civil rights revolution among Native Americans, Asians, and Latinos.
6. The emergence of second-wave feminism and the movement for gay and lesbian rights, inspired by the civil rights revolution.
7. The expansion of the hippie counterculture on and off campus, committed to an expressive, libertarian, communal approach to life and learning, most especially one advocating sexual freedom and drug experimentation.
8. The less publicized but significant emergence of a student New Right, gathering resources in its anticipation of New Left self-destruction.
9. The emergence of an environmental movement.
10. The rise of a heightened awareness of ethnic identity among white, immigrant stock Catholics and Jews.

These ten currents mixed and matched, merged and clashed, with individuals shifting and evolving and, sometimes, leaping into a new set of roles and expectations on a dime. The times were truly revolutionary insofar as history seemed to have accelerated; what more normally developed over years or decades seemed to form in weeks or months. A student who arrived on campus an apolitical preppie could find him or herself suddenly engrossed in a "Clean for Gene" campaign and then, just as quickly, flirting with the Revolutionary Youth Movement (RYM) of SDS, chanting slogans about Mao and Ho and Fidel. Some were just flirting with what seemed the flavor of the month, but many were responding to the troubled times, to the ways the war seemed to be brought home on the violent streets of Newark and Detroit and Chicago. The authority of parents, teachers, professors, administrators, and national leaders was being called into question by perceived hypocrisies concerning the consequences of marijuana usage, *loco parentis* rules in the dormitories, and the revelations of university complicity with the military-industrial complex. There were hippies and New Leftists and liberals, but sometimes the distinctions blurred; in addition, the racial and gender challenges further complicated matters. How was one to respond to a new, developing identity politics, which asked less what one believed than what one *was*?

A few things were clear: campus politics seemed to be moving left, right, and center simultaneously; the center was besieged and pulled from both ideological ends; and identity-based movements fundamentally altered the playing field. The movement, universalistic albeit generational, was becoming a disparate if fluid constellation of social movements with both conflicting and converging interests.

One way to approach the complexities of late 1960s and early 1970s activism is to recall that for many there seemed to be more continuity than discontinuity. George W. Bush, for example, Class of 1968 at Yale University, was oblivious to social upheavals, claiming that "There wasn't a lot of protest at Yale in 1968." Bush describes Yale in that period as "a fairly placid place." Of course some of that placidity would be challenged within the next few years, but it is critical to keep in mind that even at the most radical moments on American campuses, including those associated with the Cambodian invasion and the subsequent killings of young demonstrators by the National Guard at Kent State University in 1970, the traditional undergraduate elite— the jocks, the leading Greeks—still dominated student government and campus social life. New and unprecedented was the rising challenge from the New Left and related movements against the social dominance of the jocks and Greeks, who deeply resented this threat to their status. Such traditionalists made some accommodations in the form of longer hair, casual drug usage, and either a more liberal approach to the prevailing issues or, often, a resentful silence in the face of these new and often shrill challenges. At Yale, for example, the Dekes always ruled, as did the Red and Blue at the University of Pennsylvania. And on less elite campuses the great silent majority of students paid little heed to student activism, instead focusing on what mattered to them, that is, everyday matters of dating, friends and family, courses and majors, possibly the fortunes of the school's basketball team, and longer-term decisions about marriage and career.[3]

## Philadelphia Campuses, 1968–1969

On Philadelphia area campuses, there was significant variation consistent with the histories of these very different institutions. The Catholic colleges—Villanova, St. Joseph's, and LaSalle—became much more of a part of the larger upheavals, at least for a time. It became less unusual that there were at least some challenges to campus authorities, often related to the war. Temple University, following the brown bag boycott of 1968, continued to participate in a wide variety of New Left and related activities in the midst of what remained a largely apathetic commuter school for upwardly mobile, nonelite students. The Quaker schools continued to be essentially antiwar in sentiment but disorganized and often cerebral in their means of expression. And in all of the above there was the pervasive influence of the counterculture, including the call for a more relaxed response to sexual, drug, and dress choices and an increasing emphasis on youth culture, particularly rock music.

In 1968 and the spring term of 1969, it was surprising to still hear on most Philadelphia campuses the complaint of student apathy. A Swarthmore *Phoenix* editorial bemoaned "anti-war apathy" in April 1968, and in October a frustrated activist declared, "Swarthmore has not changed. Rhetoric still reigns supreme while apathy festers ubiquitously."[4] At St. Joseph's, the *Hawk* editors described the campus as "a social corpse, a vacuum, a Death Valley of social development and entertainment"; several months later associate editor Michael Wentiel lamented, "What this place needs is a riot."[5] The campus environment in fall 1968, following the tumultuous events of the spring and summer, was remarkably placid.

This apathy was most frustrating to those increasingly radical activists moving toward various versions of revolutionary communism. Swarthmore activist Hank Levy began a column in the student paper called "Up Against the Wall, M.," which asserted that "action, not words, is what is going to change this country." Another activist added, "We must stop asking questions and take some action. We can't always wait for all the facts to be in, for all the facts are never in. Succinctly, stop being so rational and move."[6] Some of Penn's activists tried to establish a new SDS chapter that would emphasize campus democracy and the ongoing struggle over the university's affiliation with defense-oriented research projects, but although an impressive 150 people came to the first meeting, many left dissatisfied and unlikely to return.[7] Temple University was coming off an active spring term during which students had rallied to protest the nontenuring of Professor Sidney Simon with an impressive teach-in featuring Paul Goodman and SDS's Carl Davidson, and had been able to take advantage of the missteps of newly inaugurated president Paul Anderson, whose call for a court injunction bailed out an increasingly dwindling sit-in and reenergized outraged faculty and students. But by fall, Temple seemed to fall back to commuter apathy; a November teach-in drew a meager thirty participants.[8] Temple's radical activists, who established their own independent newspaper, the *Temple Free Press*, after the administration placed the *Temple News* under the control of the School of Communications and Theater, were inspired by the Columbia University building takeovers that same spring as well as the subsequent protests during the Democratic Convention in Chicago. The rhetoric became more revolutionary and cruder, as the Temple activists evoked Black Panther ideology and imagery. Chicago became "Pig City" and readers were exhorted to "Stay in the Streets!"; the logo became four raised red fists with the Mexican revolutionary Emiliano Zapata's picture on a cover page proclaiming, "Viva la Revolución."[9]

One factor that frustrated the increasingly and self-consciously revolutionary student activists was the competition during the 1968 presidential campaign from liberal alternatives Eugene McCarthy and Robert Kennedy. Even considering the demoralizing impacts of the assassinations of RFK and King, and the ways such disasters reduced the possibilities of a liberal resurgence, the New Left, moving "from protest to resistance" and toward more dogmatic forms of Marxism, seemed to be inspiring but often losing many students open to reform and social change but not necessarily to revolution.[10] At LaSalle, for example, a McCarthy campaign meeting drew 125 students; in addition, both student and faculty organizations endorsed the Poor People's Campaign. At Penn, about 800 showed up in support of the Democratic challenger from Minnesota, called "a man of courage" in a *DP* editorial. When Lyndon Johnson announced his withdrawal from the campaign on March 31, at least 1,000 Penn students poured out of the dorms to celebrate in front of the statue of Benjamin Franklin and then proceeded to march festively to Independence Hall in Center City, joined by hundreds more, where they sang "The Star-Spangled Banner," "God Bless America," and "We Shall Overcome." A "crushing overflow crowd" of 11,000 came to the Palestra to hear Bobby Kennedy, and, prior to his assassination, the *DP* endorsed his candidacy. At Swarthmore, a primary poll in May gave McCarthy 299 votes (60%), RFK 72, Nelson Rockefeller 58, Nixon 8, and Socialist Workers

Party candidate Fred Halstead 7. In addition, 52 percent supported a deescalation of the war and 43 percent an immediate withdrawal, with only 8 students opting for a more forceful policy.[11]

There was little liberal optimism by fall, however, and all the responses at the greater Philadelphia campuses to the November election were subdued and conflicted. The radicals at the *Temple Free Press* used the image of a gallows on what it called "Black Tuesday," quoting Black Panther Eldridge Cleaver disparaging the two capitalist candidates and offering a dispirited recommendation of either support for the Peace and Freedom ticket or a "Vote No," which was the editors' preference.[12] Swarthmore activist Frank Ackerman asked, "Who cares which one wins? Not the South Vietnamese peasants, who die in either case. Not the unemployed Black teenagers, harassed by racist police in either case. Not me." Nevertheless a mock election including 784 Haverford and Bryn Mawr students gave Humphrey 61 percent to Nixon's 13 percent, with a scattering of votes for McCarthy, Dick Gregory, Eldridge Cleaver, and George Wallace.[13]

Yet there was more to the 1968 election than the despair and contempt of the radicals and the demoralization of many liberal students. At LaSalle, for example, the mock election indicated "Wallace support strong": Humphrey won with 39 percent, Nixon followed with 28 percent, but the Alabama governor, with 105 votes, captured 17 percent. In a separate evening school mock election, the results were more striking: Nixon won with 614 votes, followed by Wallace with 378 and Humphrey at 376.

There was, indeed, a "silent majority" of students, at least at Philadelphia's Roman Catholic institutions. Conservative icon Barry Goldwater spoke to an enthusiastic crowd of 3,000 at St. Joseph's. One letter to the editor from a recent graduate, titled "Shorthair and Love of God and Country," bemoaned the contrast between the handful of bohemians during his first year, 1963, with the "more than thirty of them, some bearded, some mustachioed, and all of them with long, matted hair" by the time of his departure. Private E-2 Clifford Judge, Class of 1967, wanted them all expelled for violations of the dress code. The largest rally at LaSalle in 1968 had nothing to do with the war or race or student power; instead, it was the hanging in effigy of *Philadelphia Inquirer* sports reporter Frank Dolson for criticizing the recruiting practices of highly successful and popular basketball coach Jim Harding.[14]

These indicators of both conservative strengths and the ongoing primacy of intercollegiate sports need to be tempered by the multiple ways in which even the most traditional and mainstream campuses were experiencing new and often unsettling challenges. At LaSalle, the environment had, indeed, changed. As students and faculty protested on-campus recruiting by Dow Chemical, more mainstream undergraduates "threw rolls of toilet paper on the marchers" and voiced threats. But there was no violence. One young faculty member, Dennis McGrath, disturbed by the football-like cheers of those harassing the demonstrators, worried about the absence of any communication: "We were in the circle, they were on the fringe, and the gulf seemed quite unpassable."[15] But those within the beleaguered circle reached out to conservative students, who joined them in calling for an end to compulsory ROTC training at the college. There were protests throughout the academic year 1968–69, including a 2,000-signature petition and a Student Council vote, culminating in a sit-in involving approximately 250 in April. This was a remarkable transformation for what had been a commuter-based, sports-centered Catholic college. Indeed, as SDS leader Vince Pinto triumphantly announced, "The Movement Comes to LaSalle." Pinto was skeptical of the good intentions of the administration, who initially resisted what was clearly a student mandate, but after the four day sit-in, an ad hoc student committee won a "complete victory," with ROTC becoming voluntary in fall 1969. A *Collegian* editorial, perhaps too euphorically, celebrated the unity of "Long Hairs, Short Hairs."[16]

There were more long-hairs by 1968 and 1969; there was more coverage in all campus newspapers of countercultural events, especially rock concerts, youth-oriented films and books, new albums, and coffeehouse events. The universe had expanded such that rebels, formerly isolated, now had access to what was going on at other campuses and in the downtown scene. There was an underground press, available on all campuses, including the *Temple Free Press,* the more countercultural *Yarrowstalks,* and the *Distant Drummer.* By early 1968, dissident Villanovans, in addition to the ongoing ability to take part in Haverford and Bryn Mawr activities, could journey to the Stewed Tomato, an off-campus coffeehouse, hear Phil Berrigan speak, albeit before a "half-filled Field House" on "Non-Violence, Vietnam and the Cold War," and take courses in the new free university on the draft, Karl Marx, and the New Left.[17]

Draft counseling centers appeared at virtually all the Philadelphia colleges. Swarthmore's opened in April 1968 with twenty-two counselors; St. Joseph's Draft Information and Counseling Service began operations in October and LaSalle's a month later.[18] Some students were refusing induction and receiving sympathetic coverage, including at the Catholic schools, although more characteristically at Swarthmore, Haverford, and Penn.[19] The most comprehensive and organized activities were at Penn, beginning with the formation of a "We Won't

Go" group in March and the establishment of a Resistance campus chapter in April 1968 under the chairmanship of Marty Goldensohn. The *DP* supported those, including younger faculty like sociology instructor Phil Pochoda, who challenged the draft. In fact, Penn's activists created their own special commencement ceremonies honoring those who were refusing induction. The April 25 event featured the Rev. William Sloan Coffin, Yale's antiwar chaplain, and included a pledge by 125 to refuse induction, another 5 who required their own amended version of the pledge to refuse, and an additional 16 who signed but did not wish their names made public, and, finally, a pledge of support to draft resisters signed by 190 ineligibles, many women, 21 in an amended version, and 23 who signed but did not want their names made public.[20]

At all the area colleges, students challenged the administration to increase student power over curriculum and decision making and to liberalize rules and regulations concerning dress, parietals, and drugs. Virtually all the area schools established some variety of free or alternative structures to address experimental, radical, and countercultural interests in a more egalitarian manner. Bryn Mawr and Haverford jointly ran a three-day colloquium on coeducational possibilities, grading policies, and, more broadly, the need for student power. They made recommendations to liberalize curricula and succeeded in creating the first format for students to evaluate their courses.[21] At the start of the fall 1968 term, Swarthmore's newly expanded Student Affairs Committee called for dormitory autonomy for students, the abolition of any rules concerning sexual behavior, and a modification of rules regulating alcohol. St. Joseph's established a campuswide dialogue that same fall on "Components of the Educational Process," which raised questions about dress codes, coeducation, and student involvement in decision making.[22] There was also a new concern about how to deal with the rising popularity of recreational drugs on campus, more typically raised earlier and with a libertarian, countercultural dimension, at the more elite institutions like Haverford rather than at the Catholic colleges.[23]

The ambience of all area colleges changed by 1968, influenced by the emergence of both the New Left and the counterculture. Campus newspapers were filled with advertisements for rock concerts at new venues like the Electric Factory, with the graphics taking on more of a psychedelic flavor. Even the more conservative Catholic schools began to be filled with music and book reviews that tended to bring the most subversive messages of youth culture into the once insulated walls of the Christian Brothers and Jesuits. At Penn, Allen Ginsberg appeared before a crowd of 3,000, while Noam Chomsky drew an impressive

800 students. By 1969, the Communist historian Herbert Aptheker could give a lecture at St. Joe's and the radical philosopher Herbert Marcuse could speak to activists at a LaSalle sit-in with virtually no controversy. It would be excessive to suggest that political and cultural radicalism had achieved predominance in 1968–69, since the Catholic schools and Temple remained commuter-based, career-oriented, sports-conscious, and essentially oblivious to radical challenges. Haverford seemed to shift more toward countercultural and away from political engagements. But at all area colleges and universities, there were new challenges to authority; new demands for rights; less tolerance for *en loco parentis*; more calls for a loosening up of rules and regulations concerning language, sexuality, dress, and the general pursuit of pleasure.[24]

As such, the campus landscape had shifted by the academic year 1968–69. Though scholars have recently brought to attention the emergence of a student New Right in such organizations as Young Americans for Freedom, liberal students remain neglected.[25] As SDS moved farther left, as Black Power brought new challenges, as events seemed to spin out of control, especially in Indochina and African American ghettos, campus liberalism seemed stronger if more on the defensive from both left and right and, increasingly, from racial and gender-based criticisms. The story has yet to be told of the impact of various radicalisms on those who called for the reform of what they defended as a still impressive liberal order. In some ways, as the New Left turned "from protest to resistance" and toward increasingly Maoist versions of Marxism-Leninism, liberalism offered a less risky, less confrontational center of gravity for students willing to question established authorities on and off campus.

For example, on most area campuses, both the main student organizations and the college newspapers were dominated by liberals. Column space was always occupied by more radical and conservative voices, but the liberals tended to be decisive in generating a developing majority consensus on peace, student power, and minority issues. Sometimes they yielded to pressures from their left, but often they drew lines to limit more radical demands. The New Left and Black Power advocates were most effective when they were able either to persuade or to intimidate liberal allies. At the University of Pennsylvania, some of these shifts were apparent in terms of challenges to the more traditional power of Greeks and athletes through the dominance of the Red and Blue Party. In March 1968, the independents, reflecting rising liberal strength and spearheaded by the *Daily Pennsylvanian* staff, defeated the Red and Blue in campus elections for Student Council. Significantly, the more radical New University Party trailed in third place, although garnering a clearly respectable vote and thus demonstrating its strength. A month later, campus political parties were abolished by an overwhelming vote, 1734-315. Nevertheless, in the early 1969 rush, 46.7 percent of frosh still pledged fraternities, a slight decline but still a measure of the ongoing status of Greek life at Penn.[26] At Temple, the liberals who dominated the student paper throughout the late 1960s often chastised the New Leftists for their dogmatism, intolerance, and inconsistencies. In late 1969, an editorial defended keeping the campus open to corporate and military recruiters, reminding SDS and the Student Mobilization Committee (SMC) of the ways such restrictions had been used against the Left in the McCarthy era.[27]

## Black Power on Campus

Second only to the war in Indochina, the most significant factor driving campus politics was race and racism. As the rise of the civil rights challenge of the early 1960s inspired and politicized those who created a New Left movement, the emergence of Black Power and the various ways it impacted on college campuses, from calls for Black Studies programs to Black Panther rallies, shaped white student politics in the late 1960s and early 1970s. By fall 1968, most of the area colleges in Philadelphia had experienced the emergence of African American student organizations. At those campuses contiguous to black neighborhoods, there was an increasing sensitivity and attention paid to race relations. Since the 1964 North Philadelphia ghetto riot, campuses at Temple, Penn, and LaSalle had been alert to the moral and practical issues involved in having enclaves of mostly white students surrounded by lower-income, often crime-ridden neighborhoods. But the earlier focus by campus idealists on tutoring projects and other volunteer outreach activities was increasingly forced to shift to the challenge of black nationalism and separatism. In fall 1967 at Temple, for example, whites were turned away from attending a talk by NAACP leader Cecil Moore sponsored by the Black Student League, whose first rally had been in the previous spring term. That same semester, there were several rallies in North Philadelphia protesting Temple University expansion. At one demonstration, James Williams of CORE exclaimed that when local blacks "move on Barton Mall with torches you'd better get out of their way, if you don't want to help them." By the end of the term, African American community and campus leaders were demanding a Black Studies program created and taught by blacks, an Urban Affairs Institute, and credit for community work.[28] By the end of the 1967–68 academic year, the campus newspaper, as a measure of its concern, published one special supplement on race and Temple's responsibilities to the local community and then another on "The Temple Black Student."[29]

The developments at Temple, in the midst of other challenges relating to the war and to student power, marked the rise of a new, more aggressive identity politics. As at other campuses, there would be administrative, faculty, and white student responses, usually supportive but qualified; some disputes and harsh feelings; then settlement. The Temple University administration announced it was considering establishing a Black Studies program in early 1969; the Steering Committee of Black Students (SCBS) responded by escalating the pressure not only for a program but also for the recruitment of more black students and the special facilities and services to ensure that they would be successful. Prior to the start of the fall 1969 term, the university announced the appointment of Curtis A. Leonard, a 1961 alumnus, as director of the Special Recruitment and Admissions Program (SRAP).[30]

Although one editorial writer accurately described the SCBS as Temple's "most effective" student organization, there were indicators of tensions and resentments. The style of the African American student leaders became more rhetorically revolutionary and exclusive; the Black Panther influence can be measured by the use of epithet "pig" to excoriate the police and their white supporters. In March 1970, black students converted two cafeteria areas into a "black room" and asked whites to leave. Under challenge, the blacks agreed that whites had the right to sit there but were being asked to respect the desires of African Americans for their own space. A Temple News editorial entitled "Bullshit" criticized this rising black separatism.[31]

Clearly, larger societal forces were driving the demands by African American students, staff, and faculty for a distinct place at the campus table. In almost all cases, the result was the establishment of special recruitment programs, supportive services, and race-centered academic programs. In most instances the rhetoric of black activists reflected the times; it was extravagant, often threatening—"by any means necessary"—and strikingly at odds with their actual political behavior, strategy, and tactics, that is, their essentially pragmatic and measured willingness to compromise. There were no Cornell or Columbia occupations on Philadelphia campuses, no black students marching out of seized buildings with raised rifles and associated guerrilla paraphernalia.[32] But it is clear that the moral mandate African Americans claimed for race-based services was granted with, at the least, more ambivalence and some resentment from most whites than had been earlier integrationist demands. At the same time, white New Leftists tended to respond with solidarity to black demands,

Figure 20. Temple University evening peace vigil during the 1969 Moratorium. Temple Urban Archives.

often coupling their support with an emphasis on the depths of racism and the prevailing threat of fascism and genocide.[33] The *Temple Free Press* offered a tribute to Malcolm X with a cover picture and a follow-up affirmation of Black Power in early 1969. They devoted much of an issue to celebrating the Cornell occupation, arguing in an editorial that it represented "A New Stage in the Struggle," justified under the Maoist slogan that "power grows out of the barrel of a gun."[34]

LaSalle experienced smaller if similar challenges. In October 1968, the *Collegian* advertised a three-part lecture series on "The Urban Crisis" and announced the formation of a new Black Student Union (BSU), formed by seven undergraduates. There were renewed calls for tutors and Big Brother/Big Sister volunteers in predominantly black Germantown, and in 1969, the creation of an official Afro-American Week. A new BSU newspaper column made "the case for Black Studies," arguing that "we are justifiably a nation within a nation." In fall 1969 the BSU pressed its demands for an African American coordinator of the school's Open Door admissions program for minority students.[35]

It is difficult to know how such demands were influenced by the rising attention to neighborhood crime. At LaSalle, Temple, St. Joseph's, and Penn, the late 1960s brought the same rising crime rates that were hitting all urban areas. There were neighborhood gangs, one of which clashed with students in a resident parking lot at LaSalle. A 1970 *Collegian* editorial, "Insecurity," bemoaned the increase in campus incidents; another asked whether the college was becoming an "armed camp or communiversity," in the latter case supporting but expressing concern about whether the new Urban Center was a real commitment or merely a concession to the threat from local youth.[36] There were also criticisms of the BSU's confrontational style; Professor John F. Connors argued that the "rhetoric of insult and threat and the style of disrespect will not advance interracial justice." Editorials expressed concern with what they perceived as the BSU's refusal to join in common efforts, particularly the new Urban Center.[37]

In many ways the racial dynamics at LaSalle replicated those in the city and the nation at large. And yet the demands of African American students, stripped of their revolutionary, nationalist rhetoric, were pragmatic and consistent with the ideals and goals of equal access and opportunity. When the smoke cleared in the middle 1970s, most area colleges and universities had accommodated themselves to some form of Black Studies program and to some special recruitment efforts to attract more black faculty, staff, and students. But the process left a bitter taste all around: many African Americans were frustrated at what appeared to them to be the tokenism of what remained essentially white institutions, while many whites fixated on the separatist rhetoric of some black groups, the continuing problems in African American neighborhoods, and the poor preparation of some of the newly admitted.

## The Swarthmore Afro-American Students Society Sit-in of 1969

Almost simultaneous with a Penn sit-in was the occupation by the Swarthmore Afro-American Students Society (SASS) of the pastoral Quaker school's Admissions Office on January 9, 1969. In existence for three years, SASS had long been concerned about the situation facing African American students on a campus that, despite its history of liberalism, had essentially remained white. Between 1953 and 1963, ten African Americans enrolled at Swarthmore; there was only one black, an Ethiopian, on the faculty. SASS began to call for increased black enrollment, with support programs to ensure that entering students could maximize their chances of success, the hiring of an African American assistant dean of admissions, and a black counselor to provide supportive services.

Throughout the year before the building takeover, there were murmurings in the college press. A February 1968 editorial on Black Power defended campus blacks against the charge of "hypersensitivity" but asserted that "the only real solution is eventual assimilation of the Negro into American culture." The editors lamented that "the black power movement will probably hinder this assimilation" but agreed that militancy was needed "to scare the people in power who have been unwilling to give it before." In March, a letter criticized the paper for avoiding "the friction (sometimes only a vague irritation) that exists here between black and white students," and, following the assassination of Dr. King, the editors bemoaned the "increasingly isolated and alienated" situation of most African American students at the college. At the same time, SASS chairman Clinton Etheridge declared that "Swarthmore subverts Black minds by bringing them to the college for a White oriented objective rather than a Black one"; he distinguished "race-conscious Blacks" from "white-oriented" ones, stressing that the former reject an "integrationist ethic."[38]

But when the freshman class of 1968 included only a disappointing eight African Americans, a rift widened between the administration's Admissions Policy Committee (APC) and SASS, which had been participating in special recruitment programs. Criticized by SASS leaders Etheridge and Don Mizell, APC chair Dean Frederick Hargadon revised and distributed throughout the campus a thirty-page report on the college's efforts, aided by foundation funds, to increase minority enrollment. The report included data in tabular form, without the use of names, of at-risk African American students. Rather than ameliorating the situation, the report set off a series of protests and demands that culminated in the January 9 action.[39]

SASS walked out of the APC meeting, feeling that Hargadon was unwilling to concede to their demands for fundamental revision of the report. At the rump meeting, which included eight black students, the APC agreed to propose an increase in black applicants, with supportive services and staff, and the development of preparatory programs for "low-risk" applicants. The issue of opening Swarthmore's doors to "at-risk" students remained a stumbling block to agreement, however. But they continued to meet over the following weeks into mid-December. Meanwhile, SASS fine-tuned their demands as "preconditions for co-operation" with APC, but a meeting in early November failed to produce consensus. SASS was particularly insistent that the college agree to a serious exploration of existing and needed services for at-risk applicants.[40]

By late 1968, matters had escalated over SASS's objectives and APC's intentions. SASS was criticized for taking a "militant separatist" posture during recruitment weekends. Nevertheless, Student Council voted to endorse SASS's four demands. APC's much-awaited report was presented on December 18, urging as a target a minimum of twenty black recruits each year, with five to ten acceptable below conventional standards but "believed to possess other qualities which will enable them to 'close the gap' in their academic preparation," with supportive services available on an experimental basis. SASS escalated the conflict by describing the proposals as the product of a "white Anglo-Saxon Protestant liberal mind-set" and proceeded on December 23 to send to President Courtney Smith nonnegotiable demands, to be met by a deadline of January 7, 1969, or SASS would have to "do whatever is necessary to obtain acceptance of same." The demands called for ten to twenty at-risk black recruits per year, and a commitment to enroll 150 within six years, plus support services and staff. SASS also attacked Dean Hargadon, demanding that he be replaced by fall 1969 unless their demands were met. President Smith's initial response was that "this College has never [been] and must never be governed by demands or moved by threats."[41]

The conflicts between SASS and the Swarthmore administration were consistent with those occurring at other schools over race.[42] SASS rejected what they called "consensus-seeking, let's work it out" academic liberalism as morally flaccid and manipulative; in effect, they did not trust the integrity of the white administrators. As such, it made nonnegotiable demands, seeking evidence of goodwill through what amounted to surrender. Administrators, as well as some faculty and students, found such a posture outside the moral parameters of liberal academic culture. Moreover, at nonelite, more traditional, often publicly funded or sectarian institutions there was a deeply entrenched power structure within the administration, accustomed to being in charge and quick to react defensively and coercively to student challenges.[43] But at Swarthmore there was a tradition of open and respectful dialogue moving toward consensus, albeit within a framework that remained paternalistic. Indeed, SASS, despite its militant demands, tended to remain within the college's traditions of polite discourse. There was little revolutionary rhetoric and nothing comparable to the threats of and actual use of violence at Cornell and San Francisco State.[44]

When SASS activists did take over the Admissions Office, they systematically closed off access to others and politely but forcefully asked those present, including deans and secretaries, to leave. They then called a press conference to sharpen their demands, including black participation in all decision making and a promise of no disciplinary action taken against them for the office seizure. White students divided into moderate and radical factions; both supported the demands, but the former called for a less coercive process to determine decision-making matters. The faculty agreed to a student request for a two-day suspension of classes to address relevant issues, asked SASS to present their demands at a faculty meeting, but concluded with a note of criticism over finding itself "faced with a resort to force and a refusal to make use of rational process."

In the days following the takeover, the campus was a beehive of activity, with meetings and workshops involving all parties. Over the weekend the faculty proposed the creation of an Ad Hoc Black Admissions Committee (AHBAC) made up of three faculty, five students (including representation from SASS), and two administrators, which was to recommend the hiring of a black admissions officer and black counselor and provide supportive services for minority admissions, including approximately ten at-risk students. The faculty went so far as to offer SASS a veto over the selection of the counselor. Meanwhile students called for fundamental changes in decision making, such that groups affected could choose their own representatives.

There was an incredible amount of effort by administration, faculty, and students to resolve the crisis in ways with which all sides could live. There was considerable delicacy in agreeing to what were essentially black nationalist, even separatist demands in ways that preserved the college's ideals of inclusion and openness. The more radical students, led by John Braxton, tended to follow the lead of SASS, refraining from making nonracial student power demands and deciding not to move forward with their own direct action disruptions. In the midst of what seemed to be progress toward resolution, President Smith told an assembly of the entire Swarthmore community that he was proud of the way all parties, including SASS, were handling the crisis. He was prepared to support faculty proposals on AHBAC but concluded with a plea that all parties commit themselves to mutual respect and consensus building. Quaker liberalism was facing a severe test of the parameters of its patience at Swarthmore. Over the next few days, SASS appeared to escalate and then temper its demands, such that agreements with the faculty proposals seemed still close. SASS thanked and commended the faculty "thus far" even as it "sincerely and earnestly" noted its belief that "a lasting, genuine settlement package [had] yet to be produced." Then on January 16, a Thursday, President Smith died of a heart attack. SASS chose to leave the Admissions Office, issuing a statement calling for a moratorium on dialogue to allow the entire college community to mourn the tragedy.[45]

Among President Smith's last words was a poignant expression of hope and failure: "We have lost something precious at Swarthmore— the feeling that force and disruptiveness are just not our way. But maybe we can see to it that this one time is the exception that proves the rule." The *Phoenix* editors, while arguing that SASS's sit-in was "premature," added that "Escalation was avoided, communications never broke down, and intransigency never appeared," complimenting faculty and students for their maturity in the midst of crisis. But letters to the editor suggested a still bruised and emotionally distraught community. Some asked, "Did the protesters 'kill' President Smith?"[46] In comparison with the confrontational clashes on other campuses, involving both white radical and black militant students, the Swarthmore sit-in was negotiated with thoughtfulness and sensitivity to the feelings and interests of others. But SASS's style and demands serve as a marker of a campus activism increasingly shaped by a form of identity politics that remains with us into the twenty-first century. Liberal and radical whites yielded, characteristically defending black rhetorical and tactical excess, including contradictory calls for exclusive control and community legitimation, by invoking a history of racism. In many ways, such campus battles were consistent with the shift to affirmative action, the claim that past injustices demanded present and future forms of special consideration, and the case can be made that such demands were essential to a realistic quest for equal opportunity. Liberal institutions like Swarthmore sought to accommodate claims to both diversity and unity, group and corporate identity, separation and assimilation. Indeed, the struggle with these dilemmas continues.[47]

## The Penn Sit-in of 1969

One of the most significant later campus struggles in the Philadelphia area took place at the University of Pennsylvania in early 1969. On February 18, 1969, Penn SDS organized a demonstration and march to begin at 11 A.M. in front of College Hall. After some speeches, several hundred marchers made a series of demands in front of the University City Science Center (UCSC), including a call for the return of UCSC properties to the local African American community; the granting of significant money by UCSC, Penn, and local bankers and realtors for community housing; and, returning to an ongoing concern, a declaration within the UCSC charter that absolutely no military or classified research be tolerated. The demonstrators returned to campus to confront President Gaylord Harnwell. At one point, a black militant from the local community threatened Harnwell: "I hope you don't croak before the revolution is over, because I want you around so you can be our puppet. You're going to have to be converted or eliminated."

The politics of gesture and rhetoric could not have been more striking; the white activists offered "hearty applause," and then the militant introduced himself, shook Harnwell's hand, and, turning to the television cameras, put his arm around the Penn president's shoulders. When Harnwell then called for time to reflect on the demands, Joe Mikuliak, the SDS leader, after being shouted down for trying to persuade the crowd to move to another room to discuss the situation, called for an immediate sit-in until demands were met. And so began a six day sit-in at the University of Pennsylvania College Hall. It was not an auspicious beginning.[48]

By academic year 1968–69, there had been several developments that would influence campus organizing efforts in Philadelphia, and specifically the Penn sit-in. For one, there was by this point a much more developed coordination and integration of areawide movement activities, especially those focused on particular colleges and universities. New Left students at the Catholic colleges still felt isolated and marginal and enormous transformations on their respective campuses and a much greater openness toward dissent. But they could feel part of a larger student, peace, and countercultural movement. It had always been the case that activist Villanovans joined with Bryn Mawr and Haverford radicals; by 1968–69 such synergies enveloped all the area colleges, including many not discussed in this study, such as West Chester and Cheyney State Universities, Lincoln University, The Community College of Philadelphia, Rosemont College, Chestnut Hill College, and Philadelphia College of Textiles. As such, when Penn SDS began its sit-in at College Hall, radical students from other campuses were aware of these activities, covered them in their newspapers and underground press, and offered some solidarity and people-power in support.[49]

In addition, there was a more problematic development: the existence of several Marxist-Leninist organizations, each determined to take advantage of local struggles, each relying on a dedicated cadre, the attraction of its ideological, strategic, and tactical certainties, and a willingness to outlast and consequently wear down all adversaries in the many meetings that resulted from campus activities. This was not a new phenomenon on the Left; the Communists and Trotskyists were notorious for using such manipulative and deceptive tactics in the 1930s. Throughout the 1960s, Old Left groups made operations problematic for radical and liberal activists who eschewed disingenuous infiltration techniques, the use of fronts, and the disciplined enforcement of political stances, or "lines." By early 1969, there were also the Marxist-Leninist remnants of SDS—for example, the Weathermen, Revolutionary Youth Movement II (RYM2), Maoist Progressive Labor Party, Trotskyist Youth Against War and Fascism, and, especially involved in the Penn struggle, the Labor Committee.[50]

The National Caucus of Labor Committees (NCLC, the Labor Committee) emerged out of a June 1968 SDS national convention and formed committees in New York, Philadelphia, and a few other cities. Its leadership included ex-Trotskyist Lynn Marcus, several activists expelled from the Progressive Labor Party, and a group at Columbia University. The Labor Committee became controversial when, during the Ocean Hill-Brownsville struggles over community control of public schools, they sided with the striking American Federation of Teachers. As a result, they were expelled from SDS; however, they continued to call themselves the SDS Labor Committee in classically Old Left manipulative mode.[51] One of their key leaders, Steve Fraser, was a student at Temple University and sparked the growth of organizational support at both Swarthmore and Penn with a sharply ideological, pro-working-class analysis centering on what they called a "socialist re-industrialization" of the economy. The Labor Committee argued in favor of confiscatory taxes on what they perceived as wasteful and parasitic investment. Their sense of certainty, the appearance they gave of being more scientific, that is, more legitimately Marxist-Leninist than their rivals, the specificity of both their analysis and their proposals, made the organization attractive to some New Leftists floundering after the self-destruction of SDS and wary of the adventurism of the Weathermen and other factions. The Labor Committee was the most important sectarian force during the sit-in at the University of Pennsylvania.[52]

Penn's institutional history, especially that of the 1960s, also influenced the way the Penn sit-in unfolded. A significant number of veterans of previous student struggles—graduate students Jules Benjamin, Bob Brand, and several others—remained in the area and offered counsel on ways to resolve the crisis. There were faculty members—like Philip Pochoda, Sol Wirth, Charles Price, and Robert Rutman—with considerable experience in facilitating negotiations and effective communications between administration, faculty, students, and the community. And, although the Penn administration under Gaylord Harnwell had often handled student demands clumsily and had consequently played into the hands of the militants, there were examples of wise counsel, particularly from the Rev. Jack Russell, the university's vice provost, who played a critical role in negotiating between groups. The Christian Association (CA) also offered its experience and mediating services at all times. Last, there was the local African American community, led by Herman Wrice of the Young Great Society (YGS), Andrew Jenkins of Mantua Community Planners (MCP), the Rev. Ed Sims from the Volunteer Community Resources Corporation (VCRC), and Forrest Adams from the Mantua Mini School, all of whom contributed to the negotiated outcome.[53]

The sit-in began as did many others of the late 1960s: impulsively, without a clear sense of direction but with the air filled with abstract and revolutionary rhetoric. Indeed, those involved were looking over their shoulders to possible worst-case scenarios, all of which focused on the risks of violent confrontation between this elite Ivy institution and the surrounding, low-income African American community. In that sense, the Penn sit-in was a permutation of the prototype—the Columbia University strike of April 1968. Yet the results sharply differed, in part because virtually all parties worked cooperatively to avoid the Morningside Heights outcome of a police assault on barricaded students and the ever-present concerns about the actions spilling over into Harlem.[54]

Joe Mikuliak, the SDS leader, noting that prior to the sit-in his group "had never had more than 150 people at a rally and . . . was often heckled to absurdity," was surprised by the extent to which students rallied in support. The 350 became 1,000 by that first evening, a "most amazing and positive occurrence." The fruits of earlier efforts, including the Christian Association, Project Mississippi, and the 1967 sit-in over secret research, all contributed to the outpouring of support in College Hall.[55] Immediately, conciliating forces, spearheaded by the Rev. John Scott of the CA, began to reach out to radical and liberal students, administrators, and community activists. Late in the evening, SDS leaders negotiated guidelines for the sit-in, including procedures for discussion and, importantly, the ongoing access of all parties to College Hall at all times. A later CA report describes these agreements as setting "this demonstration apart from other campus demonstrations across the country" and setting "a tone of dialogue for all that followed."[56]

Others saw things differently. The SDS Labor Committee always saw the issue of demands as "not goals or ends in themselves" but "a mobilization of student forces to be immediately linked as an organizing and rallying point, to members of the disorganized and fragmented black community," all to be ultimately linked to the white working class. They wanted to focus attention on the ways the local corporate elite controlled the University City Science Center (UCSC) and, therefore, to hold them fiscally responsible for exploiting local blacks. As such, they demanded that UCSC construction be stopped and that its corporate sponsors provide 1,200 units of low-income housing as part of their reparations. From their perspective, the CA was engaged in liberal cooptation in alliance with the corporate elite, the university administration, SDS and liberal student leaders, and corrupt African American self-styled leaders.[57]

In fact, those seeking to manage the sit-in were initially concerned about disruptive responses from both angry mainstream students involved in Interfraternity Weekend and Frank Rizzo's police. A rumor control center was established, and the striking students organized to ensure that College Hall remained clean and orderly. Perhaps most significantly, student leaders, including Dina Portnoy from the College of Women, persuaded both the Interfraternity Council and the Panhellenic Sorority Council to support the sit-in's demands. Therefore, at an early stage, the radicals were able to portray themselves accurately as representing the majority of students. There was always a tension between radicals and liberals, but in this case they united against what they perceived as a common enemy: those like the Labor Committee and others, mostly not from Penn, who called for "barricading" the hall and preparing for violent confrontation.[58] The liberal editorial board at the *DP* supported the sit-in but issued its own warning: "The University of Pennsylvania is a great university. We seek to improve it by cleansing it. We do not seek to destroy it."[59]

This was important in that the Columbia strikers were prone to define the university in reductionist terms as merely the instrument of

capitalist, imperialist, and racist power. Many radicals by the late
1960s were viewing notions of academic freedom and an open campus
as fraudulent, even pernicious covers for the university's underlying
repressive nature. They welcomed stripping away the veneer of tolerance to demonstrate the true fascist core to those they considered
naive. In brief, they had utter contempt for higher education, seeing it
exclusively as an instrument of class power. Those who held such a
view at Penn never achieved ascendancy.[60]

African American community leaders proceeded cautiously, with the
City-Wide Black Community Council rallying behind West Philadelphians Wrice, Jenkins, Sims, and Adams. On the fourth day, Friday,
February 21, Wrice offered the requests of a united black community
for land, a community development fund, and a role in the decision-
making process concerning university expansion. This became the
students' position as well. That same day, the university trustees made
their counter-offer, which included appointing students to a UCSC
advisory committee; authorizing Renewal Housing, Inc., the non-
profit organization created by African Americans to address lower-
income housing needs, to do a needs assessment; approving faculty
condemnation of military research at UCSC; and forming a new council, including administrators, faculty, students, and community leaders, to advise on university-community development.[61]

Whereas most believed that negotiations were moving toward a
successful resolution, the Labor Committee and other New Left elements were disturbed and sought to disrupt what they saw as a sellout.
They criticized Penn SDS for saying, "We don't want another Columbia here." Others claimed, "The sitters-in settled for procedural modi-
fications, instead of intensifying the struggle to force acceptance of
their substantive demands."[62] The Labor Committee countered with
an Alliance for Jobs, Education, and Housing, which they claimed represented the true interests of area residents and had the support of
the local Black Panthers. Over the weekend, as the black community
successfully addressed what turned out to be exaggerated Labor
Committee assertions of community support, the student negotiators
fended off Labor Committee demands, most being voiced by students
representing other area colleges. As a result, the Labor Committee
people walked out and, soon thereafter, the student negotiators
achieved consensus. They then met with trustees and African American leaders on Sunday to finalize the agreement, which brought the
six-day sit-in to a close.[63]

Those involved in the settlement claimed victory. Sociologist Phil
Pochoda suggested that the outcome "may be the single greatest internal and external change in an American university." Anthropology

professor Sol Wirth concluded, "Nobody lost. Everyone won. The University has gained in stature. It was a learning experience of unparalleled magnitude." The quadripartite commission, made up of five local residents chosen by Renewal Housing, five students chosen by the organizers of the sit-in, five faculty representatives of their senate, "all but one of whom must be resident in West Philadelphia," and five trustees or their representatives, was mandated to implement the agreement that the university would match all housing demolitions with equivalent replacements, that a sizable community development fund would come from the private sector, and that $75,000 and appropriate office space would be pledged annually by the university to the commission for staffing and operations. Finally, sensitive to the criticisms from the Labor Committee and others about placing a tax burden on the white working class, the agreement called for new housing to "be funded not at the expense of a wage tax increase . . . nor a general lowering of the standard of living of the people of Philadelphia."[64]

Mikuliak called the sit-in "one of the greatest victories for a radical movement at an American university," concluding, "We ain't stopping now, we got a movement now." Reflecting on the settlement years later, College of Women activist Lynne Hoagland, by then married to Mikuliak, recalled, "We had a very 'bust head' police commissioner, and Penn could have easily called the police and said, 'get these kids outta here,' and they never did." And yet years later, liberal student leader Ira Harkavy, by then director of the Penn Center for Community Partnerships, noted that "nothing was really institutionalized" and that the trend of inner-city deterioration continued, despite the settlements and promises. As opposed to the earlier Penn struggle over secret military research, the College Hall sit-in produced more the appearance than the substance of change.

Mikuliak's hopes for a growing New Left student movement were stilled by the complete disintegration of SDS. Penn, like many campuses, would explode in reaction to President Nixon's invasion of Cambodia in April 1970 and the subsequent killing of students at both Kent State and Jackson State. But for the most part student activism began to decline as the Vietnam War drew toward its end.[65] As "acute apathy" reigned and a disappointing 200 students showed up for discussions of the quadripartite commission's plans, acid guru Timothy Leary drew 2,500 at the Irvine Auditorium, while 100 African American students called the Penn administration racist for firing a black administrator and failing to fund an essentially separatist advising program.[66]

Penn did not return to normal following spring 1970; indeed, the very nature of normalcy had been transformed by the movements and events of the preceding half decade.

## Frank Rizzo and the New Left Movement

At some distance in both geography and spirit from the Ivy League campus at Penn or the bucolic setting of Swarthmore, Police Commissioner Rizzo responded to black and white challenges with threats, scare tactics, intimidation, and, sometimes, the framing of activists. As he had moved against SNCC, the Revolutionary Action Movement (RAM), and the Black Panthers, so he went after NCLC while the University of Pennsylvania College Hall strike was being peacefully resolved.[67]

In February 1969, the Philadelphia police arrested eight members of the Labor Committee for distributing leaflets about the UCSC protests in front of two West Philadelphia public schools. Commissioner Rizzo justified the arrests by charging that evidence existed indicating that the Labor Committee was planning to blow up public schools, a ludicrous charge in light of the strikingly anti-adventurist public politics of this very small group. Two months later, the Civil Disobedience (CD) Squad raided the apartment of Labor Committee leaders Steve Fraser and Richard Borgman, claiming to find explosives they had heard about from an informant. Historians, as well as many Rizzo observers at the time and since, believe that the explosives were planted. A skeptical court reduced bail, and four years later the charges were dropped when the police failed to produce their informant.[68]

By the early 1970s, there were a variety of Marxist-Leninist sects in addition to the Labor Committee. There were a handful of SDS Weatherpeople, RYM2 activists, the youth affiliates of the Communists and Trotskyists—the Young Workers Liberation League (YWLL) and the Young Socialist Alliance (YSA) respectively—and a number of essentially local Communist groups seeking to reach out to the working class by moving into the river wards, especially blue-collar Kensington, and/or becoming what the Old Left called "colonizers," that is, middle-class activists taking jobs in industry to connect with the proletariat. The most important of the latter was the Philadelphia Workers Organizing Committee (PWOC), some of whose leaders had been involved with People for Human Rights before it disintegrated and with the *Free Press*. Many of these activists understood that an essentially white, middle-class movement made up mostly of Quakers, WASPs, and Jews, strong on elite campuses and in affluent, educated neighborhoods like Center City and Mount Airy and seeking to align itself with the emerging African American political community, was at a

Figure 21. Marchers in Center City, 1969 Moratorium. Robert J. Brand

disadvantage in winning the loyalties of white ethnics—Catholics and working-class Jews—away from Frank Rizzo. Over the next decade, possibly several hundred activists were involved in such community and workplace organizing. Most left unsuccessful and frustrated. But some stayed, learned how to listen rather than preach the secular gospel of Marx, Lenin, and Mao, and found that they had the talent to become effective voices of working people. A few went on to become leaders in Philadelphia's trade union movement; others played major roles in community organizations, several being appointed or elected to important citywide positions. Those who continued to privately affirm their identifications as "movement lefties" found that they were inexorably forced to come to terms with everyday political realities and learned to function, very effectively, as liberal reformers.[69]

Commissioner Rizzo tried to smear the *Free Press* group by having his close associate Albert Gaudiosi, a *Philadelphia Bulletin* reporter and later his campaign manager, write a series of articles about "The New Revolutionaries" in July 1970.[70] The articles spoke of the "10,000 or so members of the New Left Movement in the area, only about 100 . . . considered 'hardcore' revolutionaries—that is, persons devoting full time to organizing to overthrow the government." The most demonized of the hardcore was the *Free Press* and its leaders Bill and Judy Biggin, alleged to be allies of the Black Panther Party. Bill Biggin was a Canadian national and a graduate student at Temple University, where he had been a radical campus leader before starting what began as the *Temple Free Press*. The *Free Press* group, never particularly effective but highly visible because of their weekly newspaper, were merely a foil Frank Rizzo used to heighten the sense of crisis and, consequently, the persuasiveness of repressive measures, prior to the Black Panther convention scheduled in the weeks following the *Bulletin* series. At one point, Rizzo, who ordered surveillance, arrests, harassment, beatings, pressure on advertisers and printers, and deportation proceedings against members of the group, stated on television that "Bill Biggin and the *Free Press* are even more dangerous than the Panthers."[71] Only a 1972 court-ordered consent decree ended the police harassment of the *Free Press* group.

On an NBC network news special, Rizzo bragged of having files of 18,000 names; as he spoke, the cards of six peace activists were actually visible on home screens. Historian Frank Donner concludes, "There is no city in the United States where legal advocacy on behalf of minorities and the poor was subjected to such pressures—surveillance, smears, and abuse, not to speak of attacks by lower court judges who permitted themselves to become instruments of Rizzo's program of reprisal." It would not be accurate, however, to suggest that police

Figure 22. Overbrook High School demonstrators, 1969 Moratorium. Temple Urban Archives

repression was decisive in the decline of the white New Left movement in Philadelphia. In some ways, Rizzo's authoritarian and arbitrary actions lent credibility to organizations whose dogmatic politics destined them to marginality. But it is also the case that the repressive environment directed from the Roundhouse (police headquarters) and, later, City Hall threatened the constitutional rights of all Philadelphians, especially liberals and radicals, white and black. New Left activists, despite their characteristic contempt for mainstream reformers, found themselves forced to work in tandem with liberals in what became a decade-long struggle against the Rizzo administration and its tendency to run roughshod over constitutional guarantees of free speech and freedom of assembly.[72]

## The 1969 Mobilization and Moratorium

Despite the rhetorical and ideological excesses within the white New Left movement, there were impressive accomplishments in opposing the Indochina War in 1969 and 1970. The Moratorium and the Mobilization, and the responses to both the Cambodian invasion and then the Kent State killings, demonstrated the ability of antiwar activists to bring together an extraordinary number of people. In particular, Philadelphia peace activists, influenced by a Quaker ecumenism and spearheaded by the essentially pragmatic, inclusive organizing of the Philadelphia Resistance, with considerable support from Old Left and liberal organizations such as Americans for Democratic Action (ADA), were able to minimize the destructive influence of what the anarchist Murray Bookshin called "all the old crap of the thirties," that is, the crude reductionism and ideological arrogance that was the worst of the old—and now the new—Communist movement.[73]

In Philadelphia, there was impressive coordination between the more liberal Moratorium and more radical Mobilization efforts, influenced by leaders like Stuart Meacham, peace education secretary of AFSC, and supported by the anchors of the peace movement—SANE, Women Strike for Peace (WSP), Women's International League for Peace and Freedom (WILPF)—and by the younger activists in the Philadelphia Resistance and A Quaker Action Group (AQAG). On Good Friday 1969, Meacham participated in a draft board silent protest only broken when he and others read the names of those Americans GIs killed in the war. It took seventeen hours. This Philadelphia innovation became the extraordinary March of Death, preceding the Moratorium demonstration in November, during which thousands marched solemnly up to the main entrance of the White

House to speak the name of a killed American soldier and then place a placard with that name into a casket. It was one of the most moving and effective efforts in the history of the peace movement.[74]

By 1970, the Philadelphia movement could mobilize or reach into every university, college, and many public and private secondary schools; into most Montgomery, Delaware, and Bucks County suburban communities; into churches and synagogues; into progressive unions. There were developing voices, caucuses, and advocacy groups among teachers, attorneys, social workers, planners, artists, businesspeople, physicians, and other health-care and mental health professionals. And there were alliances, sometimes difficult but nevertheless significant, with African American and other minority community and student organizations; with a developing feminist network of both academics who created Women's Studies programs and activists who established health centers, rape counseling and reproductive rights services, and consciousness-raising groups; and with the beginnings of gay and lesbian organizations.[75] Of course, as the war began to wind down, the broader peace movement suffered considerable decline and its New Left component collapsed. There remained, however, a sizable legacy of activists and organizations. Certainly Frank Rizzo would dominate the political landscape, especially with his 1971 election as mayor, but the city of Philadelphia and its colleges, city and suburban, had been transformed by the challenges raised by the New Left and its allies.

## The Legacy of Philadelphia's New Left Movement

How is one to assess the significance and the legacy of Philadelphia's New Left? There is also the question how to formulate the stages of New Left history, much of which, unfortunately, remains mired in ideological disputes over the claims by some veteran New Leftists of a falling away over time from quintessential values, that is, from participatory democracy. Finally, there is the issue of how to coordinate considerations of the New Left with overlapping movements and institutions, like the broader peace movement, the movement against the war in Indochina, the civil rights and Black Power movements, second-wave feminism, the gay and lesbian movements, environmentalism, the counterculture, and liberalism.[76]

The massive responses to Cambodia and Kent State marked the peak influence of the New Left and peace movements in Philadelphia.[77] But as the Indochina wars moved toward a U.S. withdrawal in 1973, campuses began to quiet down. There were still the major peace organizations, Quaker and liberal, and the McGovern campaign in 1972;

there was also a Vietnam Veterans Against the War movement and a host of new coalitions pushing the nation toward a withdrawal from the war. The peace movement in 1973 looked fundamentally different from 1963; it had been transformed by the events of the 1960s, including the rise of a New Left. The center of gravity had shifted leftward. For example, by 1969, Philadelphia SANE, an essentially liberal organization sensitive to being red-baited in the early 1960s, was being chaired by University of Pennsylvania professor and longtime activist Robert J. Rutman, who called on the organization to "play a unique role developing a broad based anti-imperialist peace movement . . . based on opposition to the imperialist character of U.S. policy" and rejecting "the entire fabric of cold-war anti-communist policy."[78] Organizations such as SANE and AFSC were deeply affected by 1960s radicalism, although one must add that to some extent the times simply encouraged the full and open expression of pre-1960s Old Left and pacifist views as older McCarthyist fears receded. There were staffing influences that would extend over the following decades; many New Leftists, as the tides of radicalism receded, found places of employment within the institutional structures of the Society of Friends and more secular organizations. Others, reflecting on the limited class composition of the New Left, sought to build bridges to the traditional working class, establishing community organizing projects and sometimes taking factory jobs. Many more struggled with the old Christian dilemma of living in the world but not being of it. They sought to find ways to make a living consistent with their skills and interests as teachers, academics, doctors, lawyers, and social workers, but in the service of "the people," a value that continued to inspire and motivate activists.

The New Left was formed by the coming together of three challenges: the challenge of racism, that of the Vietnam War, and, finally, the broader notion that even an affluent social order and culture based on the modern corporation and the suburb left much to be desired in terms of empowerment, solidarity, community, and meaning. In the argument over whether there was a "good" older New Left and then a "bad" later New Left, one must conclude that such a dichotomy is essentially counterproductive to any understanding of what is a contradictory and complex phenomenon. The early New Left in Philadelphia was, indeed, inspired by the civil rights revolution in its nonviolent, integrationist period. It was also framed by a radical critique of bourgeois culture, a rejection of the cash nexus. Finally, it began to grow from its essentially elite constituencies at colleges like Swarthmore and Haverford with the Americanization of the Vietnam

War in 1965. At the same time, a deep reading of the available historical record suggests that it is somewhat of a conceit to suggest that the
early New Left, especially SDS, in the period 1962–65 was a model
against which later degeneration should be judged. Early SDS, including its Economic Research and Action Project (ERAP) component in
Chester and Philadelphia, was already self-consciously radical, con-
temptuous of both liberal and Old Left elements, and enamored with
Third World revolutionary developments in Cuba and China. The
seeds of a later tendency toward Maoism can be found in the early period. In addition, the all too characteristic American claim of inno-
cence, the metanarrative of naivete shattered by historical reality,
always should be taken with a sizable grain of salt.[79]

What historians of the New Left need to assess is the contradictory
unfolding of such dispositions, something that I hope I have done in
this book. At precisely the moment when the Vietnam War would lead
a large number of youth toward dissent and possible activism, the
New Left lunged forward "from protest to resistance." It also moved
away from a tentative exploration of the humanist dimensions of
Marxism—that is, the young Marx; new working-class theory; radicals
in the professions—which might have been more appropriate to a
postindustrial order, to either new versions of the worst of Marxist reductionism or various forms of adventurism inspired by Mao Zedong,
Fidel Castro, Che Guevara, Régis Debray, Frantz Fanon, and others in
the Third World pantheon. The move toward rhetorical excess, abstraction, and self-righteousness ensured that opposition to the war
would be trumped by hostility to the antiwar movement, at least to
those aspects of it most influenced by the above. The impressive
demonstrations of 1969 and 1970 brought out thousands of people,
most of whom found the directions offered by the New Left to be out
of touch with their everyday lives. Like the Old Left, the New Left
became a turnstile; events brought in many recruits, but sectarian
practices ensured that most of them would not remain.

Within this national profile of emergent possibility and lost opportunity, the Philadelphia New Left had some decided advantages.
Philadelphia's Quaker-based peace institutions were always a ballast
against the worst of Left—Old or New—ideological dogmatisms. As
such, there was a weaker SDS influence in the City of Brotherly Love:
Swarthmore in the early ERAP period, Temple and Penn much more
unevenly in the late 1960s. The Philadelphia Resistance was able to resist many of the ideological pitfalls that plagued and finally destroyed
SDS; although it imbibed some of the intoxicating Third World romantic brew, it kept its eyes on the prize: the war, the draft, and complicit

institutions. Employing humor and solid organizing, the Philadelphia
Resistance sustained the higher moral ground throughout its years of
existence.

It is this higher moral ground that the early New Left held, even as
it remained limited to elite campuses. It stood for participatory democracy, an interracial movement of the poor, and the beloved community of racial integration and nonviolence. That many early New
Leftists, both red-diaper babies and those from liberal homes, were already looking toward a more revolutionary politics sometimes as manipulative as that of the Old Left does not deny the compelling
qualities of that earlier message.

It was between early 1965 and late 1967, between the first teach-ins
and the March on the Pentagon, that the New Left found itself moving from relative marginality to high visibility. And it was precisely
during that short window of opportunity, following the defeat of de
jure segregation, that the New Left was forced to confront the explo-
sive and volatile legacy of race and racism. The six-year trajectory of
ghetto riots and the emergence of a Black Power politics exacerbated
the tendency of the white New Left toward more apocalyptic and essentially impatient strategies and tactics. In Philadelphia, People for
Human Rights (PHR) was created by those seeking to come to grips
with what seemed to them to be the pervasiveness of white racism, especially in a city increasingly dominated by the political ascendancy of
Frank Rizzo. By fall 1967, "long, hot summers" seemed to be more
prevalent, more violent. Black people were dying on the streets of
Newark and Detroit; black students were being beaten in front of
Philadelphia's school board building. Soon there would be a state
of emergency and martial law in nearby Wilmington, and the war
in Indochina, despite a rising crescendo of protests, petitions, and
demonstrations, continued to grind on, the death toll mounting for
Americans, Vietnamese, Cambodians, and Laotians. It is no wonder
that the movement responded with desperation and often lost its way.
How could one focus attention on the painfully slow work of political
education and institution building when there was such an immediate
need to act, to stop the war, to end racism? And how could young people, never renowned for their patience, take the longer view?

The schizophrenic qualities of the later 1960s, among the New Left
in Philadelphia and the nation at large, rest on the simultaneous eu-
phoria of revolutionary expectations and the deep, abiding despair of
feeling helpless, utterly ineffective, even facing the triumph of a
home-grown fascism. That New Leftists misread the political landscape is indisputable and tragic. That they had difficulty in understanding how their own confrontational style was playing into the

Figure 23. Three young demonstrators, 1969 Moratorium. Temple Urban Archives.

hands of those like George Wallace, Richard Nixon, Ronald Reagan, and Frank Rizzo is perfectly clear. That they often mistook the extraordinary emergence of a youthful counterculture of hippies and freaks, rock 'n' rollers and dopesters, underground papers and head shops, for a revolutionary youth movement was unfortunate. Without indulging in a "best of times, worst of times" cliché, it is clear that there was an intensity of events and forces during the late 1960s that made it appear to be either and both revolutionary and counter-revolutionary. The times were, indeed, intense and millennial, especially to the young.

As such, the times from 1967 until the end of the war were extraordinarily contradictory. Those who criticize the early SDS memoirists for denigrating the accomplishments of that period, especially regarding the rise of the women's movement, the gay and lesbian movements, environmentalism, and Black Power, make a compelling point. It is not until at least 1968–69 that one discovers any trace of these movements. What is noteworthy is that all of these political formations were both influenced *by* and simultaneously reacted *against* the white New Left. By the late 1960s, the New Left tendency toward a Third World revolutionary model—with important partial exceptions like the Philadelphia Resistance—framed much of the rhetoric and ideological posturing of at least the women's and gay and lesbian movements and, decidedly, the Black Power movement. In many ways this revolutionary élan inspired and sharply limited the appeal of all of these social movements. What indeed was the meaning of the notion of a gay liberation front, other than to mistranslate the need to proclaim and expand the boundaries of equality into the theatrics of playing at guerrilla war?[80] Given what we know about the horrors of Mao's Great Proletarian Cultural Revolution, not to speak of the Great Leap Forward of the late 1950s, the millions killed and ravaged by utopian repression, it is sobering to come to grips with the extent to which the New Left and related movements found inspiration in such fanaticism.[81]

And yet beneath the rhetoric, a more substantial core of purpose and meaning spearheaded the most radical and transformational movements: those seeking to ensure equality between men and women, straights and gays, blacks and whites, and all the others inspired by the civil rights movement—Latinos, Indians, Asians, the disabled—to complete the promise of the Declaration of Independence, and those seeking to reconcile Promethean conquest with the need not to destroy the natural environment. This was quite a challenge, much of it growing out of the civil rights movement but much of it an outgrowth of a New Left idealism, a vision of a less alienating, more inclusive democratic community.

## The Philadelphia Story

Philadelphia has rarely been featured in the histories of political radicalism, perhaps because of its proximity to New York to its north and Washington to its south, perhaps because it lacks the intellectual-academic complex of Boston or the hardscrabble asphalt of the Chicago of Nelson Algren and Studs Terkel. Unfortunately, all too much of the attention Philadelphia receives rests on the sensationalist and unrepresentative stories regarding the hippie murderer Ira Einhorn and the destruction of the idiosyncratic black group MOVE. Philadelphia's New Left certainly shared most of the features of the national movement, but it was distinctively local insofar as it existed within a Quaker pacifist nexus. In that regard, Philadelphia reinforces the need to pay attention to the links historian Doug Rossinow has drawn between the New Left and Protestant Christianity. The City of Brotherly Love produced a morally consistent, pragmatically grounded antiwar movement dominated by the Philadelphia Resistance and a base of rock solid organizations like SANE, WSP, WILPF, AFSC, AQAG, Friends Peace Committee, and its many community-based peace groups.[82]

The overriding economic, social, and political reality within which the Philadelphia New Left must be understood is the process of deindustrialization that ravaged both white and black working-class and poor communities. Indeed, it is important for students of the New Left and of 1960s social movements in general to anchor analyses in this fundamental urban crisis, which exacerbated all efforts to build cross-racial, class-based alliances. In Philadelphia, the New Left and related movements were ill equipped to respond to the collapse of the belatedly arriving New Deal coalition of elite Quaker WASPs and Jews, southern and eastern European Catholic workers, and African Americans. The Philadelphia Resistance never intended to become a grass-roots organization; its strength was its élan, its circle of friends, often living together, organizing together, consistent with the New Left's notion of a prefigurative community. Despite valiant efforts to reach out to GIs, community-based blacks, and working-class students, the Resistance was limited by its natural constituency of conscience, direct action, and risk-taking. It remained on the moral high ground but was not able to compete with the right-wing and often demagogic low ground personified by Frank Rizzo. Indeed, it would be unfair to impose that enormous burden on an organization whose focus was always the war.

People for Human Rights suffered from its increasing tendency toward romantic revolution, but even more from the ways in which its emphasis on racism reinforced an ideological divide, which played into the hands of conservative populism. To the extent that figures like Frank Rizzo could argue that they represented a new configuration of "the people," that is, the hard-working, nonprotesting producers, blue-collar and executive—Nixon's "silent majority"—they succeeded. Their foil was always the newly constructed and cynical alliance of "limousine liberals" and rioting blacks; the noisy demonstrators who hated America; those who did not understand family, church, community, or work. Many of those who followed PHR recognized the need to counter this critique, to incorporate social class into their analysis of racism, to reach out to white working people in the river ward. Several would go on to leadership positions in union locals and community-based, multiethnic organizations. Nevertheless, progressive movements, in Philadelphia and elsewhere in the nation, continue to suffer from the ways in which a conservative producerist strategy and metaphor marginalized them.[83]

British historian Eric Hobsbawm found his inspiration for what he called the "age of revolution" in the twin volcanos of the French and industrial revolutions.[84] For the New Left movement, the two decisive eruptions were the civil rights revolution and the Vietnam War. Without either, there might have been a New Left; after all, as historian Irwin Unger suggests, "the New Left was a phenomenon common to all the affluent industrial countries," and yet none shared the American centrality of civil rights and Vietnam.[85] The New Left was not alone in responding to these twin volcanos nor to the concatenation of other social forces—corporatization, deindustrialization, suburbanization, mass higher education, mass advertising, sexual liberalization—that transformed the nation and its culture. But it left an indelible mark on American responses to foreign policy crises—the "Vietnam syndrome" that George Bush proclaimed as transcended by the Gulf War—and in the greater inclusiveness of our culture.

Historian Michael Denning argues that the Old Left created a cultural front, what he calls "a laboring of American culture," a "proletarianizing" of that culture both in terms of pervasive themes and in terms of influence, participation, organization, and ideology. It may be fruitful to think of the New Left as enriching and transforming that essentially social-democratic cultural front. Think for a moment of a joint concert by Pete Seeger and Arlo Guthrie, Seeger's Old Left earnestness juxtaposed with Arlo's sly and boyish pranks: "Goodnight Irene" meets "Alice's Restaurant." The New Left's influence was bohemian, libertarian, communitarian, and utterly contradictory. The Old Left's moral strenuousness remained but was tempered by everything from *Mad* magazine to the Beatles, with added ingredients from figures as diverse as George Carlin, Country Joe McDonald, and Bruce Springsteen.[86] I do not mean to suggest that all the above was narrowly New Left; I do wish to suggest that one legacy of the New Left was a movement culture that increasingly merged, not always comfortably, with the Popular Front posture of the 1930s, to embody beleaguered yet continued utopian hopes of post-capitalist possibilities. Such a movement culture in progressive America was surely complicated by the simultaneous emergence of identity politics, which both participated in this reconfigured cultural front and challenged it in terms of gender, race, and other forms of identity. Finally, it is difficult to disentangle this Old Left/New Left entity both from countercultural legacies and from the ways those images have been incorporated into the highly sophisticated commodification of Madison Avenue.[87]

In Philadelphia one of the best embodiments of this legacy of what one might call a movement culture is Judy Wicks's White Dog Café at 3420 Sansom Street within the campus of the University of Pennsylvania, and long a meeting place for activists, radical intellectuals, and cultural rebels. A 2001 newsletter includes articles on Dutch marijuana policy, a dinner honoring the memory of Dr. King, an Earth Day Eco Tour and Picnic, a Freedom Seder, and events addressing feminism, racism, U.S. foreign policy, and health foods.[88] In addition, there have been scores of institutions throughout the city, such as the Bread and Roses Community Fund, the People's Fund, peace and solidarity organizations, women's and gay and lesbian organizations, and radical and progressive caucuses in the professions, some of which survive and all of which have carried the legacy of the New Left and its central notions of participatory democracy and a prefigurative politics.

## The Myth of the Big Chill

The New Left legacy, now intertwined with Old Left, identity politics, and more recent dissident political activism focusing on the issues of globalization, can be measured by the remarkable continuities in the lives of many of Philadelphia's most important New Left veterans. A pernicious and inaccurate myth that undermines the movements of the 1960s claims that most New Left radicals have either burned out or sold out. This conservative mythology emphasizes the "second thoughts" of another "God that failed" generation—David Horowitz, Peter Collier, and Ronald Radosh being the most visible, and the strange paths that figures such as Jerry Rubin and Eldridge Cleaver have taken. Movies such as *The Big Chill* ask: Is that all it was—a fashion, a transitory moment out of which chastened activists returned to mainstream notions of work, family, and community?[89]

In fact, it is striking how many of Philadelphia's leading New Left activists have found ways to remain consistent with their movement values. There are attorneys who have played leading roles in civil liberties, civil rights, and labor litigation since completing law school in the late 1960s and early 1970s, most prominently David Rudovsky (PHR), winner of a MacArthur "genius" Award in 1986 for his work in defense of prisoner rights; David Kairys, author of several books on the law and social justice; Judith Chomsky (Resistance), who has worked in defense of workers' rights; and Steve Gold (PHR), long involved in advocacy for the disabled and in efforts to support parents and students within Philadelphia's troubled school system. There are a sizable number of former New Leftists, like Eva Gold (Resistance), Ron Whitehorn (PHR), Dina Portnoy (Resistance), Lynn Strieb (Resistance), and Rhoda Kanevsky (Resistance), who have become teachers and educators, long committed to addressing the abysmal failures of the city's public school system, especially regarding minority children. In the field of public health, there are planners like Bob Brand (Resistance), once a staffer with Hospital Workers Union 1199 and now heading Solutions for Progress, Inc.; and socially conscious physicians, nurses, and health care professionals like Barbara Gold (PHR), Carol Rodgers (PHR), Muffin Friedman (SDS Labor Committee), Frank Ackerman, a Swarthmore activist now working in Cambridge, Massachusetts, and Jean Hunt, a Bryn Mawr dropout who became an RN and is now Program Director for Children, Youth, and Families with the William Penn Foundation. Several New Left activists became significant trade union leaders: Roger Tauss (Penn), former president of the Transport Workers Union local, Tom Cronin (Cheyney State) with AFSCME, and Wendell Young (West Chester), of the Food and Commercial Workers. John Braxton (Swarthmore), who served prison time for his resistance to the draft, has been active in Teamsters democratization movements and, more recently, the Jobs for Justice Coalition. Michael DiBerardinis, a St. Joseph's graduate and Catholic peace activist who moved to Kensington to organize working people in a multicultural alliance, went on to become Philadelphia's commissioner of recreation under Mayor Ed Rendell and most recently vice president for programs of the William Penn Foundation. Tony Avirgan (Resistance) is director of the Global Policy Network of the Economic Policy Institute in Washington, D.C.; Martha Honey (Resistance) is a Fellow at the Institute for Policy Studies, director of its Peace and Security Program, and codirector of its Foreign Policy in Focus Program. I have been impressed with how many of the most active figures of the 1960s have found ways to sustain their essential values, even though sobered by events and most assuredly with compromises and an occasional hiatus to come to grips with personal issues.[90] There have been some tragic deaths, most notably Peter Countryman (NSM, PHR), Leo Kormis (Penn SDS), Bob Edenbaum (Temple Draft Counseling Center, SANE), Ariel Loewy (Haverford faculty and peace activist), Kiyoshi (Steve) Kuromiya, a Penn SDSer who became the city's most important AIDS activist, and, most recently, David Gracie, who was without doubt the most influential and important adult influence on Philadelphia's New Left.[91]

The legacy of Philadelphia's New Left remains impressive, if in some regards problematical. Radical visions have been tempered by the collapse of the socialist project associated with the fall of Soviet Communism, the crises of welfare state economies, the revival of conservative, free-market capitalism, the politics of the "third way" associated with Bill Clinton and Tony Blair, and the anti-utopianism that characterizes recent times. For all practical purposes, veterans of the New Left work with those they formerly held in contempt—liberals. Oddly, the Old Left Popular Front euphemism of being a "progressive" has been restored as the least problematical way to describe those who still seek some kind of social democratic welfare state. But movement aspects still reveal themselves, at their worst, in romantic and too often uncritical identifications with Third World revolutionary movements, whether Sandinista or Zapatista; in refusals to acknowledge the ways markets, private property, free trade, and profits remain essential to building a society and a world both productive and free; in tendencies to romanticize and embrace any and all forms of deviance as resistance to capitalism and bourgeois forms of social control; in adherence to aspects of political correctness that too facilely suppress expression of differences. In brief, the New Left declined in many ways because of its own difficulties in coming to grips with the values of liberal democracy and its carriers—the American middle and working classes. Perhaps most striking in reconsidering the history of Philadelphia's New Left and its legacy is an obliviousness to, if not a contempt for, the suburbs and their mostly middle-class residents. Philadelphia movement veterans, like those throughout the nation, but especially those in cities, have paid an enormous price for their ambivalence and often hostility toward that fully one-half and growing part of the American voting population who live in the suburbs.

At the same time, Philadelphia's New Left can stand proud of its role in opposing the Indochina wars; in being part of that vanguard of whites who recognized the centrality of confronting race and racism in order to truly fulfill the American promise of becoming a democratic society; in the contributions of movement activists who were central in the creation of women's and gay and lesbian movements and organizations; and in consistently struggling, particularly during the tenure of Frank Rizzo, to uphold the rule of law, First Amendment constitutional protections, and the rights of all minorities, children, the disabled, and prisoners. The notions of participatory democracy, of an inclusive and involved citizenry, of living one's life consistent with one's core values—these remain as relevant in the twenty-first century as they were when proclaimed during the 1960s.

Reflecting on my research, I most recall a conversation with Dennis Foreman, a late 1960s graduate of St. Joe's who went on to become one of southern New Jersey's very best social studies teachers and school principals. Foreman told me that he had been initially inspired by the challenges he encountered in classes with Jack Malinowski, at that time a young philosophy instructor and a draft and tax resister, now a staffer at the AFSC. The ethical focus he associated with Malinowski's teaching and personal witness, the moral imperative to stand up for justice and equality, to struggle against oppression and violence—against evil—led him to become a teacher of the Holocaust and other horrors, most especially racism. Foreman's life and the ways the movement influenced him force us toward a fuller recognition of the complexities in assessing the 1960s, the ways the New Left movement offers a legacy of good works that go well beyond the continuing efforts of its veterans. It must include those they have influenced in multifold ways to take citizenship seriously. For that, Philadelphians owe a measure of gratitude to those who have fought the good fight. They have made Philadelphia a little less of a "private city" and a little more able to justify its claim to be the City of Brotherly (and Sisterly) Love.

# Notes

*Introduction: The Movement and the City of Brotherly Love*

1. Paul Lyons, *Philadelphia Communists: The Movement and the City of Brotherly Love* (Philadelphia: Temple University Press, 1982), 160–68; Maurice Isserman, *If I Had a Hammer: The Death of the Old Left and the Birth of the New Left* (New York: Basic Books, 1987), 9–11.

2 James Miller, *"Democracy in the Streets": From Port Huron to the Siege of Chicago* (New York: Simon and Schuster, 1987), appendix, "The Port Huron Statement," 329–74; William Julius Wilson, *The Truly Disadvantaged: The Inner City, the Underclass, and Public Policy* (Chicago: University of Chicago Press, 1987), chap. 2; Barry Bluestone and Bennett Harrison, *The Deindustrialization of America: Plant Closings, Community Abandonment, and the Dismantling of Basic Industry* (New York: Basic Books, 1982); Thomas J. Sugrue, *The Origins of the Urban Crisis: Race and Inequality in Postwar Detroit* (Princeton, N.J.: Princeton University Press, 1996), esp. chap. 5 and conclusion, 259–71.

3. Doug Rossinow, *The Politics of Authenticity: Liberalism, Christianity, and the New Left in America* (New York: Columbia University Press, 1998); Kenneth J. Heineman, *Campus Wars: The Peace Movement at American State Universities in the Vietnam Era* (New York: New York University Press, 1993). Also David Farber, *Chicago '68* (Chicago: University of Chicago Press, 1988); Tom Bates, *Rads: The 1970 Bombing of the Army Math Research Center of the University of Wisconsin and Its Aftermath* (New York: HarperCollins, 1992); Anthony O. Edmonds, "The Tet Offensive and Middletown: A Study of Contradiction," *Viet Nam Generation* (1994): 119–22; Marc Jason Gilbert, "Lock and Load High School: The Vietnam War Comes to a Los Angeles High School," *Viet Nam Generation* (1994).

4. Eric Hobsbawm, *The Age of Extremes: A History of the World, 1914–1991* (New York: Pantheon, 1994).

5. Daniel Bell, *The End of Ideology* (New York: Free Press, 1962); Chaim I. Waxman, ed., *The End of Ideology Debate* (New York: Simon and Schuster, 1969).

6. Richard A. Posner, "The Moral Minority," Review of Gertrude Himmelfarb, *One Nation, Two Cultures, New York Times Book Review*, December 19, 1999, 14.

7. The most influential work on modernization remains Harold Wilensky and Charles Lebeaux, *Industrial Society and Social Welfare* (New York: Free Press, 1965). Also see my *New Left, New Right, and the Legacy of the Sixties* (Philadelphia: Temple University Press, 1996), esp. chap. 2. On Malvina Reynolds's "Little Boxes," see Pete Seeger with Peter Blood, *Where Have All the Flowers Gone* (Bethlehem, Pa.: Sing Out, 1993), 107, 206. Also, Sloan Wilson, *The Man in*

*the Gray Flannel Suit* (New York: Simon and Schuster, 1955); William H. Whyte, *The Organization Man* (New York: Simon and Schuster, 1956; reprint Philadelphia: University of Pennsylvania Press, 2002); Newton Minow, *Equal Time: The Private Broadcaster and the Public Interest* (New York: Atheneum, 1964); David Reisman, *The Lonely Crowd* (New Haven, Conn.: Yale University Press, 1955).

8. W. W. Rostow, *The Stages of Economic Growth: A Non-Communist Manifesto* (Cambridge: Cambridge University Press, 1960).

9. Alan Wolfe, *America's Impasse: The Rise and Fall of the Politics of Growth* (New York: Pantheon, 1981); Robert M. Collins, "Growth Liberalism in the Sixties: Great Societies at Home and Grand Designs Abroad," in David Farber, ed., *The Sixties: From Memory to History* (Chapel Hill: University of North Carolina Press, 1994), 11–44.

10. Lionel Trilling, *The Liberal Imagination* (Garden City, N.Y.: Doubleday, 1957), Louis Hartz, *The Liberal Tradition in America* (New York: Harcourt, Brace, 1955).

11. Miller, *"Democracy in the Streets"*, 329–74; C. W. Mills, "Letter to the New Left," in Judith Clavir Albert and Stewart Edward Albert, eds., *The Sixties Papers* (New York: Praeger, 1984), 86–92.

12. Miller, *"Democracy in the Streets"*, 329.

13. Godfrey Hodgson, *America in Our Time: From World War II to Nixon—What Happened* (New York: Vintage, 1976), chap. 4, "The Ideology of the Liberal Consensus," 67–98.

14. For Thomas Ginsberg, "Experts Creating a Vision of a Smaller Philadelphia," *Philadelphia Inquirer*, December 19, 2000, A1, A4, on the shrinking of the city by more than a half million between 1960 and 2001; Sam Bass Warner, Jr., *The Private City: Philadelphia in Three Periods of Its Growth* (Philadelphia: University of Pennsylvania Press, 1968; 2nd ed. 1987), esp. 214–23, where he concludes that " no powerful group had been created in the city which understood the city as a whole and who wanted to deal with it as a public environment of a democratic society" (223); John Lukacs, *Philadelphia: Patricians and Philistines, 1900–1950* (New York: Farrar Straus Giroux, 1981), 336.

15. Lukacs, *Philadelphia*, 9.

16. E. Digby Baltzell, *Puritan Boston and Quaker Philadelphia* (1979; New Brunswick, N.J.: Transaction Books, 1998), 6, 9.

17. Walter Licht, *Getting Work: Philadelphia, 1840–1950* (Cambridge, Mass.: Harvard University Press, 1992; reprint Philadelphia: University of Pennsylvania Press, 1999).

18. Lukacs, *Philadelphia*, 13; Licht, *Getting Work*, 249; Carolyn Adams, David Bartelt, David Elesh, Ira Goldstein, Nancy Kleniewski, and Willam Yancey, *Philadelphia: Neighborhoods, Division, and Conflict in a Postindustrial City* (Philadelphia: Temple University Press, 1991), 76.

19. Adams et al., *Philadelphia*, 75; Mark H. Haller, "Recurring Themes, " in Allen F. Davis and Mark H. Haller, eds., *The Peoples of Philadelphia: A History of Ethnic Groups and Lower-Class Life, 1790–1940* (1973; reprint Philadelphia: University of Pennsylvania Press, 1998), 282.

20. Lincoln Steffens, *The Shame of the Cities* (New York: Hill and Wang, 1957), 134; Warner, *Private City*, 214–23; Lukacs, *Philadelphia*, 406–14; Dennis Clark, *The Urban Ordeal: Reform and Policy in Philadelphia, 1947–1967*, Philadelphia: Past, Present, and Future (Philadelphia: Center for Philadelphia Studies, 1982).

21. Lukacs, *Philadelphia*, 21, 25; Adams et al., *Philadelphia*, 124–53.

22. Clark, *The Urban Ordeal*, 3, discusses unsuccessful but promising mayoral challenges in the 1930s and 1940s by John B. Kelly and then Richardson Dilworth.

23. Clark, *The Urban Ordeal*, 23, discusses "ethnic grievances," noting that the Irish never felt comfortable with the "Anglo-Protestant and Jewish reformers." During one of his campaigns, Dilworth once referred to Italians as "greasers" (24).

24. Clark, *The Urban Ordeal*, 20.

25. Clark, *The Urban Ordeal*, 5–8, 12, 23.

26. Kirk Petshek, *The Challenge of Urban Reform* (Philadelphia: Temple University Press, 1973); Nancy Kleniewski, "From Industrial to Corporate City: The Role of Urban Renewal," in William K. Tabb and Larry Sawyers, eds., *Marxism and the Metropolis: New Perspectives in Urban Political Economy* (New York: Oxford University Press, 1984), 205–22; James Reichley, *The Art of Government: Reform and Organizational Politics in Philadelphia* (New York: Fund for the Republic, 1959); Clark, *The Urban Ordeal*, 23.

27. Baltzell, *Puritan Boston*, 448–49; for examples, "The Peacemongers," *Greater Philadelphia Magazine*, May 1963, 36–38, 78–83; "Quakers Provide the Mainspring of the Peace Movement Here," *Philadelphia Bulletin*, December 15, 1963, 20.

28. S. A. Paolantonio, *Frank Rizzo: The Last Big Man in Big City America* (Philadelphia: Camino Books, 1993), 109.

29. See Fred J. Hamilton, *Rizzo* (New York: Viking Press, 1973), also Frank Donner, *Protectors of Privilege: Red Squads and Police Repression in Urban America* (Berkeley: University of California Press, 1990), esp. chap. 6, "Rizzo's Philadelphia: Police City," 197–244.

30. Nicholas Lemann, *The Promised Land: The Great Migration and How it Changed America* (New York: Knopf, 1991); Joe William Trotter, ed., *The Great Migration in Historical Perspective* (Bloomington: Indiana University Press, 1991).

31. Conrad Weiler, *Philadelphia: Neighborhood, Authority, and the Urban Crisis* (New York: Praeger, 1974), 18.

32. Arthur C. Willis, *Cecil's City: A History of Blacks in Philadelphia 1638–1979* (New York: Carlton Press Hearthstone, 1990), 91–102. Also Vincent P. Franklin, *The Education of Black Philadelphia: The Social and Educational History of a Minority Community, 1900–1950* (Philadelphia: University of Pennsylvania Press, 1979), 203.

33. Willis, *Cecil's City*, 75, 69–75, 81.

34. Willis, *Cecil's City*, 100, 135. For example, after jousting for leadership in early 1965, the local NAACP joined in an injunction against CORE picketing of a Trailways bus terminal, *Philadelphia Bulletin*, January 5, 1965. On Philadelphia CORE, see August Meier and Elliott Rudwick, *CORE: A Study in the Civil Rights Movement, 1942–1968* (New York: Oxford University Press, 1973), 187, 192, 230, 290, 308, 358, 377, for consideration of its shift toward a more grass-roots and nationalist model and for discussion of its rivalry with Cecil B. Moore and the Philadelphia chapter of the NAACP.

35. Paul Lyons, *Philadelphia Communists, 1936–1956* (Philadelphia: Temple University Press, 1982), chap. 7, esp. 153–60; Sherman Labovitz, *Being Red in Philadelphia: A Memoir of the McCarthy Era* (Philadelphia: Camino Books, 1998), chaps. 8, 9; Michal R. Belknap, *Cold War Political Justice: The Smith Act,*

*the Communist Party, and American Civil Liberties* (Westport, Conn.: Greenwood Press, 1977), 167–68; Joseph S. Lord III, "Communists' Trials," and Harry Lore, "Apostasy at the Bar: Lawyers and McCarthyism," both in *The Shingle* (November 1978).

36. Weiler, *Philadelphia*, 77–78.

37. Peter Binzen, *Whitetown USA* (New York: Vintage Books, 1970), 146, 149; Weiler, *Philadelphia*, chap. 5.

38. Binzen, *Whitetown USA*, 274–76.

39. Binzen, *Whitetown USA*, 273–305 in a chapter aptly labeled "The Ivies and the Alienated Whites"; Weiler, *Philadelphia*, chap. 5.

40. For example, *NSM News*, Special Issue, October 19, 1962, 4; December 14, 1962, 1–2, in no. 113 Northern Student Movement, reel 9, T2532, Students for a Democratic Society (SDS) Papers, ser. 2A, Swarthmore Peace Collection (SPC).

41. Paolantonio, *Frank Rizzo*, 91–94; Paul M. Washington with David McI. Gracie, *"Other Sheep I Have": The Autobiography of Father Paul M. Washington* (Philadelphia: Temple University Press, 1994), chap. 7; Weiler, *Philadelphia*, 88–89; Hamilton, *Rizzo*, 79–82.

42. Washington, *"Other Sheep"*, 67–68.


*Chapter 1. The Old Left and the 1960s*

1. David A. Shannon, *The Decline of American Communism* (New York: Harcourt, Brace, 1959), 248; Nathan Glazer, *The Social Basis of American Communism* (New York: Harcourt, Brace, 1975), 93; Paul Lyons, *Philadelphia Communists, 1936–1956* (Philadelphia: Temple University Press, 1982), 160–68.

2. Maurice Isserman, *If I Had a Hammer: The Death of the Old Left and the Birth of the New Left* (New York: Basic Books, 1987), 176–78.

3. Peter Drucker, *Max Shachtman and His Left: A Socialist's Odyssey Through the "American Century"* (Atlantic Highlands, N.J.: Humanities Press, 1994), 276; Isadore Reivich, interview, January 9, 1997. Unless otherwise stated, all interviews were conducted by the author.

4. Students for a Democratic Society, *The Port Huron Statement* (New York: Students for a Democratic Society, 1962, 2nd printing), 4. See Doug Rossinow, *The Politics of Authenticity: Liberalism, Christianity, and the New Left in America* (New York: Columbia University Press, 1998), introduction, for an intriguing thesis on the focus on anxiety in New Left thought.

5. For an example, see Marty Jezer, *The Dark Ages: Life in the United States, 1945–1960* (Boston: South End Press, 1982), 208–18.

6. *Philadelphia Bulletin*, May 14, 16, 17, 18, 1957, Temple University, Paley Library Urban Archives (TUA); Lyons, *Philadelphia Communists*, 169–89.

7. Drucker, *Max Schachtman*, 249–50, 262–63; Isserman, *If I Had a Hammer*, 57–65.

8. Martin Oppenheimer, "Pages from the Journal of the Middle Left," in Martin Oppenheimer, Martin J. Murray, and Rhoda Levine, eds., *Radical Sociologists and the Movement* (Philadelphia: Temple University Press, 1991); interviews with Martin J. Oppenheimer, August 19, 1997, Princeton, N.J.; Tom Barton, April 23, 1997, New York. Oppenheimer kindly provided the author with copies of his FBI files. Also, clippings in the *Philadelphia Bulletin* morgue on Oppenheimer, Barton, and Leo Kormis, TUA

9. Barton interview. On Paul Booth, see SDS Papers., ser. 2A, reel 3, T2526, no. 19, Taminent/NYU, Paul Booth, esp. letter from Steve Max to "Paul Truth," April 28, 1964, referring to both of them as "us electoral action people." Also see James Miller, *"Democracy in the Streets": From Port Huron to the Siege of Chicago* (New York: Simon and Schuster, 1987), 71–72, 219–20. On Marty Oppenheimer, see "Pages from a Journal of the Middle Left," in Oppenheimer, Murray, and Levine, eds., *Radical Sociologists*, 113–27. On Leo Kormis, I was impressed by the comments of Bob Brand, interview, October 16, 1998, and Josh Markel, interview, July 16, 2001.

10. *Philadelphia Bulletin*, December 15, 1963, 20; Isserman, *If I Had a Hammer*, 196–202; also, see Student Peace Union records, 1959–1964, collection 57, box I, Tamiment/NYU.

11. Milton S. Katz, *Ban the Bomb: A History of SANE, the Committee for a Sane Nuclear Policy, 1957–1985* (New York: Greenwood Press, 1986), 14.

12. Katz, *Ban the Bomb*, 21–22.

13. Katz, *Ban the Bomb*, 29, 43.

14. Katz, *Ban the Bomb*, 30.

15. Minutes, West Philadelphia-Main Line SANE Chapter, June 6, 1960 Papers, West Philadelphia-Main Line Committee of SANE and Greater Philadelphia Council of SANE, Administrative Records, ser. 1, box 1, Abraham Egnal (AE) Papers, SPC.

16. Charter of West Philadelphia-Main Line Chapter, Executive Board-Greater Philadelphia Council SANE, AE Papers, Administrative Records, ser. 1, box 1, SPC.

17. Biography, AE Papers, SPC.

18. Lynn Litterine, "A Rebel in White Gloves," *Philadelphia Inquirer*, March 14, 1978; Marilyn Lois Polak, interview, October 11, 1981, *Philadelphia Inquirer*; Ethel Taylor's Papers, Women Strike for Peace Papers, ser. A8, box 1, SPC. The memoirs of Ethel Barol Taylor, *We Made a Difference: My Personal Journey with Women Strike for Peace* (Philadelphia: Camino Books, 1998) unfortunately provide no discussion of the initial composition of either Philadelphia SANE or Philadelphia WSP, instead holding to the notion that the latter arose from a coming together of concerned mothers and housewives (1–4). This phenomenon, the understandable reluctance of former Old Leftists to admit to their radical pasts, is most recently marked in Daniel Horowitz, *Betty Friedan and the Making of the Feminine Mystique* (Amherst: University of Massachusetts Press, 1998), esp. introduction and chap. 11.

19. Claude Lewis, column, *Philadelphia Bulletin*, October 16, 1977; Joe Miller Papers, box 1, SPC; Isadore Reivich and Elizabeth Reivich, interview, January 9, 1997.

20. Katz, *Ban the Bomb*, chap. 3, esp. 45–60.

21. Katz, *Ban the Bomb*, 56.

22. Ethel Taylor, Report on National Conference, Chicago, October 14–16, Minutes, Main Line-West Philadelphia Committee of SANE & Greater Philadelphia Council of SANE, October 26, 1960; A. Egnal, letter to Norman Cousins, May 29, 1960; Main Line-West Philadelphia Committee of SANE & Greater Philadelphia Council of SANE, Administrative Records, ser. 1, box 1, AE Papers, SPC.

23. Ethel Taylor, Report on National Conference; Robert Rutman, interview, July 19, 2001.

24. Minutes, June 13, 1961, August 7, 1961, AE Papers, SPC.

25. Minutes, June 13, 1961; also see "Seeger Performance Cancelled by SANE," *Temple News*, October 10, 1961.

26. A. Egnal, letter to Mr. Clarence Pickett, Mr. Norman Cousins, Mr. Homer Jack, August 1961, AE Papers, SPC.

27. Katz, *Ban the Bomb*, 87–88.

28. "Viet Nam," *A SANE Report*, Greater Philadelphia Council of SANE, January 1963, AE Papers, SPC.

29. *A SANE Report*, esp. May 1962, September 1963, September 1964, AE Papers, SPC.

30. Sanford Gottlieb, letter to Abe (Egnal), July 1, 1963, ser. 1, box 2, AE Papers, SPC.

31. Turn Toward Peace Minutes, February 2, 1964, Turn Toward Peace Minutes, 1963–1967 Folder, ser. 1, box 2, AE Papers, SPC. Rutman confirmed the insularity of Philadelphia SANE's Old Left founders and early leaders, Rutman interview.

32. Isserman, *If I Had a Hammer*, 195–98; Charles DeBenedetti, *An American Ordeal: The Antiwar Movement of the Vietnam Era* (Syracuse, N.Y.: Syracuse University Press, 1990), 95; "Philadelphia Summer Tutorial Project," *NSM News*, Special Issue, October 19, 1962, 4, Northern Student Movement, no. 113, reel 9, T2532, SDS Papers, Tamiment/NYU. There is extensive material on the Swarthmore SDS ERAP in Chester under "Chester," no. 104, ser. 2B, reel 15, T2538. Also see Miller, *Democracy in the Streets*, 188–89; and Kirkpatrick Sale, *SDS* (New York: Random House, 1973), 104–5. On WSP, see Amy Swerdloff, *Women Strike for Peace: Traditional Motherhood and Radical Politics in the 1960s* (Chicago: University of Chicago Press, 1993), esp. 141. On prefigurative politics, see Wini Breines, *Community and Organization in the New Left, 1962–1968: The Great Refusal* (New York: Praeger, 1982), 6–7, 47–50. Also see SDS, *Port Huron Statement*, 3–4. On the shifting sensibility from Old to New Left as it pertains to folk music, see David Hajdu, *Positively Fourth Street: The Lives and Times of Joan Baez, Bob Dylan, Mimi Baez Farina, and Richard Farina* (New York: Farrar, Straus and Giroux, 2001); and Robbie Lieberman, *My Song Is My Weapon: People's Songs, American Communism, and the Politics of Culture* (Urbana: University of Illinois Press, 1989).

33. "Greater Philadelphia SANE Membership Status," November 5, 1964, Financial Records, 1965–1968, Administrative Records, ser. 1, box 1, AE Papers, SPC.

34. Nancy Zaroulis and Gerald Sullivan, *Who Spoke Up? American Protest Against the War in Vietnam, 1963–1975* (New York: Holt, Rinehart and Winston, 1984), xii.

35. Zaroulis and Sullivan, *Who Spoke Up*, 9–12; interviews, David Eldredge, Isadore and Elizabeth Reivich. Isserman concludes that SANE "served briefly in the late 1950s as a kind of surrogate party of the Left" (*If I Had a Hammer*, 180); Robert Kleidman argues that the Left "provided an activist core" for SANE, in *Organizing for Peace: Neutrality, the Test Ban, and the Freeze* (Syracuse, N.Y.: Syracuse University Press, 1993), 133. I would argue that at least in Philadelphia the activist core of Old Leftists remained a surrogate party on issues of peace throughout the 1960s and in many ways in the following decades as well.

36. Sale, *SDS*, 170–72, discusses how Booth and Todd Gitlin brought Stone to the December 1964 SDS meeting to bring attention to the issue of the Viet-

nam War, something in which most their comrades expressed minimal interest compared with the more prefigurative if already collapsing ERAP projects.

37. There has been little exploration of what might be called an "in-between generation," those too young to have experienced the 1930s, who came of age between the end of World War II and the election of JFK in 1960. In addition to Oppenheimer, Barton, and Kormis in Philadelphia, there would be a number of academics and other professionals who would play significant roles in both SANE and other, more radical peace and social justice organizations. See *Philadelphia Bulletin*, March 25, 1965, B11, for "While There Is Still a Choice in Vietnam" ad.

38. Martin Oppenheimer, "The Origins of the New Left," *Critical Sociology* (Summer 1988): 158. By 1969, SANE's executive committee included David Gracie, Bill Wisdom, Bob Edenbaum, Thompson Bradley, and David Marshall, all 1950s generation activists from the Episcopal Church, Temple University (2), Swarthmore College, and St. Joseph's College respectively. The following year, Mark Sacharoff, a Temple University English professor who would become a stalwart with the organization, joined the executive committee. There was enormous continuity: for example, Bob Rutman, Iz Reivich, Abe Egnal, Joe Miller, and Ethel Taylor remained central players. There was also some new blood from baby boomers including Tony Avirgan, a founder of the Philadelphia Resistance, and Jack Malinowski, an instructor at St. Joseph's. SANE Papers, Urb 50, box 1, folder 8, 14, TUA.

39. See, e.g, Robert J. Rutman, Statement to the Executive Board, June 13, 1969, SANE Papers, Urb 50, box 1, folder 8, TUA, which calls for SANE to develop "a broad anti-imperialist peace movement" and argues that SANE should abandon its "current position "as an independent front for left-wing Democratic Party politics." Also, Abe Egnal to SANE Executive Committee, December 18, 1967, folder P.A., 1966–1968, AE Papers, SPC, in which he asserts, "Any candidate who does not unqualifiedly call for the withdrawal of U.S. forces from Vietnam is not a peace candidate" and warns against a SANE endorsement of "the weakling and ambiguous positions" of those—presumably McCarthy and Kennedy—"posing" as peace candidates; Rutman interview.

*Chapter 2. The Quaker Schools*

1. *Phoenix*, October 30, 1956, 1; November 12, 1956, 2; November 20, 1956, 1; March 12, 1957, 2; March 18, 1957, 1; April 16, 1957, 1; April 29, 1957, 1; April 30, 1957, 1.

2. *Phoenix*, February 23, 1960, 1, 2.

3. *Phoenix*, March 8, 1960, 1; March 15, 1960,1, April 6, 13, 1960 for a series by Jon Van Til on the Nashville Movement; April 19, 26, 1960 for Jerry Gelles articles on the Raleigh conference of young civil rights activists out of which SNCC emerged.

4. *Phoenix*, September 23, 1960, 1; October 25, 1960, 1; December 6, 1960, 1; December 13, 1960, 1; January 10, 1961, 1; March 7, 1961, 1; May 16, 1961, 1, May 19, 1961, 1. Also see Robert Meeropol and Michael Meeropol, *We Are Your Sons: The Legacy of Ethel and Julius Rosenberg* (Boston: Houghton Mifflin, 1975), 285–86, 393–96, in which Michael cites historian James O'Brien's

estimate that more than "one quarter to one third of politically active students were second generation radicals." See James Putnam O'Brien, "The Development of a New Left in the United States, 1960–1965," Ph.D. dissertation, University of Wisconsin, 1971, 3 and in a 1974 private letter to Michael Meeropol.

5. Penny Patch, "Sweet Tea at Shoney's," in Constance Curry et al., *Deep in Our Hearts: Nine White Women in the Freedom Movement* (Athens: University of Georgia Press, 2000), 138–39.

6. Kenneth Keniston, *Young Radicals: Notes on Committed Youth* (New York: Harcourt, Brace and World, 1968); *Phoenix*, September 25, 1961, 1, 2; September 29, 1961, 1, 2, 3; October 6, 1961, 1; October 13, 1961, 1; October 20, 1961, 2; November 3, 1961, 1, 2. The November 7, 1961 issue covered the fund-raising visit from the Southern Student Freedom Fund by SDS' Tom Hayden and SNCC's Charles McDew (1), with editorial support for their efforts (2).

7. *Phoenix*, February 9, 1962, 1; February 13, 1961, 1; February 16, 1961, 1; September 28, 1962, 2.

8. *Phoenix*, May 1, 1962, 1; October 2, 1962, 1; October 16, 1962, 4; October 30, 1962, 1; December 7, 1962, 1, 2; January 8, 1963, 1; February 26, 1963, 1, where Carl Wittman, defending Castro's revolutionary dictatorship, quoted Mao on revolutions not being dinner parties; May 9, 1963, 1; May 14, 1963, 1; October 1, 1963, 2.

9. *Phoenix*, May 5, 1963, 1; May 9, 1963, 1, reporting that 12 of the 37 arrested were Swarthmore students; April 16, 1963, 1; May 14, 1963, 1; Annette K. Brock, "Gloria Richardson and the Cambridge Movement," in Vicki Crawford, Jacqueline Anne Rorese, and Barbara Woods, eds., *Women in the Civil Rights Movement: Trailblazers and Torchbearers, 1941–1965* (Bloomington: Indiana University Press, 1993), 121–44; James Miller, *"Democracy in the Streets": From Port Huron to the Siege of Chicago* (New York: Simon and Schuster, 1987), 71, chap. 6, 188–91.

10. *Phoenix*, September 28, 1963, 1; October 1, 1963, 1; October 26, 1963, 1. On the Chester Movement, see Val Chambers, "Past and Future Activities of Chester," prepared for the Cleveland Community People's Conference, n.d., ser. 2B, reel 15, T2538, SDS Papers, Tamiment/NYU; Danny Pope, Alain Jehlen, and Evan Metcalf with Cathy Wilkerson, "Chester, Pa.: A Case Study in Community Organization," SDS-ERAP, n.d.; and SDS, "Chester, Pa.— Jobs—Freedom Now—Community Organization in the Other America," December 1963, ser. 3, sec. 5, reel 26, T2549, SDS Papers, Tamiment/NYU.

11. See Chambers, "Past and Future," 1–4; Pope et al., "Chester Case Study," 1–3; "Chester, Pa. Jobs," 1–4.

12. Chambers, "Past and Future," 2–4.

13. Pope et al., "Chester Case Study," 9; "Prospectus for Economic Research and Action Project in Chester, Pennsylvania, During the Summer of 1964, " ERAP, March 1, 1964, SDS Papers, ser. 3, sec. 4, reel 26, T2549, Tamiment/NYU.

14. Pope et al., "Chester Case Study, 2: "The bulk of Chester's problems are shared by many older industrial cities; similarly, until this Fall, Negro organization consisted only of the NAACP. Thus the backdrop against which the Committee for Freedom and SPAC work may be typical of a large part of the North, and the program for Chester may be applicable to much of the rest of the nation." For a thoughtful history of ERAP, including the Chester project, see Jennifer Frost, *"An Interracial Movement of the Poor": Community Organizing*

*and the New Left in the 1960s* (New York: New York University Press, 2001), esp. 13–14, 45–46, 83–84.

15. Ad Hoc Committee, "Triple Revolution," SDS/ERAP Pamphlet, n.d.; and Richie Rothstein, *E.R.A.P. and How It Grew* (Boston: New England Free Press, n.d.), 2–3; Vertical Files, OF-SDS-Newark Project, Tamiment/NYU; Kirkpatrick Sale, *SDS* (New York: Random House, 1973), 99–100; Miller, *"Democracy in the Streets"*, 192; Tom Hayden, *Reunion: A Memoir* (New York: Random House, 1988), 124–26.

16. Rothstein, *E.R.A.P.*, 2–3. Also see David Milton Gerwin, "The End of Coalition: The Failure of Community Organizing in Newark in the 1960s," Ph.D. Dissertation, Columbia University, 1998, esp. chap. 1.

17. Sale, *SDS*, 102–9; Miller, "Democracy in the Streets," 188–94.

18. Wini Breines, *Community and Organization in the New Left, 1962–1968* (New York: Praeger, 1982), esp. chap. 1 on "key terms," chap. 2 on the "emergence of the New Left," chap. 4 on "prefigurative politics," 46–52, "Conclusion," 150–52.

19. Hayden, *Reunion*, 98.

20. Gail Malmgreen, interview, New York, April 30, 1997; Tom Barton, interview, New York, April 23, 1997. Also, Maurice Isserman, *If I Had a Hammer: The Death of the Old Left and the Birth of the New Left* (New York: Basic Books, 1987), 198–203.

21. Letter from Grizzard to Rennie, Paul, Clark, Carl, August 10, 1964; letter from Grizzard to Clark, October 1, 1964; Vernon Grizzard correspondence no. 24, SDS Papers, ser. 2B, reel 7; Letter from Nick to Rennie, October 13, 1964, no. 109, ser. 2B, reel 15, ERAP 1963–1965, Philadelphia, SDS Papers, Tamiment/NYU.

22. Northern Student Movement folder, no. 113, ser. 2A, reel 9, SDS Papers, Tamiment/NYU, especially "Northern Student Movement" (mimeo), *NSM News*, Special Issue, October 19, 1962; and Thomas P. Roman, "Negroes Helped to Gain College," *New York Times*, November 25, 1962.

23. Letter to SDS through Todd Gitlin and Lee Webb, n.d., NSM folder, SDS Papers, Tamiment/NYU.

24. Letter from Lee Webb to PC, n.d., NSM folder, SDS Papers, Tamiment/NYU.

25. Peter Countryman, "The Philadelphia Experience," n.d., NSM folder, SDS Papers, Tamiment/NYU; Steve Gold, interview, Philadelphia, April 17, 1998.

26. "Philadelphia Report," June 16–24, 7; "Chester ERAP Report," July 1964, Membership Lists, no. 129, ser. 2A, reel 10, SDS Papers, Tamiment/NYU.

27. ERAP Reports, August 1964—Chester, Membership Lists, no. 129, ser. 2A, reel 10, SDS Papers, Tamiment/NYU.

28. Letter, VG (Vernon Grizzard), June 1964, Chester, no. 104, SDS Papers, ser. 2B, reel 15, Tamiment/NYU.

29. Letter, October 23, 1964, Vernon Grizzard, Correspondence, no. 24, ser. 2A, reel 7, SDS Papers, Tamiment/NYU.

30. "ERAP Project Report, Report from Chester," June 20–July 1, esp. 2–3; "Chester Report," September 28, 1964, 2; "Prospectus for Summer Organizing Project in Chester, Pennsylvania," n.d.; Membership Lists, no. 129, ser. 2A; letter from Grizzard to Rennie Davis, March 11, 1965, no. 5, ser. 2A;

Letter from Grizzard to Clark, Helen, Paul, Rennie, October 26, 1964, Vernon Grizzard Correspondence, no. 24, ser. 2A; Val Chambers, "Past and Future Activities of Chester," n.d., no. 92, ser. 2B, reel 15; Letter, VG, June 1964; Don, Molly and Peter to Sharon & All, October 22, 1964, Chester, no. 104, ser. 2B (all SDS Papers, Tamiment/NYU).

31. Letter to Clark, Helen, Rennie, Paul, October 23, 1964, Vernon Grizzard Correspondence, no. 24, ser. 2A, SDS Papers, Tamiment/NYU.

32. Letter to Rennie, Paul, Clark, Carl, August 10, 1964, Vernon Grizzard Correspondence, no. 26, ser. 2A; "ERAP Reports(August)—Chester," Membership Lists no. 129, ser. 2A, SDS Papers, Tamiment/NYU.

33. Letter to Rennie, Paul, Clark, Carl, August 10, 1964; Letter to Clark, Helen, Rennie, Paul, October 23, 1964, Vernon Grizzard Correspondence; no. 24, Peter to Rennie, October, 1964, no. 104, Chester, ser. 2A, SDS Papers, Tamiment/NYU.

34. Letter from Carol Jablon to Richie, May 15, 1965, no. 121; Letter from VG to Rennie, n.d., Chester, no. 104, ser. 2B; Letter to Clark, Helen, Rennie, Paul, October 23, 1964, Vernon Grizzard Correspondence, no. 24, ser. 2A, SDS Papers, Tamiment/NYU.

35. Letter from Johnny to P. Booth and R. Rothstein, October 29, 1965; Letter to Ellen, Chapter Report, December 10, 1965, Philadelphia & Pennsylvania, no. 60, ser. 3, reel 25, SDS Papers, Tamiment/NYU.

36. Don, Molly and Peter to Sahron & All, October 22, 1964, Chester, no. 104, ser. 2A, SDS Papers, Tamiment/NYU.

37. Peter to Rennie, October 1964; VG to Rennie, November 17, 1964, Chester, no. 104, ser. 2A, SDS Papers, Tamiment/NYU.

38. Peter to Helen, December 1964, Molly to Rennie, February 1, 1965, Chester, no. 104, ser. 2A, SDS Papers, Tamiment/NYU.

39. Peter Countryman, "Race and the Movement," and Donald W. Jackson, "An Open Letter to ERAP," New Left Notes, July 15–22, 1966, New Left Notes, no. 1., ser. 4A, reel 33, SDS Papers, Tamiment/NYU.

40. Haverford News, October 22, 1956, 1; March 11, 1957, 2.

41. Haverford News, March 20, 1959, 2; October 9, 1959, 2.

42. Haverford News, February 18, 1957, 1–2; April 15, 1960, 1; April 22, 1960, 1.

43. Haverford News, April 29, 1960, 1, a campus poll of 73 Democrats, 67 Republicans, and 128 Independents found that Adlai Stevenson was the choice over JFK among Democrats 55–10 and among Independents 77–22, with 43 for Nixon and 60 for Nelson Rockefeller; November 4, 1, 1960, the election poll favored Kennedy by 60–40. There was no coverage or editorials on the election.

44. William Davidon biography, ser. A, box 1, William Davidon, Ann Morrissett Davidon and William C. Davidon Papers, DG144, SPC.

45. Philadelphia Bulletin, May 3, 1962; Philadelphia Inquirer, May 4, 1962, ser. A, box 1, Davidon Papers, SPC; letter from Don McKelvey to Bill Davidon, January 21, 1964, At-Large, no. 88, ser. 2A, reel 8, SDS Papers, Tamiment/NYU.

46. Haverford News, February 23, 1962, 1.

47. Thomas Goldstein, independent studies paper on Vietnam protests, 1988, 17–20, 1988, box 4, Thomas M. Goldstein Papers, 1962–1988, Haverford College Archives (HCA). I especially thank Russell Stetler for providing me with his recollections of his experiences during the 1960s at Haverford

and elsewhere in a series of letters dated October 24, 26, 27, 28, 29, 30, 31, November 6, 13, 2001, in the author's possession. Stetler notes that (October 29 letter), although Jim Garahan came from "a conservative Irish working class family . . . his father was a police officer," but he had "been exposed to left-wing activists of all sorts growing up in New York."

48. Goldstein paper, 24–25; Sasan Meharra, "Russell D. Stetler and the Student Anti-War Movement," 21–24, Honors thesis, University of Pennsylvania, HCA.

49. Josiah Thompson and Pancho Carner, interviews, in Meharra, "Russell D. Stetler"; Bruce Kuklick, interview, May 4, 2001.

50. Meharra, "Russell D. Stetler," 9–10; Kuklick interview.

51. Meharra, "Russell D. Stetler," 13–15.

52. Meharra, "Russell D. Stetler," 16–19; Sale, SDS, 121–23.

53. Letter from Don McKelvey to Russell Stetler & Russ, Joe, Jim, Paul et al., January 21, 1964, letter from Russ Stetler to McKelvey, December 22, 1963, At-Large, no. 88, ser. 2A, Reel 8, SDS Papers, Tamiment/NYU; Stetler letter, October 29, 2001.

54. Letter from Stetler to McKelvey, March 8, 1964, At-Large, no. 88, ser. 2A, reel 8, SDS Papers, Tamiment/NYU; Kuklick interview.

55. Meharra, "Russell D. Stetler," 21–24, 29; Stetler letter, October 30, 2001.

56. Meharra, "Russell D. Stetler," 32–51. Bill Davidon also testified in Stetler's behalf.

57. Meharra, "Russell D. Stetler," 51–52.

58. Meharra, "Russell D. Stetler," 65–66; Goldstein paper, 36, 39, 46.

59. Meharra, "Russell D. Stetler," 60, 65–67; Goldstein paper, 46; *Haverford News*, April 23, 1965, 8; October 2, 1964, 8.

60. Letter to Bruce Kuklick, April 4, 1964, HCA; Meharra, "Russell D. Stetler," 60.

61. *Haverford News*, November 13, 1964, 3; Goldstein paper, 41; Meharra, "Russell D. Stetler, 65, 68; letter from Stetler to McKelvey, April 1, 1964, At-Large, no. 88, ser. 2A, reel 8, SDS Papers, Tamiment/NYU; Stetler letters, October 26 and November 6, in which he states that Haverford's emphasis on "personal stances based on . . . moral beliefs . . . reflected the absence of a political culture at Haverford, compared to, say, Swarthmore."

62. *Haverford News*, October 23, 1964, 1.

63. *Haverford News*, February 28, 1964, 1; October 9, 1964, 7; October 23, 1964, 3; January 19, 1965, 4.

64. Meharra, "Russell D. Stetler," 72, 75, 85–88; Kuklick interview; Goldstein paper, 45, 50; Stetler letter, November 6, 2001.

65. *Haverford News*, October 2, 1964, 1; February 12, 1965, 1; February 18, 1965, 1—Eyer was elected by a vote of 215–205, February 26, 1965.

66. *Haverford News*, February 26, 1965, 3.

67. *Haverford News*, February 18, 1965, 1, 3, 8; February 19, 1965, 2; February 26, 1965, 8; April 23, 1965, 8.

68. *Haverford News*, April 9, 1965, 1, 3–4.

69. David Harris, *Our War* (New York: Times Books/Random House, 1996).

70. One of the best analyses of this rejection of liberalism remains Godfrey Hodgson, *America in Our Time: From World War II to Nixon—What Happened and Why* (New York: Vintage Books, 1978), esp. parts III and IV; also Paul Lyons, *New Left, New Right, and the Legacy of the Sixties* (Philadelphia: Temple University Press, 1996), esp. chaps. 1–3, 9; Maurice Isserman and Michael Kazin, *America*

*Divided: The Civil War of the 1960s* (New York: Oxford University Press, 2000), esp. chaps. 10, 13.

71. Isserman and Kazin, *America Divided*, chaps. 6, 7, 10; Lyons, *New Left, New Right*, chap. 5.

72 *Haverford News*, January 14, 1966, 1; February 11, 1966, 1–2; April 29, 1966, 1; June 3, 1966, 2, 5.

73. Richard Alpert and Allen Ginsburg spoke on campus, *Haverford News*, October 14, 1966, 1; November 4, 1966, 1, 2; March 17, 1967, 7. Bud Alcock, in a letter to the editor, charged that "The problem of drugs on campus is severe," and that "perhaps even heroin is being used," February 16, 1967, 4.

74. *Haverford News.*, March 17, 1967, 12; April 28, 1967, 1.

75. *Haverford News*, September 29, 1967, 1; October 28, 1967, 1–3, 10.

76. *College News*, September 30, 1956, 1.

77. *College News*, October 10, 1956, 1; October 17, 1956, 1; October 31, 1956, 1; October 23, 1957, 2; September 9, 1959, 2; April 17, 1957, 3.

78. Ruth Rosen, *The World Split Open: How the Modern Women's Movement Changed America* (New York: Viking, 2000), chap. 5, "Hidden Injuries of Sex," obviously playing off Richard Sennett and Jonathan Cobb's still extraordinarily influential *The Hidden Injuries of Class* (New York: Knopf, 1972).

79. *College News*, January 9, 1957, 3.

80. *College News*, February 11, 1959, 4; October 8, 1958, 3; October 24, 1958, 2.

81. *College News*, March 23, 1960, 2; April 6, 1960, 2; April 20, 1960, 1, 2.

82. *College News.*, November 2, 1960, 1, 2. Students supported JFK with 58%, 443–285, with faculty at 93% for Kennedy; 64% of administration and staff, however, supported Nixon. May 2, 1960, 2, letter to the editors from five seniors criticizing pro-sit-in editorial.

83. *College News*, March 7, 1962, 2; November 15, 1961, 2, 4; February 21, 1962, 5; Jean Hunt, interview, November 17, 2000; Barbara Gold, interview, March 24, 2001.

84. *College News*, May 8, 1963, 1, 2; October 4, 1963, 1; October 18, 1963, 1; October 25, 1963, 2; November 15, 1963, 1, when four Bryn Mawr students— Kathy Boudin, Edna Perkins, Dana Purvis, Barbara Ranney—were arrested, fifteen altogether picketed in Chester at the Franklin School (1).

85. *College News*, February 7, 1964; Special Conference Issue, February 21, 1964, 1, April 10, 1964, 1.

86. *College News*, April 17, 1964, 1; October 1, 1964, 5; October 15, 1964, 3, 4, in which students voted 476–59 for Johnson over Goldwater.

87. *College News*, January 15, 1965, 1.

88. *College News.*, February 19, 1965, 2, an editorial called "Confused"; February 26, 1965, 1, 2; March 14, 1965, 1; April 30, 1965, 2.

89. Elizabeth Kolbert, "The Prisoner," *New Yorker*, July 16, 2001, 48, where Boudin recalls, "I worked hard, but I always felt there were other people that were more talented," and who, despite the good grades that seemed to meet her ambitions to go to medical school, "had come to believe that she wasn't talented enough."

90. *College News*, May 31, 1965, 3; Kolbert, "The Prisoner."

91. *College News*, April 15, 1966, 3.

92. *College News*, April 22, 1966, 2; November 19, 1965, 1; January 14, 1966, 1.

93. *College News.*, May 16, 1966, 6; October 21, 1966, 4.

94. *College News*, May 8, 1963, 1.

95. *College News*, February 10, 1967, 2.

96. *College News*, February 24, 1967, 3.

97. *College News*, March 3, 1967, 1; April 4, 1967, 3; May 1, 1967, 1.

98. *College News.*, October 27, 1967, 2.

99. *College News*, October 27, 1967, article by Kit Bakke, 4.

100. Isserman and Kazin, *America Divided*, 183–86; Hodgson, *America in Our Time*, 349–52.

101. *College News*, November 3, 1967, 1; February 2, 1968, 2.

102. Feminist scholar Joan Mandle confirms (e-mail, August 28, 2000) that Philadelphia remains virtually invisible in the histories of second-wave feminism. For examples, see Rosen, *The World Split Open*, with no references, and Susan Brownmiller, *In Our Time: Memoir of a Revolution* (New York: Dial Press, 1999), which has two minor mentions of Philadelphia, one noting the opening of a third rape crisis center, the other referencing a chapter of the National Black Feminist Organization (208, 215).

103. Hunt interview; Carol Rogers, interview, May 14, 2001; "Women's Liberation Conference," *Resister*, October 15–November 15, 1969, 7; *Temple Free Press*, March 30, 1970, 5; *Philadelphia Bulletin*, March 10, 1970, 13; April 22, 1970, 19; and a series by Kitsi Burkhart on the emerging women's liberation movement, March 8, 9, 10, 11, 1970.

104. *The News* (combined Bryn Mawr and Haverford colleges), December 5, 1969, 1, 4; January 30, 1970, 1; September 15, 1970, 1; September 18, 1970, 1; Joan Mandle, e-mail correspondence, December 8, 2000.

105. *The News*, February 6, 1970, 1; February 20, 1970, 2; February 13, 1970, 3; September 18, 1970, 3.

*Chapter 3. The Catholic Schools*

1. For characteristic examples, see Todd Gitlin, *The Sixties: Years of Hope, Days of Rage* (New York: Bantam Books, 1987); Barbara L. Tischler, ed., *Sights on the Sixties* (New Brunswick, NJ.: Rutgers University Press, 1992); Charles DeBenedetti, *An American Ordeal: The Antiwar Movement of the Vietnam Era* (Syracuse, N.Y.: Syracuse University Press, 1990); Nancy Zaroulis and Gerald Sullivan, *Who Spoke Up? American Protest Against the War in Vietnbam, 1963–1975* (New York: Holt, Rinehart, 1984); On the activism of Catholic clergy (other than the Berrigans), see James Carroll, *An American Requiem: God, My Father and the War That Came Between Us* (Boston: Houghton Mifflin, 1996) and Michael B. Friedland, *Lift Up Your Voice Like a Trumpet: White Clergy and the Civil Rights and Antiwar Movements, 1954–1973* (Chapel Hill: University of North Carolina Press, 1998). For a particularly insightful examination of modern American Catholic culture, see John T. McGreevy, *Parish Boundaries: The Catholic Encounter With Race in the Twentieth-Century Urban North* (Chicago: University of Chicago Press, 1996). On more case study approaches, see Tom Bates, *Rads: The 1970s Bombing of the Army Math Research Center of the University of Wisconsin and Its Aftermath* (New York: HarperCollins, 1992); Doug Rossinow, *The Politics of Authenticity: Liberalism, Christianity and the New Left in America* (New York: Columbia University Press, 1998); W. J. Rorabaugh, *Berkeley at War: The 1960s* (New York: Oxford University Press, 1989); Kenneth J. Heineman, *Campus War: The Peace Movement at American State Universities in the*

*Vietnam Era* (New York: New York University Press, 1993). There is no consideration of Roman Catholic experiences in Rossinow's fine study, despite its subtitle.

2. See McGreevey *Parish Boundaries*, for insight into the corporate dimensions of American Catholic practices.

3. Carroll, *American Requiem*, 73–76, 127–133.

4. I want to thank Brother Joseph L. Grabenstein, F.S.C., the archivist at LaSalle University's University Archives, interview, October 16, 1998; Brother Daniel Burke, interview, July 30, 2001; Bert Strieb, interview, July 18, 2001. Also, see Mark Clark, "School Devotes 100 Years to Enrichment of Intellect," *Hawk*, October 31, 1962, 2; *Collegian*, November 14, 1956, 1 on Hungary, November 2, 1960, 1, on the mock election. Both LaSalle and St. Joseph's have become universities since this period.

5. *Collegian*: on the pro-Castro articles, see a series by Juan V. Artiles, February 25, 1959, 2; March 4, 1959, 2, on Kirk, March 14, 1962, 1; on Day, April 4, 1962, 8, April 11, 1, 1962; on the new Conservative Club, December 6, 1963, 9; John XXIII's "Pacem In Terris," December 13,1963.

6. *Collegian*, October 11, 1961, 2.

7. *Collegian*, February 28, 1962, 1; April 24, 1963, 2; October 4, 1963, 1.

8. *Collegian*, November 5, 1964, 1, 4.

9. *Collegian*, October 1, 1965, 3; October 8, 1963, 1.

10. *Collegian*, October 29, 1965, 1, 2.

11. *Collegian*, November 5, 1965, 1.

12. *Collegian*, December 3, 1965, 1; December 6, 1965, 1; May 13, 1966, 2.

13. *Collegian*, October 14, 1966, 6.

14. *Collegian*, December 16, 1966, special Christmas Issue; March 10, 1967, special supplement "The College Within the City in Crisis".

15. *Collegian*, February 14, 1967, 1; March 3, 1967, 1; March 10, 1967, 4.

16. *Collegian*, April 21, 1967, 1 and 4; October 13, 1967, 6.

17. *Collegian*, October 30, 1967, 5; Letter from Downs to Philadelphia Mobilization Committee, April 16, 1967, February 1967–June 1967 folder, Abraham Egnal Papers, DG 136, TUA.

18. *Collegian*, October 13, 1967, 1, 6; October 20, 1967, 1; September 18, 1967, 5, 6; September 19, 1967, 3.

19. *Collegian*, October 30, 1967, 2, November 17, 1967, 1–2.

20. *Collegian*, December 1, 1967, 1 and 4; December 11, 1967, 2; December 15, 1967, 3. I would also like to thank the following LaSalle graduates for providing me with valuable insight about the college during the 1960s: Frank Battalgia (Class of '63), interview, May 1, 1998; Steve Gold (Class of '64), interview, April 17, 1998.

21. *Hawk*, January 7, 1957, 1, April 16, 1957, 1, October 28, 1957, 1 on Hungary; October 16, 1958, 2 on Pius XII; May 14, 1959, 2 on Schwarz; October 31, 1962, 2 on the college's history; December 6, 1962, 2 on the feeder schools.

22. *Hawk*, October 20, 1960, 2 on JFK; October 19, 1961, 2 on "dead over red"; on developing signs of a new idealism, see October 3, 1962 editorial, 3, "Join Our Voices to Support Dignity and Rights of Man," on the University of Mississippi barring James Meredith.

23. *Hawk*, March 8, 1962, 1; February 26, 1962, 3.

24. *Hawk*, April 5, 1962, 3; May 17, 1962, 6.

25. *Hawk*, October 3, 1962, 3; October 17, 1962, 3, 4, 6; December 6, 1962,

9; December 12, 1963, the entire issue "In Memoriam" on JFK's death; April 16, 1964, 1; April 28, 1965, 6. Johnson Collins, Class of 1965, was elected Student Council president; he also maintained a 3.96 average. All three of the Catholic colleges examined had very few African American students through 1967, the majority of them athletes in basketball or track.

26. *Hawk*, May 21, 1964, 7; October 22, 1964, 3; November 2, 1964, 3.

27. *Hawk*, May 20, 1965, 1, 5; November 18, 1965, 1, 4; December 16, 1965, 1; December 15, 1966, 2.

28. *Hawk*, January 19, 1966, 2; March 17, 1967, 1; April 11, 1967, 1, 3.

29. *Hawk*, May 16, 1967, 2; November 2, 1967, 1.

30. *Hawk*, April 25, 1967, 5; October 4, 18, 1967 issues are filled with energy and controversy on Vietnam and cultural events. See Edward Mahlman, "Are Hippies Hippy or the Morality of Living Off the Fat of the Land," Oct. 18, 3.

31. *Hawk*, November 2, 1967, 1; November 8, 1967, 2; November 15, 1967, 2. Also, Dennis Foreman, interview, July 17, 2001. Foreman organized Dr. King's talk and introduced Dr. King at the fieldhouse.

32. *Hawk*, November 22, 1967, 1, 2. In fall 1967 Marshall was joined by John (Jack) Malinowski, an instructor of theology who would also become an antiwar faculty leader.

33. *Hawk*, November 22, 1967, 1, 2.

34. *Hawk*, January 17, 1968, 1.

35. *Hawk*, December 6, 1967, 1.

36. *Villanovan*, "A Freshman Becomes a Gentleman," September 18, 1956, 2, history of Villanova, 6; March 4, 1959, p. 5; February 27, 1958, 7.

37. *Villanovan*, October 4, 1967, 3.

38. *Villanovan*, April 19, 1961, 1.

39. *Villanovan*, February 21, 1962, 4; October 17, 1962, 2; November 13, 1963, 3; December, 11, 1963, 3; October 21, 1964, 1; March 24, 1965, 4.

40. *Villanovan*, November 3, 1965, 2, 5; November 10, 1965, 6 "Letters from Vietnam," included four from GIs; April 22, 1964, 4; May 5, 1965, 4.

41. *Villanovan*, March 2, 1966, 4, editorial critical of required Freshman Theology course; 5; *Villanovan* reporter and soon-to-be editor in chief Ron Javers proposed student evaluations of faculty; April 27, 1966, seniors with 3.0 GPAs or better were exempted from compulsory attendance; December 7, 1966, 1 on a call for a more liberal disciplinary code regarding expulsions, dormitory visits, and privacy rights; February 8, 1967, 2; February 8, 1967, 4, an editorial "Women's Rights," expressing concern about the dean of women dictating to the Student Government Association (SGA) about the newly formed Committee on Women's Discipline.

42. *Villanovan*, September 28, 1966, 1; October 12, 1966, editorial "Better Than Napalm," 4, 5 on Peace Corps volunteers.

43. *Villanovan*, October 19, 1966, 4, 5, 7; entitled "The American Negro Issue," this issue included a remarkable number of articles reflecting a Catholic humanism shaped by the Second Vatican Council and, of course, by the civil rights movement.

44. *Villanovan*, April 19, 1967, 4; April 26, 1967, 3; September 20, 1967, includes the announcement of the first lay dean of students and of the establishment of the Experimental Free School of Villanova (EFSV), which featured a course on Ayn Rand.

45. *Villanovan*, April 26, 1967, an article by Fred Trietsch, "No Room at the

'In,' " comments on the minimal Novan presence at the be-in: "Villanova stands in the group with St. Joe's and LaSalle that rejects the 'new generation' bag," despite there being a few "Haverford types," 5; April 26, 4; September 27, 1967, 3.

46. *Villanovan*, October 11, 1967, 1, "For the first time since the beginning of the Vietnam War an organized protest was held on the Villanova Campus, involving at first about a dozen, and then as many as twenty faculty, students, and priests."

47. *Villanovan*, November 15, 1967, 1, 8; November 22, 1967, 1, 4–5.

48. *Villanovan*, October 11, 1967, 1; January 31, 1968, 1, 2, 3; February 14, 1968, 1; December 1, 1967, "Basketball Edition"; October 25, 1967, 2; November 8, 1967, 4.

*Chapter 4. From Subway School to Ivy League*

1. Ellen W. Schrecker, *No Ivory Tower: McCarthyism and the Universities* (New York: Oxford University Press, 1986), 209–12; also transcripts of interviews with Sidney Axinn, dated January 5, 1977, and Dirk Bodde, dated February 24, 1978, Fred Zimring Collection, Conwelliana-Templana Collection, Temple University Libraries, copies in Tamiment/NYU.

2. *Temple University News*, September 28, 1956, 2; October 19, 1956, 1; November 17, 1956, 1.

3. *Temple University News*, see May 3, 6, 13, 17, 1957 issues.

4. *Temple University News*, see October 10, 18, 1961 issues.

5. *Temple University News*, see September 25, October 16, 23, 26, 27, 1961 issues.

6. Eisman, *Temple University News*, September 25, 1962, 1 and in regular op-ed columns over the next few years; see esp. November 1, 1962 on the Cuban missile crisis. Elizabeth Zakroff, in an editorial "Lost Generation Isn't Really," September 28, 1962, 2, proposed the PTP as her foremost example.

7. *Temple University News*, September 26, 28, 1962 issues; on Yipsel, February 26, 1963, 2; on CORE, March 7, 1963, 1.

8. *Temple University News*, October 24, 1963, 1; March 12, 1964, 1; Carl Gilbert, phone interview, September 27, 2000.

9. *Temple University News*, April 21, 24, 1964, issues on Barnett; December 4, 1964, 2.

10. *Temple University News*, October 7, 9, 13, 1964; November 11, 13, 1964; November 20, 1964, including Carl Gilbert, "Liberals Ignore the Plight of the Northern Negroes," 2; December 3, 18, 1964.

11. *Temple University News*, October 20, 1964; December 10, 16, 1964. Until 1965 there was little mention of Temple in the SDS records; no registrants from Temple were recorded at the 1964 Convention. Collection 24, box 11, 1964-NC and Convention folder, SDS Papers, Tamiment/NYU. However, SDS membership lists note three Temple students as of September 10, 1964, including Bob Kernish. Philadelphia had a strong SDS presence by that point, particularly rooted in the Swarthmore-initiated ERAP in both Chester and Philadelphia; in neither project, the focus of much effort in the summer of 1964, was there any notable Temple participation (no. 88, ser. 2A, reel 8). Intriguing is a letter from Nick Egleson, Swarthmore SDS and Philadelphia ERAP leader, to Rennie Davis, October 13, 1964, which discusses organizing

an SDS chapter in Temple "where we will have to work closely with the Du Bois Club people. We don't have much choice," and another letter from Vernon Grizzard, Swarthmore SDS and ERAP leader, to Clark Kissinger on October 23, indicating that "Work at Temple is fine, and SDS-DuBois Club rivalry has not materialized at all" (no. 109, ser. 2B, reel 15; no. 24, ser. 2A, reel 3, no. 24); Art Rosenfeld, interview, August 13, 2001.

12. *Temple University News*, February 10, 1965, 1; February 9, 1965, 1; March 19, 1965, 1; March 4, 1965, 1; March 24, 30, April 1, 8, 13, May 4, 1965 issues; also October 19, 23, 1965 and esp. November 1, 1965 issue, which featured such involvements.

13. *Temple University News*, March 9, 1965, 1.

14. *Temple University News*, March 16, 1965, 1, 4; March 17, 1965, 1, 4.

15. *Temple University News*, April 6, 1965, 1; April 7, 1965, 1, 2; April 9, 1965 issue, which devoted much space to the teach-in. The editorial "The New Era at the University-and WHY" spoke of a "political awakening" measured by "the rise of many 'action' organizations with the promise of more to come" (1, 3).

16. *Temple University News*, May 5, 1965, 1; May 13, 14, 18, 1965 on the referendum; May 18, 19 on the debate.

17. *Temple University News*, October 13, 1965, 1. By fall 1965, Temple SDS claimed about 30 members and expressed gratitude to the Swarthmore people for their assistance. Letter from Judy Blank, chapter secretary to the National Office, October 2, 1965, ser. 2B, reel 15, SDS Papers, Tamiment/ NYU.

18. *Temple University News*, October 22, 1965, 1; November 4, 1965, 1; November 5, 1965, 1; November 16, 1965, 1, December 9, 1965, 1. Pro-war responses included October 19, 1; the pen pal letter, November 4, 2; Halstead's letter, December 8, 1.

19. *Temple University News*, November 9, 1965, 1, 2.

20. *Temple University News*, January 11, 1966, 4–5.

21. SCPVN member Art Rosenfeld recalls more success at tempering sectarian factionalism, Rosenfeld interview.

22. *Temple University News*, February 18, 1965, 1; March 11, 1965, 2; May 20, 1966, 1; June 29, 1966, 1; September 28, 1966, 2.

23. *Temple University News*, September 29, 1966, 3; October 18, 1966, 1; October 28, 1966, 1; November 2, 1966, 1.

24. *Temple University News*, November 9, 10, 16, 1966 issues; January 6, 1967, 1.

25. *Temple University News*, October 25, 1966, 4; September 29, 1966, 1; February 21, 1967, 1; February 21, 1967, 6.

26. *Temple University News*, March 1 2, 1967 issues.

27. *Temple University News*, April 5, 1967, 1, 3; April 11, 1967, 1, 4, 6; April 12, 1967, 1, 4.

28. *Temple University News*, April 6, 1967, 4.

29. *Temple University News*, March 3, 1967, 1; May 8, 10 issues on Free University. Art Rosenfeld remembers new activists being initially awed by Gilbert's knowledge but that it "wore thin after a while," Rosenfeld interview.

30. *Temple University News*, April 13, 1967, 1; May 5, 1967, 1.

31. See Wini Breines, *Community and Organization in the New Left, 1962–1968: The Great Refusal* (New York: Praeger, 1982) for what are still the best

definitions of how the New Left differs from the Old. Breines quotes Richard Flacks: "the New Left may be defined as a *particular segment* of young activists who were self-consciously radical ideologically, but disaffected from all 'established radicalisms,' and who self-consciously sought to provide political direction, theoretical coherence and organizational community to the student movement" (9). Breines suggests that "Existentialism and not Marxism was relevant to them and captured their mood. Symptomatically, for the new left corporate capitalism and liberalism were the enemies, whereas for the old left the enemy was the right wing" (16). Breines highlights a "prefigurative politics" embodied in the notion of participatory democracy, a politics that demands authenticity, a living of one's politics in the moment; see esp. chaps 1–4. See also Doug Rossinow, *The Politics of Authenticity: Liberalism, Christianity, and the New Left in America* (New York: Columbia University Press, 1998), esp. introduction, 1–20. For examples of Temple hosting visiting civil rights activists, see *Temple University News*, October 13, 1964, 3; December 18, 1964, 3.

32. *Temple University News*, July 6, 1967, 2. Gilbert had previously devoted a column to a defense of Black Power, "Black Power Not Anti-White," November 2, 1966, 2.

33. *Temple University News*, July 12, 1967, 1. See David Caute, *The Year of the Barricades: A Journey Through 1968* (New York: Perennial Library, 1988), 41.

34. *Temple University News*, September 20, 1967, 1; September 28, 1967, 1; September 27, 1967, 2. One might note that Goldberg seemed oblivious to the gendered aspects of the draft controversies, at least in her editorial. Up to this point, there had been no indicators of second-wave feminism in the campus newspaper.

35. *Temple University News*, October 10, 1967, 1.

36. *Temple University News*, October 10, 13, 1967 issues.

37. *Temple University News*, October 7, 1967, 1; October 19, 1967, 1; October 20, 1967, 1; October 26, 1967, 1.

38. *Temple University News*, October 27, 1967, 1; November 1, 1967, 1; November 3, 1967, 1.

39. *Temple University News*, November 14–17, 1967 issues offered extensive coverage of the boycott.

40. *Temple University News*, November 17, 1967, 2; November 21 22, 1967 issues.

41. *Temple University News*, September 21, 1967, 1; October 12, 1967, 4, in which the League sponsored a speech by the NAACP's Cecil Moore on "Black Liberation and Politics"; October 13, 1967, 1; November 30, 1967, 4; December 14, 1967, 1. There were extensive efforts within the Social Work Department to work with grass-roots African American groups in the neighborhood, but also including the National Welfare Rights Organization chapter, Rosenfeld interview.

42. *Temple University News*, January 5, 1968, 3; March 15, 1968, 1; March 21, 1968, 1; April 4, 1968, 1; April 19, 1968, 1; April 23, 1968, 1; May 8, 10, 14, 15 on the CFA forum and subsequent injunction.

43. *Temple University News*, November 3, 1967, p. 3.

44. *Temple University News*, January 4, 1968, 2 for an example of Aguilar's column, "View from the Left," a developing radicalism that rejected ameliorative efforts like that of Eugene McCarthy and Robert Kennedy, but is written

in simple, clear prose bereft of the overlay of Marxist or Marxist-Leninist jargon.

45. The Temple University Special Collection Department Contemporary Culture Collection includes *Yarrowstalks*, the *Distant Drummer*, and the *Temple Free Press*, which became the *Philadelphia Free Press*. For an example of *Free Press* ideological and rhetorical style, see the September 30, 1968 issue and Chapter 9.

46. *DP*, August 16, 1965, 29, 3.

47. *DP*, September 2, 1958, 2–3; September 30, 1958, 2; February 25, 1960, 2.

48. *DP*, January 7, 1959; May 1, 1961, 1; December 4, 1961, 1.

49. *DP*, February 25, 1960,1; March 8, 1960, 1; March 22, 1960, 1; October 10, 1960, 1; September 23, 1963, 1; February 4, 1964, 1, October 3, 1964, 4.

50. *DP*, November 11, 1963, 1.

51. *DP*, November 18, 1964, 1; March 5, 1965, 3; September 13, 1965, 1–2; February 3, 1966, 3; March 7, 1966, 1.

52. *DP*, editorial, "Barcusing Up The Wrong Tree," February 7, 1966, 3.

53. Adam Corson-Finnerty (Dan Finnerty), interview, February 12, 1998; *DP*, November 4, 1963 on the rowbottom riots; January 27, 1964, 6 on fraternities and pledges (597 in a class of 1425).

54. "Reverend Scott Reflects on 30 Years of Sanctuary at St. Mary's," *The Press-Center City/University City/West Philadelphia*, January 15, 1993, 1, 3; "John Scott, Priest and Social Activist," *Pennsylvania Episcopalian*, February 2, 1993, 1.

55. Finnerty interview.

56. William K. Mandel, "A Tradition, Not Time," *DP*, April 24, 1968, 2; Finnerty interview.

57. *DP*, April 1, 1963, 4; Dennis Wilen, "Underground at the Catacombs," Dennis Wilen, "Subterranean Satire," Charles Krause, "Gold Underground," April 15, 1966, 1 ; Joan Gero, "The Catacombs: A Campus Coffee House," *Penn Comment*, March, 1965, 19. A special thanks to Adam Corson-Finnerty (Dan Finnerty) for providing me with his collection of original Underground scripts and memorabilia. For an insightful study of the battle for hegemony at one of the first campuses to experience such challenges, see Larry Colton, *Goat Brothers* (New York: Doubleday, 1993), an account of five Berkeley undergraduates, Greek and jock leaders, and their complicated responses to the challenge posed by the free speech movement and its New Left and countercultural heirs. The ways campuses became contested terrain between the Greek/jock elite and the emerging movement counter-elite have yet to be systematically examined.

58. Bob Brand, interview, October 16, 1998; Marty Oppenheimer, interview, August 19, 1997.

59. *DP*, September 30, 1963, 1; October 7, 1963, 3; October 22, 1963, 1 on a Civil Rights Forum on campus sponsored by student government; December 30, 1964, 7; January 21, 1964, 1; January 28, 1964, 1; January 30, 1964, 1; February 12, 1964, 8; April 23, 24, 1964, 1; March 23, 1965, 2. Also "Kiyoshi Kuromiya, 57, Fighter for the Rights of AIDS Patients," obituary, *New York Times*, May 28, 2000, 34; "K. Kuromiya, Tireless AIDS Activist, Dies," *Philadelphia Inquirer*, May 12, 2000, A1, A10.

60. *DP*, September 19, 1961, 1; August 15, 1962, 19; October 3, 1962, 2; February 8, 1966, 1.

61. *DP*, October 8, 1963, 4; November 13, 1963, 1; November 19, 1963, 7;

October 9, 1964, 1; October 12, 1964, 1; October 21, 1964, 1; October 30, 1964, 1.

62. *DP*, December 3, 1964, 2; December 8, 1964, 1, 2.

63. *DP*, August 16, 1965, 1, 2.

64. See Rossinow, *The Politics of Authenticity*, introduction; Breines, *The Great Refusal*, esp. 8–9, 46–52 on the New Left's prefigurative politics of authenticity.

65. Brand, interview.

66. Martin Oppenheimer, "Pages from a Journal of the Middle Left," in Martin Oppenheimer, Martin J. Murray, and Rhoda Levine, eds., *Radical Sociologists and the Movement* (Philadelphia: Temple University Press, 1991), 113–27; Martin Oppenheimer, "The Movement: A 25–Year Retrospective," *Monthly Review* 36, 9 (February 1985): 49–65; Martin Oppenheimer, "The Origins of the New Left," *Critical Sociology* 15, 2 (Summer 1988): 155–60; Oppenheimer interview; FBI File of Martin Oppenheimer, in the author's possession.

67. Brand interview; also many conversations over time with Josh Markel between 1997 and 2000.

68. Finnerty interview; *DP*, October 12, 1965, 2; October 22, 1965; Project Mississippi Scrapbook, n.d., provided to the author by Dan Corson-Finnerty and in the author's possession.

69. *DP*, October 12, 1965, 7; October 29, 1965, 1.

70. *DP*, November 11, 1965, 2; November 2, 1965, 1; November 4, 1965, 1; November 11, 1965, 1; November 22, 1965, 1.

71. *Colloquy* (Publication of the Christian Association), February 1966, 2; *DP*, October 10, 1965, 1.

72. Dan Finnerty, "What Does Philadelphia Have to do with Mississippi?" *Colloquy*, February 1966, 9.

73. *DP*, January 26, 1966, 1; February 1, 1966, 1.

74. *DP*, August 16, 1965, 3, 4.

75. *DP*, February 11, 1965, 4; February 12, 1965, 1; February 17, 1965, 1.

76. *DP*, February 12, 1965, 2; February 15, 1965, 2; March 2, 1965, 3; March 26, 1965, 1.

77. *DP*, April 2, 1965, 1, 5; April 6, 1965, 2; April 8, 1965, 1.

78. *DP*, August 16, 1965, 19; September 14, 1965, 1; September 15, 1965, 1; September 17, 1965, 1; September 20, 1965, 1; September 24, 1965, 1, "Jonathan returned from 16 days in S. Viet predicting a U.S. defeat"; September 30, 1965, 2, concerning an SPU antiwar rally attended by 200; October 8, 1965, 1, concerning Penn getting a variance from the City Planning Commission to proceed with the Fine Arts Building.

79. *DP*, October 11, 1965, 1; Jonathan Goldstein, "Agent Orange on Campus: The Summit-Spicerack Controversy at the University of Pennsylvania, 1965–1967," in Barbara Tischler, ed., *Sights on the Sixties* (New Brunswick, N.J.: Rutgers University Press, 1992), 43–61. See also "Secret Report Policy at the University of Pennsylvania," prepared by the Student Government Committee on External Affairs, April 1967. This committee was chaired by Dan Finnerty and included Bob Brand among its seven members.

80. Goldstein, "Agent Orange," 48; *DP*, October 11, 1965, 1; October 12, 1965. Traveling to Toronto were Robert Rutman, Jonathan and Rhona Mirsky, Dick Fernandez, Dan Finnerty, Bob Brand, and five other students.

81. Goldstein, "Agent Orange," 49–51; *DP*, October 13, 1965, 4; October 20, 1965, 2; October 25, 1965, 2, on the pro-war "Victory Day" rally.

82. *DP*, October 12, 1965, 3; October 20, 1965, 2; October 22, 1965, 1; October 27, 1965, 2; December 7, 1965, 1, covering the Red and Blue sweep of the campus elections.

83. *DP*, October 21, 1965, 2.

84. *DP*, October 18, 1965, 1; October 27, 1965, 1; December 13, 1965, 1.

85. *DP*, December 13, 1965, 1, 5, letter to the editor from Andrew Cuhn '68, 2.

86. *DP*, December 13, 1965, 4; January 26, 1966, 1.

87. *DP*, January 18, 1966, 1; January 19, 1966, 1; January 24, 1966, 1.

88. Goldstein, "Agent Orange," 52–53.

89. *DP*, November 3, 1966, 4.

90. Richard Lesnick, "Condemn War in Vietnam," *DP*, November 3, 1966, 6. Lesnick was identified as a member of Penn SDS.

91. *DP*, August 15, 1966, 15.

92. *DP*, August 15, 1966, 15. Also, Diane Ravitch, *The Troubled Crusade: American Education, 1945–1980* (New York: Basic Books, 1983) on the importance of the GI Bill.

93. *DP*, September 27, 1964, 4; November 5, 1966, 1. Also see Kenneth Kenniston, *Youth and Dissent: The Rise of a New Opposition* (New York: Harcourt Brace, 1971).

94. Goldstein, "Agent Orange," 56–58; *DP*, April 14, 1967, 1.

95. Goldstein, "Agent Orange," 58; *DP*, April 20, 1967, 1, 4; April 27, 1967, 1.

96. Goldstein, "Agent Orange," 57–61; *DP*, April 27, 1967, 1, 3.

97. *DP*, August 25, 1967, 1.

98. *DP*, April 13, 1967; September 28, 1967, 3; October 2, 1967, 1; March 26, 1968, 1; April 4, 1968, 1.

99. "What Is Resistance?" four-page flyer, n.d., from the collection of Josh Markel and Eva Gold, who graciously supplied materials to the author.

100. "Vietnam Commencement," April 25, 1968, in the author's possession.

101. *Philadelphia Bulletin*, March 6, 1966, in the *Bulletin* Morgue, Leo Kormis file, TUA.

102. Dennis Berman and Scott Gallin, "The 1969 College Hall Sit-in," *Thirty-Fourth Street*, September 15, 1994, 7–9.

103. *DP*, September 27, 1964, 4.

104. "Record," December 1, 1966, The Diary of Daniel Finnerty, November 7, 1966–August 11, 1967, in the author's possession.

105. Finnerty Diary, January 24, 1967.

106. Finnerty Diary, January 23, 1967; April 5, 1967.

107. On the notion of a new working class, see Greg Calvert and Carol Neiman, *A Disrupted History: The New Left and the New Capitalism* (New York: Random House, 1971), esp. chaps. 2, 3; André Gorz, *Strategy for Labor* (Boston: Beacon Press, 1967); Kirkpatrick Sale, *SDS* (New York: Random House, 1973), 338–43; Serge Mallet, *Essays on the New Working Class*, ed. and trans. Dick Howard (St. Louis: Telos Press, 1976).

108. See Maurice Isserman and Michael Kazin, *America Divided: The Civil War of the 1960s* (New York: Oxford University Press, 2000), chap. 12; David Farber, *The Age of Great Dreams: America in the 1960s* (New York: Hill and Wang, 1994), chaps. 8, 9.

109. Finnerty diary, January 26, 1967; March 7, 1967.

110. Finnerty diary, March 2, 1967.

111. Finnerty diary, March 27, 1967.

112. Finnerty diary, April 19, 1967.

113. Daniel Finnerty, "Cops Versus Kids," n.d., paper in the author's possession.

114. Isserman and Kazin, *America Divided*, chaps. 9, 12; Farber, *The Age of Great Dreams*, chaps. 7–9; James Miller, *"Democracy in the Streets": From Port Huron to the Siege of Chicago* (New York: Simon and Schuster, 1987), 281–82 on the slogan "From Protest to Resistance" associated with the Pentagon March.

115. *DP*, February 24, 1967, 1; April 4, 1967, 1; November 1, 1967, 4.

116. *DP*, January 24, 1966, 1, 4; February 15, 1966, 3; September 27, 1966, 4; October 19, 1966, 1; December 6, 1966, 1; October 9, 1967, 1. There was also an "LSD Raid" including five arrests in early 1967, January 23, 1967, 1.

117. *DP*, October 4, 1966, 1; February 25, 1966 on Penn's Community Involvement Council headed by junior Tom Perloff, which coordinated twenty local projects.

118. *DP*, October 10, 1966, 1. See also Wayne Glosker, *Black Studies in the Ivory Tower: African American Student Activism at the University of Pennsylvania, 1967–1990* (Amherst: University of Massachusetts Press, 2002), esp. chap. 2.

119. *DP*, October 10, 1966, 1, 5; S. A. Paolantonio, *Frank Rizzo: The Last Big Man in Big City America* (Philadelphia: Camino Books, 1993), 91–94; Frank Donner, *Protectors of Privilege: Red Squads and Police Repression in Urban America* (Berkeley: University of California Press, 1990), esp. chap. 6, "Rizzo's Philadelphia—Police City," 197–244; Paul Washington with David McI. Gracie, *"Other Sheep I Have": The Autobiography of Father Paul M. Washington* (Philadelphia: Temple University Press, 1994), chap. 7; Conrad Weiler, *Philadelphia Neighborhoods, Authority, and the Urban Crisis* (New York: Praeger, 1974), 88–89.

120. Washington, *"Other Sheep I Have"*, 67.

121. David Farber, *Chicago '68* (Chicago: University of Chicago Press, 1968); David Caute, *The Year of the Barricades: A Journey Through 1968* (New York: Harper Row Perennial Library, 1988); Stephen Spender, *The Year of the Young Rebels* (New York: Vintage, 1969).

*Chapter 5. The Beloved Community Goes to War*

1. "The Peacemongers," *Greater Philadelphia Magazine*, May 1963, 36–39, 78–83, box 37, folder 36, "Advertisements and Articles," Philadelphia SANE Papers Urb50, TUA.

2. "Peacemongers," 37, 38, 78.

3. "Peacemongers," 39, 79, 81, 82.

4. Box 37, folder 36, Philadelphia SANE Papers, Urb50, TUA. Note that individuals sometimes listed more than one affiliation.

5. Philadelphia SANE Papers, Urb50, TUA.

6. "Peacemongers," 78.

7. "Vietnam Meeting, March 25, 1965," DG 136, ser. 1, box 2, folder Correspondences, Minutes, Releases, AE Papers, SPC.

8. Ann Morrissett Davidon and William C. Davidon Papers, DG 144, ser. A, box 20, SPC; AE Papers, box 2, SPC.

9. Folder "Philadelphia Mobilization Committee, Feb. 1967–June 1967," AE Papers, box 2, SPC.

10. Charles De Benedetti with Charles Chatfield, *An American Ordeal: The Antiwar Movement of the Vietnam Era* (Syracuse, N.Y.: Syracuse University Press, 1990), 182–83; Nancy Zaroulis and Gerald Sullivan, *Who Spoke Up? American Protest Against the War in Vietnam, 1963–1975* (New York: Holt, Rinehart and Winston, 1984), 118.

11. Vietnam Summer, Administrative Files DG67, ser. 1, box 2, SPC.

12. Reports, May 24, 25, 28, 1967, Vietnam Summer, DG67, SPC.

13. Vietnam Summer committee meeting, June 7, 1967, Vietnam Summer, DG67, SPC.

14. Tony Avirgan interview, Washington, D.C., August 14, 1998.

15. Avirgan interview.

16. Vietnam Summer committee meeting, Vietnam Summer, DG67, SPC.

17. WATS Reports, July 17, 24, 1967, Vietnam Summer, DG67, SPC.

18. *Talk Out*, newsletter of the Mantua-Powelton Vietnam Project, June 17, July 14, 18, 1967 issues; WATS report, July 26, 1967; Mid-Atlantic-States report (n.d.), Vietnam Summer, DG67, SPC.

19. Letter from Lambert to Andy Rotstein, National Vietnam Summer, Cambridge, Mass., August 23, 1967, Vietnam Summer, DG67, SPC.

20. Todd Gitlin, *The Sixties: Years of Hope, Days of Rage* (New York: Bantam Books, 1987), 244–49; Terry H. Anderson, *The Movement and the Sixties* (New York: Oxford University Press, 1998), chap. 3; David Burner, *Making Peace with the 60s* (Princeton, N.J.: Princeton University Press, 1996), 205–8. On the extraordinary life of Guevara, see Jon Lee Anderson, *Che Guevara: A Revolutionary Life* (New York: Grove Press, 1998).

21. Gitlin, *The Sixties*, 249–81; Anderson, *The Movement*, chap. 3; Burner, *Making Peace*, 205–8.

22. Gitlin, *The Sixties*, chap. 8; Anderson, *The Movement*, 170–76; Burner, *Making Peace*, chap. 4. Art Rosenfeld, interview, Philadelphia, August 13, 2001, in which this red-diaper baby and SDS activist expressed the view that the emergence of the hippie movement did great damage to both the New Left and the antiwar movement by its essential immaturity and alienating behaviors.

23. Gitlin, *The Sixties*, 245–46; Burner, *Making Peace*, chap. 2, 208; Tom Wolfe, *Radical Chic & Mau-Mauing the Flak-Catchers* (New York: Bantam Books, 1971).

24. National Mobilization, Minutes FPC, June 1, 1967, DG136, box 5, AE Papers, SPC.

25. S. A. Paolantonio, *Frank Rizzo: The Last Big Man in Big City America* (Philadelphia: Camino Books, 1993), 91–94; Fred Hamilton, *Rizzo* (New York: Viking Press, 1973), 79–82; Paul M. Washington with David McI. Gracie, *"Other Sheep I Have": The Autobiography of Father Paul M. Washington* (Philadelphia: Temple University Press, 1994), chap. 7.

26. Avirgan interview; David Gracie, interview, Philadelphia, August 17, 2000; Bob Brand, interview, Philadelphia, October 16, 1998; Eva Gold and Judy Chomsky, interviews, Philadelphia, August 23, 2000; Martha Honey (Westover), phone interview, October 6, 2000; Josh Markel, interview, Philadelphia, July 16, 2001; Dina Portnoy interview, Philadelphia, February 10, 2001; Lisa Schiller, interview, Philadelphia, March 24, 2001.

27. Letter from Gordon Fels, "Toward a Philadelphia Draft Council #2," October 26, 1967, Draft Resistance, 1967–1968 and Philadelphia Peace Calendar, August 15–September 15, September 15–October 15, 1967, box 50, T167, National Peace Center, TUA.

28. "What Is Resistance? Strategy, Tactics, Purpose," n.d., personal papers of Josh Markel and Eva Gold, in the author's possession.

29. "What Is Resistance?" See "Channeling" in Alexander Bloom and Wini Breines, eds., *"Takin' It to the Streets": A Sixties Reader* (New York: Oxford University Press, 1995), 240–41.

30. Bob Brand interview.

31. Beth Brockman, "An Analysis on a Reweaving: A Quaker Action Group—Movement for a New Society & Philadelphia Life Center," Swarthmore College Politics 314 paper, January 13, 1987, Folder AQAG, DG144, ser. B, box 2, Davidon Papers, SPC.

32. Brockman, "An Analysis," 2–4.

33. Lawrence Scott, "A Proposed Quaker Action Group," n.d., DG74, box 1, AQAG Papers, SPC.

34. "Eaton Available for Speaking," n.d., DG74, box 44, AQAG Papers, SPC.

35. Fred Halstead, *Out Now! A Participant's Account of the American Movement Against the Vietnam War* (New York: Monad, 1978).

36. Kirkpatrick Sale, *SDS* (New York: Random House, 1973), esp. chaps. 22, 23, 24.

37. Elliott Shore, "Decade of Dissent: The Alternative Press in Philadelphia, 1966–1976," Contemporary Culture Collection, Temple University Special Collection Department; also Bayard Brunt and Albert V. Gaudiosi, "The New Revolutionaries," *Philadelphia Evening Bulletin*, July 28–31, 1970.

38. David Farber, *The Age of Great Dreams: America in the 1960s* (New York: Hill and Wang, 1994), chap. 9; Martin Nicolaus, "The Unknown Marx," in Carl Oglesby, ed., *The New Left Reader* (New York: Grove Press, 1969).

39. Gregory Calvert, "In White America: Radical Consciousness and Social Change," and Carl Davidson, "Student Power: A Radical View," in Bloom and Breines, eds., *"Takin' It to the Streets"*, 126–31, 131–34; Sale, *SDS*, 338–40.

40. David Farber, *Chicago '68* (Chicago: University of Chicago Press, 1994); Norman Mailer, *Miami and the Siege of Chicago* (New York: Signet Book, New American Library, 1968), Part II.

41. 1968 activities are from the Community Peace Calendar, Philadelphia Peace Center, January 15–February 15, 1968, December 1968–June 1969, box 22, folder 205, SANE Papers, Urb50, TUA; *Resistance*, August 1968; *Philadelphia Resistance Review*, September, October 1968, December 1968–January 1969 issues. All issues of *Resistance*, *Philadelphia Resistance Review*, and *The Resister* from the personal papers of Josh Markel and Eva Gold in the author's possession.

42. Avirgan interview; Gold and Chomsky interview.

43. *Resistance*, August 1, 1968, 1; *Philadelphia Resistance Review*, October 1968, 11; December 1968–January 1969, 10; February 1969, 13.

44. "Resistance Carols to Cops," *Philadelphia Resistance Review*, February 1969, 7.

45. *Philadelphia Resistance Review*, September 1968, 1; October 1968, 9.

46. "Cops vs. Kids," *Philadelphia Resistance Review*, October 1968, 14.

47. "Chicago: The Dog Beneath the Skin," *Philadelphia Resistance Review*, October 1968, 1, 4.

48. "Chicago: The Dog Beneath the Skin," 4–5.

49. Dan Finnerty, "Catonsville 9 vs. Boston 5: A Question of Tactics," *Philadelphia Resistance Review*, October 1968, 1–3, in which he proclaimed, "These people are crazy. Crazy like Jesus. Crazy like Che Guevara. Crazy like all of us said we would be had we lived in Germany under Hitler."

50. "Hemisphere Vietnam Meeting," *Philadelphia Resistance Review*, December 1968–January 1969, 1–4.

51. *Philadelphia Resistance Review*, September 1968. One can look far and wide to find New Left media that gave as much attention to Prague Spring as they increasingly provided to such stellar regimes as North Korea and Albania.

52. "Meeting the Vietnamese" and "Budapest Diary," *Philadelphia Resistance Review*, October 1968, 19, 22–24.

53. "Our Man in Vietnam," *Philadelphia Resistance Review*, October 1968, 1–3.

54. "Philadelphia Regional Conference: A View of What Happened and Why," *Resister*, November 1970, 6–7.

55. "Philadelphia Regional Conference," 7.

56. "Chain of Life," *Philadelphia Resistance Review*, September 1968, 6; *Philadelphia Resistance Review*, February 1969, 2; *Resister*, May 1969, 3. On George Fencl, see Paolantonio, *Rizzo*, 95–96.

57. "Bob Eaton Sentenced to Three Years," *Resister*, October 15, 1969, 9; David M. Gracie, "Coinherence, Chain-ins and the Original Conspiracy," n.d.

58. Avirgan interview.

59. Avirgan interview; "A Year in the Life," *Philadelphia Resistance Review*, March 1969, 15, 18–20.

60. Avirgan interview; *Resister*, October 1969, 7, including flyers on the benefits; June-July 1970, with flyer on the picnic.

61. *Resister*, October-November 1969, February 1970 for examples. Information on the Draft Information Center, led by Temple University English professor Robert Edenbaum, and Weekly Action Project (WAP), flyers, from Markel-Gold papers.

62. Gold and Chomsky interview; Steven Levy, *The Unicorn's Secret: Murder in the Age of Aquarius—A True Story* (Englewood Cliffs, N.J.: Prentice Hall, 1988); David Gracie, "The Warlock Affair," *Philadelphia Resistance Review*, February 1969, 27.

63. Lisa Schiller, "Washington Demobilization," *Philadelphia Resistance Review*, March 1969, 31.

64. Ruth Rosen, *The World Split Open: How the Modern Women's Movement Changed America* (New York: Viking Press, 2000), 132–35.

65. *Philadelphia Resistance Review*, December 1968–January 1969, for a piece covering draft-card turn-ins and analyzing the effectiveness of such noncooperation as well as of civil disobedience, makes no mention of any gender dimensions of such choices, 14; "Women's Liberation Conference," *Resister*, October 15–November 15, 1969, 7. The article did end with a call for those "interested in further examining the interest of women in social change" to contact Resistance staffer Marilyn Griffiths about the formation of a permanent organization forming out of the conference.

66. Gold and Chomsky interview; Schiller interview; Portnoy interview; Markel interview; Honey interview.

67. There is an ongoing debate concerning the development of the New Left that too often breaks down into unproductive dichotomies between an

earlier "good" New Left and a later "bad" New Left; see Wini Breines, "Whose New Left?" *Journal of American History* 75 (1988): 528–45 and Todd Gitlin, *The Twilight of Common Dreams: Why America Is Wracked by Culture Wars* (New York: Metropolitan Books, 1995). There is truth in both sides of the debate, in particular, that the early New Left—through 1967—maintained the moral high ground through its more indigenous, American style and its commitment to participatory democracy, but also that many of the most important advances, especially the rise of the women's movement, the gay and lesbian movement, and the environmental movement, did not emerge until the latter 1960s and early 1970s. What strikes this author is how much the latter developments were shaped and distorted by the turn toward Third Worldism, abstract rhetoric, and dogmatism, but also how the roots of such developments already existed within the ostensibly more pragmatic, existential early New Left.

68. *Resister*, October 15–November 15 1969, 2.

69. Markel interview. See *Philadelphia Bulletin*, October 15, 16, 1969 for extensive coverage of the impressive Mobilization efforts in greater Philadelphia.

70. Gold and Chomsky interviews; Schiller interview; Portnoy interview; Markel interview. Also see Jerry Lembcke, *The Spitting Image: Myth, Memory, and the Legacy of Vietnam* (New York: New York University Press, 1998) on the problematic nature of such assertions, and Paul Lyons, "Toward a Revised Story of the Homecoming of Vietnam Veterans," *Peace & Change* (April 1998): 193–200, in which I survey local Vietnam veterans whose experience belies the myth of mistreatment but supports the idea that uncomfortable silences with family, friends, and neighbors were the most characteristic experience of those returning from Vietnam.

71. *Resister*, October 15–November 15, 1969, 6.

72. *Resister*, October 15–November 15, 1969, 6, 10.

*Chapter 6. The Politics of White Antiracism: People for Human Rights*

1. Students for a Democratic Society, *The Port Huron Statement* (New York: Students for a Democratic Society, 1962, 2nd printing), 3.

2. SDS, *Port Huron Statement*, 54.

3. James W. Silver, *Mississippi: The Closed Society* (New York: Harcourt, Brace and World, 1963).

4. Among the most astute accounts of the beginnings of the movement are E. J. Dionne, Jr., *Why Americans Hate Politics* (New York: Simon and Schuster Touchstone, 1991), esp. chap. 3; Thomas Byrne Edsall and Mary D. Edsall, *Chain Reaction: The Impact of Race, Rights, and Taxes on American Politics* (New York: W.W. Norton, 1991), esp. chaps. 2, 3; Thomas J. Sugrue, *The Origins of the Urban Crisis: Race and Inequality in Postwar Detroit* (Princeton, N.J.: Princeton University Press, 1996), esp. Introduction and Conclusion.

5. Dennis Clark, *The Urban Ordeal: Reform and Policy in Philadelphia, 1947–1967*, Philadelphia: Past, Present, and Future 19 (Philadelphia: Center for Philadelphia Studies, 1982), 3–8, 20, 23, 24; Kirk Petschek, *The Challenge of Urban Reform* (Philadelphia: Temple University Press, 1973); Nancy Klieniewski, "From Industrial to Corporate City: The Role of Urban Renewal," in W. K. Tabb and L. Lawyers, eds., *Marxism and the Metropolis* (New York: Ox-

ford University Press, 1984), 205–22; James Reichley, *The Art of Government: Reform and Organizational Politics in Philadelphia* (New York: Fund for the Republic, 1959).

6. In addition to the above, see S. A. Paolantonio, *Frank Rizzo: The Last Big Man in Big City America* (Philadelphia: Camino Books, 1993); Arthur C. Willis, *Cecil's City: A History of Blacks in Philadelphia, 1638–1979* (New York: Carlton Press Hearthstone, 1990); Peter Binzen, *Whitetown, USA* (New York: Vintage Books, 1970); Conrad Weiler, *Philadelphia: Neighborhood, Authority, and the Urban Crisis* (New York: Praeger, 1974).

7. "Chester Report," September 23, 1964, ERAP 1963–1965, ser. 2B, reel 10, SDS Papers, Tamiment/NYU.

8. Philadelphia, no. 109, ERAP 1963–1965, ser. 2B, reel 10, SDS Papers, Tamiment/NYU.

9. Northern Student Movement, no. 113, ser. 2A, reel 9, SDS Papers, Tamiment/NYU.

10. Letter from Peter Countryman to Lee Webb and Todd Gitlin, NSM, no. 113, SDS Papers, Tamiment/NYU.

11. Peter Countryman, "The Philadelphia Experiment," NSM, no. 113, SDS Papers, Tamiment/NYU.

12. "Philadelphia Tutorial Project Progress Report," December 1962 to April 1963, Philadelphia, no. 111, SDS Papers, Tamiment/NYU.

13. Don (Jackson), Molly (Pratt), and Peter (Friedman) to Sharon & all (Sharon Jeffries) October 22, 1964, Chester, no. 104, ser. B, reel 15, SDS Papers, Tamiment/NYU.

14. The late Rev. David McI. Gracie graciously gave me access to his personal papers regarding his Detroit experiences with People Against Racism.

15. "Friends of N.S.M. Statement of Purpose" (Provisionally Adopted), n.d., Gracie Papers in the author's possession.

16. "People Against Racism," n.d., mimeo, Gracie Papers.

17. "People Against Racism"; David Gracie, interview, August 17, 2000, Philadelphia.

18. Gracie interview; John F. Morrison, "Part-Time Priest, Full-Time Rebel," *Discover—Sunday Bulletin,* January 20, 1974, 7–9, 17.

19. *Philadelphia Inquirer,* August 20, 1967, 16; *Philadelphia Bulletin,* September 2, 3, 1969.

20. "Growing Up in Detroit," July 1967, PAR mimeo, Gracie Papers.

21. "A Final Call to Repentance," sermon preached at St. Joseph's Church, Detroit, July 30, 1967, mimeo, Gracie Papers.

22. Hans Knight, "Should a Bishop Get Involved?" *Sunday Bulletin Magazine,* January 14, 1968, 4–7.

23. Letter, 12 Noon, Tuesday, November 7, 1967, mimeo. The signers, who eventually numbered 145, were from Temple, Penn, Swarthmore, Beaver, LaSalle, Moore College of Art, Lehigh, Bryn Mawr, Philadelphia College of Art, Haverford, St. Joseph's, Chestnut Hill College, and and Immaculata College.

24. "200 Honor Gracie," *Philadelphia Resistance Review,* February 1969, 16.

25. Author's personal recollections of a Vietnam Summer workshop in Newark, New Jersey, early summer 1967.

26. Maurice Isserman and Michael Kazin, *America Divided: The Civil War of the 1960s* (New York: Oxford University Press, 2000), 175–83.

27. Paolantonio, *Rizzo,* 91–94; Paul M. Washington with David McI. Gracie,

*"Other Sheep I Have": The Autobiography of Father Paul M. Washington* (Philadelphia: Temple University Press, 1994), chap. 7, "A Divided City."

28. Paolantonio, *Rizzo*, 89–93; Washington, *"Other Sheep I Have"*, 65–69.

29. Paolantonio, *Rizzo*, 92.

30. Washington, *"Other Sheep I Have"*, 68.

31. Peter Countryman, "Race and the Movement," *ERAP Newsletter*, August 21, 1965; Countryman, "Race and the Movement," *New Left Notes* (July 15–22, 1966), with a critical response "An Open Letter to ERAP," from Donald W. Jackson, Chester CORE and a Frank Joyce Letter to the Editor, ser. 4A, reel 33, SDS Papers, Tamiment/NYU.

32. Ron Whitehorn, interview, Philadelphia, January 18, 2001, Philadelphia; Gracie interview.

33. Mary MacColl Wentworth, "Turning Point," 11–12, part of a memoir graciously made available to the author and in the author's possession.

34. Wentworth, "Turning Point," 13–15. Another organization, Philadelphians for Equal Justice (PEJ), was simultaneously formed as a response to the School Board incident. It was an integrated group that rallied volunteer attorneys to represent those victimized by police misbehavior. PEJ claimed that "some of the city's communities exist under virtual military rule—where citizens are under constant surveillance and suspicion" and demonstrators are treated as "guilty until proven innocent." PEJ's program included an emergency action committee of lawyers ready twenty-four hours a day to provide immediate legal assistance to "victims of unfair and unconstitutional police practices." It also established a bail and legal defense fund and a program of public education especially directed "to demonstrate to the still largely unaware and comfortably illusioned white middle class" the need for police reform. "Philadelphians for Equal Justice–A Statement of Purpose," n.d., Joe Miller Papers, Box 2, SPC.

35. William L. Van Deburg, *New Day in Babylon: The Black Power Movement and American Culture, 1965–1975* (Chicago: University of Chicago Press, 1993), 164.

36. Wentworth, "Turning Point," 17.

37. Wentworth, "Turning Point," 1–5.

38. Wentworth, "Turning Point," 32–33; "Chapter 12—Moving On," 17–18.

39. Whitehorn interview.

40. *PHR Newsletter*, October 25, December 11, December 18, 1968, March 13, 1969, PHR Folder, Ann Morrissett Davidon and William C. Davidon Papers, DG144, box 8, SPC.

41. Wentworth, "Turning Point," 34–37, 40–42, "Moving On," 11; Dina Portnoy, interview, Philadelphia, February 10, 2001.

42. *PHR Newsletter*, October 25, 1968, 5; March 13, 1969, reviews by David Gracie and Bob Hecht, 2, 4, 6; Steering Committee Notes, January 1, 1969, Davidon Papers, SPC.

43. *PHR Newsletter*, October 25, 1968, 4, 5, 6; December 18, 1968, 2; March 13, 1969, 1, Davidon Papers, SPC.

44. See Leo P. Ribuffo, *Right, Center, Left: Essays in American History* (New Brunswick, N.J.: Rutgers University Press, 1992) on "brown-baiting"; Paul Lyons, *Philadelphia Communists, 1936–1956* (Philadelphia: Temple University Press, 1982), 157–60.

45. Wentworth, "Turning Point," 43.

46. Kayla Weiner, *PHR Newsletter*, December 18, 1968, 4–5. See Wini

Breines, *Community and Organization in the New Left, 1962–1968: The Great Refusal* (New York: Praeger, 1982), 6, 13–17 on prefigurative politics.

47. *PHR Newsletter,* December 18, 1968, 4–5, SPC; Breines, *Community and Organization.*

48. Wentworth, "Turning Point," 51–52; Portnoy interview; Whitehorn interview; Jean Hunt, interview, Philadelphia, November 17, 2000.

49. Arnold Schuchter, *Reparations: The Black Manifesto and Its Challenge to White America* (Philadelphia: Lippincott, 1970), chap. 1 and appendix A, Part I, 191–202.

50. Washington, *"Other Sheep I Have",* chap. 9; also see Robert L. DeWitt, "Decade of Crises in a Stormy See, 1964–1974," *Witness* (July 1984): 6–8, 23; Willard S. Randall, "Bishop DeWitt Awakens Diocese to Issues Long Kept Under Wraps," *Philadelphia Evening Bulletin,* September 2, 1968; "Gracie and Woodruff Shake Up Old Order," September 3, 1969; "In Bryn Mawr, Rector Sails; in N. Phila., He Scrounges for Aid," September 4, 1969.

51. Washington, *"Other Sheep I Have",* 92–93.

52. Whitehorn interview.

53. For insights into this racial moment, see Fred Siegel, *The Future Once Happened and Here* (San Francisco: Encounter Books, 1997), esp. "New York," 19–71; Donald Alexander Downs, *Cornell '69: Liberalism and the Crisis of the American University* (Ithaca, N.Y.: Cornell University Press, 1999); Tom Wolfe, *Radical Chic and Mau-Mauing the Flak-Catchers* (New York: Bantam Books, 1971); Sandy Vogelgesang, *Long Dark Night of the Soul: The American Intellectual Left and the Vietnam War* (New York: Harper and Row, 1974) for the Sontag quotation; Tamar Jacoby, *Someone Else's House: America's Unfinished Struggle for Integration* (New York: Free Press, 1998), esp. section 1 on New York City. Peter and Marian Wright Edelman embodied the interracial ideal through their marriage; she is most known as director of the Children's Defense Fund, he as a law professor at Georgetown University and Clinton administration Justice Department official who resigned in protest over the elimination of AFDC— Aid to Families with Dependent Children in 1996. Abraham Heschel, a prominent Jewish theologian and rabbi, was among the most impressive clerical participants in the civil rights struggle, Nelson Mandela, of course, is the former president of the newly integrated South Africa, Barbara Jordan, an eloquent voice for social justice, was an African American Representative from Texas. See Marian Wright Edelman, *The Measure of Our Success: A Letter to My Children and Yours* (Boston: Beacon Press, 1992); Abraham Heschel, *A Passion for Truth* (New York: Farrar, Straus, and Giroux, 1973); Nelson Mandela, *Long Walk to Freedom: The Autobiography of Nelson Mandela* (Boston: Little, Brown, 1994).

54. David L. Lewis, *King: A Biography* (Urbana: University of Illinois Press, 1978), chaps. 11, 12; Jervis Anderson, *Bayard Rustin: Troubles I've Seen, a Biography* (New York: HarperCollins, 1997), 289–90. See Alexander Bloom and Wini Breines, eds., *"Takin' It to the Streets": A Sixties Reader* (New York: Oxford University Press, 1995), for Carl Oglesby's October 1965 speech at the SANE-sponsored antiwar demonstration in Washington, "Trapped in a System," in which he responded to charges that protests were anti-American, "To these, I say: Don't blame *me* for *that!* Blame those who mouthed my liberal values and broke my American heart" (220–25). Also see Paul Lyons, *New Left, New Right, and the Legacy of the Sixties* (Philadelphia: Temple University Press, 1996), chap. 5, esp. 96–121.

55. Reggie Schell, "A Way to Fight Back: The Black Panther Party," in Dick Cluster, ed., *They Should Have Served a Cup of Coffee: 7 Radicals Remember the 60s* (Boston: South End Press, 1979), 49–50.

56. Schell, "A Way to Fight Back," 51–60; Washington, *"Other Sheep I Have"*, chap. 10, "The Black Panther Convention," 126–28.

57. On the Black Panthers, see Elaine Brown, *A Taste of Power: A Black Woman's Story* (New York: Pantheon, 1992), David Hilliard, *This Side of Glory: The Autobiography of David Hilliard and the Story of the Black Panther Party* (Boston: Little, Brown, 1993); High Pearson, *The Shadow of the Panther: Huey Newton and the Price of Black Power* (Reading, Mass.: Addison-Wesley, 1994); Charles E. Jones, ed., *The Black Panther Party (Reconsidered)* (Baltimore: Black Classics Press, 1998). Also, Frank Donner, *Protectors of Privilege: Red Squads and Police Repression in Urban America* (Berkeley: University of California Press, 1990), 213–14.

58. Fred Hamilton, *Rizzo* (New York: Viking Press, 1973), 85; Allen J. Matusow, *The Unravelling of America: A History of Liberalism in the 1960s* (New York: Harper and Row, 1984), 392.

59. Hamilton, *Rizzo*, 85–92, which argues that the Panthers intentionally removed their clothing to embarrass the police; Washington, *"Other Sheep I Have"*, 125–34; Paolantonio, *Rizzo*, 99–102, which suggests that the strip searches were not Rizzo's orders; Schell, "A Way to Fight Back," 64–66; Donner, *Protectors of Privilege*, 213–16.

60. Nora Sayre, "Black Panthers and the White Radicals, Philadelphia, September 1970," *Sixties Going on Seventies*, rev. ed. (New Brunswick, N.J.: Rutgers University Press, 1996), 47–49.

61. Schell, "A Way to Fight Back," 61–62.

62. David Farber, *The Age of Great Dreams: America in the 1960s* (New York: Hill and Wang, 1994), 211.

63. Whitehorn interview, Portnoy interview.

64. Paolantonio, *Rizzo*, 109.

65. Paolantonio, *Rizzo*, chap. 6, "The Campaign (1971)."

*Chapter 7. The Rise and Fall of the New Left*

1. For the conservative view, Richard J. Ellis, *The Dark Side of the Illiberal Egalitarianism in America* (Lawrence: University Press of Kansas, 1998); Myron Magnet, *The Dream and the Nightmare: The Sixties' Legacy to the Underclass* (New York: William Morrow, 1993). For the good early, bad later New Left, Todd Gitlin, *The Sixties: Years of Hope, Days of Rage* (New York: Bantam Books, 1987); Tom Hayden, *Reunion: A Memoir* (New York: Random House, 1988); James Miller, *"Democracy in the Streets": From Port Huron to the Siege of Chicago* (New York: Simon and Schuster, 1987); Irwin Unger, *The Movement: A History of the American New Left, 1959–1972* (New York: Dodd, Mead, 1974); David Farber, *The Age of Great Dreams: America in the 1960s* (New York: Hill and Wang, 1994). For a kinder view of the late period, Edward P. Morgan, *The 60s Experience: Hard Lessons About Modern America* (Philadelphia: Temple University Press, 1991); Terry H. Anderson, *The Movement and the Sixties: Protest from Greensboro to Wounded Knee* (New York: Oxford University Press, 1995). For a critique of the old boy view, Wini Breines, "Whose New Left?" *Journal of*

*American History* (September 1988): 528–45; Alexander Bloom and Wini Breines, eds., *"Takin' It to the Streets": A Sixties Reader* (New York: Oxford University Press, 1995); Wini Breines, "Of This Generation: The New Left and the Student Movement," in Alexander Bloom, ed., *Long Time Gone: Sixties America Then and Now* (New York: Oxford University Press, 2001).

2. David Farber, *Chicago '68* (Chicago: University of Chicago Press, 1988), David Caute, *The Year of the Barricades: A Journey Through 1968* (New York: Harper and Row Perennial Library, 1988); Ronald Fraser, ed., *A Student Generation in Revolt: International Oral History* (New York: Pantheon, 1988); Maurice Isserman and Michael Kazin, *America Divided: The Civil War of the 1960s* (New York: Oxford University Press, 2000), chap. 12.

3. Carter Wiseman, "In The Days of DKE and SDS," *Yale Alumni Magazine*, February 2001, 34–39. Also see Larry Colton, *Goat Brothers* (New York: Doubleday, 1993) for an interesting examination of Berkeley jocks and Greeks as they respond to the challenges of the 1960s social movements on campus, and Paul Lyons, *Class of '66: Living in Suburban Middle America* (Philadelphia: Temple University Press), esp. chaps. 4 and 7 for how "silent majority baby boomers" experienced college in the late 1960s.

4. *Phoenix*, April 16, 1968, 2; October 1, 1968, 3.

5. *Hawk*, December 5, 1968, 4; February 21, 1969, 4.

6. *Phoenix*, September 24, 1968, 4, October 1, 1968, 3

7. *DP*, September 11, 1968, 1.

8. *Temple News*, March 21, 1968, 1; April 3, 1968, 3; April 4, 1968, 1; April 19, 1968, 1; April 23, 1968, 1; May 2, 1968, 1; May 10, 1968, 1; May 15, 1968, 1; September 13, 1968, 4; November 7, 1968, 1; *Temple Free Press*, May 31, 1968, entire issue; July 8, 1968, 4–6.

9. *Temple Free Press*, September 3, 1968, 8; September 9, 1968, 1, 5–7; September 30, 1968, 1.

10. Isserman and Kazin, *America Divided*, 219–24; Farber, *Chicago '68*, 86–114.

11. *Collegian*, March 5, 1968, 1; March 26, 1968, 1; May 10, 1968, 1; *DP*, March 7, 1968, 4; March 21, 1968, 1; April 2, 1968, 1; April 13, 1968, 1; *Phoenix*, May 14, 1968, 1.

12. *Temple Free Press*, November 4, 1968, 1, 3.

13. *Phoenix*, November 5, 1968, 2, 4; *The News* (combined Bryn Mawr-Haverford paper), January 12, 1968, 5; October 25, 1968, 1. McCarthy received 18 votes, Gregory 27, Cleaver 8, and Wallace 14.

14. *Collegian*, September 27, 1968, 2; October 25, 1968, 2; *Hawk*, February 15, 1968, 1; March 1, 1968, 1, with 400 participating and three arrests.

15. *Collegian*, February 9, 1968, 1, 5.

16. *Collegian*, March 22, 1968, 1; May 10, 1968, 1, 3; October 25, 1968, 1; December 6, 1968, 1; March 18, 1968, 1; April 22, 1969, 1, 2.

17. Elliott Shore, "Decade of Dissent: The Alternative Press in Philadelphia, 1966–1976," *Drexel Library Journal* (July 1976): 59–74; *Villanovan*, January 31, 1968, 2, 3; February 14, 1968, 1.

18. *Phoenix*, March 1, 1968, 1; *Hawk*, October 18, 1968, 3; *Collegian*, November 1, 1968, 2.

19. *Collegian*, September 17, 1968, 3; *Phoenix*, May 10, 1968, 1; *The News*, October, 1969, 1; *DP*, March 21, 1968; April 5, 1968.

20. *DP*, March 26, 1968, 1; April 2, 1968, 1; April 4, 1968, 4; April 5, 1968,

1; April 19, 1968, 3; April 22, 1968, 1; "Vietnam Commencement," April 25, 1968, mimeo, provided to the author from the personal papers of Josh Markel and Eva Gold.

21. *College News*, March 11, 1969, 1; March 18, 1969, 1; April 11, 1969, 4–7.

22. *Phoenix*, September 24, 1969, 1; *Hawk*, September 27, 1968, 1; October 11, 1968, 1; November 22, 1968, 5.

23. *The News*, February 7, 1969, 2.

24. *Phoenix*, March 1, 1968, 3 on the opening of the Electric Factory at 22nd and Arch Streets, featuring Cream, Frank Zappa, and the Mothers of Invention; *DP*, January 19, 1968, 1; February 12, 1968, 1; *Hawk*, November 21, 1969, 1; *Collegian*, April 22, 1969, 6.

25. John Andrew, "Pro-War and Anti-Draft: Young Americans for Freedom and the War in Vietnam" and Jonathan Shoenwald, "No War, No Welfare, and No Damn Taxation: The Student Libertarian Movement, 1968–1972," in Marc Jason Gilbert, ed., *The Vietnam War on Campus : Other Voices, More Distant Drums* (Westport, Conn.: Praeger, 2001), 1–53; John A. Andrew III, *The Other Side of the Sixties* (New Brunswick, N.J.: Rutgers University Press, 1997).

26. *DP*, March 28, 1968, 1; April 26, 1968, 1; February 5, 1969, 1.

27. *Temple News*, November 18, 1969, 4. Also see April 30, 1970, 3, 7, for an overview and critique of the New Left groups.

28. *Temple News*, July 19, 1967, 1; October 12, 1967, 1; October 13, 1967, 1; November 7, 1967, 1; November 8, 1967, 1; December 14, 1967, 1.

29. *Temple News*, April 30, 1968; May 15, 1968. There was also an organized BSL protest against a fraternity's use of minstrels; 500 demanded the censuring of Tau Epsilon Pi fraternity, March 29, 1968, 1; April 2, 1968, 1; *Temple Free Press*, July 8, 1968, 5.

30. *Temple Free Press*, March 31, 1969; 6, April 7, 1969, 2; *Temple News*, February 27, 1969, 1; April 4, 1969, 1; August 26, 1969, 1.

31. *Temple News*, October 27, 1970, 4; March 5, 1970, 1, 4.

32. Donald Alexander Downs, *Cornell '69: Liberalism and the Crisis of the American University* (Ithaca, N.Y.: Cornell University Press, 1999).

33. *Temple Free Press*, October 7, 1968, 8; October 21, 1968, 3; January 13, 1969, 1, 3.

34. *Temple Free Press*, February 17, 1969, 8–9; February 24, 1969, 3; April 21, 1969, 2, 3, 4.

35. *Collegian*, October 11, 1968, 1; October 18, 1968, 1; November 15, 1968, 3; March 18, 1969, 1; July 7, 1969, 4; September 9, 1969, 1.

36. *Collegian*, November 4, 1969, 1; March 25, 1970, 2; November 17, 1970, 2.

37. *Collegian*, October 7, 1969, 2; November 17, 1969, 2. On crime on other campuses, see "Security Director Promises Better Job," *Hawk*, December 6, 1967, where three freshman were jumped "by a group of twelve Negro youths"; September 24, 1971, 1. The *DP* of 1968–69 is filled with reports of crime problems on and around campus.

38. *Phoenix*, February 27, 1968, 2; March 5, 1968, 2; April 9, 1968, 2; January 29, 1969, 7; Jeffrey Lott, "Swarthmore's Crisis of 1969: A Look Back," *Swarthmore College Bulletin*, March 1999, 21, a copy of which is in the author's possession from the personal papers of John Braxton.

39. *Phoenix*, January 29, 1969, 4; Lott, "Swarthmore's Crisis of 1969," 21.

40. *Phoenix*, January 29, 1969, 4.

41. *Phoenix*, January 29, 1969, 4.

42. See Karen K. Miller, "Negroes No More: The Emergence of Black Student Activism," in Bloom, ed., *Long Time Gone*, 123–44.

43. Kenneth J. Heineman persuasively makes such an argument in *Campus Wars: The Peace Movement at American State Universities in the Vietnam Era* (New York: New York University Press, 1993), esp. epilogue, 257–74.

44. Miller, "Negroes No More," 132–40; also see Downs, *Cornell '69*.

45. *Phoenix*, January 29, 1969, 4–6.

46. *Phoenix*, January 29, 1969, 2, 3; Lott, "Swarthmore's Crisis of 1969," 20.

47. See John David Skrentny's brilliant *The Ironies of Affirmative Action: Politics, Culture, and Justice in America* (Chicago: University of Chicago Press, 1996); Paul Sniderman and Thomas Piazza, *The Scar of Race* (Cambridge, Mass.: Belknap Press of Harvard University Press, 1993); David Hollinger, *Post-Ethnic America: Beyond Multiculturalism* (New York: Basic Books, 1995).

48. *Bulletin!* Diocese of Pennsylvania, March 11, 1969; "Some significant aspects and sidelights of the recent student demonstration at the University of Pennsylvania as seen from the perspective of and related by Christian Association personnel," from the personal papers of Adam Corson-Finnerty in the possession of the author; "The 1969 College Hall Sit-in," *Thirty-Fourth Street*, September 15, 1994; *DP*, February 19, 1969, 1; *Temple Free Press*, February 19, 1969, special "Join the Sit-in at Penn" issue.

49. *Phoenix*, February 21, 1969, 1 notes that 50 Swarthmoreans joined the Penn sit-in; *Collegian*, February 14, 1969, 5, editorial in support of the Penn sit-in; *Hawk*, February 21, 1969, 4, editorial support for the Penn sit-in; also, *Temple Free Press*, February 19, 1969 special issue.

50. Kirkpatrick Sale, *SDS* (New York: Random House, 1973), chaps. 20–24, esp. 514, 552, 621 on the Labor Committee. On Old Left manipulation within the peace movement see Charles DeBenedetti, *An American Ordeal: The Antiwar Movement of the Vietnam Era* (Syracuse, N.Y.: Syracuse University Press, 1990) and Nancy Zaroulis and Gerald Sullivan, *Who Spoke Up?* (Garden City, N.Y.: Doubleday, 1984); Fraser-Borgman Defense Committee mimeo, including "Origins of the Labor Committee," 12–13, SANE Papers, Urb50, TUA.

51. Sale, *SDS*, 514.

52. Fraser-Borgman mimeo, 18.

53. *Bulletin!*, March 11, 1969, 1–3; *DP*, February 24, 1969, 1, 2.

54. On the Columbia University events, see Dotson Rader, *I Ain't Marchin' Anymore* (New York: Paperback Library, 1969); Farber, *Chicago '68*, 96–97; Sale, *SDS*, 430–47; Jerry Avorn et al., eds., *Up Against the Ivy Wall* (New York: Atheneum, 1969). In the months prior to the sit-in, the *DP* was filled with stories of the spillover of crime from the community to campus—assaults, burglaries, robberies, theft.

55. "Penn Sit-in Challenges Urban Renewal Expansion," *New Left Notes*, February 28, 1969, 9, SDS Papers, ser. 3, sec. 5, reel 26, Tamiment/NYU.

56. *Bulletin!*, March 11, 1969, 2–3.

57. Fraser-Borgman mimeo, 19–23.

58. *Bulletin!*, 4, 6. Indeed at nearby Drexel, Penn activists were initially shouted down, heckled, and faced with snowballs from hostile fraternity members who were won over to the extent that, in the following days, the Interfraternity Council apologized for their unfriendly behavior; *DP*, February 19, 1969, 1–2.

59. *DP*, February 19, 1969, 2.

60. On attitudes about higher education, see Sale, *SDS*, 430–47; Isserman and Kazin, *America Divided*, 229–30; David Burner, *Making Peace with the 60s* (Princeton, N.J.: Princeton University Press, 1996), 149–50; Gitlin, *The Sixties*, chaps. 13–17.

61. *Bulletin!*, March 11, 1969, 5–6.

62. *New Left Notes*, February 28, 1969, 9, 11; March 7, 1969, 3, a letter from Ed Aguilar of Temple SDS, viewing the agreement as driven by the moderate faculty and community leaders like Wrice and noting that Penn's Society of African-American Students (SAAS) was not involved in the process. In fact, SAAS played a quiet role and helped fend off Labor Committee claims of black support. They would focus on their own issues with the University, especially the establishment of a black studies program, *DP*, March 25, 1969, 1.

63. *Bulletin!*, March 11, 1969, 7–9.

64. *Bulletin!*, March 11, 1969, 10, Appendix C.

65. "The 1969 College Hall Sit-in," *New Left Notes*, February 28, 1969, 8–9. The *DP* described Penn SDS as "leaderless and directionless," still wracked by ideological splits, Labor Committee pressures by the following term, September 30, 1969. Although a Student Plenum narrowly voted to support the creation of a sanctuary in Houston Hall for military deserters and resisters, the student body voted 2764–1873 against, *DP*, October 8, 1969, 1; October 15, 1969, 1.

66. *DP*, November 11, 1969; 1, November 13, 1969; 1, April 4, 1970, 1.

67. Frank Donner, *Protectors of Privilege: Red Squads and Police Repression in Urban America* (Berkeley: University of California Press, 1990), chap. 6, "Rizzo's Philadelphia—Police City," 197–244.

68. Fraser-Borgman mimeo, 23–24; S. A. Paolantonio, *Frank Rizzo: The Last Big Man in Big City America* (Philadelphia: Camino Books, 1993), 99.

69. Ron Whitehorn interview, January 18, 2001, John Braxton interview, August 28, 2000, David Gracie interview, August 17, 2000, Michael DiBerardinis interview, June 15, 2001, Lisa Schiller interview, March 24, 2001, Dina Portnoy interview, February 10, 2001.

70. *Philadelphia Bulletin*, July 29–31, 1970.

71. Paolantonio, *Frank Rizzo*, 98–99; *Bulletin!*, July 28, 1970, 1; Donner, *Protectors of Privilege*, 217–22.

72. Donner, *Protectors of Privilege*, 227.

73. Murray Bookchin, "Listen, Marxist!" in Arthur Lothstein, ed., *All We Are Saying: The Philosophy of the New Left* (New York: Capricorn Books, 1970), 92.

74. Nancy Zaroulis and Gerald Sullivan, *Who Spoke Up? American Protest Against the War in Vietnam, 1963–1975* (New York: Holt, Rinehart and Winston, 1984), 281–84; Stewart Meacham, "The New Mobilization—The Fall Offensive—1969—November Action—Washington—The Death March—November 14–15, 1969—A Proposed Plan of Organization," mimeo, Joe Miller Papers, DG144, B5, SPC. Also, see *Plain Dealer*, May 7, 1970, 4–5; *Resister*, October 15–November 15, 1969, issue on the Moratorium and Mobilization in Philadelphia.

75. See *Community Peace Calendar*, Philadelphia Peace Center, March 15–April 15, 1969; September 15–October 15, 1970, for the density of movement activities in those years; as late as 1972, see the list of community-based organizations as recipients of People's Fund grants, February 17, 1972, Urb50, B22, F205, TUA. On gay and lesbian movements, see Marc Stein, *City of Sisterly and*

*Brotherly Loves: Lesbian and Gay Philadelphia, 1945–1972* (Chicago: University of Chicago Press, 2000), esp. Parts 3, 4.

76. Barbara Tischler, ed., *Sights on the Sixties* (New Brunswick, N.J.: Rutgers University Press, 1992); Doug Rossinow, *The Politics of Authenticity: Liberalism, Christianity, and the New Left in America* (New York: Columbia University Press, 1998); Gilbert, *The Vietnam War on Campus*; Heineman, *Campus Wars*; Gitlin, *The Sixties*; Wini Breines, *The Great Refusal: Community and Organization in the New Left, 1962–1968* (New York: Praeger, 1982), Breines, "Whose New Left?"

77. *Plain Dealer*, May 7, 1970; *Philadelphia Free Press*, May 4, 11, 1970, entire issues.

78. Robert J. Rutman, "Statement to the Executive Board of SANE," June 13, 1969, SANE Papers, Urb50, box 1, folder 8, TUA.

79. Sale, *SDS*, chaps. 21–25 on "Revolution"; Isserman and Kazin, *America Divided*, chap. 9.

80. See Stein, *City*, 295 and chap. 12 for a different interpretation of the notion of liberation fronts.

81. Stein, *City*, 7–9, 17; Paul Lyons, *Philadelphia Communists, 1936–1956* (Philadelphia: Temple University Press, 1982). Philadelphia's women's movement rarely appears in any of the studies of the origins and history of second-wave feminism; some Philadelphia feminists suggest that part of the reason is that they never generated their own media (feminist journals or newspapers), were less academic and campus-centered, and simply focused on the more practical tasks of building supportive institutions addressing women's needs and interests, Hunt, Rogers, Shalleck interviews.

82. Rossinow, *Politics of Authenticity*, Introduction.

83. On producerism, see Daniel T. Rodgers, *The Work Ethic in Industrial America, 1850–1920* (Chicago: University of Chicago Press, 1978) and Nancy MacLean, *Behind the Mask of Chivalry: The Making of the Second Ku Klux Klan* (New York: Oxford University Press, 1994), 84–85.

84. E. J. Hobsbawm, *The Age of Revolution, 1789–1848* (New York: Vintage, 1996), Introduction.

85. Unger, *The Movement*, vii.

86. Michael Denning, *The Cultural Front* (London: Verso, 1997), xvi–xvii.

87. Thomas Frank, *The Conquest of Cool: Business Culture, Counterculture, and the Rise of Hip Consumerism* (Chicago: University of Chicago Press, 1997) and virtually any issue of his interesting magazine the *Baffler*.

88. *Tales from the White Dog Café: A Tri-Annual Newsletter*, Winter–Spring 2001.

89. Peter Collier and David Horowitz, *Second Thoughts: Former Radicals Look Back at the Sixties* (Lanham, Md.: Madison, 1991).

90. *Philadelphia Inquirer*, April 28, 2000, B22 on Rudofsky, Friedman, Braxton, Portnoy. Other information from the relevant interviews.

91. See obituary for Kuromiya, *Philadelphia Inquirer*, May 12, 2000, A1, A10; Stein, *City*, for Kuromiya's role in the founding of the Philadelphia Gay Liberation Front, 316–18; Gracie obituary, *Philadelphia Inquirer*, May 24, 2001, B8.

# Index

# Acknowledgments

I have been most fortunate in having so many people to thank for offering me advice, guidance, and criticism over the seven years during which this book was written. Let me start with my students at the Richard Stockton College of New Jersey, those studying social welfare policy, U.S. history since 1920, the Vietnam War, the 1960s, race and ethnic relations, and Holocaust and genocide. They have inspired me to help them recognize that there have been moments when it seemed as though young people could make a difference in this world by making their own history.

The University of Pennsylvania Press encouraged me to write this book. Most particularly, Robert Lockhart , the history editor, played a central role in the revising and reconfiguring of what I believe to now be a much superior work. I would also like to thank Managing Editor Alison A. Anderson and Assistant Editor Samantha Foster for their advice and assistance.

Perhaps my largest debt is to the archivists and librarians who provided me with their gracious and generous aid in my quest to reconstruct the historical record: Dan McCole, archivist at St. Joseph's University Archives; a number of staffers from the Falvey Memorial Library of Villanova University and from the University of Pennsylvania Library; Loretta Treese and Eric Pumroy from Bryn Mawr College Library. A special thank you to archivist Brother Joseph L. Grabenstein, F.S.C. of LaSalle University, a dear and thoughtful man who runs the best small university archive I have ever had the good fortune to use.

Also, to those ever helpful staffers at the Temple University Urban Archives, Paley Library: Margaret Jerrido, Brenda Galloway-Wright, George Brightbill, Evan Towle, and Thomas M. Whitehead from the Contemporary Culture Collection. The staff at Haverford College Special Collections Magill Library—Emma Jones Lapsansky, Ann Wetherill Upton, and Diana Franzusoff Peterson—provided me with considerable assistance. Those who have made the Swarthmore Peace

Collection of the Swarthmore College Library so extraordinary and who were essential to my work include Wendy E. Chmielewski, Barbara Addison, and Anne Yoder. The archivists at the State Historical Society of Wisconsin and the University of California at Berkeley were also helpful. My archival investigations began at New York University's Tamiment Institute Library of the Ernest Holmes Bobst Library, and I remain much appreciative of the assistance I received from Peter Filardo, Gail Malmgreen, and Andrew H. Lee.

Certainly my college has been always supportive of my scholarly efforts; it has remained, fundamentally, a teaching institution, but one that recognizes the ways research enriches pedagogy. In particular, I wish to thank our outgoing president, Vera King Farris, and our vice president for academic affairs, David Carr, for their gracious support. To the Stockton faculty—so many wonderful and dedicated teachers!—I just want to say that there is nothing I value more than being considered one of your colleagues.

Over the years a number of dear friends and colleagues have been there to provide me with both support and invaluable criticism. Burt Weltman, Jay Mandle, Joan Mandle, Louis Ferleger, Joe Walsh, Josh Markel, Eva Gold, and Stephen Dunn have read all or extensive parts of this manuscript. They bear no responsibility for the results, but I must declare my deepest regard for their friendship and critical support.

Good friends tell me that I am strikingly single-minded in focusing on my research efforts. Indeed, I impose the brunt of that intensity upon those closest to me—my family. As such, I ask their forgiveness and express my deepest love for my wife Mary Hardwick, the best public school science teacher in the land, my sister-in-law Emily McDonald, my stepson Nate Zelnick, and my youngest Max Lyons.

Over the course of the seven years writing this book, I interviewed in person in most instances, but by phone or e-mail on a few occasions, the following fifty-two people: Frank Ackerman, Tony Avirgan, Tom Barton, Frank Battaglia, Thompson Bradley, Robert Brand, John Braxton, Father Daniel Burke, Ken Campbell, Frank Carner, Judith Chomsky, Adam Corson-Finnerty, Michael DiBerardinis, Bob Eaton, David Eldredge, Rev. Richard Fernandez, Dennis Foreman, Debbie Frazier, Muffin Friedman, Carl Gilbert, Barbara Gold, Eva Gold, Steve Gold, Brother Joseph Grabenstein, Rev. David Gracie, Ira Harkavy Martha Honey, Jean Hunt, Bruce Kuklick, Emma Lapsansky, Jack Malinowski, Gail Malmgreen, Jay Mandle, Joan Mandle, Josh Markel, Joe Mikuliak, Marty Oppenheimer, Dina Portnoy, Jim Quinn, Iz Reivich, Liz Reivich, Carol Rogers, Art Rosenfeld, David Rudovsky, Robert Rutman, Lisa Schiller, Russell Stetler, Bert Streib, Mary L.

Wentworth, Ron Whitehorn, Roger Wood, Shelly Yanoff. This is not primarily an oral history—memories from thirty to forty years ago are inherently problematic—but I much appreciate the time these people allowed to my curiosity. And I admire their candor in reflecting on their experiences. They are the reason I wrote this account, although, of course, none of them are responsible for its content or analysis.